Books for You

NCTE Bibliography Series

Books for You

An Annotated Booklist for Senior High Students

1995 Edition

Leila Christenbury, Editor,
and the Committee on the Senior High School Booklist
of the National Council of Teachers of English

With a Foreword by

Jerry Spinelli

National Council of Teachers of English
1111 W. Kenyon Road, Urbana, IL 61801-1096

Manuscript Editor: Jane M. Curran
Production Editor: Rona S. Smith
Series Cover Design: R. Maul
Cover Illustration: Carlton Bruett
Interior Design: Doug Burnett

NCTE Stock Number: 03677-3050

It is the policy of NCTE in its journals and other publications to provide a fo-
rum for the open discussion of ideas concerning the content and the teaching
of English and the language arts. Publicity accorded to any particular point of
view does not imply endorsement by the Executive Committee, the Board of
Directors, or the membership at large, except in announcements of policy, where
such endorsement is clearly specified.

Library of Congress Cataloging-in-Publication Data
Books for you : an annotated booklist for senior high students / Leila
    Christenbury, editor, and the Committee on the Senior High School
    Booklist of the National Council of Teachers of English. —1995 ed.
        p.   cm. — (NCTE bibliography series, ISSN 1051-4740)
    Includes indexes.
    Summary: An annotated bibliography of fiction and nonfiction books
of interest to high school students. Includes author, title, and subject
indexes.
    ISBN 0-8141-0367-7 (pbk.)
    1. Young adult literature—Bibliography. 2. High school libraries—
United States—Book lists. I. Christenbury, Leila. II. National Council of
Teachers of English. Committee on the Senior High School Booklist.
III. Series.
Z1037.B724 1995
[PN1009.A1]
011.62′5—dc20   95-4579
                                                                         CIP

About the NCTE Bibliography Series

The National Council of Teachers of English is proud to be part of a process that we feel is important. It begins when an educator who knows literature and its value to students and teachers is chosen by the NCTE Executive Committee to be a booklist editor. That editor then works with teachers and librarians who review, select, and annotate hundreds of new trade books sent to them by publishers. It's a complicated process, one that can last three or four years. But because of their dedication and strong belief in the need to let others know about the good literature that's available, these professionals volunteer their time in a way that serves as an inspiration to all of us. The members of the committee that compiled this volume are listed on one of the first pages, and we are grateful for their hard work.

In our bibliography series are five different booklists, each focused on a particular audience, each updated regularly. These are *Adventuring with Books* (pre-K through grade 6), *Kaleidoscope* (multicultural literature, grades K through 8), *Your Reading* (middle school/junior high), *Books for You* (senior high), and *High Interest—Easy Reading* (middle school, junior/senior high reluctant readers). Together, these volumes list thousands of the most recent children's and young adult trade books. Although the works included cover a wide range of topics, they all have one thing in common: they're good books that students and teachers alike enjoy.

Of course, no single book is right for everyone or every purpose, so inclusion in this booklist is not necessarily an endorsement from NCTE. However, it does indicate that the professionals who make up the booklist committee feel that the work in question is worthy of teachers' and students' attention, whether for its informative or aesthetic qualities. On the other hand, exclusion from an NCTE booklist is not necessarily a judgment on the quality of a given book or publisher. Many factors—space, time, availability of certain books, publisher participation—may influence the final shape of the list.

We hope that you will find this booklist a useful resource in discovering new titles and authors, and we hope that you will collect the other booklists in the NCTE series. Our mission is to help improve the teaching and learning of English and the language arts, and we feel the quality of our booklists contributes substantially toward that goal. We think you will agree.

Dawn Boyer
Director of Acquisitions
and Development in Publications

Contents

Foreword: Why Read?

When I was a little kid I never read outside of the classroom. Except for comic books. *G.I. Joe. Superman. The Heap.* In sixth grade I even had a subscription to *Bugs Bunny.* I thought that wisecracking rabbit was the funniest thing. Still do.

In eleventh grade, on one college application, I was asked to list three books I'd read recently. I could list only two: *The Adventures of Robin Hood* and *Kon-Tiki,* the account of an explorer's voyage by raft across the Pacific Ocean. I remember liking those two books, especially *Kon-Tiki,* but if I had the itch to read more, plowing through *Silas Marner* in English class cured me.

Even in college, except for the obligatory *Catcher in the Rye* and *Lord of the Flies,* I rarely read beyond course requirements. And now here I am—the kid who didn't read books—writing them.

What happened?

I think it had something to do with baseball. Back in my comic book days, my ambition was to be a major league shortstop. But after tenth grade my batting average went down, my strikeout totals went up, and I started shopping around for something else to become.

Biologist, Navy pilot, reporter, lawyer—I toyed with them all before finally settling on writer. But still I did not read. Until graduate school, when my old interest in baseball took a peculiar turn. *The Natural,* a novel by Bernard Malamud, was recommended to me. I read it, and was stunned at the power of the story to draw me into the game as thoroughly as putting on a Little League uniform once had. I discovered that a book could be more than a course requirement or a time-killer. I discovered that reading need not be a passive non-activity, such as napping, but that it is an authentic experience in and of itself, as exercising as dancing, as crunchy as biting into an apple.

And best, I made the happy discovery that during those years of my search for a vocational identity, I had in fact been something all along: a reader. I possessed the only two credentials needed: I knew how to read, and I enjoyed it. For whatever reason, I simply hadn't done it.

And now I began to consider what I had missed. How many boring hours had I spent wondering what to do? How many excited impulses—for exotic adventure, for mystery, for knowledge—had withered and died between my ears? How much richer might my life have been had I spent less time with *TV Guide* and more with the card catalog?

Finally, I began to read.

And write.

And when I got around to writing about a character named Maniac Magee, I saw a chance to re-do my own kidhood. I made Maniac as good at baseball as I wished I had been. I made him a pitcher's nightmare. But that wasn't all. When I walked Maniac up to the plate in Chapter 7 to face the fearsome McNab, I did what I had never done the first time around: I put a bat in one hand—and a book in the other.

Jerry Spinelli

Jerry Spinelli's first published book, Space Station Seventh Grade, *was written with adults in mind; but because the protagonist is a thirteen-year-old boy, it was steered into the young adult market. He has been writing for young people ever since. His sixth novel,* Maniac Magee, *was awarded the 1991 Newbery Medal. His other young adult novels include* Who Put That Hair in My Toothbrush?, Jason and Marceline, There's a Girl in My Hammerlock, School Daze: Report to the Principal's Office, School Daze: Who Ran My Underwear Up the Flagpole?, School Daze: Do the Funky Pickle, School Daze: Picklemania!, *and* Tooter Pepperday.

Introduction

There is no single activity which will have a more lasting, positive effect on your life than reading. Regardless of your plans for the future, or what you think you may be doing after graduation, reading can play an integral part. Architects and engineers have to read specifications; historians need to read primary accounts. Nurses and physicians must read descriptions of illnesses and treatments; athletes read game plans and strategic analyses. Computer scientists read manuals; teachers read books in their field. Artists of all kinds read, as do scientists and journalists and technicians. Reading is also important to your personal life, and whether your private interest is poetry, romance, cyberspace, Formula One racing, vampires, baseball, or the history of the Russian republics, books can inform, entertain, and elevate. Books are, in all their many manifestations, a universe of the mind, and all of us who selected and reviewed the many books represented in this volume invite you to browse, savor, and read.

As you look through this book, you will note that it is arranged in chapters according to topic, and each chapter contains brief descriptions or annotations of books related to that subject area, such as "Science Fiction" or "Dating and Sexual Awareness." The books are listed alphabetically according to the author's or editor's last name. Each entry also lists the publisher, the number of pages, the International Standard Book Number (ISBN), and whether a book is fiction or nonfiction.

Most of the books listed in this volume were published between 1990 and 1994; all are quality works that we hope you will like. In total, we have selected over 1,000 books to recommend to you. One hundred fifty-seven of these books—on a range of subjects and culled from other chapters in *Books for You*—are repeated in the chapter called "Multicultural Themes." We hope that this arrangement allows you to see the diversity of works represented in this booklist and to locate more easily books that have a multicultural focus.

If you are looking for books by a particular author, look for his or her name in the Author Index at the back of the book. If you are looking for a certain title, check for it in the Title Index. If you are hunting for books on a particular topic, first check the list of chapter titles on the Contents pages for a general rundown of topics. If you are searching for a specific topic, such as AIDS, polar bears, the Gulf War, or slavery, look for that topic in the Subject Index. To aid you in finding a particular book, each book listed in the booklist has been assigned an annotation number, and the three indexes list entries by annotation number. The full names and ordering addresses of the many publishers who generously donated their books for us to read and review are listed in the Directory of Publishers at the back of the book.

We, the people who read and reviewed these books, are teachers and librarians and, most importantly, readers. We have worked hard on this project for three years, but it has been a true labor of love. More than anything, we want you to enjoy reading as we do and to use this booklist to find books that you feel are worthwhile to read. As you can see from the dedication at the beginning of this volume, our work is for people, like yourself, who read and love books. Through this 1995 edition of *Books for You*, we send our best wishes for happy reading.

Leila Christenbury
Editor, 1995 *Books for You*

to the typesetters and proofreaders

to the illustrators and photographers

to the publishers and printers

to the editors and reviewers

to the booksellers and book buyers

to the writers

to the readers

to all who love

books

1 Adventure and Survival

1.1 Adkins, Jan. **A Storm without Rain.** William Morrow/Beech Tree Books, 1993. 179 pp. ISBN 0-688-11852-6. Fiction.

Fifteen-year-old Jack does not want to give a speech at his grandfather's birthday party, so he sails off to a nearby island. In the midst of a dream, he is transported back to his grandfather's boyhood years by a "storm without rain." He cannot trust anyone with his secret until he meets his grandfather as a youth. Will he survive life in the early 1900s? How will he get back home?

1.2 Baillie, Allan. **Little Brother.** Illustrated by Elizabeth Honey. Viking, 1992. 144 pp. ISBN 0-670-84381-4. Fiction.

Vithy is separated from his older brother, Mang, when they escape a Khmer Rouge firing squad during the 1970s. With the rest of his family already killed by the Khmer, Vithy must find Mang before he leaves the country. His efforts put him in danger and cause him difficulties. While Vithy always counted on Mang to get him through, now he must deal with hunger and constant fear as he tries to cross the miles of war-torn Cambodia on his own. First published in Scotland, 1985; in Australia, 1990.

Notable 1992 Children's Trade Books in the Field of Social Studies

1.3 Banks, Lynne Reid. **One More River,** rev. ed. Morrow Junior Books, 1992. 243 pp. ISBN 0-688-10893-8. Fiction.

Lesley is an intelligent, wealthy, pretty, and popular Jewish girl living a comfortable life in Canada. But after an extravagant party celebrating her fourteenth birthday, her life takes some dramatic turns. It all starts when Lesley's father tells her the family is moving to Israel, a country at war with its Arab neighbors. Lesley at first refuses to go, but she has no choice. Relations with her parents become strained when she has to leave her friends and home, learn a new and difficult language, adjust to living in a kibbutz with other Israeli teenagers, and survive the Six-Day War of 1967. First published in 1973.

1.4 Beatty, Patricia. **Lupita Mañana.** William Morrow/Beech Tree Books, 1992. 190 pp. ISBN 0-688-11497-0. Fiction.

Lupita's nickname is "Mañana" because she always thinks life will be better *tomorrow*. After their father dies in a fishing accident, Lupita's brother mocks her optimism when their family must take desperate steps to survive. The only way to get money is for Lupita and her brother to leave Mexico and work in the United States. Sneaking across the border, however, is dangerous and difficult, and they risk imprisonment or death in trying.

1.5   Bezine, Ching Yun. **On Wings of Destiny.** Penguin/Signet Books, 1992. 396 pp. ISBN 0-451-17320-1. Fiction.

Qing, Sumiko, and Te fight their individual struggles, growing up in oppression and fear. Qing's wealthy family loses its power and possessions when the Communists take over China in the late 1940s; her parents and her brother Te leave her behind when they flee to Taiwan. There Te learns painfully that the Nationalist Chinese and the Taiwanese hate and fight each other. In Hawaii, Sumiko opposes her mother's desire for her to marry into wealth and success. The three end up in America struggling to achieve their dreams together. Mature language and situations.

1.6   Blair, David Nelson. **Fear the Condor.** Dutton/Lodestar Books, 1992. 137 pp. ISBN 0-525-67381-4. Fiction.

In war-torn Bolivia in the 1930s, Bartolina, an Amarya Indian, experiences difficulties. Her father is taken from the large farm where they work in order to fight for the army, leaving her to take care of herself. Bartolina's grandmother teaches her many Indian superstitions that add to her fears and keep her from making friends. When her grandmother tries to organize a rebellion among the farm workers, Bartolina runs away to find a life that is not lived as a slave to others.

1.7   Buss, Fran Leeper (with Daisy Cubias). **Journey of the Sparrows.** Dutton/Lodestar Books, 1991. 155 pp. ISBN 0-525-67362-8. Fiction.

Nailed into a crate and loaded into the back of a truck, Maria, her younger brother, and her pregnant sister make their escape to the United States. Even in Chicago they still must be "invisible," or the immigration officials will return them to their brutal existence in El Salvador. Maria is the best hope for her family. Her father and brother-in-law were murdered, and she must help her mother and baby sister make an escape soon from their hiding place in Mexico.

Jane Addams Award, 1992
ALA Best Books for Young Adults, 1992
Booklist Editors' Choice, 1991
Notable 1991 Children's Trade Books in the Field of Social Studies

1.8   Campbell, Eric. **The Place of Lions.** Harcourt Brace Jovanovich, 1991. 183 pp. ISBN 0-15-262408-2. Fiction.

Chris and his dad are on their way to a new life in Africa. As the small plane takes them across the immense and beautiful Serengeti Plain of Tanzania, an accident sends them crashing into the lonely land. Fourteen-year-old Chris must find a way to survive the harsh environment and threatening animals in order to get help for his dad and the pilot. But what is watching him and following him on his journey? First published in Great Britain, 1990.

ALA Best Books for Young Adults, 1993
Notable 1991 Children's Trade Books in the Field of Social Studies

1.9   Campbell, Eric. **The Year of the Leopard Song.** Harcourt Brace Jovanovich, 1992. 160 pp. ISBN 0-15-299806-3. Fiction.

When Alan returns to his Tanzanian home after a year of schooling in England, he senses tension in the air. His good friend, Kimathi, disappears, the native workers on his father's coffee plantation leave the fields, and a bloody message is scrawled on the barn wall. A strange feeling drives Alan to search for his friend on the slopes of Mt. Kilimanjaro, where Kimathi has gone to fulfill a tribal ritual. The two boys are drawn to an encounter that changes their lives forever.

1.10   Choi, Sook Nyul. **Echoes of the White Giraffe.** Houghton Mifflin, 1993. 137 pp. ISBN 0-395-64721-5. Fiction.

Sookan, her mother, and her younger brother flee south from Seoul to Pusan, in American-occupied Korea. They end up living in a paper shack on the mountain along with many other refugee families. The war with Japan is over, but now civil war has erupted in Korea. During this period of her life, without her father and three older brothers, Sookan works hard to keep her goal of going to an American university. Sequel to *Year of Impossible Goodbyes.*

1.11   Cole, Brock. **The Goats.** Farrar, Straus and Giroux / Aerial Books, 1992. 184 pp. ISBN 0-374-42576-0. Fiction.

Summer camp. A time for fun and friends. But not for Howie and Laura. Singled out for a practical joke, Howie and Laura are left for the night, without clothes, on a deserted island. They cannot stand the thought of returning to the camp, so the two escape from the island. Being on the run is not easy, but Howie and Laura discover strengths and resources no one knew they had. They are no longer the "goats."

1.12   Cooney, Caroline B. **Flight #116 Is Down.** Scholastic, 1992. 201 pp. ISBN 0-590-44465-4. Fiction.

"How many human beings had that plane held? How many seats must have been crammed into that smashed cylinder? How many passengers . . . ?" Heidi is the first person to arrive at the site of an airplane crash. What can she do alone? The story moves through the terrifying time after the crash as Heidi, joined by local rescue squad volunteers, frantically tries to save as many lives as possible. In the midst of the tragedy, Heidi finds a bravery she did not know she had and makes friends with Patrick, who helps her keep the unforgettable night in perspective.

ALA Best Books for Young Adults, 1993
ALA Quick Picks for Young Adults, 1993

1.13   Cossi, Olga. **Adventure on the Graveyard of the Wrecks.** Pelican, 1991. 160 pp. ISBN 0-88289-808-6. Fiction.

Dave, Jim, and Carl have been beachcombing for fishing floats many times. This time they invite Shari. She cannot see all the excitement about "float fever" until she finds her first one. The only damper to her spirits is the raging storm pounding the beach—and her friends—and churning up the sea. Then everything gets worse when Carl starts acting strangely, the weather intensifies, and the trip becomes a struggle to survive and a lesson in trust.

1.14   Cross, Gillian. **The Great American Elephant Chase.** Holiday House, 1993. 193 pp. ISBN 0-8234-1016-1. Fiction.

It is the 1880s, and Tad is drawn to the elephant show when it arrives in town. He does not intend to run away when he hides in the elephant's train car. But the next thing he knows, he is locked in with the elephant, and the train is pulling out of town. When the elephant's owner is killed in a train accident, Tad gets caught up in rescuing the great animal from the evil, ill-tempered Hannibal Jackson. Tad and the elephant travel by foot, by flatboat, and by steamboat in their hair-raising flight from the cruel Jackson. First published in Great Britain as *The Great Elephant Chase,* 1992.

School Library Journal Best Books, 1992

1.15   Dickinson, Peter. **Tulku.** Dell/Laurel-Leaf Library, 1993. 286 pp. ISBN 0-440-21489-0. Fiction.

After his father's mission in China is destroyed, Theodore is on his own, fleeing from the rebels of the Boxer Uprising of 1898–1900. When he encounters Mrs. Jones, a strong, kind botanist, he hears and sees things that are startling because of his religious background. Mrs. Jones takes Theodore along, escaping from the rebels and bandits and traveling to Tibet and the Lama. Yet once again they are into trouble because the Lama thinks they hold magical powers that will lead to Tulku. First published in Great Britain, 1979.

1.16   Garland, Sherry. **Song of the Buffalo Boy.** Harcourt Brace Jovanovich, 1992. 243 pp. ISBN 0-15-277107-7. Fiction.

Loi can hardly remember the American soldier-father who kissed her goodbye in Da Nang when she was very young. Now she is seventeen and an outcast in Vietnam because of her mixed-race status. The love she and Khai share is forbidden, and she must marry the cruel Officer Hiep. The only solution is to run away to Ho Chi Minh City and try to get to America. But Loi must decide if she can stand to leave the only family she knows and the country she loves in the hopes of finding her father and a better life.

ALA Best Books for Young Adults, 1993
Notable 1992 Children's Trade Books in the Field of Social Studies

1.17   Grover, Wayne. **Ali and the Golden Eagle.** Greenwillow Books, 1993. 150 pp. ISBN 0-688-11385-0. Fiction.

Ali and his family live in a remote Saudi Arabian village that lies at the bottom of a deep valley. Wayne is an American working in the area. Ali's family are great falconers, training and competing with other villages. One day Wayne uses his skills to catch a young eagle, which Ali and his father carefully train to hunt. Through the fame and attention Ali gains with his eagle, the lives of Ali and his entire village are changed dramatically.

1.18   Hesse, Karen. **Letters from Rifka.** Henry Holt, 1992. 148 pp. ISBN 0-8050-1964-2. Fiction.

Through letters written to her cousin Tovah in Russia, young Rifka tells of her family's dramatic escape from persecution in Russia in 1919 and their immigration to America. The journey entails numerous setbacks: humiliating physical examinations, typhus, separation from her family, and a year's delay in Belgium when she contracts the skin disease ringworm and is not allowed to board the ship for America. Bright and determined, Rifka finds comfort in her one book, a volume of Pushkin's poetry, and faces each setback with renewed courage. This story is based on the immigrant experiences of the author's grandparents.

ALA Best Books for Young Adults, 1993
ALA Notable Books for Children, 1993
IRA Children's Book Award, 1993
School Library Journal Best Books, 1992

1.19   Hiçyilmaz, Gaye. **Against the Storm.** Little, Brown/Joy Street Books, 1992. 198 pp. ISBN 0-316-36078-3. Fiction.

When farm life in their Turkish village becomes too difficult, Mehmet and his family move to Ankara to live at the mercy of his successful uncle. The new way of life is a threat to everything dear to Mehmet—his family, his best friend, his dog, and his own idealism and outlook on life. The shantytown existence that traps Mehmet's family and steals their dreams is not the rich, abundant life they expected. Mehmet learns how to survive from a streetwise orphan friend and discovers within himself the strength to escape. First published in Great Britain, 1990.

ALA Notable Books for Children, 1993
Notable 1992 Children's Trade Books in the Field of Social Studies

1.20   Hiller, B. B. **Shipwrecked.** Scholastic/Point Books, 1991. 122 pp. ISBN 0-590-44775-0. Fiction.

This novelization of the movie *Shipwrecked* finds Haakon Haakonsen, a small, frightened fourteen-year-old, leaving home to make his way as a ship's boy aboard a merchant ship. His two-year adventure is filled with pirates, shipwrecks, and a pretty, willful stowaway named Mary. Initiation into the ranks of the ship's crew and surviving alone on a deserted island bring Haakon to the realization that he can do just about anything.

1.21   Hobbs, Will. **Beardance.** Atheneum, 1993. 197 pp. ISBN 0-689-31867-7. Fiction.

When Cloyd learns that grizzly bears have been spotted in his Colorado mountains, he heads off in search of them. He feels responsible for the death of a male grizzly the previous summer, and helping these endangered bears may give him the chance to right things. His Native American grandmother taught him, "To live right, give something back." With dangers from weather and men threatening Cloyd and the bears, he must decide how much of himself to give in order to save the grizzlies.

ALA Best Books for Young Adults, 1994

1.22 Hobbs, Will. **Changes in Latitudes.** Avon/Flare Books, 1993. 162 pp. ISBN 0-380-71619-4. Fiction.

Travis, his younger brother and sister, and their mother travel to Mexico for a dream vacation. Why doesn't his father go with them? What appointments keep taking their mother off on side trips alone? While his brother, Teddy, gets caught up with the area's endangered sea turtles and Travis concentrates on meeting a beautiful female, his sister, Jennifer, tries to hold the family together. Before the trip is over, a nightmare of tragedy, anger, betrayal, and discovery replaces Travis's old way of life.

1.23 Hobbs, Will. **Downriver.** Bantam Books, 1992. 204 pp. ISBN 0-553-29717-1. Fiction.

"Discovery Unlimited" is the name of Al's nine-week course for delinquent kids, who dub themselves "the Hoods in the Woods." On a boat trip through the rapids of the Grand Canyon, "the hoods"—four guys and four girls—leave Al, take the boats, and set off on their own down the Colorado River. With a lot of luck and great determination, they manage to navigate the dangerous waterfalls and roaring rapids on a wild trip that has unforeseen challenges and consequences.

ALA Best Books for Young Adults, 1992
ALA Quick Picks for Young Adults, 1992

1.24 Hosie-Bounar, Jane. **Life Belts.** Delacorte Press, 1993. 117 pp. ISBN 0-385-31074-9. Fiction.

Nita, Molly, and Eddie love the beach on which they live. But during their thirteenth summer, the long, hot days of late August change their lives dramatically. Carefree, adventurous Nita tries to comprehend the pending death of her mother; Molly, already insecure and shy, experiences unexpected physical changes; and Eddie, born with a birth defect, grapples with guilt over a tragedy he might have prevented.

1.25 Howe, Norma. **Shoot for the Moon.** Crown, 1992. 217 pp. ISBN 0-517-58151-5. Fiction.

Gina has few friends, feels her parents wish she were not around, and has no goals beyond high school. When she wins a trip to Italy, Gina encounters the difficulties of foreign money and language and the pleasure of places she never imagined existed. She also meets a handsome, young Dutchman who joins her for the week and helps her take a fresh look at her life.

1.26   Karl, Herb. **The Toom County Mud Race.** Delacorte Press, 1992. 151 pp. ISBN 0-385-30540-0. Fiction.

Mud races in four-wheel drive pickups, fights with snakes and alligators, and racial hostility—these are part of the excitement that Jackie, Bonnie, and Snake encounter in Toom County. The action-packed adventure begins when Snake finds a package, unloaded from a plane, that belongs to X Slocum. X sends his boys after the package, and after Jackie, Bonnie, and Snake as well. X does not care what his goons have to do—he wants that package.

ALA Quick Picks for Young Adults, 1993

1.27   Laird, Elizabeth. **Kiss the Dust.** Dutton Children's Books, 1992. 279 pp. ISBN 0-525-44893-4. Fiction.

First Tara sees a teenage boy shot at close range by the Iraqi secret police; then her father has to escape in the middle of the night because of his involvement with the Kurdish resistance movement. Finally, Tara and her mother must leave their home and seek sanctuary in the hills of Kurdistan, giving up the comforts Tara has known for thirteen years and becoming fugitives from the Iraqis. It is 1984, and the family's flight takes them from one refugee camp to another, one frightening situation to the next, while Tara wonders if they will ever find a safe place to live. First published in Great Britain, 1991.

ALA Best Books for Young Adults, 1993
Notable 1992 Children's Trade Books in the Field of Social Studies

1.28   Landsman, Susan. **Survival! At Sea.** Illustrated by Rose Water. Avon/Camelot Books, 1993. 114 pp. ISBN 0-380-76603-5. Nonfiction.

The first days of Maralyn and Maurice's sailing trip from Panama to New Zealand are perfect. But on the sixth day, a sperm whale rams their boat. What should have been a two-week trip stretches into 117 days of starvation, dehydration, and determination to live. The odds are impossible, but Maralyn and Maurice triumph because they learn survival techniques the hard way.

1.29   Mahy, Margaret. **Underrunners.** Viking, 1992. 169 pp. ISBN 0-670-84179-X. Fiction.

Tris, abandoned by his mother and misunderstood by his father, has few friends. He meets Winola, however, who joins in his fantasy life of suspense and danger in the underrunners, a vast network of tunnels running through the land near his isolated home. But when Winola runs away from the Children's Home, she turns their make-believe danger into reality as she is pursued by a frightening person.

ALA Notable Books for Children, 1993
Booklist Editors' Choice, 1992

1.30 McClung, Robert M. **Hugh Glass, Mountain Man: Left for Dead.** William Morrow/Beech Tree Books, 1993. 156 pp. ISBN 0-688-04595-2. Fiction.

Hugh Glass has survived many dangers and attacks, but the brutal attack of a grizzly bear leaves him near death. Two fellow trappers traveling with him agree to stay behind to bury him. However, Hugh continues to live, and his companions fear an attack from hostile Native Americans as they wait. In panic, they finally abandon Hugh, leaving him without food, supplies, or water. When Hugh recovers, he vows revenge on the two men and begins a 200-mile journey across the American frontier of 1823 to find them.

Notable 1990 Children's Trade Books in the Field of Social Studies

1.31 McLaughlin, Frank. **Yukon Journey.** Scholastic/Point Books, 1991. 99 pp. ISBN 0-590-43538-8. Fiction.

Sixteen-year-old Andy is bullied at school but cannot talk about it to his dad, who still blames Andy for the death of their dog, Sammy. Andy feels he is a coward and a disappointment to his father. When his dad's plane crashes in the Yukon during a snowstorm, Andy knows he has to find his father. He is scared to go alone, but he must not give up until he finds his dad . . . or dies trying.

1.32 Murphy, Claire Rudolf. **To the Summit.** Dutton/Lodestar Books, 1992. 156 pp. ISBN 0-525-67383-0. Fiction.

Being seventeen years old and a part of the first father-daughter team to climb Alaska's Mount McKinley is a thrilling adventure. Or is it? Does Sarah have the physical endurance and the mental toughness to make the twenty-one-day climb? As someone who likes to be alone, can she work as a team member to survive the hidden crevasses that swallow people forever, the subzero temperatures and high altitude that numb the body and the brain, and the avalanches that bury climbers in a few seconds? To survive, Sarah must overcome the obstacles within herself.

IRA Young Adults' Choices, 1994

1.33   Newth, Mette (translated by Tiina Nunnally and Steve Murray).
The Abduction. Farrar, Straus and Giroux/Aerial Books, 1993.
248 pp. ISBN 0-374-40009-1. Fiction.

The foreigners have never invited Osuqo's people onboard their
ship before. She is suspicious when they do; but she, her father,
and her fiancé, Poq, cannot refuse. The innocent trading quickly
changes to murder and kidnapping, and Osuqo and Poq are taken
from their country and their people. When they arrive in Norway,
they are treated like wild animals. Only Christine and Henrik see
them as human beings in need of help. But what can they do
alone? First published in Norway, 1987.

School Library Journal Best Books, 1989

1.34   Obstfeld, Raymond. **The Joker and the Thief.** Delacorte Press,
1993. 230 pp. ISBN 0-385-30855-8. Fiction.

Eric and Didra have planned a special weekend together, their
first since Didra went away to college. When they get to her parents' cabin, however, they find Griffin, an escapee from the juvenile detention home. Eric has always done the right thing, always
done what was expected of him. But for some reason, when the
sheriff comes looking for the youth, Eric cannot make himself turn
Griffin in. Soon he is caught up in helping Griffin leave the area,
and he finds himself on an adventure that changes his own life.

1.35   Pettit, Jayne. **My Name Is San Ho.** Scholastic, 1992. 149 pp. ISBN
0-590-44172-8. Fiction.

San Ho has lived with the terrors of war since his first breath.
When his father is taken away to fight and die for the Vietcong
and the bombings and killings get too close to home, San Ho's
mother sends him to Saigon to live. Then his mother marries an
American soldier, moves to the United States, and sends for San
Ho. Another frightening time begins as he makes the journey to
a new life with a confusing language, a stepfather, strange foods,
and racism. San Ho must overcome his fears in order to experience happiness in his new home.

1.36   Pike, Christopher. **The Immortal.** Pocket Books/Archway Paperbacks, 1993. 213 pp. ISBN 0-671-74510-7. Fiction.

A vacation in Greece with her best friend seems the perfect gift
to Josie. Yet while touring the ancient island of Delos, Josie feels
the strange sensation of having been there before in another life.
After the tour, trouble starts—Josie goes boating with a boy and
they almost drown in a storm; she has haunting dreams about

living in ancient Greece; a goddess statue that she removes from the island changes form. Josie is not sure what is happening, but she knows she is involved with the gods and goddesses in a dangerous way. Mature language and situations.

1.37   Raven, James. **The Best Enemy.** Illustrated by Eric Velasquez. Bantam Books, 1993. 135 pp. ISBN 0-553-29930-1. Fiction.

When an explosion shakes their neighborhood, Keith, Davina, Kim, and Joel fear that the Nemesis gang is seeking revenge. A second attack on the local junk dealer sends the Dojo Rats in defense of their neighborhood again. But some pieces are missing from the puzzle—finding those clues puts Kim in danger and tests her karate skills. Second book in the Dojo Rats series.

1.38   Raven, James. **Entering the Way.** Illustrated by Eric Velasquez. Bantam Books, 1993. 136 pp. ISBN 0-553-29929-8. Fiction.

Keith, Davina, Kim, and Joel, best friends from karate class, call themselves the Dojo Rats. When Keith spots Rikki beating up a street person, he uses his karate to attack Rikki. Soon the four friends find themselves fighting Rikki's gang, Nemesis, which is determined to take over their neighborhood. The four want to save their neighborhood through their karate—beating an opponent without violence—but first Keith must conquer his anger. First book in the Dojo Rats series.

1.39   Raven, James. **Test of Wills.** Illustrated by Eric Velasquez. Bantam Books, 1993. 146 pp. ISBN 0-553-56243-6. Fiction.

Davina has her Dojo Rat karate friends, but she struggles with who she is as she seeks more independence. Her absent father's visit to town only adds to her confusion. In the midst of her troubles, a newcomer to the neighborhood brings another form of danger for the Dojo Rats: his family is being pursued by a murderous gang seeking revenge. As Davina helps Vang, she learns about family hardships and finds some answers to her own struggle with identity. Fourth book in the Dojo Rats series.

1.40   Rhodes, Judy Carole. **The Hunter's Heart.** Macmillan/Bradbury Press, 1993. 184 pp. ISBN 0-02-775935-0. Fiction.

At eighteen, Benjy King finds himself the owner of a small farm left to him by his grandfather. The work is harder than he imagined, and he encounters other problems as well. Benjy meets Sara, who comes to town looking for a father she has never seen, and Benjy wants to help her. Also, the land around his farm is being worked by logging companies, threatening the way of life of his friends Coot Hunter and Wolf. Ben wonders how he can help.

1.41   Roberts, Libby. **Survival Skills.** Lerner, 1993. 48 pp. ISBN 0-8225-2481-3. Nonfiction.

If you want to learn how to make your outdoor adventure safe and practical, you will enjoy this book. Learn to anticipate dangerous situations and how to prevent accidents, whether you are hiking in the mountains, spending the day at the beach, camping in the desert, or traveling through an unfamiliar city. Wilderness expert Libby Roberts discusses survival and wilderness skills with your safety as the number one priority. The book includes a glossary and listings of additional books and videos. Part of the All Action series.

1.42   Serraillier, Ian. **Escape from Warsaw.** Illustrated by Erwin Hoffmann. Scholastic/Point Books, 1990. 218 pp. ISBN 0-590-43715-1. Fiction.

Ruth and Edek's lives are changed completely when war comes to their Polish homeland. Their mother is taken away in the night by Nazi Storm Troopers, and their father is confined in a war prison. After Ruth and Edek escape with their little sister, they struggle to exist on their own in war-torn Warsaw. When they hear that their father has escaped to Switzerland, the three children attempt to cross Poland and Germany to find him. Their travels are dangerous and long, but they are determined to reach Switzerland. First published as *The Silver Sword*.

1.43   Strasser, Todd. **The Diving Bell.** Scholastic Hardcover Books, 1992. 157 pp. ISBN 0-590-44620-7. Fiction.

Set during the Spanish occupation of the Americas, *The Diving Bell* demonstrates the courage, wit, and determination of a young Native American girl, Culca, who takes on the Spanish government. Culca devises a plan to save her brother and other village divers from being forced to dive for gold at the site of a shipwreck that is too deep for the divers to reach and survive.

1.44   Swindells, Robert. **Fallout.** William Morrow/Beech Tree Books, 1992. 151 pp. ISBN 0-688-11778-3. Fiction.

As he takes shelter in a concrete bunker from a sudden rainstorm, Danny is knocked to the ground by a blinding flash of light, a hot rush of wind, and a tremendous thundering of the earth. He looks out from his shelter to see the fearful—but recognizable—sight of the mushroom-shaped cloud lifting from the English horizon. With fear and dread, Danny starts out for home to learn the fate of his family and his town. First published as *Brother in the Land*, 1985.

1.45   Taylor, Theodore. **Timothy of the Cay.** Harcourt Brace, 1993. 161 pp. ISBN 0-15-288358-4. Fiction.

In April 1942, Phillip Enright, an eleven-year-old white boy, and Timothy Gumbs, a black man of seventy, are shipwrecked in the Caribbean when their ship is torpedoed. Phillip is blinded by the blast. He and Timothy survive for three months on a tiny island, but when a hurricane strikes, Timothy dies. Phillip must manage alone for two months before he is rescued. Years later, remembering and recalling Timothy's wisdom, Phillip returns to Timothy's burial site. Sequel to *The Cay.*

ALA Best Books for Young Adults, 1994
Notable 1994 Children's Trade Books in the Field of Social Studies

1.46   Townsend, Tom. **Queen of the Wind.** Eakin Press/Panda Books, 1989. 142 pp. ISBN 0-89015-715-4. Fiction.

Because sailing is her only love, Blaze McKenzie leaves her New England home to be a sailing instructor on the Texas Gulf Coast. But Jack, her new boss, is difficult to please, especially when Blaze keeps breaking rules and pulling pranks. Then she is selected to sail a racing yacht in a single-handed ocean race, a dangerous competition, and Jack is her sailing coach. The grueling training becomes complicated when Blaze falls in love with Jack.

1.47   Ure, Jean. **Plague.** Harcourt Brace Jovanovich, 1991. 218 pp. ISBN 0-15-262429-5. Fiction.

Fran returns from a month-long camping trip to find her parents dead and London deserted. From the scant newscasts, she knows that a germ warfare accident is suspected of causing the terrible plague that is killing everyone. Fran's best friend Harriet is still alive but almost insane from watching her mother die. As the two girls set out in search of food and safety, they are joined by a school friend. The three begin a journey of danger as they travel across London. First published in Great Britain as *Plague 99*, 1987.

ALA Best Books for Young Adults, 1993

1.48   Voigt, Cynthia. **The Wings of a Falcon.** Scholastic, 1993. 467 pp. ISBN 0-590-46712-3. Fiction.

He was different from the other boys on the island—he never
cried, even when he was whipped; he never showed fear; and he
had no name. But he would be the next ruler of the island, the
seventh Damall, because he had beaten Nikol and had been
named heir. But when the sixth Damall dies, the boy and friend
Griff decide to leave the island forever, taking with them the
Damall's greatest treasure and protection, the green gemstone.
They seem safe—but will Nikol come after them to reclaim the
stone?

School Library Journal Best Books, 1993

1.49   Westall, Robert. **The Kingdom by the Sea.** Farrar, Straus and
Giroux/Aerial Books, 1993. 176 pp. ISBN 0-374-44060-3. Fiction.

When his family disappears in a German bombing attack during
World War II, Harry Baguely decides to strike out on his own
rather than live with an aunt he does not like. His best friend is a
stray dog that he adopts as he makes his way up the English seacoast to get away from the bombing. Harry meets many people
along the way—some who befriend him, some who try to kill
him—and learns to survive the dangers of nature and those who
would harm him. When he thinks he has finally found a home, a
new surprise awaits him. First published in Great Britain, 1990.

ALA Best Books for Young Adults, 1992

1.50   Williams, Michael. **Into the Valley.** Putnam/Philomel, 1993. 191
pp. ISBN 0-399-22516-1. Fiction.

At age seventeen, Walter does not understand what is happening in his South African country. Then he reads about a seventeen-year-old general who is responsible for saving his village.
When his brother dies, Walter begins a search for the youthful
general whom no one claims to know. He wants to understand
his country's problem and his part in it—but first he must fight
for his life. First published in South Africa, 1990.

2 Animals and Pets

2.1   Ackerman, Diane. **The Moon by Whale Light: And Other Adventures among Bats, Penguins, Crocodilians, and Whales.** Random House, 1991. 249 pp. ISBN 0-394-58574-7. Nonfiction.

Few people consider bats or alligators to be attractive, fewer still travel to the Antarctic to watch penguins, and hardly anyone swims with a whale. The exception is the author of these essays, Diane Ackerman. Her exquisite descriptions of nature range from the spiraling ascent of bats as they leave their cave for nocturnal foraging to the delicate courtship of alligators, those creatures who have outlived dinosaurs. The respect and admiration that Ackerman feels for animals is obvious in every adventure she relates in this beautifully written book.

Booklist Editors' Choice, 1991

2.2   Ball, Zachary. **Bristle Face.** Holiday House, 1991. 206 pp. ISBN 0-8234-0915-5. Fiction.

In this story set in the South in the early 1900s, fourteen-year-old Jase is sent to live with a cruel uncle after his parents are killed. Tired of being beaten by his uncle, Jase runs away, finding a funny-looking dog on his journey. He and Bristle Face find a home with Lute, a storekeeper who later becomes sheriff of their town. Though Bristle Face looks odd, he proves to be a wonderful dog and helps Jase find a new family.

2.3   Brandenburg, Jim (edited by Joann Bren Guernsey). **To the Top of the World: Adventures with Arctic Wolves.** Walker, 1993. 44 pp. ISBN 0-8027-8220-5. Nonfiction.

Spending a summer on Canada's Ellesmere Island, author Jim Brandenburg had a unique opportunity to study and photograph a family of wolves. Since Ellesmere Island is only 500 miles from the North Pole, it is an uninhabited, seldom-visited spot that provides a look at nature unhampered by the effect of humans. For this one summer Brandenburg followed a family of seven adult wolves and six pups, recording and observing their hierarchical structure, hunting techniques, training of the pups, and all other aspects of their routine—including howling. He returned to civilization impressed by the intelligence exhibited by the wolves as well as their concern for all members of their family unit. Breathtaking photographs illuminate the work.

ALA Best Books for Young Adults, 1994
ALA Quick Picks for Young Adults, 1994
NCTE Orbis Pictus Honor Book, 1994
School Library Journal Best Books, 1993

2.4   Bruant, Nicolas, photographer (text by John Heminway). **Wild Beasts.** Chronicle Books, 1993. 149 pp. ISBN 0-8118-0490-9. Nonfiction.

Nicolas Bruant, tells the story of African animals through photos: "I like the idea of zeroing in on a subject, drawing the tightest possible line between the animal and myself, and getting directly to each animal's essence, or my own, as the animal's intermediary." Beginning in 1970, Bruant photographed in Africa for twenty years, noting the differences brought on by wars, poaching, and anarchy. The photos are supplemented with both field notes and information text, highlighting habit and habitat of elephants, hippos, reptiles, zebras, birds, and other animals.

2.5   Burgess, Melvin. **The Cry of the Wolf.** William Morrow/Tambourine Books, 1992. 128 pp. ISBN 0-688-11744-9. Fiction.

When young Ben meets the Hunter, he is so in awe of him that he unthinkingly blurts out the fact that wolves live near his family's farm in Surrey. Since wolves are thought to be extinct in England, the Hunter's interest is piqued, and he goes in search of them. Finding the wolf family, the Hunter kills all of them except Graycub. Once Ben realizes what has happened, he is so upset that he makes it a personal quest to hunt the Hunter. First published in Great Britain, 1990.

2.6   Cerullo, Mary M. **Sharks: Challengers of the Deep.** Photography by Jeffrey L. Rotman. Dutton/Cobblehill Books, 1993. 57 pp. ISBN 0-525-65100-4. Nonfiction.

Do you worry about sharks when you go swimming in the ocean? Though sharks are feared by many people, they seldom attack humans, preferring to feed upon marine plants or other marine animals. As illustrated in this book, sharks have been around for over 400 million years and range in size from less than the width of one's hand up to the size of a bus. Sharks are well adapted for hunting for food since they can smell blood up to a quarter-mile away, can see shapes in dim light, and can react to sounds and vibrations. Their ability to sense electric fields given off by other animals means they sometimes bite through telephone cables lying at the bottom of the ocean. The book warns that some sharks should be avoided, and it helps readers understand how humans have used sharks, ranging from a source of vitamin A to a temporary skin for covering burns. Ironically, just as the value of sharks is being realized, their numbers are diminishing because of increased fishing, both commercially and recreationally.

School Library Journal Best Books, 1992

2.7   Clutton-Brock, Juliet. **Horse.** Alfred A. Knopf/Dorling Kindersley, 1992. 64 pp. ISBN 0-679-81681-X. Nonfiction.

In only sixty-four photo-laden pages, all aspects of the horse are introduced. Two-page spreads are devoted to a variety of topics, including the horse's evolution, its skeletal structure, and its use as a warhorse, mount for knights, draft animal, and in sporting events. The importance of the horse in exploration, in the settlement of the American West, and as a means of both travel and transport is detailed. Horse accoutrements are well illustrated with pages devoted to shoes and shoeing, riding equipment (including ancient spurs, bits, and stirrups), and horse-drawn vehicles. This slim book in the Eyewitness Books series includes a wealth of information that is sure to bring browsing pleasure to readers.

2.8   Douglas-Hamilton, Iain, and Oria Douglas-Hamilton (edited by Brian Jackman). **Battle for the Elephants.** Viking, 1992. 368 pp. ISBN 0-670-84003-3. Nonfiction.

When young Iain married Oria back in the late 1960s and they joined together in elephant research, neither thought that for the next twenty years they would be fighting just to keep the elephants from being decimated, first in Kenya, where they lived, and then throughout Africa. Now, however, they wage a battle worldwide against the ivory trade. It is a trade so lucrative that elephants are slaughtered merely to hack off their tusks and whole African villages give up their traditional farming merely to hunt and kill elephants. It is a trade that reaches all the way to Asia, where the ivory is sold. Because of the efforts of the Douglas-Hamiltons, as well as conservationists and park rangers, a ban on trade in ivory went into effect in 1989, slowing the rapid decimation of the largest mammals on earth today.

2.9   Durrell, Gerald. **The Aye-Aye and I: A Rescue Mission in Madagascar.** Arcade, 1993. 175 pp. ISBN 1-55970-204-4. Nonfiction.

Endangered animals have friends in Gerald Durrell and his wife. On their latest adventure, the Durrells travel to the island nation of Madagascar in search of the aye-aye, a toothy mammal once thought extinct. As they travel, they also collect gentle lemurs to take back to their Jersey, England, wildlife shelter, where they will try to breed the lemurs and send the offspring to zoos around the world. As usual, the unusual happens. Only Durrell would make light of his raging diarrhea while hunting for lemurs, or the "rear" attack he withstands from ducks while in an outside bathroom. Reading a Durrell book is just like being on the journey with him—lively, funny, and adventuresome.

2.10   Edwards, Elwyn Hartley. **The Ultimate Horse Book.** Photographs by Bob Langrish. Alfred A. Knopf/Dorling Kindersley, 1991. 240 pp. ISBN 1-879431-03-3. Nonfiction.

Have you heard of an Ardennais, Haflinger, or Knabstrup? Do you know how to curry a horse or determine its conformation? If "no" is your answer to one or both of these questions, this is the book for you. Following background information on the origin, evolutionary development, and early uses of the horse, glorious color photographs highlight horse characteristics, such as markings, coat colors, gaits, and behavior. Then follows a two-page layout for each of over eighty different breeds, including the Ardennais, Haflinger, and Knabstrup. This is a book for everyone, not just horse lovers.

2.11   Guravich, Dan, photographer (text by Downs Matthews). **Polar Bear.** Chronicle Books, 1993. 110 pp. ISBN 0-8118-0050-X. Nonfiction.

What eats 140 pounds at one meal, swims hundreds of miles, and loves to take naps? The creature is *Ursus maritimus* (sea bear), more popularly known as the polar bear. Forever roaming the ice, or swimming in chilly waters, the polar bear's body is well suited for life in the cold. Feeding almost entirely on seals, adults eat only the skin and blubber, leaving the red meat for their young or the Arctic foxes that follow them. Females are ferociously protective mothers, keeping their cubs by their side for several years before sending them off to forage on their own. Few people have the stamina to camp out on the ice just to have a glimpse of this bear in its home near the Arctic Circle, where frigid temperatures are the norm. Thus this book is a great alternative. The charming photos, perfectly matched with the text, were collected over several decades and provide a complete look at the polar bear's lifestyle.

2.12   Hall, Lynn. **The Soul of the Silver Dog.** Harcourt Brace Jovanovich, 1991. 125 pp. ISBN 0-15-277196-4. Fiction.

When her younger sister was born, Cory felt as though the love had been removed from her life. Her parents did not mean to ignore her, but bedridden Bethy demanded all their time. Bethy is now dead, her parents are divorced, and Cory feels more alone than ever. Alone, that is, until Sterling enters her life. Sterling is a champion Bedlington terrier left blinded by glaucoma. His owners cannot show a blind dog, so he is given to Cory, who loves him and trains him for competition in the obstacle course, offering him one last chance to be in a show ring.

ALA Quick Picks for Young Adults, 1993

2.13   Hall, Lynn. **Windsong.** Charles Scribner's Sons, 1992. 73 pp. ISBN 0-684-19439-2. Fiction.

Marty hates her spoiled younger brother and is unhappy about her mother's affair with a preacher, so she looks for any excuse not to be at home. Luckily her job at the greyhound kennel occupies most of her time. One puppy catches her eye, the runt of a litter of greyhounds, and she knows the puppy will soon be destroyed. She manages to save it, names it Windsong, and tries to take the puppy home—but she immediately runs into trouble because of her brother's allergies.

2.14   Iwago, Mitsuaki. **Whales.** Chronicle Books, 1994. ISBN 0-8118-0585-9. Nonfiction.

This unusually designed book piques one's curiosity about whales. A short introduction explains that the humpback whales portrayed in the book were photographed in three locations—southeastern Alaska, the Hawaiian Islands, and the Bonin Islands off the coast of Japan—and that the photographs were possible only because of the 1966 prohibition on whale hunting. Following are page after page of incredible color photos of the humpback whale—breeching, feeding, migrating, tending its calf. To avoid distracting from the impact of these photos, small black-and-white duplicate photos with captions are found in the back of the book. The unconventional design heightens the reader's impression of the humpback whale's magnificence.

2.15   Knight, Linsay. **The Sierra Club Book of Great Mammals.** Sierra Club Books for Children, 1992. 68 pp. ISBN 0-87156-507-2. Nonfiction.

This overview of mammals introduces the three major groups— monotremes, marsupials, and placental mammals—and then presents a history of their evolution, behavior traits, and a list of mammals currently endangered. Various types of mammals, from oxen to orangutans, donkeys to zebras, and bears to cats, are described in the remainder of the book, with each species accompanied by color photographs or illustrations. Fun facts, such as the many uses for an elephant's trunk, the difference between roaring and purring in cats, and the explanation of body odor in gorillas, make the book a browser's delight.

2.16   MacQuitty, Miranda. **Shark.** Photographs by Frank Greenaway and Dave King. Alfred A. Knopf/Dorling Kindersley Books, 1992. 63 pp. ISBN 0-679-91683-0. Nonfiction.

Did you know that there are about 375 species of shark, ranging in size from 6.5 inches to over 40 feet in length? If you want to learn about sharks and their behavior, you will find this book in the Eyewitness Books series to be a comprehensive introduction. Filled with numerous color photographs, the book reveals different species of sharks in their natural environments and dispels common misconceptions about them.

2.17   Monson, A. M. **The Deer Stand.** Lothrop, Lee and Shepard Books, 1992. 171 pp. ISBN 0-688-11057-6. Fiction.

For citified Bits, having to move up to northern Wisconsin is a horrible experience. The quiet is eerie, the kids at school laugh at her multipierced ears, and no one wants to be her friend. One afternoon Bits climbs into a deer stand located on their property, sees a deer she names Buck, and sets out to befriend him. Her continual food offerings gradually tame him until she realizes the damage she has done to the animal—right before hunting season. Bits is frantic as she tries to find a way to save her deer from hunters.

2.18   Newton, David E. **Hunting.** Franklin Watts/Impact Books, 1992. 142 pp. ISBN 0-531-13022-3. Nonfiction.

This book is not a guide to hunting. Rather, it is an overview of hunting from its origins as a means for humankind's survival to its current status as a sport. In addition to providing historical background about hunting traditions in Europe, Asia, and North America, author David E. Newton explores the laws and regulations currently controlling hunting and details the problems involved with poachers. Several chapters provide alternating viewpoints between hunters and nonhunters with regard to harassment, wildlife conservation, and ethical issues. Whether you are a hunter or a nonhunter, this book is useful for anyone interested in animals or the sport of hunting.

2.19   Paine, Stefani. **The World of the Sea Otter.** Photographs by Jeff Foott. Sierra Club Books, 1993. 132 pp. ISBN 0-87156-546-3. Nonfiction.

The sea otter lives most of its life in the ocean, where its dense coat and fastidious grooming provide the buoyancy needed to survive. But that luxurious coat also contributed to the animal's near demise in the 1700s, when the Aleuts and the Russians hunted it almost to extinction. Now that the sea otter is legally protected from hunting, its population along the Pacific coast from Mexico to Alaska is up to about 150,000—but that is only half of its original number. As the color photos illustrate, the sea otter is a playful creature that is content to spend its life eating, diving, grooming, and sleeping. These charming animals have returned to the coastal waters of California, where those interested in conservation are determined to see these creatures thrive.

2.20   Peck, Sylvia. **Kelsey's Raven.** Morrow Junior Books, 1992. 234 pp. ISBN 0-688-09583-6. Fiction.

When Kelsey Martine and her mother hear a strange noise coming from behind their boarded-up fireplace, they hire Dustin, a chimneysweep. Behind the fireplace they discover an injured raven, which Kelsey keeps in an aerie, or nest, on their roof while taking a class on birds at the museum. A first romance for Kelsey, an argument with her best friend Sam, and her mother's eventual engagement to Dustin mark Kelsey's summer, all of which are overshadowed by her care for the aging raven.

2.21   Polikoff, Barbara Garland. **Life's a Funny Proposition, Horatio.** Henry Holt, 1992. 103 pp. ISBN 0-8050-1972-3. Fiction.

Horatio has had difficulty adjusting to the death of his father and his family's subsequent move to a small town. Now his life changes again as his grandfather (called O. P. for Old Professor) moves in with them, displacing Horatio from his own bedroom. But Horatio finds they have a common bond in death as he still grieves over his father and O. P. grieves for his dog Mollie, who dies during a winter storm.

ALA Notable Books for Children, 1993
School Library Journal Best Books, 1992

2.22   Richardson, Nan, and Catherine Chermayeff. **Wild Babies.**
Chronicle Books, 1994. 80 pp. ISBN 0-8118-0477-1. Nonfiction.

Wild babies fill many niches within the structure of their species.
The baby white rhino is fiercely defended by its mother, while a
baby snow monkey may be offered to an aggressive male as a sign
to halt the aggression. The dominant ostrich hen ensures that her
eggs lie in the center of the collective nest, where they have the
best chance for hatching. Manatee and koala offspring can spend
up to two years being cared for by their mothers, while other
wildlife babies, such as male langurs, are driven out of their troop
within their first year. Other babies featured include hedgehogs,
lemurs, musk ox, and crocodiles, all of which are raised in
uniquely individualistic ways, as portrayed in captivating color
photographs.

2.23   Sakurai, Atsushi, Yohei Sakamoto, and Fumitoshi Mori (translated
by Takeshi Shimizu, with Neal M. Teitler). **Aquarium Fish of the
World: The Comprehensive Guide to 650 Species.** Chronicle
Books, 1993. 300 pp. ISBN 0-8118-0269-8. Nonfiction.

The 650 species of aquarium fish described in this book are divided among eleven chapters, organized by their fish family. A
map precedes each chapter to show the normal distribution of
each fish family and is followed by information on the native surroundings. Many photos illustrate these aquarium fish and are
accompanied by notes describing their needs in an aquarium and
the difficulty in raising and/or breeding them. Readers can imagine these fish, usually seen only in tanks, swimming in their natural habitats of the Amazon River, the Zaire River, or Lake
Tanganyika, to name just a few spots where they are found.

2.24   Savage, Candace. **Peregrine Falcons.** Sierra Club Books, 1992.
145 pp. ISBN 0-87156-504-8. Nonfiction.

The peregrine falcon is one of the most wide-ranging birds, as well
as one of the rarest. Its unusual place at the top of the food pyramid enables it to serve as a warning signal for the environment.
Through history, falcons have been tamed and trained to hunt for
their keepers. In recent years, predatory birds were eradicated to
allow better sport hunting of game; their numbers were further
diminished when the use of DDT caused thin-shelled eggs to
crack before the chicks were hatched. But humans are also responsible for the peregrines' resurgence through reduction of DDT
usage and an increase in specialized breeding programs. Gorgeous photographs capture the beauty of the bird, from their nest

sites on steep cliffs with their fluffy chicks to their soaring flight, feeding habits, use by falconers, and striking plumage.

2.25 Shachtman, Tom. **Driftwhistler: A Story of Daniel au Fond.** Henry Holt, 1992. 176 pp. ISBN 0-8050-1285-0. Fiction.

In this third volume of the Daniel au Fond trilogy, the sea lion Daniel and his tribe of sea lions finally come to the end of their search for a legendary cove called Pacifica, where animals and people can coexist. Daniel becomes more of a shaman and eventually a driftwhistler, one who is able to bring unity to the thirteen tribes of sea mammals. Through the thoughts of Daniel and his fellow sea lions, the book highlights concern about pollution, the exploitation of animals and natural resources, and a need for cooperation.

2.26 Sherlock, Patti. **Four of a Kind.** Holiday House, 1991. 196 pp. ISBN 0-8234-0913-9. Fiction.

Ever since Andy was a young boy, he has wanted his own team of Percheron horses, those big, beautiful draft horses that are often seen pulling wagons in commercials. When a neighbor's Percheron has twin foals that have to be sold, Andy knows that this is his chance to achieve his dream. First he has to convince his grandfather, with whom he lives, to buy them, and then he has to train them. Andy has inherited his grandfather's stubbornness and is determined to succeed in this endeavor. When the two Percherons are added to his family, the result is "four of a kind."

IRA Young Adults' Choices, 1993

2.27 Sherlock, Patti. **Some Fine Dog.** Holiday House, 1992. 153 pp. ISBN 0-8234-0947-3. Fiction.

Terry lives with his single mother in a household that is always concerned about money. He sings in the choir partly because his mother hopes that one day he will win the annual choir scholarship and have a chance to escape from poverty by attending college. Terry finds a stray border collie and wants to keep it, though the family budget does not allow for extras such as dog food. A frightening experience while caught in a snowstorm in the mountains enables Terry to decide what is best for everyone.

2.28 Smith, Roland. **Inside the Zoo Nursery.** Photographs by William Muñoz. Dutton/Cobblehill Books, 1993. 58 pp. ISBN 0-525-65084-9. Nonfiction.

Though zoo nurseries are popular with the public, zoo staff members are happiest when the nursery is empty, for that means the young are being raised by their mothers. But if a mother is too weak, dies, or has too many babies, zoo nursery personnel are prepared to step in and raise the young. Read about Mandy, a young baboon rejected by her mother, who spends thirteen months in the zoo nursery, where she encounters many other animal youngsters, such as baby leopards, cheetahs, kangaroo rats, and ostriches.

School Library Journal Best Books, 1992

2.29   Zwaenepoel, Jean-Pierre. **Tigers.** Chronicle Books, 1992. 80 pp. ISBN 0-8118-0136-5. Nonfiction.

Stretched out on overlooks, camouflaged in the tall grass, or cooling off in a muddy stream are various specimens of tigers, another endangered species. Captivated by these large felines, the author spent several years in a national park in central India observing different tiger families and their interconnectedness with their surroundings. Although Belgian Jean-Pierre Zwaenepoel is not a trained scientist, his beautifully illustrated work is a reminder of the cost to the world when human populations encroach on a wild animal's territory.

3 Archaeology and Anthropology

3.1 Avi-Yonah, Michael. **Dig This! How Archaeologists Uncover Our Past.** Lerner/Runestone Press, 1993. 96 pp. ISBN 0-8225-3200-X. Nonfiction.

Ancient civilizations and people hold the key to today's art, rituals, and customs of everyday life. Archaeologists, working with highly scientific systems and methods, have found ways to "read" these secrets and preserve the information for the future. *Dig This!* defines archaeology and describes what diggers have discovered that links great civilizations with modern times. A pronunciation key, glossary, and index make this easily read book both usable and informative.

3.2 Brown, David J. **The Random House Book of How Things Were Built.** Random House, 1992. 140 pp. ISBN 0-679-92044-7. Nonfiction.

Saddam Hussein is rebuilding the ancient city of Babylon. Flush toilets were in existence 3,500 years ago. What are the architectural secrets behind these structures? From cobels to ziggurats to flying buttresses—from Roman roads to cathedral bells—this colorfully illustrated text carries us through the history of the world's man-made structures, some of which are still surrounded by mystery. This is a good beginner's book, with its nontechnical glossary and helpful index of architectural methods and styles. First published in Great Britain, 1991.

IRA Children's Choices, 1993

3.3 Gonen, Rivka. **Fired Up! Making Pottery in Ancient Times.** Lerner/Runestone Press, 1993. 72 pp. ISBN 0-8225-3202-6. Nonfiction.

What can a pot, shaped by hand from wet clay, tell us about its maker and the civilization that influenced its creation? As artists paint scenes depicting everyday life on the sides of clay bowls and vases, cooking utensils become records of lost civilizations. An entire army of clay soldiers protects a Chinese emperor in the afterlife. Ancient pottery becomes a calendar for the past. An index and glossary aid in this clear history of the techniques of pottery making.

3.4   Hoig, Stan. **People of the Sacred Arrows: The Southern Cheyenne Today.** Dutton/Cobblehill Books, 1992. 130 pp. ISBN 0-525-65088-1. Nonfiction.

The Sacred Arrow Renewal ceremonies and the annual Sun Dance bring Oklahoma's Southern Cheyenne back to the lands where their tribes once roamed freely, before the white man's prejudices and restrictions separated their communal nation. The struggle to retain old values and customs while adjusting to conditions brought on by the settlement of the West are told with personal insight by a native Oklahoman who grew up near the Cheyenne territories. Photographs and old prints add to the telling.

3.5   Hubbard-Brown, Janet. **The Disappearance of the Anasazi: A History Mystery.** Illustrated by Lino Saffioti. Avon/Camelot Books, 1992. 90 pp. ISBN 0-380-76845-3. Nonfiction.

The ancient civilization of Anasazi tribes once existed in great numbers in the southwestern United States. They built superhighways—yet they did not possess the wheel. They were known as a gentle people but are thought to have participated in cannibalism at some point. They carved great cities from the canyon walls. This easy-to-read book sets forth many facts known about Anasazi rituals and customs, but it cannot solve the mystery of their disappearance.

3.6   Macaulay, David. **Ship.** Houghton Mifflin, 1993. 96 pp. ISBN 0-395-52439-3. Fiction.

Small streamlined sailing ships known as caravels explored and shaped the world in the fifteenth century; they were the equivalent of our space shuttles. Modern underwater archaeologists painstakingly explore remains of an ancient caravel and record through illustrations, charts, and diagrams how a caravel might have looked. Through a fictional sixteenth-century diary and colorful, detailed illustrations, we witness the day-to-day construction of such a ship.

Booklist Editors' Choice, 1993
IRA Teachers' Choices, 1994

3.7   Monroe, Jean Guard, and Ray A. Williamson. **First Houses: Native American Homes and Sacred Structures.** Illustrated by Susan Johnston Carlson. Houghton Mifflin, 1993. 137 pp. ISBN 0-395-51081-3. Fiction.

Tepees of the Plains Indians were decorated with disks that represented Whirlwind Woman, an entity who helped create the earth. The Delaware Ceremonial Dwelling was built to specifications from instructions received in dreams by men of the tribe. A Grizzly-Bear House grew to accommodate any number of guests. The forms that Native American houses and spiritual dwellings have taken reflect myths and legends from what Native Americans call the Beginning Time. A glossary, bibliography, and index add information.

Notable 1994 Children's Trade Books in the Field of Social Studies

3.8   Pearson, Anne. **Ancient Greece.** Alfred A. Knopf/Dorling Kindersley, 1992. 63 pp. ISBN 0-679-91682-2. Nonfiction.

Brief descriptions of every aspect of the ancient Greek world are accompanied by numerous colorful drawings and photographs in this Eyewitness Book. The beauty of Greek art, the temples of the gods, and everyday life of women and athletes are some of the topics covered in this fact-filled presentation. If you are just beginning to learn about the ancient world or if you are looking for some little known fact, such as who Nike is, this volume is a good place to begin.

Notable 1994 Children's Trade Books in the Field of Social Studies

3.9   Pellegrino, Charles. **Unearthing Atlantis: An Archaeological Odyssey.** Random House/Vintage Books, 1993. 325 pp. ISBN 0-679-73407-4. Nonfiction.

Thera is a Mediterranean island buried for 3,000 years under a layer of volcanic ash spewed forth by one of the earth's most violent upheavals. Thera had flush toilets and multistoried buildings that could easily be a part of modern cities. Were the inhabitants of the island of Thera citizens of the lost city of Atlantis? A chronological history of the earth and an extensive bibliography make this book a valuable resource for anyone interested in the mystery of Atlantis.

3.10   Reeves, Nicholas, with Nan Froman. **Into the Mummy's Tomb.** Scholastic/Madison Press Books, 1992. 64 pp. ISBN 0-590-45752-7. Nonfiction.

Egyptologist Nicholas Reeves tells of modern-day discoveries of ancient Egyptian treasures at the family estate of Lord Carnarvon, grandson of the man who financed Howard Carter in his search for and discovery of King Tutankhamen's tomb in 1922. Reeves relates events leading up to the 1922 discovery of the greatest treasure find of modern times—a king's treasure buried for 3,000 years. Colorful photographs, drawings, and diagrams lead us through the burial chambers as they were found.

ALA Quick Picks for Young Adults, 1993
Booklist Editors' Choice, 1992
IRA Teachers' Choices, 1993
School Library Journal Best Books, 1992

4 Art and Architecture

4.1   Bindman, Catherine. **Designer's Guide to French Patterns.** Chronicle Books, 1993. 128 pp. ISBN 0-8118-0472-0. Nonfiction.

Do you have questions about what patterns and colors to use in designing or remodeling? This volume in the Guide to Color series examines the evolution of French design, from medieval manuscripts to contemporary textiles and wallpaper. It is replete with 125 color illustrations of patterns and with explanations that reflect the cultures and styles of French patterns, including religious, royal, and popular sources. First published in Great Britain, 1993.

4.2   Bolton, Linda. **Hidden Pictures.** Dial Books, 1993. 57 pp. ISBN 0-8037-1378-9. Nonfiction.

See if you can find the hidden messages or pictures in paintings and other works of art in this entertaining and intriguing book. Use the reflecting mirror included to help solve some of the mysteries. Learn about anamorphic pictures, distorted pictures, and curious pictures. Learn as well to make your own mysterious pictures. View the works of the famous—Leonardo da Vinci, Salvador Dali, Pablo Picasso, Paul Gauguin, for example—and the unidentified artists who created these visual riddles.

IRA Children's Choices, 1994

4.3   Cole, Alison. **Color.** Alfred A. Knopf/Dorling Kindersley, 1993. 64 pp. ISBN 1-56458-332-5. Nonfiction.

This essential visual guide to the use of color is part of the Eyewitness Art series. Author Alison Cole examines the unique use of color in the works of the great masters, from Giotto and Raphael to Jackson Pollock and Andy Warhol. She describes a variety of ways to mix pigments in different media to achieve different effects. The book was prepared in collaboration with the National Gallery of Art, Washington, D.C.

4.4   Cummings, Pat. **Talking with Artists.** Macmillan/Bradbury Press, 1992. 96 pp. ISBN 0-02-724245-5. Nonfiction.

Fourteen famous illustrators of books for children—artists such as Leo and Diane Dillon, Steven Kellogg, and Chris Van Allsburg—talk with author Pat Cummings. In a short chapter on each artist, she provides a two-page autobiographical statement, responses to eight questions ("Where do you get your ideas from? Do you have any children? Any pets? How did you get to do your first book?"), and illustrations by the artist.

ALA Notable Books for Children, 1993
Booklist Editors' Choice, 1992
Boston Globe–Horn Book Nonfiction Award, 1992
IRA Teachers' Choices, 1993
NCTE Orbis Pictus Honor Book, 1993

4.5   Deem, George. **Art School: An Homage to the Masters.** Illustrations by George Deem. Chronicle Books, 1993. 64 pp. ISBN 0-8118-0414-3. Nonfiction.

Building on the concept of "schools of art," George Deem recasts the work of thirty-eight renowned painters—Vermeer, Modigliani, Rembrandt, Velazquez, Matisse among them—as imaginary classrooms in which he imitates, in vivid color, the style and typical subject matter of each artist. An introduction by Irene McManus informs readers of Deem's schoolroom theme.

4.6   Freeman, Judi. **Mark Tansey.** Los Angeles County Museum of Art and Chronicle Books, 1993. 116 pp. ISBN 0-8118-0468-2. Nonfiction.

Judi Freeman presents an interpretive essay on fifty Mark Tansey paintings reproduced in photographs and drawings. Tansey, an American artist, created twenty-two drawings, and Alain Robbe-Grillet, French author and photographer, wrote an introduction expressly for this publication. Freeman describes much of Tansey's work as conveying imaginary narratives through their dense detail.

4.7   Guliayev, Vladimir. **The Fine Art of Russian Lacquered Miniatures.** Chronicle Books, 1993. 287 pp. ISBN 0-8118-0325-2. Nonfiction.

As a more open society develops in the former Soviet Union, we are now privy to a number of previously "hidden" treasures, including the intricate art form of Russian lacquers—boxes and objects typically painted with scenes of folk myth or peasant life. The text and 250 photographs trace the history of the lacquers and shed light on Russian history.

4.8   Heiferman, Marvin, and Carole Kismaric. **My Day: A Tale of Fear, Alienation and Despair.** Chronicle Books, 1993. 93 pp. ISBN 0-8118-0270-1. Nonfiction.

The authors take a "visually literate approach to bookmaking," combining photography, art, and tongue-in-cheek messages to black-and-white photography on the topic of *anxiety.* They examine the turmoil and tension of everyday life—in particular, American white-collar life.

4.9   Heller, Steven, and Louise Fili. **Italian Art Deco: Graphic Design between the Wars.** Chronicle Books, 1993. 134 pp. ISBN 0-8118-0287-6. Nonfiction.

Art Deco, a synthesis of ancient motifs, Cubism, and machine-age symbols, dominated design from 1925 to 1939. Artists such as Marinetti, Depero, and Munari turned the commonplace into allegory, or symbols, through their graphics, and they also influenced car posters, fashion designs, and other artistic expressions. Art Deco peaked in 1939, but the style still influences many of today's graphic designers.

4.10   Hess, Alan. **Viva Las Vegas: After-Hours Architecture.** Chronicle Books, 1993. 128 pp. ISBN 0-8118-0111-X. Nonfiction.

How did a small town in the desert boom into a neon strip? Not only does Alan Hess trace the development of Las Vegas as an urban center with an economy largely built around gambling, but he also examines the evolution of the architecture of "the strip" over several decades. Archival and contemporary photographs graphically illustrate the "neon capital"—Las Vegas is the only city in which signage qualifies as architecture—and provides an interesting perspective on urban architecture.

4.11   Hockney, David (edited by Nikos Stangos). **That's the Way I See It.** Chronicle Books, 1993. 248 pp. ISBN 0-8118-0506-9. Nonfiction.

Artist David Hockney shares his art, theories, personal insights, and working techniques in this book, tying these subjects together with the narrative of his life. Inspired by the Cubist movement, Hockney explains how he uses photo snapshots to include narrative elements in a work. Selling his house in London and moving to California influenced his use of color. Working on the set design for the Stravinsky opera *Rake's Progress* made him reconsider space as a function of perspective. Even the copy machine gets serious consideration as it influences the way artists create in our world today.

4.12   Isaacson, Philip M. **A Short Walk around the Pyramids and through the World of Art.** Alfred A. Knopf/Borzoi Books, 1993. 122 pp. ISBN 0-679-91523-0. Nonfiction.

What is a work of art? Is a pyramid art? Is a kachina doll? What constitutes sculpture? Are cities and towns art? The author brings to life a real understanding of different kinds of art and presents this in a clear, readily understood manner. Extensive use of color photographs adds to the book.

ALA Best Books for Young Adults, 1994
ALA Notable Books for Children, 1994
Notable 1994 Children's Trade Books in the Field of Social Studies
School Library Journal Best Books, 1993

4.13   Lorenz, Richard. **Imogen Cunningham: Ideas without End: A Life in Photographs.** Chronicle Books, 1993. 180 pp. ISBN 0-8118-0390-2. Nonfiction.

Imogen Cunnningham was one of the first women to achieve status as a photographer. A pioneer and compelling artist, she traced stark realities of life as well as more attractive aspects over a seventy-year career. Her nudes are bold; her still lifes are imaginative. This work contains 200 of her photographs, including many never published previously.

4.14   Parsons, Thomas. **Designer's Guide to Scandinavian Patterns.** Chronicle Books, 1993. 128 pp. ISBN 0-8118-0495-X. Nonfiction.

Thomas Parsons examines the contribution of Danish, Finnish, Norwegian, and Swedish artists to the field of design. He examines Scandinavian motifs from filigreed Viking brooches to today's bold graphic designs. The book includes 125 color illustrations, as well as black-and-white images.

4.15   Peeters, Benoît. **Tintin and the World of Hergé.** Bulfinch Press, 1992. 165 pp. ISBN 0-316-69752-4. Nonfiction.

George Remi, the Belgian artist Hergé, creates Tintin, a gallant reporter who traverses the globe. From their first publication in 1929, Hergé's cartoons became popular for their story lines and dialogue. In a beautifully illustrated text, Benoît Peeters does an admirable job of presenting a biography of the artist as well as a detailed interpretation of his immensely successful books. With over 120 million books sold in almost forty languages for a period of over sixty years, the Tintin success is phenomenal.

4.16   Platt, Richard. **Stephen Biesty's Incredible Cross-Sections.** Illustrated by Stephen Biesty. Alfred A. Knopf/Dorling Kindersley, 1992. 53 pp. ISBN 0-679-81411-6. Nonfiction.

What fantastic views of the interior architecture of a castle, galleon, the Empire State Building, and even a space shuttle! Stephen Biesty's intricately detailed illustrations are based on actual plans. The text blends history and humor and equals the richness of the architect's drawings. Several illustrations are an added bonus because they fold out to an amazing three feet. This book pleases anyone who wants to know the intricate details of past or present places and objects that fascinate.

ALA Quick Picks for Young Adults, 1994

4.17 Schwartz, Gary. **Rembrandt.** Harry N. Abrams, 1992. 92 pp. ISBN 0-8109-3760-3. Nonfiction.

Through a series of color and black-and-white photographs of Rembrandt Harmenszoon van Rijn's paintings and with information about his life, Gary Schwartz provides an intriguing portrait of this seventeenth-century artist. In this book in the First Impressions series, the photographs reveal much about Rembrandt's interests and his techniques. Of special interest is the attention given in the text to the circumstances surrounding the artist's creations that reveal the human soul.

4.18 Sexton, Richard, photographer (text by Randolph Delehanty). **New Orleans: Elegance and Decadence.** Chronicle Books, 1993. 222 pp. ISBN 0-8118-0074-1. Nonfiction.

New Orleans is an eclectic mixture of people, food, and architecture thanks to its unique geography and history. There are the French and Spanish fur traders, the Caribbean and African slaves and free men, and the working-class German and Irish to thank for the beauty of New Orleans. The photos by Richard Sexton and the narrative by Randolph Delehanty capture both the elegance and decadence of the Crescent City.

4.19 Smith, Ray. **An Introduction to Acrylics.** Alfred A. Knopf/ Dorling Kindersley, 1993. 72 pp. ISBN 1-56458-373-2. Nonfiction.

This volume in the Dorling Kindersley Art School series, in association with the British Royal Academy of Art, provides a practical guide to a wide range of acrylic painting techniques. Author Ray Smith, an internationally noted artist, describes how to use this relative newcomer to the world of painting media, including selecting colors, picking brushes and other painting tools, choosing paper, composing the image, achieving color balance in a painting, and using light, shade, and tone.

4.20   Smith, Ray. **An Introduction to Oil Painting.** Alfred A. Knopf/
Dorling Kindersley, 1993. 72 pp. ISBN 1-56458-372-4. Nonfiction.

In association with the Royal Academy of Art, this book in the
Dorling Kindersley Art School series explores how to paint with
oils. The step-by-step instructions are designed for those who
wish to learn, improve, or master oil painting. Full-color photographs and easy-to-follow exercises guide "armchair" art students
all the way from selecting materials to presenting the finished
artwork. A glossary explains the painting terms, and there is a
cautionary note about the toxicity of oil paints.

4.21   Tuchman, Maurice, and Joseph Campbell. **Masquerade: The
Mask as Art.** Chronicle Books, 1993. 107 pp. ISBN 0-8118-0445-3.
Nonfiction.

More than sixty sculptors and painters present "the mask as art"
in this fascinating book. Masks are a form of expression, identity,
authenticity, and social comment. Illustrations show the diverse
materials and rich colors used in masks.

4.22   Tudor, Tasha, and Richard Brown. **The Private World of Tasha
Tudor.** Little, Brown, 1992. 134 pp. ISBN 0-316-11292-5. Nonfiction.

What is it like to be a successful illustrator of children's books?
To be able, for the most part, to shape your own life, build your
ideal home, raise flora and fauna? Richard Brown spent one year
on Tasha Tudor's farm photographing the seasons, the illustrator, and her lifestyle. Brown weaves a rich portrait of Tudor
through her own words and his photography and captures her
"uniquely appealing personality and way of life." The color photographs are splendid, as are the examples of her work, some of
which have not been previously published.

4.23   Wiggins, Colin. **Post-Impressionism.** Alfred A. Knopf/Dorling
Kindersley, 1993. 64 pp. ISBN 1-56458-334-1. Nonfiction.

This is an essential visual guide to Post-Impressionist painters—
such as Cézanne, Gauguin, Picasso, and van Gogh—and the influences that shaped their work. The book is one volume in the
Eyewitness Art series and was done in collaboration with the Art
Institute of Chicago.

4.24   Wright, Michael. **An Introduction to Pastels.** Alfred A. Knopf/
Dorling Kindersley, 1993. 72 pp. ISBN 1-56458-374-0. Nonfiction.

Pastels—sticks of pure pigment in a wide range of vivid colors and subtle tints—are ideal for the beginning artist wanting to make the transition from drawing and sketching to painting. British artist Michael Wright introduces readers to working with pastels. Full-color photographs show the range of pastels and types of paper available and the effects that can be achieved. Step-by-step instructions help readers learn to create and frame their artwork. Terms are further explained in the glossary. This is one of six books in the Dorling Kindersley Art series in association with the British Royal Academy of Art.

4.25 Wright, Patricia. **Goya.** Alfred A. Knopf/Dorling Kindersley, 1993. 64 pp. ISBN 1-56458-333-3. Nonfiction.

Patricia Wright examines the life and art of Francisco Joseph Goya and the influences that shaped his work. The Spanish painter Goya worked in the late 1700s and early 1800s, and some consider him a genius and the greatest painter of his age. This book in the Eyewitness Art series was done in collaboration with the National Gallery of London.

4.26 Zamora, Martha (translated by Marilyn Sode Smith). **Frida Kahlo: The Brush of Anguish.** Chronicle Books, 1990. 143 pp. ISBN 0-8118-0485-2. Nonfiction.

Seventy-five art reproductions tell Frida Kahlo's life story. Her art graphically depicts her tragic life, including a streetcar accident, an unhappy marriage to famous artist Diego Rivera, and a debilitating back operation. In spite of her injuries, Kahlo's spark for life shines through in her art, including self-portraits in native Mexican outfits and accompanied by monkeys, ancient relics, and beautiful flowers. Discover both the source and results of Frida Kahlo's self-absorption.

5 Autobiography and Biography

5.1   Anderson, Madelyn Klein. **Edgar Allan Poe: A Mystery.** Franklin Watts/Impact Books, 1993. 137 pp. ISBN 0-531-13012-6. Nonfiction.

Like so much of his writing, Edgar Allan Poe's life was a mixture of speculation and mystery. Born to a theatrical mother and a father who played at acting, Poe was orphaned early in his life and went to live with the Allans of Richmond, Virginia. How he was treated by the Allans is a source of conjecture, as the story varies according to which critic tells the tale. This biography relates the many jobs Poe held and how he was not always fairly compensated, the claims of plagiarism against him, the personal life and loves of the young man, and the mystery of his early death. Whether fact or fantasy conjured by the young Poe himself, his story is the sad saga of a man whom life did not treat well.

5.2   Andronik, Catherine M. **Kindred Spirit: A Biography of L. M. Montgomery, Creator of Anne of Green Gables.** Atheneum, 1993. 145 pp. ISBN 0-689-31671-2. Nonfiction.

Every year, tourists take the ferry from the Canadian mainland to Prince Edward Island to visit a quaint house with green trim. It is the birthplace of Lucy Maud Montgomery, author of the much loved *Anne of Green Gables*. This biography reveals the constant struggle Montgomery faced living in an era when women were not expected to become serious writers. She never gave up her dreams, and when she died in 1942, her books were known around the world.

5.3   Archer, Chalmers, Jr. **Growing Up Black in Rural Mississippi: Memories of a Family, Heritage of a Place.** Walker, 1992. 147 pp. ISBN 0-8027-1175-8. Nonfiction.

Chalmers Archer Jr. shares with the reader his life as an African American child growing up in the Deep South during the 1940s and 1950s. Although he mentions some of the discrimination his family faced, he does not dwell upon it. Instead, he focuses on his close-knit family and the rich heritage passed on to him. The book is filled with family history, legends, and descriptions of a lifestyle that has all but disappeared.

5.4 Baldwin, Joyce. **To Heal the Heart of a Child: Helen Taussig, M.D.** Walker, 1992. 144 pp. ISBN 0-8027-8167-5. Nonfiction.

Illustrating the fact that the fight for women's rights is not a new one, this biography of Dr. Helen Taussig (1898–1986) explores the obstacles she faced in her personal life and professional life. Joyce Baldwin has successfully captured the die-hard spirit of a feisty lady who fought for the safety of infants suffering from congenital heart defects and, in the process, won for herself a distinguished position among many acclaimed doctors. Born to affluent parents, Taussig fought against dyslexia, hearing loss, and prejudice to ascend to heights few have achieved. At a time when women were not admitted to medical schools in this country, Helen Taussig defied tradition when she decided upon her career. Her long hours of work and her complete devotion to her research on "blue babies" netted her the distinction of being a pioneer in preserving the lives of hundreds who would otherwise have died.

5.5 Bentley, Judith. **Archbishop Tutu of South Africa.** Enslow, 1993. 83 pp. ISBN 0-89490-180-X. Nonfiction.

A combination of the political history of South Africa and the personal life of Desmond Tutu, this biography traces the life of Tutu and tells of his crusade to show his South African countrymen the evils of apartheid. Maps of the country and vivid pictures of inhumane treatment of its citizens illustrate the political turmoil that has beset South Africa for years. A product of a religious family, Tutu worked as a teacher for a time. Yet when the need arose for a priest in his village, he filled the position and remained until he was named the first black Archbishop in the Anglican Church of South Africa. Tutu's valiant efforts to bring harmony among the people of his country won him the 1984 Nobel Prize for Peace.

5.6 Bober, Natalie S. **Thomas Jefferson: Man on a Mountain.** Macmillan/Collier Books, 1993. 274 pp. ISBN 0-02-041797-7. Nonfiction.

This thorough tribute to the accomplishments of a great man recounts the political, social, and economic rise of Thomas Jefferson from his early years in Shadwell to his death on his beloved mountain at Monticello. His life as a student at the College of William and Mary, his courtship of and marriage to Martha Wayles, his political life first in Virginia and then on a national level, and his keen interest in practical inventions are all part of this intriguing story of a man whose skills and talents enabled him to rise to the ultimate position as president of the United States. Despite his prominence as a statesman and a politician, Jefferson's greatest pride lay in the role he played in writing the Declaration of Independence, in his love for his family and his Monticello, and in the construction of the University of Virginia, his "academical village." It is through these three accomplishments that the reader is able to see this giant as a real person.

5.7   Broman, Sven. **Conversations with Greta Garbo.** Viking, 1992. 259 pp. ISBN 0-670-84277-X. Nonfiction.

If you are fascinated by the elusive Greta Garbo, one of Hollywood's most famous stars, you will enjoy this collection of photographs and conversations with her. The author, a Swedish journalist, met Garbo in a hotel in 1985. The chance meeting was the beginning of a friendship that lasted until Garbo's death in 1990. Sven Broman's book offers a better understanding of the real Greta Garbo. First published in Great Britain as *Greta Garbo.*

5.8   Byars, Betsy. **The Moon and I.** Simon and Schuster/Julian Messner, 1991. 94 pp. ISBN 0-671-74165-9. Nonfiction.

Novelist Betsy Byars's memoirs are warm, amusing, and filled with talk about writing and good advice for young writers. Byars shares her personal writing habits, filling the reader in on when and where she likes to write and how she gets her ideas for new books. Byars also weaves in entertaining childhood memories and stories of her adult encounters with a snake named Moon.

ALA Notable Books for Children, 1993

5.9   Cantwell, Mary. **American Girl: Scenes from a Small-Town Childhood.** Random House, 1992. 209 pp. ISBN 0-394-57502-4. Nonfiction.

Mary Cantwell, a writer for the *New York Times,* offers an entertaining look at what it was like to grow up in a small American town during the 1940s and 1950s. She takes her readers back to a gentler time of family get-togethers, Fourth of July parades, first dates, and proms. We also witness unhappy moments, such as a bout with polio, school fights, and the death of loved ones. Her memories will make us smile and perhaps question today's fast-paced, impersonal lifestyle.

5.10   Coil, Suzanne M. **Harriet Beecher Stowe.** Franklin Watts/Impact Books, 1993. 157 pp. ISBN 0-531-13006-1. Nonfiction.

Born in New England of Puritan heritage in 1811, Harriet Elizabeth Beecher was reared to hold the steadfast religious beliefs of her father, a minister. Her schooling, first in New England and then in Cincinnati, molded her into a fine teacher and later a renowned writer. Always a strong-willed person, Stowe saw inequities and felt a need to do what she could to eliminate them. In 1850, she embarked upon her greatest triumph, writing *Uncle Tom's Cabin,* a book about slavery that changed both her world and the world around her. Although she wrote other works, nothing else produced the volume of reviews, both favorable and unfavorable, as *Uncle Tom's Cabin.* This biography gives an introspective look at the many facets of Harriet Beecher Stowe—wife, author, teacher, mother, daughter, and friend.

Notable 1994 Children's Trade Books in the Field of Social Studies

5.11   Colman, Penny. **Breaking the Chains: The Crusade of Dorothea Lynde Dix.** Betterway/Shoe Tree Books, 1992. 131 pp. ISBN 1-55870-219-9. Nonfiction.

Dorothea Dix devoted her life to helping the ill. Described by some as strong-willed, opinionated, and demanding, she traveled the country exposing the inhumane treatment of the mentally ill and pressuring state legislatures to build hospitals. During the Civil War, she became superintendent of female nurses and worked to train women to care for the thousands of wounded men. A woman of strong moral convictions, Dorothea Dix was tireless in her efforts to help those who could not help themselves.

School Library Journal Best Books, 1992

5.12   Colman, Penny. **A Woman Unafraid: The Achievements of Frances Perkins.** Atheneum, 1993. 113 pp. ISBN 0-689-31853-7. Nonfiction.

Beginning her career as a teacher, Frances Perkins soon became aware of the many social ills that existed in this country—a fact that prompted her to switch to social work. Thereafter she worked in both Chicago and Philadelphia, striving to right social injustices, especially for young women and children. After witnessing a destructive fire that killed workers in a shirt factory, Perkins resolved to fight for the rights of laborers. It was Perkins's role as the country's first female cabinet member, Secretary of Labor in the administration of President Franklin D. Roosevelt, that netted her the greatest recognition. Under her leadership, America saw such accomplishments as the establishment of the forty-hour work week, safer working conditions, a minimum wage, and the passage of the Social Security Act.

Notable 1994 Children's Trade Books in the Field of Social Studies

5.13   Conklin, Thomas. **Muhammad Ali: The Fight for Respect.** Millbrook Press, 1992. 94 pp. ISBN 1-56294-112-7. Nonfiction.

Muhammad Ali is one of the most well known sports figures of our time. Thomas Conklin not only details Ali's life in the ring, but also explains how Ali was affected by the political events of the 1960s and 1970s. Race relations, the Vietnam War, and the Nation of Islam all played a part in changing Cassius Clay, the fighter, into Muhammad Ali, a political symbol.

5.14   Constantine, Mildred. **Tina Modotti: A Fragile Life.** Chronicle Books, 1993. 189 pp. ISBN 0-8118-0502-6. Nonfiction.

An Italian by birth, Tina Modotti became a world traveler as a result of her work as a photographer and political activist. Her beauty and sexuality captivated many, but her photography occupied her life in Mexico for a decade. Drawn into the social and political arenas of that country, Modotti found herself in opposition to governmental officials, who sought to expel her from the country. Exiled, she traveled to Germany, the Soviet Union, Spain, and eventually back to Mexico, where she spent her final days. Her life is pieced together in this book through the photographs she took in Mexico, along with letters and more photos taken by her long-time friend, teacher, and lover, renowned photographer Edward Weston.

5.15   Cook, Blanche Wiesen. **Eleanor Roosevelt: Volume One, 1884–1933.** Viking, 1992. 500 pp. ISBN 0-670-80486-X. Nonfiction.

By gaining access to new archives and through interviews with the family and friends of Eleanor Roosevelt, author Blanche Wiesen Cook has created one of the most complete pictures yet of this former first lady. Previously unpublished information about her relationship with friends, such as Esther Lape and Lorena Hickok, enables readers to see Eleanor Roosevelt as an individual, not just as the wife of President Franklin D. Roosevelt.

5.16   Corrigan, Grace George. **A Journal for Christa: Christa McAuliffe, Teacher in Space.** University of Nebraska Press, 1993. 191 pp. ISBN 0-8032-1459-6. Nonfiction.

In July 1985, Christa McAuliffe, a New Hampshire social studies teacher, was selected to become the first teacher in space. She spent the next six months in a rigorous training program in preparation for the spaceflight and readying the science lessons that she would teach from space to American schoolchildren. On January

28, 1986, Christa and six NASA astronauts had barely begun the historic spaceflight when the *Challenger* spacecraft exploded, killing all aboard. Grace George Corrigan, McAuliffe's mother, tells her daughter's life story in journal format. This personal biography relates McAuliffe's childhood in Boston as the oldest of five children, her first teaching jobs in Maryland, her life in New Hampshire prior to selection for the Teacher-in-Space program, and her preparation for the flight. The glimpses into Christa McAuliffe's life reveal her as a dedicated teacher and a warm, generous individual. The book includes family photographs.

5.17 Cytron, Barry, and Phyllis Cytron. **Myriam Mendilow: Mother of Jerusalem.** Lerner, 1994. 123 pp. ISBN 0-8225-4919-0. Nonfiction.

A member of a spiritual Jewish family, Myriam Mendilow grew up in Israel, where she saw both peace and war. She had the advantage of being educated in Europe and later returned as a teacher to Israel, where she married and lived a comfortable existence. Observing the abandoned and forlorn elderly crouched in doorways, idle and begging, made Mendilow wonder how to help these people. She began her "Lifeline for the Old" to provide a few hours of daily entertainment for the elderly, but the project grew into a real humanitarian effort to involve skilled individuals who had been cast off simply because they were old. For these people, Myriam Mendilow represented a true friend who helped to restore their dignity and their worth as human beings.

5.18 Devaney, John. **Bo Jackson: A Star for All Seasons.** Walker, 1992. 127 pp. ISBN 0-8027-8179-9. Nonfiction.

The multitalented, successful, and sometimes humorous Bo Jackson was not always the hero he is today for many athletic-minded young men. As a child growing up in Alabama, young Vincent Jackson posed more problems than his mother felt able to handle, and she worried that her young son would wind up in prison. However, Jackson discovered he was able to control his sometimes brutal nature through his talents in baseball, football, and track and to use these sports to rise above his poverty and problems. This biography is a warm story of how Bo Jackson overcame a speech problem, how he resisted the offers of instant money at the expense of his education, and how he strove to be the best in each sport in which he participated. Included in the account are diagrams and photos of high points in the life of Bo Jackson—

great moments that should appeal not only to sports buffs but also to anyone interested in the accomplishments of a true winner.

5.19   Eckert, Allan W. **A Sorrow in Our Heart: The Life of Tecumseh.** Bantam Books, 1992. 862 pp. ISBN 0-553-08023-7. Nonfiction.

The Shawnee chief Tecumseh proved himself a valiant leader early in his life. Skilled as a hunter and a warrior, he nevertheless opposed cruel torture of other humans, even captives, and demonstrated that disdain by taking a strong stand against such brutal acts that the Shawnee customarily inflicted. He was able to influence other Native Americans because of his eloquence and the high esteem in which he was held. Respect for Tecumseh was not confined merely to the tribes of the midwestern area but extended to the white villages as well. As a result of his reputation for decency, he was able to gather and to provide information that would lead to victory over American military forces who intended to annihilate the Native American population in the late 1700s and early 1800s.

5.20   Faragher, John Mack. **Daniel Boone: The Life and Legend of an American Pioneer.** Henry Holt, 1992. 362 pp. ISBN 0-8050-1603-1. Nonfiction.

Historian John Mack Faragher has utilized numerous sources in an attempt to separate truth from myth in this biography of frontier hero Daniel Boone. Starting with the arrival of Boone's father in America from England, Faragher traces the childhood years of Daniel Boone, beginning with his birth in Pennsylvania in 1734, the Boone family affiliation with the Quakers, Boone's own marriage and family life, and his many hunting trips and land deals, some of which caused brushes with the legal system. His heroic dealings with Indian nations are highlighted, as is his political service in Virginia and Kentucky before he settled in Missouri, where he died in 1820. Informative and sometimes comical, the book presents an account of the life of Daniel Boone that may be largely plausible, even if it fails in total accuracy.

5.21   Fleming, Thomas. **Harry S. Truman, President.** Walker, 1993. 130 pp. ISBN 0-8027-8269-8. Nonfiction.

A man of humble beginnings, Harry S. Truman was thrust into the office of president of the United States upon the death of Franklin D. Roosevelt in 1945. Truman, a decisive and independent thinker, did not always say or act as politicians wanted him to, but his homespun common sense has reserved a place in history for him. From Missouri to Washington, D.C., and back to Missouri, Truman's life reflects his underlying belief in America and the welfare of its people, even when his decisions were unpopular. Truman's dispute with General Douglas MacArthur, his hard-fought battle with Senator Joseph McCarthy over Communist infiltration in this country, and the steel strike that he sought to avoid during the Korean War are among the accounts given in this biography of the thirty-third president of the United States.

Notable 1994 Children's Trade Books in the Field of Social Studies

5.22 Flynn, Jean. **Lady: The Story of Claudia Alta (Lady Bird) Johnson.** Eakin Press/Sunbelt Media, 1992. 130 pp. ISBN 0-89015-821-5. Nonfiction.

Who would have believed that Claudia Taylor, the shyest girl in Marshall, Texas, High School's class of 1928, would become Lady Bird Johnson, wife of the thirty-sixth president of the United States? When Lady Bird married Lyndon Johnson, whom she described as "the most determined young man I have ever met," she faced many challenges. She evolved into an astute businesswoman, a political campaigner, a mother, a first lady, and, eventually, a conservationist, responsible for beautification projects across the country.

5.23 Freedman, Russell. **Eleanor Roosevelt: A Life of Discovery.** Houghton Mifflin/Clarion Books, 1993. 198 pp. ISBN 0-89919-862-7. Nonfiction.

Those who knew Eleanor Roosevelt as a child were probably amazed to see her become Eleanor Roosevelt, First Lady of the World. She was so timid and "afraid of almost everything" in her early years that even her parents grew impatient with her. Through adversity she became strong—she lost both parents when she was quite young, and her husband, Franklin Roosevelt, contracted polio. She grew into the roles of political activist, writer, and humanitarian even before her husband became the thirty-second U.S. president. In this book, award-winning writer Russell Freedman chronicles her growth.

ALA Best Books for Young Adults, 1994
ALA Notable Books for Children, 1994
Booklist Editors' Choice, 1993
Boston Globe–Horn Book Nonfiction Award, 1994
Newbery Honor Book, 1994
Notable 1994 Children's Trade Books in the Field of Social Studies
School Library Journal Best Books, 1993

5.24   Gilbert, Martin. **Churchill: A Life.** Henry Holt, 1991. 959 pp. ISBN
        0-8050-0615-X. Nonfiction.

        Using information drawn from personal correspondence of Win-
        ston Churchill and his wife, government archives, friends, and
        colleagues, this biography attempts to give a full, unbiased ac-
        count of the life of the great British statesman. Beginning with his
        birth and childhood during Britain's Victorian era and covering
        his life and accomplishments until his death in 1965, the biogra-
        phy presents a massive portrait of the highs and lows of a career
        that spanned more than fifty years of service to his country.
        Churchill's candid, outspoken nature and his sometimes brutal
        criticism are evident in the biography. However, the book also
        recognizes his ability to foresee the nature of war and society and
        his compassion for humanity. Churchill is portrayed here as the
        great individual and respected world leader that he truly was.

5.25   Hamilton, Nigel. **JFK: Reckless Youth.** Random House, 1992.
        898 pp. ISBN 0-679-41216-6. Nonfiction.

        Those who question whether John F. Kennedy deserved his rep-
        utation as a womanizer will have many of those questions
        answered by reading this first volume of Nigel Hamilton's biog-
        raphy of JFK. The previously unpublished letters and documents
        that Hamilton consulted, as well as the Kennedy friends and ac-
        quaintances he interviewed, create a picture of someone who was
        indeed a "reckless youth." This work chronicles much of JFK's
        behavior from his adolescence until his election as congressman
        from Massachusetts in 1946, when he was twenty-nine years old.

5.26   Hamilton, Virginia. **Paul Robeson: The Life and Times of a Free
        Black Man.** HarperCollins, 1992. 105 pp. ISBN 0-06-022189-5.
        Nonfiction.

        A multitalented African American man born in the late nineteenth
        century, Paul Robeson overcame innumerable odds to become a
        successful athlete, singer, and actor. His accomplishments did not
        come easily, but his outspoken nature enabled him to express a
        keen belief in his own ability in a society that did not recognize
        equality for all. Through his father's encouragement and his per-
        sonal drive, Paul Robeson was able to attend college and law
        school. Later he expanded his careers to include the theater and
        the concert circuit. For a time he enjoyed fame and respect, but
        when he voiced opinions that many in this country viewed as "un-
        American," he was branded as a Communist. When Robeson

would not soften his position, his passport was canceled, preventing him from traveling outside the United States. Years later the Supreme Court reversed the passport decision, and Robeson continued his foreign concerts.

5.27   Harrison, Barbara, and Daniel Terris. **A Twilight Struggle: The Life of John Fitzgerald Kennedy.** Lothrop, Lee and Shepard Books, 1992. 159 pp. ISBN 0-688-08830-9. Nonfiction.

Of the many biographies published about John Fitzgerald Kennedy, this one explores all aspects of the man and the president. Born into wealth, JFK enjoyed luxuries few Americans can afford; however, these advantages did not ease his suffering. His private life was lived in the shadow of his older brother, Joseph, and a domineering father who charted a course for his son early on. Moreover, the authors do not glorify Kennedy's presidency. Instead, they write of his mistakes during critical times and his downfalls as well as his crowning moments, making him a human figure whose eloquence endeared him to many and made him an object of contempt for others.

ALA Notable Books for Children, 1993
Booklist Editors' Choices, 1992
Notable 1992 Children's Trade Books in the Field of Social Studies

5.28   Haskins, James. **The Life and Death of Martin Luther King, Jr.** William Morrow/Beech Tree Books, 1992. 182 pp. ISBN 0-688-11690-6. Nonfiction.

Divided into two distinct parts, this biography represents yet another author's research into the life and times of Martin Luther King Jr. James Haskins reports the usual events of King's birth in 1929, his youth, and his manhood; his interest in and study of the teachings of Christ, Gandhi, and Thoreau; and his desire for a life better than the one that he and other African Americans in the South had come to despise. Biographer James Haskins covers King's preparation for the ministry, his leadership in the early Civil Rights movement, the zenith of his power and influence, and his assassination in 1968. Part two deals with the aftermath of his assassination and the unanswered questions regarding both King's presumed killer, James Earl Ray, and the possibility of a conspiracy.

5.29   Haskins, Jim. **One More River to Cross: The Stories of Twelve Black Americans.** Scholastic, 1992. 200 pp. ISBN 0-590-42896-9. Nonfiction.

This book chronicles the lives of twelve African Americans, eight men and four women, who have made major contributions to American life. Beginning with Crispus Attucks and ending with Ronald McNair, the author writes of the great difficulties these individuals faced and their determination to succeed. Their life stories serve as role models for today's youth.

ALA Best Books for Young Adults, 1993
Notable 1992 Children's Trade Books in the Field of Social Studies

5.30   Hildebrand, Lee. **Hammertime: The True Story of Hammer's Electrifying Rise.** Avon Books, 1992. 162 pp. ISBN 0-380-76690-6. Nonfiction.

Hammertime is not only the life story of rapper Hammer; it is also a brief history of rap music. Lee Hildebrand reveals how Stanley Kirk Burrell became the little Hammer, the Holy Ghost Boy, M. C. Hammer, and, finally, Hammer. He also shows how Hammer has used his leadership skills, probably more than musical talent, to rise to stardom in the music world.

5.31   Hodges, Margaret. **Making a Difference: The Story of an American Family.** William Morrow/Beech Tree Books, 1992. 189 pp. ISBN 0-688-11780-5. Nonfiction.

Who was Mary Beattie Sherwood? She was a woman who believed that anything could be accomplished through hard work. She raised four daughters and a son on her own in the early 1900s, and each grew up to have a successful career. She fought for women's rights and environmental concerns during her lifetime. This biography of the Sherwood family provides the reader with strong female characters who believed in education, commitment, and achievement.

5.32   Ione, Carole. **Pride of Family: Four Generations of American Women of Color.** Avon Books, 1993. 217 pp. ISBN 0-380-71934-7. Nonfiction.

Carole Ione begins her memoir by telling the reader about her childhood and the three strong women of color who raised her. There was her mother, a journalist and composer; her straight-laced great-aunt Sistonie, a doctor; and her fun-loving grandmother Be-Be, an entertainer and restaurateur. The author shares her travels, her two failed marriages, and her discovery of her great-grandmother's diary. It is through this search of the past that Carole Ione gains a deeper understanding of herself and the women who raised her.

5.33   King, Coretta Scott. **My Life with Martin Luther King, Jr.,** rev. ed. Penguin/Puffin Books, 1993. 315 pp. ISBN 0-14-036805-1. Nonfiction.

Written as a tribute to her husband and as an inspiration to young African Americans of today, *My Life with Martin Luther King, Jr.* deals with the trials and the successes of the civil rights leader. In this biography, Coretta Scott King gives detailed accounts of the threats, the marches, the sit-ins, and the numerous jailings that her husband endured, along with the personal fears and other emotions that she and the family suffered. A lengthy description of the preparations for and the execution of the 1963 March on Washington, D.C., is given, as is attention to the King family and friends who assisted in the gallant effort to end racial discrimination and oppression in the United States. King's account is a commendable effort to recall her husband's accomplishments, but her narrative frequently becomes rather verbose and tiring, especially for young readers.

5.34   Kissinger, Rosemary K. **Quanah Parker: Comanche Chief.** Pelican, 1991. 129 pp. ISBN 0-88289-785-3. Nonfiction.

A daring story of a brave young Comanche chief who vowed to fight the white man for Indian land, this tale of valor and stark determination is a classic example of the struggle between the Native American's love for the land and the white man's desire for expansion. Born to a white mother and an Indian father and reared in the ways of the Comanche, Quanah Parker pledged to uphold the Comanche lifestyle and traditions and to resist the government's plan to confine his people to reservations. For a time, he was able to keep his pledge, but when he recognized the imminent danger of starvation and death for the Comanches, he realized he had to comply with the government. Parker did so, but on his own terms, and he became a liaison between his people and the white man.

5.35   Knudson, R. R. **The Wonderful Pen of May Swenson.** Macmillan, 1993. 108 pp. ISBN 0-02-750915-X. Nonfiction.

After attending college in Utah, May Swenson set out for New York City with one goal in mind—to become a writer. Her life in the big city was extremely difficult. She found herself without funds to support herself, but she continued her struggle, always with a view to attaining her goal. When national magazines finally began publishing her poems, she realized her dream. Later, her poems appeared in collections of books, and she won awards and the respect of other poets.

5.36   Krensky, Stephen. **Four against the Odds: The Struggle to Save Our Environment.** Scholastic, 1992. 96 pp. ISBN 0-590-44743-2. Nonfiction.

A collection of four mini-biographies, this easy-to-read account of the lives of John Muir, Rachel Carson, Lois Gibbs, and Chico Mendes provides young readers with vital information about saving our environment. If no other goal is accomplished, author Stephen Krensky, in simple language and illustration, has provided a clear picture of what will happen if we sacrifice the environment in the name of progress. The poignant story of Lois Gibbs as she fights to preserve the lives of the victims of toxic waste in New York's Love Canal, Rachel Carson's revelation of the dangers of the chemical DDT, John Muir's struggle to help create national parks, and Chico Mendes's determination to save the rain forests of South America are all moving tales of individuals who sought to save the planet. This book should hold the interest of readers who are concerned about the dangers to the environment both in the present and for future generations.

5.37   Lamar, Jake. **Bourgeois Blues: An American Memoir.** Penguin/ Plume Books, 1992. 174 pp. ISBN 0-452-26911-3. Nonfiction.

On first glance, *Bourgeois Blues* seems to be simply a story of how easily success came to a young man who had privileges few other African Americans enjoy. But this description is deceptive. Jake Lamar's private school education seemed an almost natural prelude to his enrollment in and eventual graduation from Harvard, where, to his father's chagrin, he displayed his journalistic talent by working on the staff of a school newspaper. It is his father, in fact, who produces the conflict in young Jake's life. Despite this conflict, Lamar succeeds in becoming the youngest writer for *Time* magazine, where he does a reputable job and also learns what it means to be a black man in middle-class America.

5.38   Little, Jean. **Stars Come Out Within.** Viking, 1990. 260 pp. ISBN 0-670-82965-X. Nonfiction.

The second installment of author Jean Little's biography, *Stars Come Out Within* continues the account of the faith and strength of a woman who has known adversity and yet finds the courage to smile through it all. In this segment, she tells of her trauma after losing sight in both eyes and the despair she felt in trying to continue her writing. Despite her blindness, she is able to count her blessings: her computer, her guide dog, her mother, and her friends. Each helps Little to view life as worthwhile; as a result, she has produced a beautifully frank and funny story.

ALA Notable Books for Children, 1992

5.39   Lyons, Mary E. **Sorrow's Kitchen: The Life and Folklore of Zora Neale Hurston.** Charles Scribner's Sons, 1990. 125 pp. ISBN 0-684-19198-9. Nonfiction.

This illustrated biography of one of America's often forgotten female authors is simply and tastefully written. *Sorrow's Kitchen* takes the reader from the rather unhappy childhood of Zora Neale Hurston as she grew up in Florida to her determination to obtain an education and her migration from the South to New York City during the height of the Harlem Renaissance in the 1920s. Hurston made frequent trips to her native Florida and the West Indies in search of folklore, and eventually returned to Florida, where she died in poverty in 1960. Excerpts from Hurston's works and photographs taken throughout her life are included.

ALA Best Books for Young Adults, 1992
IRA Teachers' Choices, 1991
School Library Journal Best Books, 1991

5.40   McKissack, Patricia C., and Fredrick McKissack. **Sojourner Truth: Ain't I a Woman?** Scholastic, 1992. 178 pp. ISBN 0-590-44690-8. Nonfiction.

Drawing upon history, this inspirational biography is ideal for teens. For the many who are unaware of the contributions of the early American slave population, this book provides insight into one woman's quest for equal rights for her race in general and for women in particular. Sojourner Truth, born a slave in 1797, traveled across the country, spreading the truth to all who wanted to hear, and left in her wake many enlightened individuals who came to realize that being a woman did not mean being weak and ineffectual. Despite her inability to read, Sojourner Truth demonstrated that she could learn, and she tapped every resource at hand to convey her message. Her determination to be regarded as a person entitled to all the privileges afforded others comes through clearly and elevates Sojourner Truth to the rank of a truly great American pioneer.

ALA Best Books for Young Adults, 1993
ALA Notable Books for Children, 1993
Boston Globe–Horn Book Nonfiction Award, 1993
IRA Teachers' Choices, 1993

5.41   McPherson, Stephanie Sammartino. **Peace and Bread: The Story of Jane Addams.** Carolrhoda Books, 1993. 89 pp. ISBN 0-87614-792-9. Nonfiction.

Despite growing up in Cedarville, Illinois, in the 1860s and 1870s with all the comforts of life, Jane Addams saw the poverty of cities and felt she had to help. After finishing college and traveling to Europe, Addams, a frail young woman with a spinal disorder, decided to live among the impoverished and help them. As a result, Hull House, a Chicago settlement home, was established in 1889. Here Addams learned to understand the many cultures within the city and to instill a sense of worth in those who frequented Hull House. Through her unselfishness, Jane Addams began a movement for peace throughout the world.

5.42   Meltzer, Milton. **Andrew Jackson and His America.** Franklin Watts, 1993. 196 pp. ISBN 0-531-11157-1. Nonfiction.

Frontiersman, Indian fighter, lawyer, politician, and U.S. president—all were jobs held by Andrew Jackson, who began life in a simple log cabin in South Carolina in 1767. Jackson became a heroic figure after defeating the British in the Battle of New Orleans. From this point he went on to assume a governorship in Florida for a short time before returning to Tennessee and Hermitage, his home, claiming ill health. After a stint in the U.S. Senate and after losing his first bid for the presidency, Jackson became the seventh president of the United States in 1829. As aggressive as he was, Jackson managed to endear himself to the American public, but not always to his political peers. His most memorable deeds include elimination of the powers of the Bank of the United States and relocation of many Native Americans from their homes to points west. After two terms as president, Andrew Jackson returned to his beloved Hermitage, where he lived until his death in 1845.

5.43   Meyer, Carolyn. **Where the Broken Heart Still Beats: The Story of Cynthia Ann Parker.** Harcourt Brace Jovanovich, 1992. 196 pp. ISBN 0-15-200639-7. Fiction.

Carolyn Meyer has taken "the key facts of the history of Cynthia Ann Parker and used them as a framework on which to fashion the story of her life, as it could have been." Historians of the American West agree that Parker was captured by Comanche warriors in the mid-1800s and lived among her captors for twenty-five years before being "rescued" by Texas Rangers and returned to her relatives. These well-meaning rescuers failed to realize that Parker was no longer a member of the white man's culture. Her heart and soul belonged to the Comanches, and she and her small daughter longed to return to her Comanche husband and two sons in their Indian settlement.

ALA Best Books for Young Adults, 1993
IRA Teachers' Choices, 1993
Notable 1992 Children's Trade Books in the Field of Social Studies

5.44   Miller, Luree, and Scott Miller. **Alaska: Pioneer Stories of a Twentieth-Century Frontier.** Dutton/Cobblehill Books, 1991. 103 pp. ISBN 0-525-65050-4. Nonfiction.

Alaskans are well known for being rugged individuals who enjoy the unspoiled wilderness and personal freedom that Alaska offers. This book introduces the reader to five fascinating pioneer families who have made their homes in the great state of Alaska, from Frank and Mary Miller, who went to Alaska in 1906 to look for gold, to Scott and Carol Reymiller, modern-day pioneers who set traps, cut wood, ice fish, and fly their own plane.

Notable 1991 Children's Trade Books in the Field of Social Studies

5.45   Morey, Janet Nomura, and Wendy Dunn. **Famous Asian Americans.** Dutton/Cobblehill Books, 1992. 162 pp. ISBN 0-525-65080-6. Nonfiction.

Besides the life stories of fourteen modern-day Asian Americans, such as architect I. M. Pei, Senator Daniel Inouye, and newscaster Connie Chung, the authors provide an explanation of the term *Asian American* and a historical perspective of the discrimination this group has faced since the Chinese arrived in this country during the California Gold Rush.

Notable 1992 Children's Trade Books in the Field of Social Studies

5.46   Myers, Walter Dean. **Malcolm X: By Any Means Necessary.** Scholastic, 1993. 200 pp. ISBN 0-590-46484-1. Nonfiction.

Walter Dean Myers gives an objective account of Malcolm X (1925–65), one of the most influential civil rights leaders of the twentieth century. By seeing Malcolm as a child in Nebraska, Wisconsin, and Michigan and a young man in Boston and Harlem, one can better understand Malcolm as an adult—how he was able to use his talents to promote the growth of the Nation of Islam and why he sought changes, "by any means necessary," in the way African Americans were treated.

ALA Best Books for Young Adults, 1994
IRA Teachers' Choices, 1994
Coretta Scott King Author Honor Book, 1994

5.47   Otfinoski, Steven. **Nelson Mandela: The Fight against Apartheid.** Millbrook Press, 1992. 118 pp. ISBN 1-56294-067-8. Nonfiction.

In 1990, Nelson Mandela was freed from prison after serving twenty-seven years for leading the fight in South Africa against apartheid. Author Steven Otfinoski begins the book by giving a brief history of the country and by describing Mandela's childhood as the son of a Thembu chief. He then traces Mandela's lifelong struggle for black rights and gives a detailed account of the world events that led to Mandela's release from prison.

5.48   Parks, Rosa, with Jim Haskins. **Rosa Parks: My Story.** Dial Books, 1992. 189 pp. ISBN 0-8037-0673-1. Nonfiction.

On December 1, 1955, Rosa Parks refused to give up a seat to a white man on a segregated bus in Montgomery, Alabama. With this act of defiance, the Civil Rights movement became a national cause. But long before that day, Rosa Parks had been fighting against injustice. She begins her story by describing the many forms of discrimination she and her family faced living in the South and ends with a discussion of the years since 1955.

ALA Best Books for Young Adults, 1993
ALA Notable Books for Children, 1993
ALA Quick Picks for Young Adults, 1993
IRA Children's Choices, 1993
IRA Young Adults' Choices, 1994

5.49   Perry, Bruce. **Malcolm: The Life of a Man Who Changed Black America.** Station Hill Press, 1992. 380 pp. ISBN 0-88268-103-6. Nonfiction.

Malcolm tells the story behind what motivated Malcolm Little, the young boy who became Malcolm X, the civil rights activist who inspired some and infuriated others. As a child, Malcolm learned to persuade others in order to get his way, and he later developed the talent to influence thinking with his orations. His hardships and struggles during his youth are explored, including his prison term in the mid-1940s, when he made the decision to leave behind his drug addiction and devote his life to being a Muslim and to speaking for the oppressed in America.

5.50   Pflaum, Rosalynd. **Marie Curie and Her Daughter Irène.** Lerner, 1993. 135 pp. ISBN 0-8225-4915-8. Nonfiction.

When Marie Curie began her research on the mysterious new "X" rays, she did not know it would lead to the winning of three Nobel Prizes—and eventually to her death. Both Marie and her daughter Irène spent most of their lives researching radioactivity, and this book explores their personal lives as well as their work in the lab. Sadly, little was known of the dangers of their research, and both died prematurely from massive doses of radioactive materials.

5.51 Rodriguez, Richard. **Days of Obligation: An Argument with My Mexican Father.** Penguin Books, 1993. 230 pp. ISBN 0-670-81396-6. Nonfiction.

In this collection of autobiographical essays, Richard Rodriguez explores his own cultural identity. The son of immigrants from Mexico, he is a native Californian, but his complexion and features clearly mark his Mexican heritage. Rodriguez feels keenly the tug of two cultures within him—what he calls the tragic vision of Mexico versus the comic, or optimistic, vision of California. Meditative, frank, poetic, these essays deal with what it means to be an American.

5.52 Rylant, Cynthia. **But I'll Be Back Again.** William Morrow/Beech Tree Books, 1993. 80 pp. ISBN 0-688-12653-7. Nonfiction.

In a world of phonies and guarded individuals, it is refreshing to find a genuine person like novelist Cynthia Rylant, who is willing to share personal feelings. Whether she is revealing positive experiences like getting her first kiss or the pain of being separated from her father, Rylant speaks as an honest, open individual who knows what it means to experience life's joys and sorrows. Her indomitable spirit permeates this book and assures the reader that the title is appropriate—it is not just a line borrowed from a song by the Beatles.

5.53 Schwarzkopf, H. Norman, with Peter Petre. **It Doesn't Take a Hero.** Bantam Books, 1992. 530 pp. ISBN 0-553-08944-7. Nonfiction.

Not only does this book chronicle General Norman Schwarzkopf's involvement in Desert Storm; it also provides insight into the people and events that shaped his early life. Beginning with his father's going off to war in August 1942 and ending with the early days of his own retirement in 1991, Schwarzkopf speaks candidly of who he is and what the U.S. Army is and has been over the years. It is clear that the man and the institution share a symbiotic relationship.

5.54 Sloan, Bill, with Jean Hill. **JFK: The Last Dissenting Witness.** Pelican, 1992. 255 pp. ISBN 0-88289-922-8. Nonfiction.

A historical biography relating the controversial death of John F. Kennedy, this account of that fateful day on November 22, 1963, in Dallas, Texas, is the basis for Oliver Stone's movie *JFK*. Jean Hill, a witness to the shooting of the president, gives an account that contradicts the Warren Commission Report and suggests that political figures in high positions may have been involved in a sinister plot to kill Kennedy. Hill poses several points for which she contends there is evidence—evidence that the Warren Commission chose not to explore in its investigation.

5.55   Soto, Gary. **Living up the Street.** Dell, 1992. 167 pp. ISBN 0-440-21170-0. Nonfiction.

To read *Living up the Street* is to come to know poet and novelist Gary Soto, at least in part. From his early childhood days, when he and his siblings took delight in teaching their friends to fight, to his adult struggles to become a writer, Soto gives the reader an honest look at what it was like to grow up as a Mexican American in the barrio of Fresno. Although it would have been easy to focus on the negative, Soto chooses instead to recall incidents and relationships that reveal a broad range of emotions—courage, jealousy, humor, love, loyalty, deceit, and determination.

5.56   Sufrin, Mark. **Stephen Crane.** Atheneum, 1992. 153 pp. ISBN 0-689-31669-0. Nonfiction.

Critic Alfred Kazin once referred to Stephen Crane as the "first great tragic figure in the modern American generation." Mark Sufrin's biography of Crane confirms Kazin's assessment. In 1893, when he was twenty-two, Crane wrote *Maggie: A Girl of the Streets*. By the time he was twenty-four, he had published *The Red Badge of Courage*, which remains one of the great war novels. Crane seemed destined for greatness. Four years later, however, he was dead. Crane was quite ill the last year of his life, and by his final days, he and his wife lived primarily on money borrowed from friends. He had been reduced to writing potboilers in an effort to sustain the extravagant lifestyle he and Cora had established. The spark of genius he possessed never reached its full potential, and Crane died at age twenty-eight.

School Library Journal Best Books, 1992

5.57   Surcouf, Elizabeth Gillen. **Grace Kelly, American Princess.** Lerner, 1992. 64 pp. ISBN 0-8225-0548-7. Nonfiction.

Before her marriage to Prince Rainier III of Monaco in 1956, American Grace Kelly had found fame and enjoyed success as an actress. However, it was not by chance that she became a star. Although she had been born into "the good life," she had worked long, difficult hours to achieve her goal. After her storybook marriage into the royal family of Monaco, she sought and found ways to contribute to the good of society. Especially fond of young people, she devoted a great deal of time to organizing programs for the needy children of her principality. In addition, she was instrumental in promoting the fine arts in Monaco, although protocol dictated that she, as a princess, could no longer directly participate. Until her death in 1982, Princess Grace remained an active woman, determined to pursue her interest in humanity.

5.58 Uchida, Yoshiko. **The Invisible Thread.** Simon and Schuster/ Julian Messner, 1991. 136 pp. ISBN 0-671-74164-0. Nonfiction.

In this book, award-winning author Yoshiko Uchida recounts not only her own life but a terrible chapter in American history, the imprisonment of thousands of Japanese Americans during World War II. Without bitterness, Uchida tells of her family's losses, both material possessions and respect. She says she writes of this horrible experience because "I want each new generation of Americans to know what once happened in our democracy. I want them to love and cherish the freedom that can be snatched away so quickly, even by their own country."

ALA Best Books for Young Adults, 1993

5.59 van der Rol, Ruud, and Rian Verhoeven (translated by Tony Langham and Plym Peters). **Anne Frank: Beyond the Diary: A Photographic Remembrance.** Viking, 1993. 113 pp. ISBN 0-670-84932-4. Nonfiction.

Anne Frank's father was an avid photographer, and thanks to his hobby and Anne's ability to write so candidly, we can come to know rather intimately the Frank family of Germany. This book consists of over 100 photographs by Otto Frank and others of the homes in which the family lived, including the Secret Annex, and segments of the diaries that Anne kept while the family was in hiding in Amsterdam from the Nazis. Additional essays provide historical background. Those who knew Anne Frank and her sister in the Bergen-Belsen concentration camp also contribute their memories. First published in the Netherlands, 1992.

ALA Best Books for Young Adults, 1994
ALA Notable Books for Children, 1994
ALA Quick Picks for Young Adults, 1994
Booklist Editors' Choice, 1993

5.60   Vogel, Ilse-Margret. **Bad Times, Good Friends: A Personal Memoir.** Harcourt Brace Jovanovich, 1992. 256 pp. ISBN 0-15-205528-2. Nonfiction.

Based on her memoirs of life in war-torn Germany during World War II, Ilse-Margret Vogel's book captures the spirit of everyday people who bond together when horrible events threaten their daily existence. In this biographical account, Vogel relates how she and friends managed to survive the ugliness and the horrors that beset them in Berlin between 1943 and 1945. Sharing a common characteristic, a hatred for Adolf Hitler, Vogel and her friends risked their lives to give shelter to others opposed to the Nazi regime.

5.61   Walesa, Lech, with Arkadiusz Rybicki (translated by Franklin Philip with Helen Mahut). **The Struggle and the Triumph: An Autobiography.** Arcade, 1992. 330 pp. ISBN 1-55970-149-8. Nonfiction.

The road that Lech Walesa traveled from Gdansk electrician to Nobel Peace Prize–winner to president of the Republic of Poland was a difficult one. In this autobiography, he cites many of the hardships he faced, but he focuses as well on the triumphs of the Solidarity Movement, which began in August 1980. Walesa credits fellow activists, his family, and his religious faith with helping him to bring freedom to Poland.

5.62   Walsh, Jill Paton. **Grace.** Farrar, Straus and Giroux, 1992. 255 pp. ISBN 0-374-32758-0. Fiction.

This narrative account, based on actual events of Grace Darling's successful efforts to assist her father in rescuing passengers from a shipwreck, is a captivating story of compassion for humanity. Realizing the dangers involved in risking their lives in a raging storm, young Grace and her father set out in rough waters to rescue shipwrecked survivors and succeed in returning them to safety. Initially, Britons hail the girl as a heroine, but the glory is short-lived, for Grace is later branded as avaricious and is accused of performing such a daring feat for the bounty and the personal glory.

5.63 Warner, Lucille Schulberg. **From Slave to Abolitionist: The Life of William Wells Brown.** Dial Books, 1993. 135 pp. ISBN 0-8037-2743-7. Nonfiction.

William Wells Brown is not a well-known name, but his life story is amazing. He began as a slave on a Missouri farm and died at age sixty-nine as a free man, an antislavery lecturer, a world traveler, and the first black American novelist. The author adapted Brown's writings to a first-person narrative that vividly describes the horrors of slavery and Brown's personal struggles to become a free man.

5.64 Witkin, Zara (edited by Michael Gelb). **An American Engineer in Stalin's Russia: The Memoirs of Zara Witkin, 1932–1934.** University of California Press, 1991. 363 pp. ISBN 0-520-07134-4. Nonfiction.

Not only was Zara Witkin a brilliant engineer; he also was an idealist. It was his idealism that took him to Stalin's Russia in 1932 with the hope that he could be a part of the great experiment called Communism. The corruption of the bureaucrats, their lack of sensitivity to the suffering of the masses, and his failure to win the heart of Russian actress Emma Tsesarskaia disappointed Witkin and led to his return to California in 1934.

5.65 Wyman, Carolyn. **Ella Fitzgerald: Jazz Singer Supreme.** Franklin Watts/Impact Books, 1993. 117 pp. ISBN 0-531-13031-2. Nonfiction.

Despite her shy nature, Ella Fitzgerald managed to overcome tremendous stumbling blocks to become one of the greatest jazz vocalists in the world. Starting out by winning a small sum of money in a Harlem music competition, Fitzgerald has since sung with top bands and renowned musicians in the United States and other countries. This straightforward, simply written biography outlines the difficulties Fitzgerald experienced with segregation when she was on tour, her failed marriages, and the weight problem that she has battled since childhood, but it also relates the happier times in her life. Source notes and a discography are included in the book for those interested in the chronology of her career.

5.66 Zatarain, Michael. **David Duke: Evolution of a Klansman.** Pelican, 1990. 304 pp. ISBN 0-88289-817-5. Nonfiction.

Unlike the stereotyped bigot most often associated with hate mongers, David Duke is presented by biographer Michael

Zatarain as an intelligent person who speaks for a cause in which he truly believes. From his days at Louisiana State University to the seat that he now occupies in the Louisiana House of Representatives, Duke has made himself a figure indelibly inscribed on the face of America. This book explores his life as a persuasive backer of white rights, his membership in the Ku Klux Klan, his distrust of Jewish and black people, and his undying devotion to what he perceives as the preservation of the white race. Writing objectively, Zatarain has captured all aspects of the man who has become a symbol of "white power" in America today.

6 Careers and College

6.1   Blumenthal, Howard J. **Careers in Baseball.** Little, Brown, 1993. 163 pp. ISBN 0-316-10095-1. Nonfiction.

You do not have to be a spectacular athlete to be a part of the baseball industry. There are many career opportunities that can turn your dreams into reality. In this book, seventeen baseball professionals talk about their jobs—how they got started, what they do every day, how they fit into the baseball industry. Profiles include the jobs of broadcaster, sports reporter, trainer, photographer, scout, stadium operations and entertainment personnel, media relations person, and video producer. Whether you love to play or just watch the game, baseball may be the industry for you.

6.2   Blumenthal, Howard J. **Careers in Television: You Can Do It!** Little, Brown, 1992. 162 pp. ISBN 0-316-10076-5. Nonfiction.

When we think of careers in television, we usually think of the performer, the news anchor, or sports broadcaster. There are, however, many behind-the-scenes jobs in the television industry. This book gives the reader a look at twenty successful people, each with a different occupation. A director, a videographer, an animation executive, and seventeen others talk about their jobs, and each concludes with some personal advice on getting started and being successful.

6.3   Drucker, Peter F. **Managing for the Future: The 1990s and Beyond.** Dutton/Truman Talley Books, 1992. 370 pp. ISBN 0-525-93414-6. Nonfiction.

Interested in knowing why so many business giants, such as the American car companies, failed in the 1980s, while so many Japanese companies succeeded? Peter F. Drucker not only explains what the managers of the 1980s did wrong, but he also tells you what the American business manager of the 1990s must know to compete in the changing world economy. This book is for the mature reader who plans a career in business management.

6.4   Dunbar, Robert E. **Guide to Military Careers.** Franklin Watts, 1992. 128 pp. ISBN 0-531-11118-0. Nonfiction.

Who is the nation's largest employer? The military is, and if you are interested in joining one of the five branches of the armed forces, this book will provide the detailed information you need to make the right choices. Whether a young person plans to join after high school or after college, he or she will find up-to-date information on admission requirements, job opportunities, and benefits in this book.

6.5 Galica, Gregory S. **The Blue Book: A Student's Guide to Essay Exams.** Harcourt Brace Jovanovich, 1991. 79 pp. ISBN 0-15-601300-2. Nonfiction.

If you need to learn how to perform well on essay exams for high school or college classes, this book will help. Author Gregory S. Galica discusses in-class and out-of-class exams. He describes the whole process of taking exams, from how to study before an exam to learning from the experience afterward. This book also contains advice about how to use your time efficiently during an exam and how to write well-organized essays.

6.6 Lantz, Fran. **Rock, Rap, and Rad: How to Be a Rock or Rap Star.** Avon/Flare Books, 1992. 215 pp. ISBN 0-380-76793-7. Nonfiction.

Interested in becoming a rock or rap star? A good way to begin is to read *Rock, Rap, and Rad.* Author Fran Lantz interviewed musicians, managers, and promoters to come up with practical advice for the would-be rock or rap star. What brand of instrument should you buy? How do you get started? What should you expect at your first audition? Do you need a manager? All these questions and more are answered, along with tips from the stars.

6.7 Rowan, N. R. **Women in the Marines: The Boot Camp Challenge.** Lerner, 1994. 70 pp. ISBN 0-8225-1430-3. Nonfiction.

The marines are looking for "a few good men." That may have been the marines' motto in the past, but now women are playing a growing role in the U.S. Marine Corps. This book takes you through the boot camp experience, using words and photographs to describe the basic training a female recruit faces. If you are looking for a challenge and risks after high school graduation, discover how the Marine Corps may be the place for you.

6.8 Tenuto, James, and Susan Schwartzwald. **Get Real! A Student's Guide to Money and Other Practical Matters.** Illustrated by Andrea Dietrich. Harcourt Brace Jovanovich/Harvest Books, 1992. 204 pp. ISBN 0-15-600595-6. Nonfiction.

The world of finances can be confusing. *Get Real!* simplifies the tangle of information on bank and charge accounts, car purchases and housing rental, various insurance policies, and budgeting time and money. Some of the information deals with practical advice about overspending, writing a resumé, avoiding campus scams and gambling temptations, and simply traveling to college. While the book is directed to the beginning college student, the money management explanations will help any high school student.

7 Cars, Planes, Boats, and Trains

7.1   Antonick, Michael. **The Corvette Black Book.** Michael Bruce Associates, 1992. 128 pp. ISBN 0-933534-35-3. Nonfiction.

This is a book for the Corvette enthusiast or the wanna-be enthusiast. From Corvette number 1, or #E53F001001, to the present, every bit of Corvette trivia seems to be covered: numbers of all kinds, prices, detail changes, historical changes, production changes. While this is not a book for everyone, it is must reading for anyone who has even a passing interest in Corvettes.

7.2   Bamsey, Ian. **The Anatomy and Development of the Sports Prototype Racing Car.** Motorbooks International, 1991. 218 pp. ISBN 0-87938-586-3. Nonfiction.

Racing car fan(atic)s will enjoy this book. It begins with a brief description of the origin of the sports car prototype—why and when it began—and a brief history of the sports car. Also included is a discussion of the chassis and engines of sports prototype racing cars from the beginning cars through the Jaguar XJR-14, a two-seat sports car as technically advanced as the contemporary Formula One car. One of the best features of the book is that it spends time on the one-offs as well as the famous Jaguars and Porsches, from both IMSA and the World Sports Car Championship.

7.3   Beattie, John. **Drama in the Air: Extraordinary True Stories of Daring and Courage.** Robson, 1990. 224 pp. ISBN 0-86051-564-8. Nonfiction.

Here is a book for anyone with an interest in aircraft or flying and in ordinary people doing extraordinary things. The suspenseful true stories cover acts of daring and courage from World War II to the present day. There is sufficient background information included with each tale for casual readers unfamiliar with each situation. First published in Great Britain, 1989.

7.4   Coiley, John. **Train.** Alfred A. Knopf/Dorling Kindersley, 1992. 64 pp. ISBN 0-679-81684-4. Nonfiction.

Part of the Eyewitness Books series, this mini-encyclopedia traces the development of trains from the early coal-powered steam engines to the high-speed electric trains of today. Bold photographs depict the trains, often with labels to indicate parts and purposes. Take a look at Queen Victoria's day carriage, built in 1869 with maple doors and trim and silk upholstery; see a suspended monorail in Germany, built in 1901 and still in operation; and read about a British steam locomotive that in 1938 set a speed record of 126 miles per hour between London and Edinburgh—a record that still stands. Not fast enough? Then check out the French electric train that set a world speed record of 320 miles per hour!

7.5   Jacobs, David H., Jr. **Engine Detailing.** Motorbooks International, 1992. 160 pp. ISBN 0-87938-610-X. Nonfiction.

This is a book for anyone who loves cars and wants them to look their best. It describes all ranges of detailing, from simple washing to in-depth cleaning, including tools, soaps, cleaners, and even paints. There are helpful finds for the hot-rodder, the sports car lover, the truck enthusiast, or those who want to keep their everyday vehicle looking new.

7.6   Kentley, Eric. **Boat.** Alfred A. Knopf/Dorling Kindersley Books, 1992. 64 pp. ISBN 0-679-81678-X. Nonfiction.

This book, one of many in the wide-ranging Eyewitness Books series, looks at the varied ways in which human beings have taken to the water, from raft to ocean liner, from hide-covered boat to paddlewheeler. Most of the text is found in captions that accompany the plentiful illustrations. The visual materials, almost all photographs, provide a rich, detailed look at the various boats, their construction, and their changing technologies and equipment.

Notable 1992 Children's Trade Books in the Field of Social Studies

7.7   Lamm, Jay, and Nick Nicaise. **Illustrated Shelby Buyer's Guide.** Motorbooks International, 1992. 128 pp. ISBN 0-87938-604-5. Nonfiction.

One of a growing number of Illustrated Buyer's Guides, this book has eliminated trying to put values on Shelby cars since the prices are out of date by the time they are published. The Shelby cars (most of which were race cars) swept all before them in SCCA Racing—both in A and B Production racing. Readers can learn about the history of Shelby cars, their differences, and even some tips for spotting counterfeits.

7.8   Remus, Timothy. **Boyd Coddington's How to Build Hot Rod Chassis.** Motorbooks International, 1992. 160 pp. ISBN 0-87938-626-6. Nonfiction.

If you can weld, you can build a hot rod chassis using this book. Boyd Coddington is a renowned artist who works in steel and aluminum. His car designs are world famous, including Chezoom and Cadzilla and a hot rod for the rock group ZZ Top. Coddington's articles and pictures have appeared in all the enthusiast publications plus magazines as divergent as *Playboy* and *Smithsonian.* This book gives the reader the necessary information to build a hot rod chassis. The photos and diagrams are comprehensive, and pitfalls and possible trouble areas are noted.

7.9   Stubblefield, Mike, and John H. Haynes. **The Haynes Emissions Control Manual.** Haynes, 1992. 192 pp. ISBN 1-85010-667-3. Nonfiction.

A good book for the do-it-yourself mechanic, this is one of a large number of Haynes Automotive Books dealing with the different areas of automobile maintenance and repair. While readers of these books should watch for occasional typographical errors associated with numbers, the emissions area should not be as critical as other engine functions.

7.10   Sullivan, George. **How an Airport Really Works.** Dutton/Lodestar Books, 1993. 112 pp. ISBN 0-525-67378-4. Nonfiction.

Busy airports are like small cities. They operate twenty-four hours a day, 365 days a year, and provide a variety of services for the traveler. Besides restaurants, shops, and banks, large airports have fire stations, police forces, and medical centers. If you would like to find out what goes on behind the scenes, you will find George Sullivan's book packed with facts and fascinating tidbits about airport design, food service, baggage handling, and animal care.

7.11   Von Dare, Gregory. **Corvette Racers.** Photographs by Dave Friedman. Motorbooks International, 1992. 192 pp. ISBN 0-87938-574-X. Nonfiction.

Still billed as America's Only Sports Car, the Corvette has contributed much to the heritage of American racing. This book briefly describes the history of the Corvette as SCCA Racer and International Racer. There is also a brief chapter on Corvette Drag Racers and Bonneville Cars. But the main focus is on sports car racing and the drivers who gained today's fame from yesterday's racing. If you are a racing fan or a Corvette fan, this book is a must.

8 Classics

8.1   Andrews, William L., editor. **The African-American Novel in the Age of Reaction: Three Classics.** Penguin/Mentor Books, 1992. 587 pp. ISBN 0-451-62849-7. Fiction.

The three classics in this collection are protest novels against the South's doctrine of "separate but equal," which governed race relations following the Civil War. *Iola Leroy*, by Frances E. W. Harper, is the story of a light-skinned young woman who discovers at the death of her southern planter father that her mother was a former slave. Charles W. Chesnutt's *The Marrow of Tradition* portrays the devastating effects of white supremacist politics on a small southern town. *The Sport of the Gods* by Paul Lawrence Dunbar tells the grim story of a southern black mother, son, and daughter who migrate to New York City to escape the disgrace they experience when the father of the family is falsely charged with robbery and sent to the state penitentiary. The themes of these novels are still timely today.

8.2   Aristotle (translated by H. C. Lawson-Tancred). **The Art of Rhetoric.** Penguin, 1991. 291 pp. ISBN 0-14-044510-2. Nonfiction.

In ancient Greek civilization, effective debate was highly prized, ranking second only to skill in warfare. In *The Art of Rhetoric*, Aristotle provided his fellow Athenians with a systematic analysis of the art of persuasion. In doing so, he created the most influential work, even to the present day, on this topic. Aristotle divides oratory into three types: deliberative (or political), laudatory, and forensic (or litigious). In addition to proofs by logical arguments, Aristotle's book includes proofs of a psychological nature—those of emotion and character. The volume ends with suggestions for improving the style and composition of speeches. Written in the style of a manual, this volume is not easy reading, but the persistent reader will gain a deeper understanding of the art of persuasion.

8.3   Baum, L. Frank. **The Emerald City of Oz.** Illustrated by John R. Neill. William Morrow, 1993. 300 pp. ISBN 0-688-11558-6. Fiction.

In this sixth and last book of the Oz series, Dorothy returns to the magical Land of Oz, taking along her dog Toto and her Uncle Henry and Aunt Em, whose mortgaged farm has failed once again. To entertain her relatives, hardworking people unused to the luxurious idleness of Oz, Dorothy and a party of Oz friends take them on a tour. Meanwhile Princess Ozma, Ruler of Oz, discovers in her magical mirror that the wicked Nome King is tunneling underground to make a surprise attack on the Emerald City. Can this fabulous city be saved by a princess who believes only in kindness? This intriguing story in the Books of Wonder series is illustrated with the colored plates from the original 1910 edition by John R. Neill.

8.4   Benjamin, Alan. **Appointment.** Illustrated by Roger Essley. Simon and Schuster/Green Tiger Press, 1993. 32 pp. ISBN 0-671-75887-X. Fiction.

A superstitious elderly man thinks he sees death, disguised as an old woman, in an ancient Middle East marketplace. In 1933, W. Somerset Maugham published the intriguing story "Appointment in Samarra." Alan Benjamin has adapted this tale of mortality into a short and easy-to-read story set in Baghdad, Iran. Roger Essley has provided rich, full-page illustrations in color.

8.5   Berger, Thomas. **Orrie's Story.** Penguin Books, 1992. 276 pp. ISBN 0-316-09220-7. Fiction.

The Greek tragedy of a brother and sister, Orestes and Electra, who plot to kill their mother is transformed into a down-to-earth story that takes place in a small American town right after World War II. Augie, an army hero, has a few surprises of his own for his wife, Esther, and her lover, E. G.; but it is Orrie who emerges as both hero and victim in this fast-paced, suspenseful story.

8.6   Carroll, Lewis. **Alice's Adventures in Wonderland.** Illustrated by John Tenniel. William Morrow/Books of Wonder, 1992. 192 pp. ISBN 0-688-11087-8. Fiction.

Feeling drowsy as she sits outdoors, Alice spies a white rabbit hurrying along, muttering, "Oh dear! Oh dear! I shall be too late!" as he checks the time on his pocket watch. Curious, Alice races after the rabbit and follows him down a large hole. Down, down she falls into a wonderful, strange world of talking creatures: a Dodo, a disappearing Cheshire Cat, a Mad Hatter, a Mock Turtle, and a King and Queen of Hearts with a retinue of card people, to name a few. Filled with exquisite wit, humor, and nonsense, the tale is the source of numerous modern-day sayings. This edition contains illustrations by John Tenniel reproduced from the original 1865 wood engravings by the Brothers Dalziel.

8.7   Carroll, Lewis. **Through the Looking Glass and What Alice Found There.** Illustrated by John Tenniel. William Morrow/Books of Wonder, 1993. 228 pp. ISBN 0-688-12049-0. Fiction.

In this delightful sequel to *Alice's Adventures in Wonderland,* Alice, leaving her kittens and chess game behind, steps through the looking glass in her drawing room and finds herself in a nonsensical world where events often happen in reverse. As she explores this strange world, she meets some very odd characters: Tweedledum and Tweedledee, Humpty Dumpty, the White Knight, the Red Queen, and the White Queen. The clever, often blunt, conversations with these characters are a challenge to Alice's wit and good manners. This book is for all age groups and merits rereading. The fifty illustrations by John Tenniel are made directly from wood blocks used in the original 1872 publication.

8.8   Conrad, Joseph. **Chance.** Penguin/Signet Classic Books, 1992. 353 pp. ISBN 0-451-52557-4. Fiction.

Flora de Barral, teenage daughter of a prominent financier, suddenly finds herself penniless and friendless when her father is imprisoned for swindling. Her governess, an unscrupulous, resentful woman, abandons Flora, declaring her now no better than a beggar. Traumatized, Flora loses her sense of self-worth and falls prey to a succession of self-interested people. Then she meets Roderich Anthony, a sea captain who falls hopelessly in love with her. This novel explores the many faces of love, false and true, and Flora's development from a vulnerable waif to a self-assured woman. It is also a study of the ways in which chance influences life's events. First published in 1914.

8.9   Kingsley, Charles. **Westward Ho!** Illustrated by N. C. Wyeth. Charles Scribner's Sons, 1992. 413 pp. ISBN 0-684-19444-9. Fiction.

Tall, strong, and intelligent, fifteen-year-old Amyas Leigh of Burrough, England, has two ambitions: to see the Indies and to fight the Spaniards. By age twenty, he has sailed around the world with Francis Drake and returned home to give God thanks. His biggest adventure comes, however, when he, his brother Frank, and other members of the League of the "Rose of Torridge" sail to the Spanish Main, the Spanish colonies of South America bordering the Caribbean, to avenge the seduction of a local belle, Rose Torridge, by a Spanish nobleman. Set in the Elizabethan period, this historical novel vividly portrays the lush natural beauty of the New World and its dangers. It is unstinting in its description of the warfare between England and Spain for domination of the seas and the New World. First published in 1920.

8.10   Kipling, Rudyard. **Kim.** Dell/Yearling Books, 1992. 312 pp. ISBN 0-440-40695-1. Fiction.

Kim, the orphaned son of a former British colonial soldier, becomes streetwise and as dark skinned as a native as he roams the bustling streets of Lahore, India. Playing one day on a cannon, a city landmark, Kim meets a Tibetan lama who is on a pilgrimage. Kim is attracted to this holy man and finds purpose in his life by becoming the lama's protector and disciple—his *chela.* But he also has an allegiance to Mahbub Ali, an influential horse trader who uses him from time to time as a spy. Living alternately in two worlds, Kim is continually caught up in adventure and intrigue as he travels with his lama on the Grand Trunk Road. First published in 1901.

8.11   Rand, Ayn. **Atlas Shrugged.** Penguin/Signet Books, 1992. 1,084 pp. ISBN 0-451-17192-6. Fiction.

Suppose the creative leaders of the world went on a "mind strike" and left the running of the world to second-rate, parasitic individuals? Such is the premise of this philosophical novel by Ayn Rand, who portrays the prime movers of business as shrugging their shoulders and walking away from duty when society does not reward their creativity. Can society survive without its great minds? Do prime movers like John Galt, mechanical genius and hero of this novel, have an obligation to save society from economic and political disaster? This story is filled with action, conflict, passion, and, in the end, hope. First published in 1957.

8.12   Rand, Ayn. **The Fountainhead.** Penguin/Signet Books, 1993. 704 pp. ISBN 0-451-17512-3. Fiction.

Strong, honest, and individualistic, young architect Howard Roark believes that a building's form must be true to its function. He refuses to imitate or borrow from the past or to compromise with the whims of his clients or his fellow architects. Because of this, he struggles to make a living. Peter Keating, on the other hand, is everything that Roark is not. A member of a prestigious architectural firm, Keating is charming and always compromising—doing, in fact, whatever is necessary to ensure his future success and fame. A powerful novel of ideas, *The Fountainhead* dramatically portrays the conflict between blunt individualism and collectivism, between creators and "second handers." First published in 1943.

8.13   Thurber, James. **The Thirteen Clocks.** Dell, 1992. 124 pp. ISBN 0-440-40582-3. Fiction.

Coffin Castle is so cold that its thirteen clocks have frozen. Princess Saralinda, the only warm person in the castle, is a virtual prisoner because her cruel possessive uncle, the Duke, delights in giving all her suitors impossible tasks. Can young Prince Zorn of Zorna, disguised as a traveling minstrel, succeed where all others have failed? He takes hope when Golux, a wizard assigned to help people in peril, becomes his adviser. This is a timeless tale of youth, love, and the pursuit of the impossible dream. First published in 1950.

8.14   Thurber, James. **The Wonderful O.** Dell, 1992. 73 pp. ISBN 0-440-40579-3. Fiction.

In this rollicksome tale, Littlejack and Captain Black sail with their sinewy pirate crew to the island of Ooroo in search of precious jewels. Having a morbid hatred of the vowel O, Captain Black, on reaching the island, issues an edict removing all O's from the islanders' vocabulary (for example, *Ooroo* becomes *R* and *coat* becomes *cat*). Confusion reigns. Black and his men devastate the town searching for the jewels and destroying all things with O in their names—buildings, trees, animals, vegetables, and flowers. Will they find the precious jewels? Will the gentle islanders survive this onslaught? This hilarious fantasy will appeal to all who enjoy wordplay and one-upmanship. First published in 1957.

8.15   Tritten, Charles. **Heidi Grows Up.** Dell/Yearling Books, 1992. 164 pp. ISBN 0-440-40107-0. Fiction.

In response to popular demand, Charles Tritten, the translator of *Heidi,* wrote this novel about Heidi's adolescent years. Because the teacher of the village school in Dörfli is strong on punishment and weak in instruction, Heidi is sent to a fashionable boarding school in Lausanna. She experiences good-humored teasing and sometimes scorn from her classmates for her quaint, peasant ways. Nevertheless, she is determined to get her education so that she can return to her alpine village to care for her aging grandfather and take over the teaching of the village youngsters.

8.16   Wharton, Edith. **Summer.** Penguin/Signet Classic Books, 1993. 196 pp. ISBN 0-451-52566-3. Fiction.

Charity Royall is restless and bored with her daily routine in a small town until she meets Lucius Harney. His entrance into her life changes her world forever. The young couple pursues a dream of first love that inevitably intersects with the harsh realities of life. Charity leaves behind innocence as her relationship with Lucius marks her journey into adulthood. First published in 1917.

9 Dating and Sexual Awareness

9.1 Bode, Janet. **Kids Still Having Kids: People Talk about Teen Pregnancy.** Illustrated by Stan Mack. Franklin Watts, 1992. 191 pp. ISBN 0-531-11132-6. Nonfiction.

Janet Bode writes for a teenage reader confronting either a surprise or planned pregnancy. She provides expert and real-life information she has gathered from asking questions about love, sex, pregnancy, abortion, foster care, adoption, and parenting. Her stories are placed in conjunction with factual information aimed at helping the reader make wise decisions. This book contains mature themes and controversial topics.

Notable 1992 Children's Trade Books in the Field of Social Studies

9.2 Gilder, George. **Men and Marriage.** Pelican, 1992. 199 pp. ISBN 0-88289-444-7. Nonfiction.

George Gilder discusses the traditional role of the family, our oldest institution, as the stable basis for a thriving society. After pointing out the importance of love and the biological differences between males and females, he shows the vast changes that have taken place in terms of marriage and the economy. In order for civilization to continue, Gilder contends that there must be a return to the original family structure. First published as *Sexual Suicide*, 1973.

9.3 Gravelle, Karen, and Leslie Peterson. **Teenage Fathers.** Simon and Schuster/Julian Messner, 1992. 98 pp. ISBN 0-671-72850-4. Nonfiction.

Thirteen case studies offer a close look at the attitudes, problems, failures, and successes of teenage fathers. The interviews range across a variety of social and cultural backgrounds. From the father who has nine children and wants nothing to do with any of them to the fathers who have only one child and are trying to be good parents, the stories illustrate the frustrations, hardships, and problems of having a child while still a teenager.

ALA Best Books for Young Adults, 1993
IRA Young Adults' Choices, 1994

9.4 Guernsey, JoAnn Bren. **Abortion: Understanding the Controversy.** Lerner, 1993. 112 pp. ISBN 0-8225-2605-0. Nonfiction.

This book presents both pro-life and pro-choice arguments on abortion. Using facts and statistics, JoAnn Bren Guernsey details the history of abortion as a surgical procedure and social issue, highlighting both the extreme and moderate views. Depicted are methods of abortion as well as methods of persuasion used by the opposing sides. Who has abortions and why? What does abortion mean economically, socially, and morally? What are the alternatives?

9.5 Jakobson, Cathryn. **Think about Teenage Pregnancy.** Walker, 1993. 160 pp. ISBN 0-8027-8128-4. Nonfiction.

The emotional, political, and personal aspects of teenage contraception and pregnancy are addressed in this book. It is informative with its history of the family life curriculum, explanation of the systems around the country for involving the teenage fathers in caring for a child, and comparisons between American responses to teenage sexuality and those of Europeans. Cathryn Jakobson poses some thought-provoking questions, such as: Is knowledge enough to combat the desire for personal fulfillment that may motivate teenage pregnancy?

9.6 Johnson, Joan J. **Teen Prostitution.** Franklin Watts, 1992. 188 pp. ISBN 0-531-11099-0. Nonfiction.

Though many teenagers turn to the streets, the act of prostitution is illegal. Joan J. Johnson discusses the teenagers who participate in prostitution and cites the obvious reasons. In addition, she presents an answer for such a serious problem. Prevention is a necessity for this group of teenagers who are neglected to the extent that they are driven to find solace by selling their bodies.

9.7 Johnson, Julie Tallard. **Making Friends, Finding Love.** Lerner, 1992. 64 pp. ISBN 0-8225-0045-0. Nonfiction.

This book uses quotations from real people to address real concerns without relying on trite phrases or ideas. It goes beyond "be a friend to yourself first" by presenting options for the reader to consider about friendship and love. To be a friend you must have trust, honesty, availability, safety, love, respect, reciprocity, and growth. Loneliness and belonging are discussed honestly, as are families' roles and setting limits on relationships.

9.8 Koertge, Ron. **Where the Kissing Never Stops.** Avon Books, 1993. 217 pp. ISBN 0-380-71796-4. Fiction.

Seventeen-year-old Sully is not having a good year. His father died a year ago; his girlfriend moved away; he still has a weight problem; and his mother is trying "to find herself." During the course of the year, Sully and his best friend Walker share many of the typical teenage anxieties and insecurities. Walker, who is being pressured by his father to become a psychiatrist, sees Sully as a perfect case study. He frequently identifies the causes of Sully's anxieties and never fails to offer a solution. One such solution is Rachel, a blind date that Walker arranges. Sully falls in love with her, and their relationship becomes a stabilizer in Sully's life. Being with Rachel makes Sully wish that he could stay forever in a place "where the kissing never stops."

9.9   Kranz, Rachel. **Straight Talk about Prejudice.** Facts on File, 1992. 124 pp. ISBN 0-8160-2488-X. Nonfiction.

Although this book deals with many forms of prejudice, the chapters on prejudice against women (Chapter 3) and homosexuals (Chapter 4) are exceptional. Chapter 3 is structured through seven vignettes that showcase prejudice, ranging from a woman not being able to walk alone at night to a woman who trains a man for a job only to learn that he will be paid more than she. Chapter 4 is structured around a sterotype- and myth-awareness test about homosexuality. For example, is it true that gay people tend to come from more privileged backgrounds?

9.10   Kuklin, Susan. **Speaking Out: Teenagers Take on Race, Sex, and Identity.** G. P. Putnam Sons, 1993. 165 pp. ISBN 0-399-22532-3. Nonfiction.

What happens when you make a high school racially balanced: 25 percent Asian, 25 percent African American, 25 percent Hispanic, and 25 percent white? Does it improve or worsen prejudice? Susan Kuklin asked a group of people to discuss prejudice, race, sexuality, and being different. When the students were given the chance to talk for themselves, they clearly showed that their feelings are the same—it hurts to be labeled. Further discussion showed they learned valuable lessons about self-esteem, compatibility, and respect.

ALA Quick Picks for Young Adults, 1994
Booklist Editors' Choice, 1993

9.11   Landau, Elaine. **Sexual Harassment.** Walker, 1993. 93 pp. ISBN 0-8027-8266-3. Nonfiction.

Sexual Harassment uses recent cases to present the meaning, source, and consequences of this issue on the job and in school.

The Clarence Thomas Supreme Court confirmation hearings in the U.S. Senate and the allegations of sexual harassment from Anita Hill are analyzed, along with other cases, to show the importance of facing this social issue. Helpful tactics are offered to avoid harassment situations, and policy statements are outlined for employees or students to implement in order to ensure their own harassment-free environments.

9.12   Mazer, Norma Fox. **Out of Control.** Morrow Junior Books, 1993. 218 pp. ISBN 0-688-10208-5. Fiction.

When does harmless teasing turn into sexual harassment? How long will boys be boys? What starts out as a game for Rollo Wingate and his friends frightens the self-assured Valerie Michon. Is it better or worse when the principal calls them all together for a formal apology? Rollo has to deal with his friends, his school, his family, his victim, and, most of all, himself when the game gets out of control.

ALA Best Books for Young Adults, 1994

9.13   McClintock, Norah. **The Stepfather Game.** Scholastic/Point Books, 1991. 190 pp. ISBN 0-590-43971-5. Fiction.

How can three half-sisters be so different? There is Brynn, the beautiful, studious, and responsible one who tries to take care of Chloe, the wild Chinese American child, and Phoebe, the youngest and plumpest. Each has obstacles to overcome. Brynn almost loses her best friend over a boy; Chloe, never dateless, finds herself without one when her boyfriend shuns her because of her mixed heritage; and Phoebe goes on a starvation diet that lands her in the hospital. Together they learn to help each other through their obstacles.

9.14   Scoppettone, Sandra. **Happy Endings Are All Alike.** Alyson, 1991. 202 pp. ISBN 1-55583-177-X. Fiction.

Jaret and Peggy are lovers. Jaret's mother knows and accepts their lesbian relationship. Peggy's sister knows, too, but she cannot accept it. Can Peggy and Jaret? After a brutal attack against Jaret, the girls, their families, and the town are all faced with handling the relationship and different ideas on sexuality.

9.15   Walker, Kate. **Peter.** Houghton Mifflin, 1993. 170 pp. ISBN 0-395-64722-3. Fiction.

Peter Dawson, a regular fifteen-year-old bloke in Australia, is interested in motorcross and men. What does not make sense to

Peter is that he is in love with David, his older brother's friend. Can he be gay? All his friends talk about scoring. Why doesn't he when he gets the chance? Is fifteen the age to figure it out? First published in Australia, 1991.

ALA Best Books for Young Adults, 1994
ALA Notable Books for Children, 1994
ALA Quick Picks for Young Adults, 1994

10 Easy Reading

10.1 Adler, C. S. **Ghost Brother.** Avon/Camelot Books, 1992. 135 pp. ISBN 0-380-71386-1. Fiction.

Wally's older brother Jon-O died trying to rescue a child. Jon-O was everything that Wally is not: a daredevil, popular, and a good athlete. Wally tries to keep his brother alive by imagining that Jon-O is with him, teasing him, urging him on. He attempts to change to be just like Jon-O, but in doing so, Wally constantly gets into trouble.

IRA Children's Choices, 1991

10.2 Ashabranner, Brent. **Land of Yesterday, Land of Tomorrow: Discovering Chinese Central Asia.** Photographs by David Paul and Peter Conklin. Dutton/Cobblehill Books, 1992. 139 pp. ISBN 0-525-65086-5. Fiction.

Through words and photographs, this book provides information about the remote northwestern area of China. Geological exploration, the journey of Marco Polo, and the lives of the Uighur and Kashgar nomadic tribes are detailed. The photographs were taken during the late 1980s, the brief period when this area was open to outsiders.

10.3 Avery, Gillian. **Maria's Italian Spring.** Illustrated by Scott Snow. Simon and Schuster, 1993. 265 pp. ISBN 0-671-79582-1. Fiction.

Twelve-year-old Maria is alone in England after her latest guardian dies. She eventually ends up with relatives in Venice, Italy, and resolves never to leave her uncle and cousin's house. Maria, however, is befriended by Cordelia, whose energetic and exotic plans both frighten and intrigue her. Both girls must learn the relationship between compromise and change.

10.4 Avi. **Windcatcher.** Map by Jim Kemp and Anita Karl. Avon Books, 1992. 120 pp. ISBN 0-380-71805-7. Fiction.

Eleven-year-old Tony Sousa has saved $300 from his paper route for a motor bike. When his parents tell him he is too young, he purchases a small Snark sailboat instead. Staying with his grandmother on the Connecticut shore of Long Island Sound, Tony learns how to sail the boat and becomes involved with treasure hunters. Then he has to decide whether to share in the treasure or see that it goes to the proper authorities.

10.5   Ballard, Robert D. **Exploring the Bismarck: The Real-Life Quest to Find Hitler's Greatest Battleship.** Scholastic/Madison Press Books, 1991. 64 pp. ISBN 0-590-44268-6. Nonfiction.

Four young German soldiers who actually sailed on the *Bismarck* and survived her sinking give firsthand accounts of the life and death of the World War II ship. The recovery of the ship, using the same method that was used with the *Titanic,* is also described. Photographs, illustrations, a glossary, and bibliography are included.

ALA Quick Picks for Young Adults, 1992
IRA Children's Choices, 1992

10.6   Block, Francesca Lia. **Missing Angel Juan.** HarperCollins, 1993. 138 pp. ISBN 0-06-023007-X. Fiction.

Angel Juan flees Los Angeles, his parents, and his friends to strike out on his own in New York City. He is followed by Witch Baby and the other members of the band he deserted. Witch Baby senses trouble, and through a series of adventures and disasters, she is eventually reunited with the boy she truly loves. She is not totally prepared, however, to accept what she finds. Sequel to *Weetzie Bat, Witch Baby,* and *Cherokee Bat and the Goat Guys.*

ALA Best Books for Young Adults, 1994
ALA Quick Picks for Young Adults, 1994
School Library Journal Best Books, 1993

10.7   Bryant, Bonnie. **The Saddle Club: Horse Trouble.** Bantam/Skylark Books, 1992. 135 pp. ISBN 0-553-48025-1. Fiction.

The loss of a valuable pen prompts the Saddle Club—three young girls bound in friendship by a common love of horses—to take over the everyday management of Pine Hollow Stables when Mrs. Reg, the owner of the pen and the manager of the stables, leaves town for a week. The girls' mismanagement and comical misunderstandings lead them through a light-hearted series of events that create havoc for the girls but only positive results for the stables.

10.8   Cavanagh, Helen. **Panther Glade.** Simon and Schuster, 1993. 144 pp. ISBN 0-671-75617-6. Fiction.

Born in New Jersey, Bill finds himself stuck for the summer in the Florida Everglades with his archaeologist aunt. Bill grows to love archaeology as he becomes interested in the legend of the cat god.

Suddenly Bill is stranded on an island after a storm, and he discovers that the lore he has grown to love is actually coming to life.

10.9   Christopher, John. **The Guardians.** Macmillan/Collier Books, 1992. 214 pp. ISBN 0-02-042681-X. Fiction.

In this novel set in the year 2050, the former Great Britain is divided into two countries—Conurb, crowded and crude, and County, seemingly peaceful and simple. Conurban Rob Randall escapes into the unknown world of the County after his father's mysterious death. Rob assumes a false identity in this alien world and sets out to find the true reason behind his father's death.

10.10   Deem, James M. **Ghost Hunters.** Illustrated by Michael David Biegel. Avon/Camelot Books, 1992. 112 pp. ISBN 0-380-76682-5. Nonfiction.

This book tells thirteen true stories about the experiences of ordinary people, researchers, scientists, and ghosts. Current research and investigations on apparitions, haunted houses, moving objects, and the afterlife are included. A bibliography is also provided.

10.11   Denenberg, Barry. **The True Story of J. Edgar Hoover and the FBI.** Scholastic, 1993. 224 pp. ISBN 0-590-43168-4. Nonfiction.

This biography of the controversial former chief of the Federal Bureau of Investigation focuses on the FBI's impact on the major law enforcement issues of the 1920s through the 1970s. Hoover was regarded by many as the nation's top law enforcer, and he ran the FBI for approximately half a century, outlasting the administrations of eight presidents.

10.12   Doherty, Berlie. **Dear Nobody.** Orchard Books, 1992. 185 pp. ISBN 0-531-08611-9. Fiction.

Helen and Chris are both eighteen and still in school when Helen discovers she is pregnant. At the same time, Chris's mother, who walked out on him and his father when he was ten, reappears and wants to make up for the past. Unable to cope with these two traumatic events, Chris flees and tries to understand both parenthood and his own parents.

ALA Best Books for Young Adults, 1993
Booklist Editors' Choice, 1992
Carnegie Medal, 1992
School Library Journal Best Books, 1992

10.13 Geller, Mark. **Who's on First?** HarperCollins, 1992. 60 pp. ISBN 0-06-021085-0. Fiction.

Alex is worried that Carol, his older sister, does not have an escort for their cousin's wedding. Secretly, he sets her up with his best friend's cousin, Leon, but then Alex discovers that he dislikes Leon very much. Caught in the middle, Alex must decide what to do. Should he tell Carol of his involvement in arranging her date and risk her getting angry with him? Or should he say nothing and possibly allow Leon to hurt her?

10.14 Hughes, Monica. **The Crystal Drop.** Simon and Schuster, 1993. 212 pp. ISBN 0-671-79195-8. Fiction.

The year is 2011. Megan's mother is dead, the family farm is doomed due to drought, Megan must look after her younger brother Ian, and civilization as the two know it is on the verge of collapse. Megan and Ian begin a journey across Canada in search of a resource that, in their futuristic world, is more precious than gold—water.

10.15 Kjelgaard, Jim. **Big Red.** Illustrated by Carl Pfeüffer. Bantam/Skylark Books, 1991. 218 pp. ISBN 0-553-15194-0. Fiction.

Danny enjoys hunting and fishing with his father, a trapper in the backwoods country. When Danny meets the champion Irish setter, Big Red, the boy and dog become fast friends. Noticing Danny's talent with handling Big Red, Mr. Haggin, the owner of a large estate and of Big Red, asks Danny to help him with his show dogs—and he allows Danny to work with Big Red on his own. After many adventures in the backwoods with the setter, Danny and Big Red face their biggest challenge and most frightening foe: Old Majesty, a bear famous for his killer instinct. First published in 1945.

ALA Notable Book, 1945

10.16 Litowinsky, Olga. **The High Voyage: The Final Crossing of Christopher Columbus.** Dell/Yearling Books, 1992. 145 pp. ISBN 0-440-40703-6. Fiction.

Fernando Columbus, youngest son of Christopher Columbus, tells the story of his famous father's fourth and final voyage across the Atlantic. Life aboard the ship, terrible weather conditions, and the various and sometimes strange customs of the cultures that Columbus encounters during his two-year trip are detailed. The book also shows the human side of Columbus, whose life ends in a widely unknown and surprising way.

10.17 Lowry, Lois. **Anastasia on Her Own.** Dell/Yearling Books, 1992. 131 pp. ISBN 0-440-40291-3. Fiction.

Anastasia's mother is not very organized, so Anastasia and her father develop a schedule to organize her mother's day. When her mother is suddenly called away, Anastasia discovers that everything does not always stick to a schedule. Her brother's bout with the chicken pox and an unexpected visit from her father's old girlfriend add to the confusion.

10.18 Montgomery, Lucy Maud (story by Gail Hamilton). **Conversions.** Bantam/Skylark Books, 1992. 123 pp. ISBN 0-553-48032-4. Fiction.

In a story adapted from Lucy Maud Montgomery's *Anne of Green Gables* about life on Canada's Prince Edward Island, Sara lives on the farm at Avonlea owned by her stern Aunt Hetty, an elderly school teacher, and her kinder Aunt Olivia. Peter, a teenage boy hired to do odd jobs around Avonlea, is invited by Sara to attend an evangelical meeting at the Presbyterian church. He must decline because he does not have the appropriate clothes. Sara's cousin makes fun of Peter, but when the flu strikes the countryside, opinions change. A book in the Road to Avonlea series.

10.19 Murphy, Jim. **The Long Road to Gettysburg.** Houghton Mifflin/Clarion Books, 1992. 112 pp. ISBN 0-395-55965-0. Nonfiction.

Nineteen-year-old Confederate Lieutenant John Dooley and seventeen-year-old Union soldier Thomas Galway were actual participants in the Civil War's Battle of Gettysburg. The battle, as well as the delivery of Lincoln's famous speech at the dedication of the National Cemetery at Gettysburg, is told through their eyes.

Booklist Editors' Choice, 1992
Notable 1992 Children's Trade Books in the Field of Social Studies

10.20 Nelson, Theresa. **The Beggars' Ride.** Orchard Books, 1992. 121 pp. ISBN 0-531-08496-5. Fiction.

Clare flees an unhappy home life and abusive stepfather and finds herself homeless, living under the boardwalk of Atlantic City, New Jersey. After joining a gang, the Cowboys, whose members have problems similar to hers, Clare is forced to participate in a scam whose victim is an old man who has also befriended her. Clare must pick the gang, her friend, or jail.

ALA Best Books for Young Adults, 1993
ALA Notable Books for Children, 1993
School Library Journal Best Books, 1992

10.21   Thesman, Jean. **The Whitney Cousins: Triple Trouble.** Avon/ Flare Books, 1992. 153 pp. ISBN 0-380-76464-4. Fiction.

The Whitney cousins—Amelia, Heather, and Erin—are together for the summer, staying with Amelia in the small town of Fox Crossing. Heather is involved with planning the town centennial. Amelia agrees to teach some of the locals clowning techniques. Erin meets Toby and falls in love for the first time. These fifteen-year-old cousins manage to enjoy an adventurous summer.

10.22   Waters, David, and Sam Hamm (adapted by Andrew Hefler). **Batman Returns.** Little, Brown, 1992. 92 pp. ISBN 0-316-17757-1. Fiction.

In this story set during the Christmas holiday season, a strange birdlike man called the Penguin emerges from the sewers. He is joined by a mysterious creature called Catwoman. Together, they begin a campaign to get the Penguin elected mayor of Gotham City. In the process, they also plan to ruin the city and the reputation of Batman, the secret alter-ego of millionaire Bruce Wayne.

10.23   Whitman, Sylvia. **V Is for Victory: The American Home Front during World War II.** Lerner, 1993. 79 pp. ISBN 0-8225-1727-2. Nonfiction.

When America entered World War II, domestic life changed drastically. The war was everywhere. Women who had stayed at home to raise families now worked around the clock in factories, children assisted with collecting metal and paper, and the government instituted food and gasoline rations. Using personal interviews, government slogans, historical accounts, songs, drawings, and photographs, author Sylvia Whitman illustrates how civilians went to work to win the war and how World War II changed life for all Americans.

Notable 1992 Children's Trade Books in the Field of Social Studies

10.24   Wolf, Joyce. **Between the Cracks.** Dial Books, 1992. 172 pp. ISBN 0-8037-1270-7. Fiction.

Cal's best friend Bentley gradually falls under the spell of a mysterious man. Cal is skeptical at first, but then she begins to see the Dark Man, too. Realizing that her friend is falling deeper and deeper into a dangerous world, Cal sets out to rescue her friend. In the process, she learns the meaning of both courage and friendship.

10.25 Zindel, Paul. **David and Della.** HarperCollins, 1993. 167 pp. ISBN 0-06-023354-0. Fiction.

David, a budding playwright who develops writer's block when his girlfriend attempts suicide, hires Della to inspire him to write again. Della is a young actress with several bad habits, including the inability to tell the truth. She comes to know herself and face her troubled past as she helps David do the same.

11 Family Relationships

11.1 Alvarez, Julia. **How the García Girls Lost Their Accents.** Penguin/Plume Books, 1992. 290 pp. ISBN 0-452-26806-0. Fiction.

Four sisters from the Dominican Republic move with their parents to New York City in the 1960s and find their new life a struggle. For Carla, Sandra, Yolanda, and Sofia, the questions about their new life in America—and the solutions—are all different. When they visit home, they are no longer Dominican; when they return to America, they feel alien. Yet the García girls prevail in this warm and wise story of two cultures colliding.

11.2 Bennett, Cherie. **The Fall of the Perfect Girl.** Penguin/Puffin Books, 1993. 212 pp. ISBN 0-14-036319-X. Fiction.

Suzanne Elizabeth Wentworth Lafayette was born with a silver spoon in her mouth. Her mother is part of an old established family in Tennessee, and her father is a famous lawyer who has just been appointed attorney general of Tennessee. Suzanne's world is perfect until the phone calls from across town start coming. Why would anyone want to destroy her world? Who are Charlene and Patsy? What is in her father's past to ruin her family's perfect life—forever?

11.3 Blacker, Terence. **Homebird.** Macmillan/Bradbury Press, 1993. 139 pp. ISBN 0-02-710685-3. Fiction.

"Sometimes the danger signals are there, but it takes time to see them." So begins the saga of thirteen-year-old Nicky Morrison and what was supposed to be his first year at boarding school. But Nicky has a hard time dealing with a school that he hates, classmates that he dislikes, and a family that is breaking up. He decides to run away from school—only to find himself in a worse position on the streets and in the company of criminals. First published in Great Britain, 1991.

11.4 Bridgers, Sue Ellen. **Keeping Christina.** HarperCollins, 1993. 281 pp. ISBN 0-06-021505-4. Fiction.

This novel is based on a true story of high school friendships. Annie, Jill, and Peter have been friends since childhood, but when Christina moves to town, Annie's sympathetic response threatens to jeopardize those friendships. As Annie learns more about Christina, she finds that Christina is not who or what she originally thought. Christina has lied, stolen, and manipulated relationships. By the conclusion of the novel, Annie has developed insights into the nature of friendship, the value of intellectual freedom, and the importance of family.

11.5 Brooks, Martha. **Two Moons in August.** Little, Brown/Joy Street Books, 1992. 199 pp. ISBN 0-316-10979-7. Fiction.

Sidonie does not lose just one parent when her mother dies of tuberculosis. Her father is gone in spirit. Her older sister, Bobbi, maintains control of the family—but just barely. When Kieran, an intense young man, plays push-me, pull-me with Sidonie, she exclaims, "I'm surrounded by intense people. What am I supposed to do, crawl under the sofa so I won't have a nervous breakdown? Stop the car right now. I want out."

ALA Best Books for Young Adults, 1993

11.6 Cannon, A. E. **Amazing Gracie.** Dell/Laurel-Leaf Library, 1993. 214 pp. ISBN 0-440-21570-6. Fiction.

Fifteen-year-old Gracie accepts a tremendous amount of responsibility trying to keep her family together after her mother's remarriage and the family's move to Salt Lake City. Everything goes along smoothly for Gracie as she meets Tiimo, her first boyfriend, and begins to settle into her new home and community. Then disaster strikes—her mother's past depression returns, leading to her attempted suicide. Through it all, Gracie struggles to keep her family together and create a sense of stability in their lives.

ALA Best Book for Young Adults, 1992
School Library Journal Best Books, 1991

11.7 Carter, Alden R. **Up Country.** Scholastic, 1991. 256 pp. ISBN 0-590-43638-4. Fiction.

Though the beginning of this book relies on stereotypes to portray Carl as an electronic genius, his mother as a promiscuous alcoholic, and Carl's cousins as wholesome hicks, the ending is sincere. Carl matures when he is sent to live with his cousins after his mother is arrested. But it is not until his own arrest that he realizes just how much his mother's alcoholism controls him: "I didn't act as an individual, I did things because I'd been programmed by the alcoholism of my parent. Hell, I wasn't an individual at all; I was a robot!" Mature language and subject matter.

11.8 Caseley, Judith. **My Father, the Nutcase.** Alfred A. Knopf, 1992. 185 pp. ISBN 0-679-93394-8. Fiction.

Zoe is fifteen, and life is a big puzzle. How do you tell a boy *no* so that he understands the meaning? How do you know when you're in love? Zoe wonders if she is wrong to detest her father's clinically depressed condition. Is he aware of the strain he is putting on the whole family? Does he care? Sometimes it seems to her that she will never have any answers—after all, even the adults cannot find them.

11.9   Cooney, Caroline B. **Operation: Homefront.** Bantam Books, 1992. 211 pp. ISBN 0-553-29685-X. Fiction.

The Herrick family leads a normal life until President George Bush calls up troops to fight in the Middle East against Iran's Saddam Hussein. Their whole world is changed when Rosalys Herrick, the mother, is sent to the Persian Gulf. Her husband and the children—Laura, fourteen, Langdon, fifteen, and Nicholas, eight—find life difficult as they try to maintain a normal homefront while news from the Gulf War is constantly on television. Will their mother return? Will she be all right?

11.10   Corman, Avery. **Prized Possessions.** Simon and Schuster, 1991. 320 pp. ISBN 0-671-69298-4. Fiction.

During Elizabeth Mason's first week at a prestigious eastern college, the talented, outgoing, and beautiful young woman is raped by Jimmy Andrews, the star of the college tennis team. The rape and ensuing struggle for justice challenge the safe and affluent life that Ben and Laura Mason have built for themselves and their children. It also challenges the assumed values and lifestyles of the Andrews family, the college, and others closely involved with the case.

ALA Best Books for Young Adults, 1992

11.11   Cossi, Olga. **The Magic Box.** Penguin/Pelican Books, 1990. 191 pp. ISBN 0-88289-748-9. Fiction.

Seniors Mara, Kate, and Jayni lead their high school basketball team to the state championship game. The day before the big game, Mara breaks a "no smoking" rule, which can get her kicked off the team. That same day she also finds out that her mother has cancer of the larynx, her "magic box of speech." Now Mara will need all her strength to focus her attention on helping both her team and her mother face these critical situations.

11.12   Cottonwood, Joe. **Danny Ain't.** Scholastic, 1992. 288 pp. ISBN 0-590-45067-0. Fiction.

Life is a series of choices, Danny Ain't learns. Forced to survive independently while his father recovers from flashbacks of the Vietnam War, twelve-year-old Danny develops his philosophy of life. In the space of three weeks, he learns that "There's a lot of traps in this life. There's poison bait and shot guns to dodge. I guess growing up is learning to make the right choices." Humorous and well written, *Danny Ain't* is a companion book to *The Adventures of Boone Barnaby*.

11.13 DeVito, Cara. **Where I Want to Be.** Houghton Mifflin, 1993. 187 pp. ISBN 0-395-64592-1. Fiction.

Kristie doesn't know where she wants to go, but she knows where she doesn't want to be—Show Low, Arizona. Last summer she was stuck in Show Low because her father died, but this summer she is determined to get out of town and away from her well-meaning half-brothers, Kyle and Derrin. She wants to find out who she really is and where she really belongs. Who is this mother who left when Kristie was two? What is her family trying to protect her from?

11.14 Doherty, Berlie. **Granny Was a Buffer Girl.** William Morrow/ Beech Tree Books, 1993. 131 pp. ISBN 0-688-11863-1. Fiction.

Eighteen-year-old Jess cannot wait to leave her home and family to study in France. The night before she leaves, her family has a celebration in which they share family stories about members who are no longer with them—Grandma Bridie and her brother, Danny—as well as about their own lives. These tales reveal both past and present hurts and joys. Slowly, Jess begins to realize that knowing your family's history is an important part of understanding who you are. First published in Great Britain, 1988.

Booklist Editors' Choice, 1988
Boston Globe–Horn Book Fiction Honor Book, 1988
Carnegie Medal Honor Book, 1988

11.15 Doherty, Berlie. **White Peak Farm.** William Morrow/Beech Tree Books, 1993. 102 pp. ISBN 0-688-11864-X. Fiction.

Nothing ever seems to change at White Peak Farm in Derbyshire, England, where Jeannie's family has worked the land for generations. This is a story, however, about change. Observing the impact of change on her family, Jeannie realizes that she, too, is changing. This realization permits her to leave her home, but allows the spirit of White Peak Farm to remain constant. Elegantly crafted, each chapter serves almost as a separate story. The characters are complex enough to seem real.

11.16   Durant, Penny Raife. **When Heroes Die.** Atheneum, 1992. 136 pp. ISBN 0-689-31764-6. Fiction.

Twelve-year-old Gary Boyden idolizes his Uncle Rob, the surrogate father who has taught him all that he knows about basketball. With the stress of seventh grade, Gary needs advice, especially about one girl. Unfortunately, Uncle Rob is dying of AIDS. Providing understanding rather than rejection, Gary's friends help him deal with his anger at Uncle Rob's death. Ironically, it is Uncle Rob's practical lessons about life that echo in Gary's mind, giving him the confidence to go on.

11.17   Ferris, Jean. **Relative Strangers.** Farrar, Straus and Giroux, 1993. 229 pp. ISBN 0-374-36243-2. Fiction.

Although Berkeley and her mother, Lily, have a good relationship, Berkeley has always wanted her father to be part of her life, too. Suddenly, right before graduation, she receives a letter inviting her to go to Europe with her father, Parker Stanton. With her mother's encouragement, she decides to go, only to learn at the airport that her father's elegant new wife and sullen stepdaughter are going along. What other surprises will Parker spring on her during their trip? Is he the kind of father Berkeley wants?

11.18   Fine, Anne. **The Book of the Banshee.** Little, Brown/Joy Street Books, 1992. 168 pp. ISBN 0-316-28315-0. Fiction.

Will Flowers has a lot in common with William Saffery, the hero in the book he is reading. Both are teenage boys who find themselves in wars—Saffery in World War I and Will in one at home. When Will is given an assignment by a visiting writer at his school, he decides to record the war that his sister Estelle, the Banshee, has declared. As he writes hilarious accounts of the skirmishes in this home war, he makes remarkable discoveries about himself.

11.19   Fleischman, Paul. **The Borning Room.** Harper and Row/Harper Keypoint, 1991. 101 pp. ISBN 0-06-023785-6. Fiction.

Georgina Lott's life is revealed to the reader from one special room in her house set aside for births, illnesses, and death—the borning room. As she gains insights into herself and the meaning of life, the world outside is full of the violence of the Civil War, the emancipation of the slaves, and the arrival of electricity to her small town in Ohio. Georgina relates the events of her life, from her birth in the 1850s to the arrival of her children and from the death of her mother to her own approaching death in the new twentieth century.

ALA Best Books for Young Adults, 1992
ALA Notable Books for Children, 1992
Booklist Editors' Choice, 1991
IRA Teachers' Choices, 1992
Notable 1991 Children's Trade Books in the Field of Social Studies
School Library Journal Best Books, 1991

11.20 Garland, Sherry. **Shadow of the Dragon.** Harcourt Brace, 1993. 314 pp. ISBN 0-15-273530-5. Fiction.

Danny Vo faces many problems caused by his Vietnamese heritage. At age sixteen, he wants to fit in with his American friends, but his grandmother tries to raise him in a traditional Vietnamese home. When his cousin, Sang Le, joins the family, many problems arise both inside and outside the home. This book reveals the difficulties and prejudices faced by a family trying to survive in a foreign culture.

ALA Best Books for Young Adults, 1994
Booklist Editors' Choice, 1993

11.21 Gibbons, Kaye. **Charms for the Easy Life.** G. P. Putman's Sons, 1993. 254 pp. ISBN 0-399-13791-2. Fiction.

Every word of southern dialect rings true in this tale of North Carolina women who are self-sufficient and intensely individual. It spans the lives of three generations of women who are quirky, humorous, and often outrageous. The narrator, Margaret, is much like her grandmother, Charlie Kate, a healer and self-proclaimed doctor. Charlie Kate's daughter, Sophia, refuses to accept her mother's plans for her life. This look at divided loyalties, personal tragedies, and triumphs will mesmerize you with its sensitivity and humor.

ALA Best Books for Young Adults, 1994
Booklist Editors' Choice, 1993

11.22 Grant, Cynthia D. **Uncle Vampire.** Atheneum, 1993. 153 pp. ISBN 0-689-31852-9. Fiction.

Carolyn believes her Uncle Toddy is a vampire who is wrecking her life. Her brother is flunking, her sister refuses to come home from college, her mother is depressed and stays in the bedroom, and her father is desperately pretending that nothing is wrong. The only one who listens to Carolyn is her perfect twin, Honey, but Carolyn loses hope when even Honey turns a deaf ear. Carolyn must solve this herself: someone must be told that Toddy is a vampire.

ALA Best Books for Young Adults, 1994
ALA Quick Picks for Young Adults, 1994

11.23   Haas, Jessie. **Skipping School.** Greenwillow Books, 1992. 181 pp. ISBN 0-688-10179-8. Fiction.

Phillip is having a hard time dealing with the pressures placed on him by his family's move from their farm to a suburban community, his new school, and his father's terminal cancer. His job at the local veterinary clinic does not provide much relief either. One day Phillip walks out of school and finds the perfect refuge—an old abandoned farmhouse within walking distance of the school. Yet, his daily skipping of school to go to the house creates even more problems.

11.24   Hathorn, Libby. **Thunderwith.** Little, Brown, 1991. 214 pp. ISBN 0-316-35034-6. Fiction.

After her mother dies, Laura Ritchie is sent to live with her father and his family, but she still feels alone. She is befriended by a dingo dog and learns that this might be her totem, her guiding animal spirit. Neil tells her so with his aboriginal stones from the Australian Dreamtime. Even so, Laura has to face her fears—of her stepmother and of Gowd, the neighbor and class officer who reads her fears instinctively. First published in Australia, 1989.

ALA Best Books for Young Adults, 1992
School Library Journal Best Books, 1991

11.25   Hopkins, Lee Bennett. **Mama.** Illustrated by Stephen Marchesi. Simon and Schuster, 1992. 106 pp. ISBN 0-671-74985-4. Fiction.

Mama is a very funny, lively, proud mother who tries to give her two boys everything despite the fact that she is a single parent. As Mama jumps from one job to another, she devises methods to get things for her sons, methods that put her oldest son into some dangerous situations. When he realizes what Mama is doing, the boy finds it hard to follow her direction: "Mama wants you to keep on smiling all through your life."

11.26 Jenkins, Lyll Becerra de. **Celebrating the Hero.** Dutton/Lodestar Books, 1993. 179 pp. ISBN 0-525-67399-7. Fiction.

Camilla Draper, a young American girl of Hispanic descent, must come to grips with the death of her mother. After receiving a letter asking her to come to her mother's hometown in Colombia to a ceremony honoring her grandfather, Camilla decides that the best way to remember her mother would be to attend this event. In the process, she learns much about her mother and her culture—complete with political repression. The story portrays the Hispanic culture, including family traditions and storytelling.

11.27 Kaye, Geraldine. **Someone Else's Baby.** Hyperion Books, 1992. 138 pp. ISBN 1-56282-150-4. Fiction.

Seventeen-year-old Terry Browning is pregnant and trying to find her way through a life that has become very complex. In her journal she records her thoughts and feelings about her pregnancy, her parents, her brothers, her friends, and, most of all, her unborn baby. Realizing that most of the decisions about the baby have been taken out of her hands, Terry decides to tell her child about the circumstances surrounding its conception, gestation, birth, and adoption through her very candid journal.

ALA Best Books for Young Adults, 1993
ALA Quick Picks for Young Adults, 1993

11.28 Koller, Jackie French. **If I Had One Wish. . . .** Little, Brown, 1991. 161 pp. ISBN 0-316-50150-6. Fiction.

Alec cannot stand his little brother, Stevie, who is always tattling on him. So when an old bag lady gives him one wish, Alec eagerly wishes Stevie away. Little does he know how this wish will change his whole life. Alec finds himself in a rich family with parents who pay little attention to him. Alec's new life is worse than the first, and he wonders if he can undo his wish and return to his normal life.

ALA Quick Picks for Young Adults, 1992

11.29 Kordon, Klaus (translated by Elizabeth D. Crawford). **Brothers Like Friends.** Putnam/Philomel Books, 1992. 206 pp. ISBN 0-399-22137-9. Fiction.

Growing up in Berlin in the 1950s, Frank, a seven-year-old tag-along, and his half-brother, Burkie, a soccer star, develop a special relationship that becomes even closer when their mother marries Uncle Willi, an abusive man. Surrounded by buildings and people who are scarred by the aftermath of World War II, the boys gain a special understanding of each other and of life as they struggle with the hard choices they face. First published in Germany, 1978.

11.30   La Puma, Salvatore. **A Time for Wedding Cake.** Penguin/Plume Books, 1992. 256 pp. ISBN 0-452-26814-1. Fiction.

Using provocative, controversial situations and mature language, *A Time for Wedding Cake* effectively conveys the story of Gene Leone, a World War II veteran who returns to Bensonhurst, Brooklyn. As Gene, the second son of a Sicilian family, tells his story, he reveals how he is controlled by lust and molded by family traditions, philosophies, and relationships. The reader's attention is held as Gene becomes both a victim and a perpetrator of marred, decadent relationships.

11.31   Lamb, Wally. **She's Come Undone.** Pocket/Star Books, 1993. 465 pp. ISBN 0-671-75921-3. Fiction.

Delores Price's life seems to be falling apart—her father leaves, her mother is institutionalized, and she is sent to live with her grandmother. She finds herself forced into many situations that threaten her security and sanity. After being raped by a person she trusts, Delores finds that her greatest fear is realized—she is institutionalized herself. Through this experience she begins to understand many things about life. In this often witty, thought-provoking novel, Wally Lamb takes his heroine through harrowing adult experiences that make her stronger.

Booklist Editors' Choice, 1992

11.32   Lee, Gus. **China Boy.** Penguin/Signet Books, 1992. 394 pp. ISBN 0-451-17434-8. Fiction.

Kai Ting is the first American-born member of his Mandarin Chinese family living in San Francisco. Respecting his mother deeply, he spends much time with her. Her death and his father's remarriage to an intolerant American leave Kai torn between the culture he was taught to respect and the culture in which he has to survive. Kai turns to the YMCA to learn how to defend himself and opens up a new world of people and self-respect.

Booklist Editors' Choice, 1991

11.33   L'Engle, Madeleine. **Certain Women.** Farrar, Straus and Giroux, 1992. 352 pp. ISBN 0-374-12025-0. Fiction.

Successful actress Emma Wheaton faces the imminent death of her father, renowned actor David Wheaton. David always wanted to play King David of the Old Testament because of the many corollaries between their lives—including the nine wives and eleven children. He keeps beside his bed an unfinished script about King David written by Emma's former husband. As David and Emma discuss the play and reminisce about the past, the Biblical story and their story become entwined, helping Emma reconcile the past.

11.34 Littke, Lael. **Blue Skye.** Scholastic Hardcover Books, 1991. 184 pp. ISBN 0-590-43448-9. Fiction.

For eleven years, Skye traveled across western America with her "freedom loving" mother, Reanna. Then Reanna returns home to Sheep Creek, Idaho, to marry Bill. Skye discovers that she is not going to travel with the new couple; instead, she is to stay with her grandfather. Although Skye resents being stuck on the family farm, she begins to realize how important a family really is from her Grandpa, a little boy named Jermer, and her "dozens of cousins."

11.35 Macdonald, Caroline. **Speaking to Miranda.** HarperCollins/ Willa Perlman Books, 1992. 251 pp. ISBN 0-06-021103-2. Fiction.

Who am I? Who was my mother—really? Who is this spirit, Miranda, that keeps speaking to me? Ruby has lived with her stepfather for most of her eighteen years, yet even he cannot answer these questions for her. He knows little about Emma Blake, her mother—except for her brief appearance in his life and then her tragic exit. Ruby is drawn from Australia to New Zealand in her quest for the answers to her questions. Will she find them? First published in Australia, 1990.

11.36 Marino, Jan. **The Day That Elvis Came to Town.** Little, Brown, 1991. 204 pp. ISBN 0-316-54618-6. Fiction.

Thirteen-year-old Wanda hates sharing her house with boarders, and she hates her father's drinking. Then one day in the early 1960s, Mercedes Washington, a black jazz singer, rents a room from them. This causes quite a commotion in their small southern town. Yet, Mercedes serves as a peacemaker in the house. Even more importantly, Mercedes knows Elvis Presley from her school days, and she might help Wanda meet Elvis in person. Life might just get better after all!

Booklist Editors' Choice, 1991
School Library Journal Best Books, 1991

11.37 Mazer, Harry. **Who Is Eddie Leonard?** Delacorte Press, 1993. 188 pp. ISBN 0-385-31136-2. Fiction.

Eddie Leonard is raised by an old woman who lies to him about his parents and sometimes locks him in closets. When she dies, he begins a search to find his parents and to determine who he is as he enters adolescence. Eddie sees a picture of a missing child and begins a search to see if he is that child.

ALA Best Books for Young Adults, 1994

11.38 McDaniel, Lurlene. **Mother, Help Me Live.** Bantam Books, 1992. 136 pp. ISBN 0-553-29811-9. Fiction.

In this book in the One Last Wish series, Sarah McGreggor has more on her mind than does the average fifteen-year-old girl. She has leukemia, and her only hope for survival is a bone marrow transplant. The doctors tell her the best donors would be her brothers or sisters—but then she finds out that she is adopted. When Sarah receives a check for $100,000, she decides to use the money to find her biological mother and possibly be cured.

11.39 Meyer, Carolyn. **White Lilacs.** Harcourt Brace/Gulliver Books, 1993. 242 pp. ISBN 0-15-200641-9. Fiction.

White Lilacs, written in the first person and based on factual events, tells a tale of segregation and violence. Rose Lee is a young black girl growing up in Dillon, Texas, in the 1920s, and her family and friends are moved from their homes so that the white citizens of Dillon may have a park to beautify the town. Rose Lee has been given the responsibility of recording the buildings before they are torn down or moved to a less fertile area. She slowly grows to realize that some of her white neighbors and employers are not concerned with her welfare or her well-being. The white lilac, a symbol of hope, flourishes throughout the story.

ALA Best Books for Young Adults, 1994

11.40 Mori, Kyoko. **Shizuko's Daughter.** Henry Holt, 1993. 220 pp. ISBN 0-8050-2557-X. Fiction.

Twelve-year-old Yuki and her mother, Shizuko, are true friends, exploring and capturing nature's beauty in words and drawings. The two find comfort in one another since Hideki, Yuki's father, is seldom home and shows little interest in his wife and daughter. Hideki's behavior eventually drives Shizuko to suicide, which devastates Yuki. Her new, critical stepmother creates a cold, distant home in which Yuki can never do anything right. Yuki learns to bear this new life by relying on memories of her mother and the way life used to be. Notes on the setting describe the Japanese cities in which the story takes place, and a glossary provides additional information.

ALA Best Books for Young Adults, 1994
Notable 1994 Children's Trade Books in the Field of Social Studies

11.41 Moulton, Deborah. **Summer Girl.** Dial Books, 1992. 133 pp. ISBN 0-8037-1153-0. Fiction.

Tamara—or Tommy, as the thirteen-year-old prefers to be called—is in the midst of two difficult situations: the terminal illness of her mother and a sudden move to Maine to live with her father, a man she has not heard from for ten years. As her mother's condition worsens, Tommy learns the true story behind her father's years of silence.

IRA Young Adults' Choices, 1994

11.42 Myers, Walter Dean. **Somewhere in the Darkness.** Scholastic Hardcover Books, 1992. 168 pp. ISBN 0-590-42411-4. Fiction.

Jimmy cannot decide what to do with his life. He knows he should stay in school but finds that some days it is easier to stay home. One afternoon a stranger calls out to him from the darkness of his Harlem tenement hallway. The voice belongs to Crab, his father, who has escaped from prison and who wants Jimmy to know who his father really is. Crab takes Jimmy from New York and his "Mamma Jean" on a trip across the country to visit his own boyhood town.

ALA Best Books for Young Adults, 1993
ALA Notable Books for Children, 1993
ALA Quick Picks for Young Adults, 1993
Booklist Editors' Choice, 1992
Boston Globe–Horn Book Fiction Honor Book, 1992
Coretta Scott King Author Honor Book, 1993
Newbery Honor Book, 1993

11.43 Naylor, Phyllis Reynolds. **The Year of the Gopher.** Dell/Laurel-Leaf Library, 1993. 201 pp. ISBN 0-440-21591-9. Fiction.

George Richards faces an incredible amount of pressure during his senior year. He has a family tradition he is expected to uphold—attend Harvard. There is only one problem: George does not want to follow in his father's footsteps. On his application form he tells the university exactly what he thinks of their institution, and he is denied entrance. He spends the following year in various "gopher" jobs while he tries to figure out who he is and what he wants to do with his life.

11.44   Newton, Suzanne. **Where Are You When I Need You?** Viking, 1991. 199 pp. ISBN 0-670-81702-3. Fiction.

Making decisions that affect your future is very difficult, as Missy Cord finds out. As a senior in high school, she has to deal with scholarship applications and college plans. To complicate matters, Missy falls in love with Jim Perkins, her best friend since childhood. Now she has to decide whether she should go away to college and run the risk of losing Jim, or stay in Tucker, North Carolina, and give up a dream she has had for years.

School Library Journal Best Books, 1991

11.45   Peck, Richard. **Don't Look and It Won't Hurt.** Dell/Laurel-Leaf Library, 1992. 178 pp. ISBN 0-440-21213-8. Fiction.

Fifteen-year-old Carol Patterson has spent all her life in the small town of Claypitts. There she lives in a rundown house on the wrong end of town with her mother, who is hostess at a truck plaza restaurant, and her two sisters. As the middle child in the family, Carol feels protective of her younger sister and often serves as a buffer between her older sister and her mother. Carol does well in school, but she has few friends. She struggles to find the inner strength to hold her family together through the reappearance of a long-absent father, the pregnancy of her older sister, and an incident that causes her mother to lose faith in her. Through her struggle, Carol begins to gain a different perspective of her life and the people in it. First published in 1972.

School Library Journal Best Books, 1993

11.46   Pfeffer, Susan Beth. **Family of Strangers.** Bantam Books, 1992. 164 pp. ISBN 0-553-08364-3. Fiction.

Sixteen-year-old Abby Talbott, through a combination of letters, diaries, and essays, reveals the desperation of the Talbott family. Abby's surgeon-father and lawyer-mother never seem to have recovered from the death of their two-year-old son. Dr. Talbott, a violently abusive man, nearly destroys his three daughters. This haunting book celebrates the indomitable human spirit as all three daughters seek to find themselves, though the effort nearly overwhelms Abby and Jessica.

IRA Young Adults' Choices, 1994
Notable 1992 Children's Trade Books in the Field of Social Studies

11.47 Plummer, Louise. **My Name Is Sus5an Smith. The 5 Is Silent.** Dell/Laurel-Leaf Library, 1993. 217 pp. ISBN 0-440-21451-3. Fiction.

Sus5an is easily bored with conventionalism, which is, of course, the reason for the silent 5 in her name. Growing up in Utah, surrounded by her parents, grandparents, a brother, and several aunts, Sus5an desires to pursue her interest in art. At age seventeen, she jumps at the chance to spend the summer in Boston. There she befriends an eccentric old woman with a dead dog in the freezer and reacquaints herself with Uncle Willy, who abandoned her mother's sister. By the summer's end, Susan drops the silent 5. Events have caused her to come to terms with some complexities in her life, and she looks forward to her plans for the future.

ALA Best Books for Young Adults, 1992
School Library Journal Best Books, 1991

11.48 Pullman, Philip. **The Broken Bridge.** Alfred A. Knopf/Borzoi Books, 1992. 218 pp. ISBN 0-679-91972-4. Fiction.

Ginny and her father have a close relationship. She believes that her mother, a black Haitian artist, is dead. Then, at age sixteen, Ginny learns some disturbing things about her father's past. Angry that he has not been totally honest, Ginny decides to find out the truth. Her search leads her to an art gallery in Liverpool where she comes face to face with the truth, only to realize that the truth is sometimes very hard to live with.

ALA Best Books for Young Adults, 1993

11.49 Qualey, Marsha. **Revolutions of the Heart.** Houghton Mifflin, 1993. 184 pp. ISBN 0-395-64168-3. Fiction.

Revolutions of the Heart is a touching story covering topics that today's teenagers might have to deal with in their lives. Cory Knutson is Summer High School's senior sweetheart, but she has to endure hardships in her senior year: racial bias associated with her boyfriend, Mac, and the death of her mother. Author Marsha Qualey shows how a young heart survives in tough times.

ALA Best Books for Young Adults, 1994
ALA Quick Picks for Young Adults, 1994
School Library Journal Best Books, 1992

11.50 Rana, Indi. **The Roller Birds of Rampur.** Henry Holt, 1993. 298 pp. ISBN 0-8050-2670-3. Fiction.

Born in India and raised in England, seventeen-year-old Shelia Mehta struggles to find a balance between the Eastern philosophy that is her heritage and the Western influences that are so familiar to her. Indi Rana presents a story of a young woman who is confused about who she really is. With a trip to India and her grandparents' help, Shelia begins to understand her relationship to an ancient culture that is complex, compelling, and full of contradictions. Then, she must discover her karma, or life force.

11.51   Reiss, Kathryn. **The Glass House People.** Harcourt Brace Jovanovich, 1992. 277 pp. ISBN 0-15-231040-1. Fiction.

Sixteen-year-old Beth and her younger brother Tom cannot understand why their mother wants to return to Philadelphia to a home from which she ran away twenty years ago. It was then that Clifton Becker died mysteriously, and his death continues to overshadow their mother's relationship with her parents and sister. Who was responsible for Clifton's death? Whose story is correct? Can a shattered family be restored? As Beth tries to find answers to these questions, she begins to realize that "truth" depends on a person's point of view.

11.52   Roy, Jacqueline. **Soul Daddy.** Harcourt Brace Jovanovich/Gulliver Books, 1992. 235 pp. ISBN 0-15-277193-X. Fiction.

Who am I? Where do I come from? How do I fit in? Fifteen-year-old Hannah Curren asks herself these questions daily. She and her twin sister, Rosie, live in a white suburb of London with their white mother. Suddenly, their father, a famous black reggae musician, and their half-sister, Nicola, appear on the scene. Hannah's life drastically changes as she finds a new extended family and begins to realize what it really means to be black. First published in Great Britain, 1990.

11.53   Ryan, Elizabeth A. **High School Help Line: Straight Talk about Parents.** Dell/Laurel-Leaf Library, 1992. 136 pp. ISBN 0-440-21300-2. Nonfiction.

Elizabeth Ryan provides liberal, contemporary advice on problems faced by today's teenagers regarding communication, changing families, freedom, privacy, and daily life in this informative book for teenagers. She includes an index organized by topic, which allows for quick reference. Also included is a list of names and addresses of organizations that readers can contact for additional help, as well as an extensive bibliography of works of fiction on these topics for the young adult reader.

11.54 Sachs, Marilyn. **What My Sister Remembered.** E. P. Dutton, 1992. 122 pp. ISBN 0-525-44953-1. Fiction.

This book illustrates the problems inherent in memory. Two sisters, separated in early childhood when their parents were killed in a car accident, are reunited eight years later for a visit. Molly was adopted by her mother's older sister and her husband and lives in a small apartment in New York City, while Beth was adopted by a wealthy couple who have a large home in San Francisco. The situation surrounding the girls' separation after the accident comes clear to Molly when Beth recounts her memories and accuses Molly's adoptive mother of neglect. Molly learns that what she has always known has not always been.

11.55 Seabrooke, Brenda. **The Bridges of Summer.** Dutton/Cobblehill Books, 1992. 143 pp. ISBN 0-525-65094-6. Fiction.

Zarah suffers from culture shock when her mother sends her from New York City to Domingo Island, South Carolina, to spend the summer with her grandmother, Quanamina, and her little cousin Loomis. How is she ever going to become Princess Zarah the dancer on this isolated island that does not even have running water or electricity? It is a remote place where the people speak Gullah, an unusual African American dialect, and where many folk traditions are still a way of life. Yet, fourteen-year-old Zarah learns many things about herself and her rich Gullah heritage from this proud, strong woman who rules her island just as her family before her.

Notable 1992 Children's Trade Books in the Field of Social Studies

11.56 Shusterman, Neal. **What Daddy Did.** Little, Brown, 1991. 230 pp. ISBN 0-316-78906-2. Fiction.

How can you love the person who ruined your life? How can you want him to take care of you and yet hate him at the same time? This book affirms the confusion of feeling two strong emotions simultaneously. Preston Scott's father murdered Preston's mother. Now, released from prison, the father comes to live with Preston and his mother's parents. Can the boy forgive his father?

ALA Best Books for Young Adults, 1992
IRA Children's Choices, 1992
IRA Young Adults' Choices, 1993

11.57 Skinner, David. **You Must Kiss a Whale.** Simon and Schuster, 1992. 94 pp. ISBN 0-671-74781-9. Fiction.

When thirteen-year-old Evelyn's father leaves, her mother moves Evelyn and her little brother to some old ruins in the middle of a desert to work on a secret project. While baby-sitting, Evelyn rummages through her mother's old chest, where she finds a story her father wrote. In the story, a boy named Kevin receives a letter that says, "You must kiss a whale." Evelyn is determined to find out what the message means.

11.58   Sleator, William. **Oddballs.** E. P. Dutton, 1993. 134 pp. ISBN 0-525-45057-2. Fiction.

"This book is dedicated . . . To my family: Please forgive me!" From the first page to the last, the reader understands why William Sleator felt compelled to make this statement. He portrays his family and their wide array of friends (whose names are changed to protect the innocent) as a group that is proud to be labeled "oddballs," people who do not fit into the popular groups by choice. The family stories relate antics that are hilarious, heartwarming, obnoxious, and true to life.

ALA Best Books for Young Adults, 1994
ALA Quick Picks for Young Adults, 1994

11.59   Staples, Suzanne Fisher. **Haveli.** Alfred A. Knopf, 1993. 259 pp. ISBN 0-679-84157-1. Fiction.

In this magnificent sequel to *Shabanu: Daughter of the Wind*, Shabanu, a Pakistani young woman, is now married to the elderly Rahim and struggles to find acceptance for herself and her daughter, Mumtaz, among the other wives of the household. Shabanu works in subtle ways to assure a better future for Mumtaz, but just when Shabanu's goals seem in sight, violence, love, and betrayal separate her from everything she holds dear. Shabanu must choose between her own dreams and her responsibilities in this mesmerizing and evocative book.

ALA Best Books for Young Adults, 1994
Booklist Editors' Choice, 1993
School Library Journal Best Books, 1993

11.60   Stevenson, Laura C. **Happily After All.** Avon/Camelot Books, 1993. 229 pp. ISBN 0-380-71549-X. Fiction.

Ten-year-old Becca has lived with her father since her mother left eight years ago. He has been her best friend and protector, treating her like a princess. When her father dies, Becca is sent to live with her mother—a woman about whom she has never heard a good word. Becca moves from her beautiful California home to a dirty old farmhouse in Vermont. There she begins to find clues to unravel the mystery that surrounds her mother's disappearance. Soon it appears that Becca's father managed to prevent her from knowing the truth about many things.

11.61 Stolz, Mary. **Go and Catch a Flying Fish.** Harper and Row/ Harper Keypoint Books, 1992. 213 pp. ISBN 0-06-025868-3. Fiction.

Taylor is nervous about a lot of things this summer—beginning high school in the fall and the constant arguing of her parents. Being uncertain about her future, she immerses herself in taking care of her two younger brothers and talking to her best friend, Sandy. As the summer passes, Taylor learns that certain things are inevitable—she will go to high school, and her parents may split up, whether she is ready or not.

11.62 Stolz, Mary. **What Time of the Night Is It?** HarperCollins/Harper Keypoint Books, 1993. 209 pp. ISBN 0-06-026062-9. Fiction.

In yet another book about Taylor Reddick, Mary Stolz tells the story of a family coping with the pain of divorce. Taylor feels all the pressure of keeping the family together while dealing with the well-meaning, nosey grandmother who insists that she run the household in the "proper" way. Instead of relieving the pressure on Taylor, her presence adds to the tension in the house. As the hurricane season approaches, Taylor wonders if her family will be blown apart.

11.63 Sweeney, Joyce. **The Tiger Orchard.** Delacorte Press, 1993. 240 pp. ISBN 0-385-30841-8. Fiction.

Zach is an eighteen-year-old senior who has been having recurring nightmares about a man in an orchard full of tigers. To determine the cause of the dreams, Zach is seeing a therapist, but he makes no real progress until he meets Clarissa, the new girl in school. As their relationship develops, they become very close as both lovers and friends. Together, they help each other reveal secrets of the past and break the bonds of silence.

ALA Best Books for Young Adults, 1994

11.64 Talbert, Marc. **The Purple Heart.** HarperCollins/Willa Perlman Books, 1992. 135 pp. ISBN 0-06-020429-X. Fiction.

After months of playing war with his friend, Luke thinks his father can teach him about war when he returns from Vietnam with a Purple Heart. But when his father shows signs of weakness and even cries from his nightmares, Luke feels betrayed and does not know how to confront him. A prank on a neighbor opens the opportunity, and through this encounter, Luke learns that in many cases courage is just doing what you have to do.

11.65   Thesman, Jean. **Rachel Chance.** Avon/Flare Books, 1992. 175 pp. ISBN 0-380-71378-0. Fiction.

On her fifteenth birthday, Rachel Chance decides to do something about the recent kidnapping of her little brother, Rider. So far her mother's constant inquiries of Police Chief Carmichael and her grandpa's cussing all over town have not brought Rider back home. Rachel decides to take the situation into her own hands during Seattle's sweltering July of 1940. With the help of Grandpa, Hank, and Druid Annie, Rachel sets her rescue plan into motion. But will it work?

ALA Notable Books for Children, 1991

11.66   Tomey, Ingrid. **Savage Carrot.** Charles Scribner's Sons, 1993. 181 pp. ISBN 0-684-19633-6. Fiction.

Thirteen-year-old Carrot has a hard time dealing with the accidental death of her father, as do the other members of her family. Carrot's mother is a living zombie; her sister pretends nothing has changed; her Gram accepts the pain of loss; and her mentally disabled uncle, Babe, seems unaware of the situation. How can one ever get over the death of a loved one and still cope with the problems of everyday life? In this tender story, Carrot learns to go on living in the present while remembering the past.

11.67   Turnbull, Ann. **Speedwell.** Candlewick Press, 1992. 119 pp. ISBN 1-56402-12-2. Fiction.

Eleven-year-old Mary is determined to make her father proud. Mary knows she cannot live up to her mother's expectations, not when her sister Phyl is so perfect. While her father goes off to search for work during the Great Depression of the 1930s, Mary volunteers to take care of his homing pigeons, including Speedwell. Little does she know how caring for the birds will affect her, from giving her new friends to stranding her in a cave. First published in Great Britain, 1992.

11.68   Whelan, Gloria. **A Time to Keep Silent.** William B. Eerdman, 1993. 124 pp. ISBN 0-8028-0118-8. Fiction.

Thirteen-year-old Clair Lothrop's world crumbles when her mother dies. Her father, an affluent minister in Westville Heights, Michigan, withdraws into a world of his own, and Clair retreats into a world of silence. Believing Clair's silence is caused by the memories of her mother, Clair's father leaves Westville to begin a church in Michigan's northern woods. Here Clair meets a new friend, Dorrie, who teaches her many ways to cope with bad circumstances. Together, the two girls form a lasting relationship.

11.69 White, Ruth. **Weeping Willow.** Farrar, Straus and Giroux, 1992. 246 pp. ISBN 0-374-38255-7. Fiction.

Growing up in the Appalachian mountains, Tiny relies on her make-believe friend, "Willa, Willa on my pilla," to get her through. Vern, her stepfather, proves his love in overly intimate ways and "does things to her." Tiny cannot tell her mother because there is no place else for Tiny to go. The problem is compounded when she is raped again, and the preacher called in by her mother to counsel the family turns the episode into gossip. Through Willa, Tiny learns to say nice things to herself.

ALA Best Books for Young Adults, 1993
IRA Young Adults' Choices, 1994

11.70 Willey, Margaret. **The Melinda Zone.** Bantam Books, 1993. 144 pp. ISBN 0-553-09215-4. Fiction.

"I'm the child of divorce, remember? . . . I'm used to keeping secrets." With these words, Melinda begins a friendship with Paul the summer she decides to find herself. What secrets do they share? Melinda tells Paul how she feels about being caught between her parents, and Paul shares his true feelings about Sharon, Melinda's cousin. Still, like most secrets, once they are shared, they need to be addressed and resolved. How can Melinda and Paul do this without hurting those they care about most?

11.71 Wills, Maralys, and Chris Wills. **Higher Than Eagles: The Tragedy and Triumph of an American Family.** Longstreet Press, 1992. 362 pp. ISBN 1-56352-025-7. Nonfiction.

Maralys and Chris Wills tell a family's story of being pioneers in the sport of hang gliding. Maralys, the mother, offers insights into her family's difficulties and conflicts with the obstinate, daring Bobby as the family learns to accept him the way he is. The family's triumphs (Bobby's part in the Smithsonian film *To Fly*) and their losses (the deaths of Bobby and his brother Eric) make this a story not only of a sport but of individuals and a family.

11.72 Wolff, Virginia Euwer. **Make Lemonade.** Henry Holt, 1993. 200 pp. ISBN 0-8050-2228-7. Fiction.

LaVaughn, fourteen, is saving her baby-sitting money for college. No one in her building and no one in her family has ever been, but that is no reason for her not to go. Yet, Jolly, seventeen and the mother of two kids, depends on LaVaughn, and when Jolly loses her job for refusing her boss's advances, she needs LaVaughn even more. Knowing that Jolly needs the money more than she does, LaVaughn encourages her friend to go back to school. Jolly begins the long, slow process of turning the lemons of her life into lemonade.

ALA Best Books for Young Adults, 1994
ALA Notable Books for Children, 1994
ALA Quick Picks for Young Adults, 1993
Booklist's Top of the List, 1993
IRA Teachers' Choices, 1994
School Library Journal Best Books, 1993

11.73 Worth, Richard. **Single-Parent Families.** Franklin Watts, 1992. 127 pp. ISBN 0-531-11131-8. Nonfiction.

While single-parent families have always been in existence in the United States, today about 40 percent of American families are headed by a single parent. This book explores the many reasons for the rise in single-parent families (divorce, death, teenage pregnancies) and discusses the impact on both children and adults. It details common problems that arise in single-parent familes and how individuals in such families can cope with the stress.

Notable 1992 Children's Trade Books in the Field of Social Studies

12 Fantasy

12.1 Alexander, Lloyd. **The Remarkable Journey of Prince Jen.** E. P. Dutton, 1991. 273 pp. ISBN 0-525-44826-8. Fiction.

Travel with young Prince Jen to the Kingdom of Tienkuo to learn princely virtues and how to live a "Heavenly Perfection." With six gifts for the Emperor—all of which are used at times of crisis along the way—Jen meets villains and outlaws, a fascinating flute girl, and many opportunities to face danger and gather wisdom.

Booklist's Top of the List, 1991
School Library Journal Best Books, 1991

12.2 Anthony, Piers. **Fractal Mode.** Ace Books, 1992. 344 pp. ISBN 0-441-25126-9. Fiction.

Although Nona is the ninth daughter of the ninth daughter of Oria and thus the recipient of the world's magic, she has to hide from the despots who wish to destroy her. Meanwhile, Colene and her companions—a telepathic horse, a woman who knows only the future, and a king—find their way to help Nona as they fulfill their own quest. Mature reading. Second book in the Mode series.

12.3 Anthony, Piers, and Robert E. Margroff. **Mouvar's Magic.** Tor Books, 1992. 310 pp. ISBN 0-812-51982-5. Fiction.

Fans of Piers Anthony's work will love this sequel to *Demons Don't Dream*. Twenty years after Kevin Knight Hackleberry and his family slay the witch Zady's body, the prophecy is fulfilled. Zady and her evil minions return to fight Kevin and his ever-growing family, including the telepathic triplets and dragons. Who will win?

12.4 Askounis, Christina. **The Dream of the Stone.** Farrar, Straus and Giroux, 1993. 291 pp. ISBN 0-374-31877-8. Fiction.

When her parents are killed in a plane accident, Sarah, nearly fifteen years old, has only her genius brother, Sam, to rely on—and he is on the other side of the country at a California institute, Cipher. When an old, hobo-like woman appears, Sarah is friendly but confused, especially when Sam tells her the woman has written some thoughtful equations on the wall of the treehouse—and speaks Latin! Sam's experiments, which he calls "The Looking Glass," involve added dimensions, wormholes, antimatter, and some still unknown particles. Sarah meets fantastic characters and monsters before Sam unravels the final secret of Cipher.

12.5   Bradshaw, Gillian. **The Land of Gold.** Greenwillow Books, 1992. 154 pp. ISBN 0-688-10576-9. Fiction.

In the middle of the night, Princess Kandaki wakes to find her parents murdered by the commander of the palace guard, who names himself king. He orders her to be sacrificed to a dragon in the Marshes of Derr, but she is rescued by Prahotep, an Egyptian, the traditional enemy of Kandaki's people. He and his lonely dragon, Hathor, are seeking dragons for companions. They join forces with the princess to achieve their goals and to win back the kingdom. Sequel to *The Dragon and the Thief.*

12.6   Brittain, C. Dale. **Mage Quest.** Baen Books, 1993. 353 pp. ISBN 0-671-72169-0. Fiction.

Daimbert the Wizard of Yurt is not sure whether he is more afraid of going or of being left behind when King Haimeric decides it is time to go on a quest. The king wants the blue rose he has heard about to add to his garden. Soon they are joined by others and form an unusual group, each questing for individual reasons and desires, everything from a pilgrimage to a search for the powerful Black Pearl of Solomon. A king's wizard should protect him from danger, and soon Daimbert must protect them all from the big blue djinn and black magic.

12.7   Brooke, William J. **Untold Tales.** HarperCollins, 1992. 165 pp. ISBN 0-06-020272-6. Fiction.

Everyone knows about the Frog Prince, the Sleeping Beauty, and the Beauty and the Beast, but William Brooke twists the tales a bit to create new "happy endings." For example, what if the princess preferred her mate when he was a frog, and the two of them played by the pond all day, free of concerns? They both have to work out a new solution, and the reader will approve. This is a book to bring smiles and chuckles.

12.8   Callander, Don. **Aquamancer.** Ace Books, 1993. 289 pp. ISBN 0-441-02816-0. Fiction.

Journeyman Pyromancer (or Fire Wizard) Douglas Brightglade goes off on a dangerous mission to vanquish a coven of witches from Far Kingdom. His fiancée, Apprentice Aquamancer Myrn Manstar, accompanies him and overcomes her own dangers. They are aided by protective spells, magical elements of air and water, and powerful and friendly plants and animals. Sequel to *Pyromancer.*

12.9 Charnas, Suzy McKee. **The Kingdom of Kevin Malone.** Harcourt Brace Jovanovich/Jane Yolen Books, 1993. 211 pp. ISBN 0-15-200756-3. Fiction.

Kevin Malone, an abused teenager, draws Amy into his fantasy world. They travel on *seelim,* horse-like creatures covered with oval-shaped, lizard-like scales. Amy does not like the journey at all, especially when Kevin insists on telling her all about Fayre Farre and its problems. The champion of this kingdom is Kevin himself. He is searching for his sword, Farfarer, and Amy helps him. In the process, Amy comes to understand her own life and adjusts to new realities.

12.10 Chetwin, Grace. **The Chimes of Alyafaleyn.** Macmillan/Bradbury Press, 1993. 234 pp. ISBN 0-02-718222-3. Fiction.

In the "Region of the Harmonies," spheres maintain a harmonious existence for its citizens, but two unusual young people, Caidrun and Tamborel, have a difficult time keeping these spheres in an acceptable manner. Tam begins by helping Caidry, but it is Caidry who bestows a final gift on Tam.

12.11 Clayton, Jo. **The Magic Wars.** DAW Books, 1993. 367 pp. ISBN 0-88677-547-7. Fiction.

Faan has finally learned to use her magic powers but cannot forget the one thing she wants most—to be reunited with her mother. Before she can find her mother, Faan and her partners in magic are caught in the middle of an evil sorcery war between gods. She and her friends are thrust through different universes where they meet new allies. Finally, they are confronted with the horrible Chained God in a decisive battle. A victory over the god could clear the way for Faan to find her mother. Third book in the Wild Magic series.

12.12 Cochran, Molly, and Warren Murphy. **The Forever King.** Tor Books, 1992. 402 pp. ISBN 0-812-51716-4. Fiction.

It is 1992, eight years before the millennium, when this modern version of the Arthurian tale begins. The evil Saladin, a man born 3,000 years before Christ and whose life has been preserved by a metal cup, is a prisoner in a hospital for the criminally insane, waiting for the right time to make his move. The Knights of the Round Table, with some help from Merlin, are just beginning to remember their identities, like Hal Woczniak, who is working for the FBI, and Arthur Blessing, who is no ordinary ten-year-old boy. Arthur has the cup by chance, though it is his by right if he realizes how to keep it. But Saladin will do anything to gain possession of it.

12.13   Crawford, Dan. **Rouse a Sleeping Cat.** Ace Books, 1993. 251 pp. ISBN 0-441-73553-3. Fiction.

Nimnestl, king's champion, must continue to guard her youthful king, Conan III of Rossacotta, as he faces intrigue, magic, and deceit in this first book in a new series. Courtly games (not the kind children play), conspiracy, and adventure twist around magical plots and fantastical creatures in this intricate tale.

12.14   Dean, Pamela. **Tam Lin.** Tor Books, 1991. 468 pp. ISBN 0-312-85137-5. Fiction.

The ancient tale of *Tam Lin* is transferred to a midwestern college, with freshman Janet Carter walking through the halls of the dormitories and classrooms with the ghosts of past days and "normal" college students. Teachers and peers become involved in unraveling the truth behind suicides and hauntings. Who is the fairy queen? What part does Thomas play in the past and in the present? Mature situations.

12.15   Deitz, Tom. **Dreambuilder.** Avon Books, 1992. 418 pp. ISBN 0-380-76290-0. Fiction.

There are many unusual elements in this mature fantasy: a white twelve-point deer, an inexplicable man in the hardware store, and a family of "Masters" who are forced to reside and reign in a small county in Georgia. Add to these a young art teacher who tries to build her dream house, which looks like a castle from Middle Earth, as she finds friends and love. Sequel to *Soulsmith.*

12.16   Doyle, Debra, and James D. Macdonald. **Knight's Wyrd.** Harcourt Brace Jovanovich, 1992. 209 pp. ISBN 0-15-200764-4. Fiction.

On the eve of his knighting, Will learns from the castle wizard that he will never inherit his father's seat as Lord of Restonbury. Instead, he will meet death as he faces battles with trolls, dragons, and ogres. What is his fate, his Wyrd? Will's quest includes tournaments, spying, and a visit with Isobel, his fiancée, who also is not what he expects. This is a well-written, well-designed fantasy.

12.17 Duane, Diane. **So You Want to Be a Wizard.** Dell/Yearling Books, 1992. 226 pp. ISBN 0-440-40638-2. Fiction.

Harassed at school by bullies and at home for being too bookish, Nita escapes into the library, where she finds a most unusual book that explains how to become a wizard. With this book, she makes contacts with other wizards and strange creatures. Eventually, Nita saves the world by finding a very special book in an alternate New York City. Author Diane Duane has created an escape that many readers will want to make.

12.18 Dunlop, Eileen. **Green Willow.** Holiday House, 1993. 160 pp. ISBN 0-8234-1021-8. Fiction.

In an updated version of *The Secret Garden*, young Kit and her friend Daniel restore an old Japanese garden that has been neglected for years. Supposedly haunted, the garden has an aura of mystery that has been prolonged by secrecy. As Kit works in the garden and tries to answer the baffling questions about the retreat, her personal problems are solved as well.

12.19 Emerson, Ru. **Night-Threads: The Craft of Light.** Ace Books, 1993. 280 pp. ISBN 0-441-58088-2. Fiction.

This first book in a new trilogy continues the adventures of the Mage—Duchesses Jennifer and Lialla and their families in an alternate magical world. Enemies sent by the evil brothers of Jennifer's husband threaten her, her unborn child, and her duchy. Jennifer tries to fight them with twentieth-century knowledge and magic.

12.20 Friesner, Esther M. **Yesterday We Saw Mermaids.** Tor Books, 1992. 155 pp. ISBN 0-812-51345-2. Fiction.

It is 1492. A young nun is chosen scribe by the lord Zamiz the Unaccountably Repulsive to record daily all that she sees and hears. The nun and some others from her convent, including the cruel Brother Garcilaso and Mother Catalina, are accidently plucked from an execution scene when the lady Rasha of the Thousand Doors saves a young captive Jewess from burning at the stake. On a golden ship, sung to full size and carried by waves sung into being by the lady Rasha, the strange group begins a long ocean journey. It is the same voyage undertaken at the same time by the *Niña*, *Pinta*, and *Santa Maria*. Can the golden ship reach Prester John and the new place in time to save it? Will the child the little Jewess is carrying be able to save them, as Prester John forecast?

Can *la Zagala*, the gypsy, bear the burden passed to her by Prester John and restore the faith of the dragons, mermaids, and other creatures of fur and talons?

12.21   Gear, W. Michael, and Kathleen O'Neal Gear. **People of the Fire.** Tor Books, 1991. 467 pp. ISBN 0-812-52150-1. Fiction.

The young man, Little Dancer, is an ancient Native American who grows up in the tribe of the Short Buffalo People. He is, however, a member of the Red Hand, bitter enemies of the People. Little Dancer has an extremely powerful gift, that of the Dreamer. While destined to be great and to lead his people to greatness, Little Dancer wants, more than anything, to be free of this fate. Unless he can reconcile his desires and his destiny, Little Dancer will lose his sanity. Mature language and situations.

12.22   Gear, W. Michael, and Kathleen O'Neal Gear. **People of the River.** Tor Books, 1992. 527 pp. ISBN 0-812-50743-6. Fiction.

Nightshade, a Native American priestess, is blessed with a special power enabling her to travel into the spirit world or the underworld to escape the pressures of a war between two sections of her village. In another village, young Lichen has a strange dream that eventually leads her to Nightshade. Together, they are able to save the ancient village of Cahokia from destruction. Mature situations.

12.23   Greeno, Gayle. **Finders-Seekers.** DAW Books, 1993. 506 pp. ISBN 0-88677-5507. Fiction.

This is a complex tale of Ghatti's catlike animals, who are able to telepathically bind to human magicians. The Bondmates who serve as judges must find who or what is killing them as they travel. First book in the Ghatti's Tale series.

12.24   Hoppe, Joanne. **Dream Spinner.** Morrow Junior Books, 1992. 228 pp. ISBN 0-688-08559-8. Fiction.

As she struggles to share her father with a new stepmother and stepbrother, Brian, Mary travels back in time in her dreams to enter the lives of the Pinkhams, who owned her family's Victorian home a century ago. Mary gets so involved with the past that she almost fails in school, becomes ill, and ends up in the hospital. Brian's diabetes and the attention of Mike, a classmate who likes her, help bring Mary back to the twentieth century.

IRA Young Adults' Choices, 1994

12.25 Hughes, Monica. **The Promise.** Simon and Schuster Books for Young Readers, 1992. 196 pp. ISBN 0-671-75033-X. Fiction.

In the palace in Malan on the desert continent of Roshan, Princess Rania is enjoying her birthday—until a chief's young son, Atbin, arrives with a message: Rania must leave her home and family to be the new apprentice to Sandwriter, the old woman who is the spiritual leader of Roshan. Atbin escorts the young girl across the sea and desert to the sacred valley where she will learn from the aged woman the rituals and lore that maintain her people. Thus Rania's parents have kept the promise that they made—to give up their daughter to serve their country—but when Rania has the chance to choose a normal life, she must decide if *she* will keep the promise. Sequel to *Sandwriter.*

12.26 Jacques, Brian. **Mariel of Redwall.** Avon Books, 1993. 387 pp. ISBN 0-380-71922-3. Fiction.

This fourth book in the Redwall series describes the adventures of Mariel, a mousemaid with the knotted rope weapon she calls Gullwhacker. She is off, over land and sea with an adventurous young mouse from Redwall Abbey, to rescue her father from the evil pirate rat Gabool the Wild. A band of companions and an ancient sword make this a fantasy quest.

12.27 James, Betsy. **Dark Heart.** E. P. Dutton, 1992. 217 pp. ISBN 0-525-44951-5. Fiction.

After fleeing her father, seventeen-year-old Kat is trying vainly to fit in with the People of the Creek, her deceased mother's people. To become a woman, she must go through painful initiation rites. Kat wonders where she should live and what her feelings are toward blind Raim and the good-looking Set. This sequel to *Long Night Dance* is a compelling, mature tale.

12.28 Jordan, Sherryl. **Winter of Fire.** Scholastic, 1993. 336 pp. ISBN 0-590-45288-6. Fiction.

Elsha, always a rebel, is a born member of the branded slave tribe, the Quelled, and is destined to spend her life mining firestones to warm all life for the Chosen, the Master Race. When she is chosen to be the Firelord's special handmaiden, Elsha discovers the power to find firestones and to change her world.

ALA Best Books for Young Adults, 1994

12.29 Kindl, Patrice. **Owl in Love.** Houghton Mifflin, 1993. 204 pp. ISBN 0-395-66162-5. Fiction.

Owl is a teenage girl; Owl is a shapeshifter; Owl is an owl in a family of witches and assorted animals. Other than the color of her blood—black—and her refusal to eat ravioli or pizza or other messes from the cafeteria, she can be a normal teenager, with a crush on Mr. Lindstrom, her science teacher. A boy she views as wild complicates her life when she realizes he, too, is a capable shapeshifter, and also Mr. Lindstrom's son. Once the reader accepts the basic premise, Owl is an adventurous fantasy.

ALA Best Books for Young Adults, 1995
ALA Quick Picks for Young Adults, 1994

12.30 Kisling, Lee. **The Fools' War.** HarperCollins, 1992. 166 pp. ISBN 0-06-020837-6. Fiction.

In this fantasy with fairy tale qualities, Clemmy, the youngest son of a peasant family, does good deeds, passes several trials, and is finally rewarded with the hand of the woman he loves. Even though he is not perfect, he is kind and honest, and he learns to read Latin to help his king.

12.31 Kurtz, Katherine, and Deborah Turner Harris. **The Templar Treasure.** Ace Books, 1993. 310 pp. ISBN 0-441-00345-1. Fiction.

McLeod, a Knight Templar and the wealthy solver of mysteries, is also a Hunter of Darkness as he travels in and out of Scotland's past. In this adventure, he seeks and discovers Solomon's Seal and rescues it from Scotland's enemies. The fantasy is combined with historical accuracy, as readers of the first two tales in the Adept series will recognize.

12.32 Lackey, Mercedes. **The Lark and the Wren.** Baen Books, 1992. 488 pp. ISBN 0-671-72099-6. Fiction.

Rune has always wanted to be a bard, or poet-singer. After defeating a demon with her music, she is encouraged to go to the city to learn. On the way, she finds a mentor, colleagues, and friends while battling evil guild masters, a magician, and the King of the Fairies. She becomes a bard, but not in the way she imagines. First book in the Bardic Voices series.

ALA Best Books for Young Adults, 1993

12.33 Lowry, Lois. **The Giver.** Houghton Mifflin, 1993. 180 pp. ISBN 0-395-64566-2. Fiction.

In a grim story set in a totalitarian community sometime in the future, Jonas is apprehensive about the life-task he will soon be assigned by the Elders. All thoughts, feelings, and dreams are controlled in this society, where sameness is valued above all else, and every aspect of life is scrutinized. But then Jonas meets the Giver and begins to glimpse a different kind of world. This is a book to be read at one sitting.

ALA Best Books for Young Adults, 1994
ALA Notable Books for Children, 1994
Booklist Editors' Choice, 1993
Boston Globe–Horn Book Fiction Honor Book, 1993
IRA Children's Choices, 1994
IRA Teachers' Choices, 1994
Newbery Medal, 1994
Notable 1994 Children's Trade Books in the Field of Social Studies
School Library Journal Best Books, 1992

12.34 MacDonald, George. **The Light Princess, and Other Stories.** Illustrated by Craig Yoe. William B. Eerdmans, 1991. 171 pp. ISBN 0-8028-1861-7. Fiction.

In George MacDonald's fantasy world, the "light princess" has no gravity to keep her on earth—she floats unless she is tied down. Also, she is lighthearted and cannot cry, so she giggles all the time. Naturally, a prince arrives to solve both problems. The author's play on words and use of well-known themes result in stories that are original and ingenious and that are certain to make the reader laugh. The three other volumes in the series are *The Golden Key, The Wise Woman,* and *The Gray Wolf.*

12.35 McCaughrean, Geraldine. **A Pack of Lies: Twelve Stories in One.** Scholastic, 1991. 168 pp. ISBN 0-590-43664-3. Fiction.

Bored with work in her mother's store, which is doing poorly, Alisa is amazed at, attracted by, and slightly afraid of the new employee, MCC Berkshire. Able to tell inventive and intricate stories that induce the customers to buy objects, and stories that somehow are true, MCC Berkshire charms everyone, especially Alisa's mother. But where does the truth start and fantasy begin? Read to find out—if you dare.

Carnegie Medal, 1989

12.36 McKillip, Patricia A. **The Cygnet and the Firebird.** Ace Books, 1993. 233 pp. ISBN 0-441-12628-6. Fiction.

Brand Saphier is a man trapped in the body of a firebird. The evil spell that has transformed him allows his human form to emerge as the moon rises each evening; his memory, however, remains shrouded. Through the labyrinths of time, Brand journeys to the land of Ro Holding, where he is befriended by Nyx Ro, the resident magician, and by her cousin, Meguet. With the aid of these two kinswomen, Brand is returned to his homeland and the dragon-inhabited desert that surrounds it. As his memory is slowly resurrected, he learns the identity of the unlikely adversary who has imprisoned him within the firebird's body.

12.37   McKinley, Robin. **Deerskin.** Ace Books, 1993. 309 pp. ISBN 0-441-14226-5. Fiction.

Deerskin is a fairy tale, an old French story of a king and queen so beloved and magnificent that their princess daughter is neglected by all, including her parents. When the queen dies, the life of the young princess changes. Suddenly everyone notices her, especially the king. His attention—a mad scene of rape—is devastating, and the princess flees the palace and her country to become a new person, Deerskin. The story of her new life in the wild is fascinating.

ALA Best Books for Young Adults, 1994

12.38   Murphy, Shirley Rousseau. **The Catswold Portal.** Penguin/Roc Books, 1992. 405 pp. ISBN 0-451-45146-5. Fiction.

In a San Francisco garden, there is a beautifully carved wooden gate featuring nine rows of nine heads of cats so lifelike that one thinks they might leap off the gate. This gate acts both as a door to a toolshed and as a portal to an underground netherworld. Evil Queen Siddonie lives underground, though her henchmen are also above ground, and she has decided that she wants to control both realms. To do so, she needs the help of a young girl who mysteriously disappeared years ago. Melissa, now a grown woman, is that girl, and she is currently shape-shifting between human and cat form in that very San Francisco garden with the underground portal.

Booklist Editors' Choice, 1992

12.39   Napoli, Donna Jo. **The Magic Circle.** E. P. Dutton, 1993. 118 pp. ISBN 0-525-45127-7. Fiction.

A talented midwife, descriptively named Ugly One, is called to deliver children of the rich and powerful. This is a dangerous task in an era when witchcraft can be charged at the least peculiarity. Forced to hide in the woods, Ugly One encounters Hansel and Gretel and faces the end of all witches, good and bad.

ALA Best Books for Young Adults, 1994
ALA Quick Picks for Young Adults, 1994

Booklist Editors' Choice, 1993
School Library Journal Best Books, 1993

12.40 Norman, Roger. **Albion's Dream: A Novel of Terror.** Delacorte Press, 1992. 209 pp. ISBN 0-385-30533-8. Fiction.

When Edward discovers a mysterious handmade board game hidden behind a bookcase in his uncle's house, little does he realize that he is entering a forbidden realm. The game, Albion's Dream, has a curious relation to reality. As Edward throws the dice and makes his moves, he is affecting the fate of those around him.

IRA Young Adults' Choices, 1994

12.41 Norton, Andre. **The Mark of the Cat.** Ace Books, 1992. 248 pp. ISBN 0-441-51971-7. Fiction.

Hynkkel, the second son of a minor noble, has completely disappointed his father, who wants him to be a great soldier. Instead, Hynkkel is tricked by his brother into appearing to kill his *kotti*, his catlike companion. The penalty for such a murder is instant death, so Hynkkel flees to the desert, where his good sense helps him befriend the great cats. They help him pass the trials to become the High King, much to the displeasure of his brother, but to the acclaim of the country and his supporters.

12.42 Norton, Andre, and Mercedes Lackey. **The Elvenbane.** Tor Books, 1991. 566 pp. ISBN 0-812-51175-1. Fiction.

Two top fantasy writers have created a believable, consistent world in which humans are slaves to long-living and evil elfkind—and dragons avoid them both. Because of the prophecy that half-breeds would be able to overcome their elfin masters, all half-breeds are put to death—except for Shana, born by accident and raised by the dragons. Finally forced to find her own way, Shana creates a world in which elves, half-elves, humans, and dragons all play a role.

12.43 Ogiwara, Noriko (translated by Cathy Hirano). **Dragon Sword and Wind Child.** Farrar, Straus and Giroux, 1993. 329 pp. ISBN 0-374-30466-1. Fiction.

This exquisite high fantasy, based on the mythology of ancient Japan, is set in a small village where Saya, an orphan, is found to be the Water Maiden. She becomes the centerpiece in the battle between the God of Light and his immortal children and the Goddess of Hardness and Earth. Saya finds Chihaya, who can sheathe and use the Dragon Sword, but the mission of the sword is hidden from all—even Chihaya. First published in Japan, 1988.

12.44   Peel, John. **Uptime, Downtime.** Simon and Schuster, 1992. 242 pp. ISBN 0-671-73274-9. Fiction.

Karyn and her younger brother, Mike, travel back and forth through time to solve their real-life problem. Orphaned, they have been adopted by their Uncle Harry, who is about to marry a much younger woman. They are shocked to overhear Harry admit that he had not wanted to adopt them. Karyn then discovers that wishing will take her and Mike first to Stonehenge and then throughout the centuries, away from today's sorrows. But how will they return to the present?

12.45   Pierce, Meredith Ann. **Dark Moon.** Little, Brown/Joy Street Books, 1992. 238 pp. ISBN 0-316-70744-9. Fiction.

This is the second book in the Firebringer trilogy, a fast-paced, exciting account of the children of the moon—a civilization of unicorns who are trying to live in harmony following ancient customs, although these are turbulent times in the Vale. Aljan, the son of Korr, who is known as Jan the Battle Prince, enjoys a brief idyllic period of courtship and mating, only to face a treacherous attack by enemy gryphons and life with the two-footed creatures, or humans, who think they are Jan's masters. When Jan returns, he finds that his friends and mates have also suffered hardships and now look to him for leadership.

12.46   Reichert, Mickey Zucker. **Child of Thunder.** DAW Books, 1993. 588 pp. ISBN 0-88677-549-3. Fiction.

Colbey, a Renshai Warrior, must come to terms with his new powers and position as western Wizard of Odin's World. Magic is alien to him, but he is very comfortable in the world of battle. As in the two previous books in the Renshai trilogy, all hands are turned against Colbey as he balances good and evil.

12.47   Salsitz, Rhondi Vilott. **The Twilight Gate.** Walker, 1993. 192 pp. ISBN 0-8027-8213-2. Fiction.

Fantasy and reality mingle as the real world becomes too difficult and painful for George when his father dies and his mother becomes ill. A unicorn mare and girls, Mindy and Leigh, help George as he helps them come to terms with their worlds.

12.48   Sherman, Josepha. **Child of Faerie, Child of Earth.** Walker, 1992. 159 pp. ISBN 0-8027-8112-8. Fiction.

Using fairy tale traditions, this novel tells of Percinet, son of Rezaila, the Queen of Faerie. Percinet falls in love with Graciosa, a twelfth-century mortal princess in a Snow White predicament: a cruel stepmother has full control of the beautiful young girl's life. Percinet offers to bring Graciosa back to the Realm of Faerie, where they will marry and where the princess will be able to develop her dormant magic powers. But life must get more difficult and impossible for Graciosa before she agrees to leave her father and the human world.

ALA Best Books for Young Adults, 1993

12.49 Sleator, William. **Others See Us.** E. P. Dutton, 1993. 163 pp. ISBN 0-525-45104-8. Fiction.

Jared is looking forward to spending another summer with his family at the beach, especially getting to see his cousin Annelise—he has secretly had a crush on her since they were kids. One day while riding his bike, Jared falls into the toxic swamp not far from his cottage and soon realizes that he suddenly has the ability to read minds. Now he sees Annelise in a different light. He finds that underneath her sweet and caring exterior is a wicked young woman who longs for control and who has been using Jared to get what she wants. She also was responsible for a girl's drowning the previous summer. What Jared does not know is that his grandmother also has mind-reading abilities and has developed the power to shield her own thoughts from others. Things get complicated when Annelise develops the power, and she and his grandmother come together with secrets that could destroy him.

ALA Quick Picks for Young Adults, 1994

12.50 Snyder, Zilpha Keatley. **Below the Root.** Dell/Laurel-Leaf Library, 1992. 231 pp. ISBN 0-440-21266-9. Fiction.

Raamo, at thirteen, is amazed to be chosen to join the ranks of the Ol-zhaan, the religious and governmental leaders of the realm of Green-sky. There the Kindar live in the great grundtrees, whose huge trunks and enormous spreading limbs reach toward the sky. The Kindar never look down to the great roots, for they have been told monsters live there. And now Raamo is to be a Chosen. But does he realize what lies ahead for him? He crosses the doorway to learn the "Forgotten," a time of violence. First published in 1975.

12.51 Vande Velde, Vivian. **Dragon's Bait.** Harcourt Brace Jovanovich/Jane Yolen Books, 1992. 144 pp. ISBN 0-15-200726-1. Fiction.

As her father lies dying, Alys is accused of being a witch. Her trial is a farce as the townspeople, led by greedy Gower, who desires her father's tinsmith shop, describe witchly misdeeds. Sentenced to be eaten by a dragon, Alys instead joins forces with the dragon to plan her revenge.

ALA Quick Picks for Young Adults, 1994

12.52   Williams, Tad, and Nina Kiriki Hoffman. **Child of an Ancient City.** Illustrated by Greg Hildebrandt. Atheneum, 1992. 137 pp. ISBN 0-689-31577-5. Fiction.

On a caravan to another town, the characters are waylaid by a vampire who offers them a Scheherazade-like proposal. They are all to tell the saddest story they can think of; if the stories are sad enough, the vampire will leave by morning without taking anyone. The tales are unusual and eerie. Make sure the lights are on when this book is read.

12.53   Winthrop, Elizabeth. **The Battle for the Castle.** Holiday House, 1993. 211 pp. ISBN 0-8234-1010-2. Fiction.

William and Jason have been friends forever, but Jason's new and competitive interest in athletics may change things. When William gets a magic token, he convinces Jason to journey with him back to the Middle Ages. Jason agrees because time in the present will stand still. He can be away for a long period, improve his muscles and his endurance, and return to the present with added skills. But what will the two friends find when they travel back in time? This is a great adventure, and a story of friendship. Sequel to *Castle in the Attic.*

12.54   Wrede, Patricia C. **Calling on Dragons.** Harcourt Brace Jovanovich/Jane Yolen Books, 1993. 244 pp. ISBN 0-15-200950-7. Fiction.

Morwen, the unconventional witch, her cats, Queen Cimorene, and their friends from two previous books reunite to save the magic sword of the queen's husband. Witches, wizards, talking cats, Kazul the dragon king, and Killer the eight-foot rabbit all combine in this humorous tale about conformity, magic, and of course, a quest. Third book in the Enchanted Forest Chronicles.

12.55   Wrede, Patricia C. **Mairelon the Magician.** Tor Books, 1991. 280 pp. ISBN 0-812-50896-3. Fiction.

Mairelon lives on the streets of London, hiding from some people and searching for others. Kim, a seventeen-year-old girl still able to disguise herself as a boy, breaks into Mairelon's wagon. Kim does not know what she is looking for, but she finds a grand adventure and some truths about herself and the world of magic and wizardry.

Booklist Editors' Choice, 1991

12.56 Wrede, Patricia C. **Searching for Dragons.** Harcourt Brace Jovanovich/Jane Yolen Books, 1991. 242 pp. ISBN 0-15-200898-5. Fiction.

In this humorous and lighthearted second book of the Enchanted Forest Chronicles, Mandanbar, King of the Enchanted Forest, does all he can think of to avoid meeting Princess Cimorene. He has a great many important concerns—dragons, wizards, and a feud between them. Princesses, usually empty-headed, ambitious bores in Mandanbar's experience, are completely unnecessary. But Cimorene, chief cook and librarian to the King of Dragons, is unique and just the perfect life partner for Mandanbar. Second book in the Enchanted Forest Chronicles.

ALA Best Books for Young Adults, 1993
ALA Notable Books for Children, 1992

12.57 Yep, Laurence. **Dragon War.** HarperCollins, 1992. 313 pp. ISBN 0-06-020303-X. Fiction.

This fourth book in the adventures of Shimmer, princess of the dragons, relates the final battles against the Boneless King in the effort to restore the dragon clan's home. Thorn, a human ally, has been imprisoned in the cauldron, and it takes all the ingenuity of the companions, including the monkey wizard who serves as narrator, to free Thorn and reclaim the throne for Shimmer. Previous titles in the series are *Dragon of the Lost Sea, Dragon Steel,* and *Dragon Cauldron.*

12.58 Yolen, Jane. **Here There Be Dragons.** Illustrated by David Wilgus. Harcourt Brace, 1993. 149 pp. ISBN 0-15-209888-7.

Dragons are taken very seriously in this collection of prose and poetry. There is a one-hundred-word story to get the readers' interest, followed by a fifty-word story, which is even more provocative. If you have read the Dragon's Blood series, you have met Jakkin, the main character. "The King's Dragon," as involved as the most complex fairy tale, is the story of three dragons who wish to earn their mother's love.

12.59   Zambreno, Mary Frances. **A Plague of Sorcerers.** Harcourt Brace Jovanovich/Jane Yolen Books, 1991. 257 pp. ISBN 0-15-262430-9. Fiction.

Coming from a family of wizards, Jermyn Graves should find it quite easy to obtain a familiar—some suitable cat—and become an apprentice wizard. But he has a difficult time of it, even with the help of Aunt Merry. Finally, Jermyn and Delia, a skunk, find each other. They set out to stop the magic plague that is putting all the wizards of the land in a coma.

ALA Best Books for Young Adults, 1993

13 Historical Fiction

13.1 Armstrong, Jennifer. **Steal Away.** Orchard Books, 1992. 207 pp. ISBN 0-531-08583-X. Fiction.

It is 1896, and thirteen-year-old Mary finds herself on a surprising journey with her grandmother: a train trip to Canada to visit a sick friend. Mary's comfortable convictions are challenged as she learns that the woman they are going to visit, Bethlehem, is a former slave. Gran and Bethlehem recount their escape together to freedom some forty years previously. Bethlehem's adopted daughter, Free, helps Mary record the event, and in the process the story becomes Mary's and Free's story as well.

ALA Best Books for Young Adults, 1993
ALA Notable Books for Children, 1993
IRA Teachers' Choices, 1993

13.2 Berry, James. **Ajeemah and His Son.** HarperCollins/Willa Perlman Books, 1992. 83 pp. ISBN 0-06-021044-3. Fiction.

In this story set in the early 1800s, Ajeemah, a native of Ghana, and his eighteen-year-old son, Atu, are abducted by fellow Africans as they walk to a neighboring village with a dowry for Atu's bride-to-be. They soon find themselves on a slave ship bound for Jamaica. Sold to different sugar plantations and separated forever, one finds freedom in death, the other in life.

ALA Best Books for Young Adults, 1993
ALA Notable Books for Children, 1993
Booklist Editors' Choice, 1992
Boston Globe–Horn Book Fiction Award, 1993
Notable 1992 Children's Trade Books in the Field of Social Studies
School Library Journal Best Books, 1992

13.3 Brady, Taylor. **Mountain Fury.** Avon Books, 1993. 298 pp. ISBN 0-380-77133-0. Fiction.

Book three of the Kincaids series follows the lives of Kitty, Meg, and Jim, children of Katherine and Byrd Kincaid, as each tries to forge a life in the American West of the 1850s. Kitty and her husband, Ben, try to establish a horse ranch, while Meg runs away from an abusive marriage to start a new life, and Jim struggles to become a man as he is stalked by an unscrupulous captain of the First Dragoons.

13.4   Brady, Taylor. **Raging Rivers.** Avon Books, 1992. 332 pp. ISBN 0-380-71082-X. Fiction.

In the early 1820s, Katherine Carlyle flees Kentucky on a flatboat in the first book of the Kincaids series. She leaves her past behind and sets out down the raging Ohio River toward an unknown future in the new western territories. Disaster strikes, and Katherine finds herself the leader of a group of women and children headed through the wilderness toward frontiersman Byrd Kincaid. He and Katherine fall in love and become the founders of a dynasty of adventurers who roam "the shining mountains" and beyond.

13.5   Campbell, Bebe Moore. **Your Blues Ain't like Mine.** Ballantine Books, 1993. 332 pp. ISBN 0-345-38395-8. Fiction.

Written for a mature audience, this novel contains graphic descriptions of sensitive situations and explicit sexual references. Based loosely on a historic case from the 1950s, the novel tells the story of the Deep South, its social injustices, and its codes of behavior. One of the characters, Armstrong Todd, a fifteen-year-old Chicago-born African American, does not fully understand these codes. It is his murder that opens the story and allows the reader to learn about the black and white families of the Delta region of Mississippi. A best-seller, Bebe Moore Campbell's novel spans the years from 1955 to 1988 and shows how one act of racist violence destroys the lives of several black and white families for three generations.

Booklist Editors' Choice, 1992

13.6   Collier, James Lincoln, and Christopher Collier. **The Clock.** Illustrated by Kelly Maddox. Delacorte Press, 1992. 161 pp. ISBN 0-385-30037-9. Fiction.

Annie Steele, age fifteen in 1806, is put to work in a Connecticut woolen mill by her father, who needs her wages to help pay his debts. At the mill, Annie discovers the harsh realities of the emerging industrial age and has to adjust to leaving behind school and domestic chores. As an eyewitness to crime and cruelty, Annie is propelled by her courage and sense of justice into a risky and frightening series of events.

13.7   Davis, Ossie. **Just like Martin.** Simon and Schuster, 1992. 215 pp. ISBN 0-671-73202-1. Fiction.

In the fall of 1963, a young man growing up in Alabama comes face to face with the reality of racial inequality in America. Issac

Stone confronts the tragedy of the racially motivated bombing of his church and then has to find a way to respond. Influenced by Dr. Martin Luther King Jr. and his doctrine of nonviolence, Issac tries to face the attitudes of others and to change them. The objections of his father make Issac's struggle personal as well as political.

Notable 1992 Children's Trade Books in the Field of Social Studies

13.8   Dubois, Muriel L. **Abenaki Captive.** Illustrated by Susan Fair Lieber. Carolrhoda/Adventure in Time Books, 1994. 180 pp. ISBN 0-87614-753-8. Fiction.

As the members of the St. Francis Abenaki tribe embark on their annual trapping and hunting expedition, Ogistin takes the place of his older brother Simi, who was recently killed by the English. When the Abenaki hunters encounter John Stark and his companions trapping on Indian lands, they capture the white men. During the time that the English captives live with the Abenaki, Ogistin experiences conflicting feelings of revenge and respect, while Stark comes to appreciate the ways of the Abenaki.

13.9   Duong Thu Huong (translated by Phan Huy Duong and Nina McPherson). **Paradise of the Blind.** William Morrow, 1993. 270 pp. ISBN 0-688-11445-8. Fiction.

The first Vietnamese novel to be translated and published in North America, this book traces the lives of three women striving to maintain "dignity in a society that expects ever greater sacrifices from them." This haunting story, set in what was then the Soviet Union, appeals to the senses with its vivid imagery and also explores the politics and culture of the 1980s. Follow Hang as she begins her reflections from a dormitory as an "exported worker" at a Russian textile factory—reflections on her childhood in Vietnam, on her family history, and on the events that led her to leave her country. The novel includes a glossary of Vietnamese food and cultural terms. First published in Vietnam, 1988.

13.10   Fleischman, Paul. **Path of the Pale Horse.** HarperCollins/Harper Trophy/Charlotte Zolotow Books, 1992. 143 pp. ISBN 0-06-021905-X. Fiction.

In Philadelphia in 1793, the optimism of the emerging nation is shaken by an outbreak of deadly yellow fever. Asclepius "Lep" Nye, apprenticed to a physician, attempts to unravel the mystery of the disease. At the same time, he is growing up and seeking answers to questions about his family and the past. He learns about human nature and himself and faces the power of death.

13.11 Forman, James D. **Becca's Story.** Charles Scribner's Sons, 1992. 180 pp. ISBN 0-684-19332-9. Fiction.

Fourteen-year-old Becca Case has two boyfriends. Alex Forman promises a stable future. Charlie Gregory is a charmer, full of adventure and laughter. Becca is content to let them compete for her attention, believing that she will eventually know who holds the key to her heart. Then the Civil War erupts, taking both Charlie and Alex away. Before the war's end, one has disappeared, and the other must work to get Becca's love. This story is based on a journal and letters of one of the author's ancestors.

ALA Best Books for Young Adults, 1993
Notable 1992 Children's Trade Books in the Field of Social Studies
School Library Journal Best Books, 1992

13.12 Gregory, Kristiana. **Earthquake at Dawn.** Harcourt Brace Jovanovich/Gulliver Books, 1992. 192 pp. ISBN 0-15-200446-7. Fiction.

It is April 1906, and Edith Irvine, a well-known photographer, is on her way to Paris for an exhibition of her work. Her companion—the narrator—is Daisy Valentine, a family employee. Daisy and Edith arrive at their first stop, San Francisco, just as a great earthquake strikes. For the next few days they experience the terror and suffering caused by this calamity and by the great fires that follow. In attempting to photograph the devastation, Edith encounters a turn-of-the-century "news coverup" by public officials.

ALA Best Books for Young Adults, 1993
Notable 1992 Children's Trade Books in the Field of Social Studies

13.13 Hansen, Joyce. **The Captive.** Scholastic, 1994. 195 pp. ISBN 0-590-41625-1. Fiction.

Kofi lives a life of privilege as the son of an Ashanti chief on the Ivory Coast of Africa. When a family slave betrays and kills Kofi's father, Kofi himself is sold into slavery. A "waterhouse" (slave ship) takes him to America, where he is purchased by a Puritan farmer. Kofi learns how to survive in a new land and attempts to gain his freedom, eventually dedicating his life to helping free other slaves.

Notable 1995 Children's Trade Books in the Field of Social Studies

13.14 Hudson, Jan. **Sweetgrass.** Scholastic/Point Books, 1991. 157 pp. ISBN 0-590-43486-1. Fiction.

Sweetgrass is a fifteen-year-old Native American of the Blackfoot tribe, who live on the prairies of western Canada in what is now Alberta. It is 1837. Her primary concern is her prospect of marriage, but Sweetgrass also faces violence and confronts a devastating outbreak of smallpox. The difficulty of the unsettled and demanding life of the Blackfoot is vividly portrayed. Sweetgrass exhibits courage, demonstrating the power of the human spirit to face such adversities as loneliness, fear, and even death, and she emerges with new strength.

IRA Young Adults' Choices, 1991

13.15 Jones, Adrienne. **Long Time Passing.** HarperCollins/Harper Keypoint/Charlotte Zolotow Books, 1993. 244 pp. ISBN 0-06-023056-8. Fiction.

Jonas Duncan grows up in a world of contrasts. His father is bound for Vietnam, and his mother is a pacifist. When his mother suddenly dies, Jonas is unwillingly sent to live with Aunt Hester, who does not approve of his new "hippie" friends. Jonas takes part in antiwar demonstrations, but he finds his new values challenged when his father is listed as MIA, missing in action. Should he enlist with the hope of finding his father?

13.16 Koller, Jackie French. **The Primrose Way.** Harcourt Brace Jovanovich, 1992. 271 pp. ISBN 0-15-256745-3. Fiction.

In 1633, sixteen-year-old Rebekah joins her missionary father in the newly established Puritan settlement in New England. She befriends the niece of the chief of the local Pawtucket Indian tribe and begins to learn about Indian culture. As time passes, Rebekah begins to question whether the "savages" she has been sent to save need to be saved at all. This book addresses the important question of whether one group has the right to judge others and force them to conform to a different way of life.

ALA Best Books for Young Adults, 1993

13.17 Matas, Carol. **Sworn Enemies.** Bantam Books, 1993. 144 pp. ISBN 0-553-08326-0. Fiction.

Zev has been jealous of Aaron since they were children: Aaron is intelligent, he lives in a prosperous Jewish family, and his father can pay to keep him out of the army of Czar Nicholas I. Zev is a weak student and makes a living by kidnapping Jewish boys for the army. Now the girl Zev loves is engaged to Aaron. But Zev has a way to get rid of Aaron—he kidnaps Aaron and sells him to the Russian army. By a turn of fate, both young men end up in captivity together. Sworn enemies, will they join forces to survive, or will they destroy each other?

ALA Quick Picks for Young Adults, 1994
Notable 1994 Children's Trade Books in the Field of Social Studies

13.18   Mazzio, Joann. **Leaving Eldorado.** Houghton Mifflin, 1993. 170 pp. ISBN 0-395-64381-3. Fiction.

Can a young girl survive on her own in New Mexico in the 1890s? With her mother dead and her father off to yet another gold rush, Maude finds employment in a boardinghouse. A school teacher, a "soiled dove," and a mute Indian girl each help Maude learn her way in an adult world. An early marriage offers security, but Maude has dreams of her own.

13.19   McCullough, Colleen. **The Grass Crown.** Avon Books, 1992. 1,077 pp. ISBN 0-380-71082-X. Fiction.

This epic saga illuminates the ancient Roman Empire, with all its political intrigue. In Colleen McCullough's tradition, she creates sympathetic characters caught up in the treachery that abounds in this early civilization as one generation slips from power and a new generation of leaders takes over. McCullough bases her novel on historically accurate facts and includes maps, illustrations, and a glossary of terms to help the reader gain insight into this magnificent era.

13.20   Means, Florence Crannell. **The Moved-Outers.** Walker, 1992. 156 pp. ISBN 0-8027-7386-9. Fiction.

Sumiko (Sue) Ohara spends the fall of 1941 doing what most high school seniors do—singing in the church choir, having fun with her lifelong best friend, Emily, dreaming about college and "the real world." But the "real world" intrudes with the bombing of Pearl Harbor on December 7, 1941, and Sue and her Japanese American family are faced with racial prejudice and overzealous patriots. The family is forced to move to an internment camp for the remainder of the war. Originally published in 1945, *The Moved-Outers* was the first book for young adults to deal with the forced internment of Japanese Americans during World War II.

Newbery Honor Book, 1946

13.21   Miranda, Ana (translated by Giovanni Pontiero). **Bay of All Saints and Every Conceivable Sin.** Viking, 1991. 305 pp. ISBN 0-670-83455-6. Fiction.

Poet Gregório de Matos narrates this story of seventeenth-century colonial Brazil. When a controversial political figure is assassinated, the corrupt governor plots revenge. An investigation begins, suspects are arrested, and people take sides. Conspirators plot. Gregório falls hopelessly in love with a woman who seems unattainable, and conflicts arise as he is drawn into the mystery and intrigue. First published in Brazil, 1989.

13.22   Namioka, Lensey. **The Coming of the Bear.** HarperCollins, 1992. 230 pp. ISBN 0-06-020289-0. Fiction.

Zenta and Matsuzo, two young Japanese samurai, find themselves stranded on an island inhabited by the primitive Ainu people. The Ainu take them to their *kotan* (village) and feed them. Eventually the two warriors realize that they must leave the island, but soon they find themselves trying to prevent conflict between the Ainu and nearby Japanese settlers. This story of cultural difference and prejudice in sixteenth-century Japan presents a timeless theme in a unique setting.

13.23   Nixon, Joan Lowery. **Land of Dreams.** Delacorte Press, 1994. 152 pp. ISBN 0-385-31170-2. Fiction.

When Kristin Swenson and her parents emigrate to Minnesota in 1902, she looks forward to the new freedoms that her life in America offers. She wants to speak English, live and work in a city, and make choices for herself. She does not want to continue living the way she did in Sweden. However, that is not the way of her parents and their community. Everyone keeps telling Kristin that change must be gradual, but she wants it immediately. She wonders if she will realize her dream of independence. Third book in the Ellis Island series.

13.24   Nixon, Joan Lowery. **Land of Promise.** Bantam/Skylark Books, 1993. 169 pp. ISBN 0-553-08111-X. Fiction.

This Ellis Island novel follows Rose Carney, a fifteen-year-old Irish farm girl who immigrates to Chicago in 1902. Rose works as a store clerk to help her father and brother raise enough money to bring her mother and sister to America. Rose's attempts are constantly thwarted by her father's drinking and her brother's obsession with giving financial support to a radical group dedicated to freeing Ireland by violent means. At Jane Addams's Hull House, Rose finds a peaceful way of social reform. Second book in the Ellis Island series.

13.25 O'Dell, Scott. **Sing Down the Moon.** Dell/Yearling Books, 1992. 137 pp. ISBN 0-440-40673-0. Fiction.

In 1863, the government of the United States sent Colonel Kit Carson west to Arizona to destroy the lives of the Navajo people. Bright Morning, a young girl tending sheep in a Navajo village, lives through this ordeal, the fleeing of her people, and the Long Walk of the Navajo people into imprisonment. Growing into adulthood and gaining independence are a part of this story of Bright Morning's struggle to return home and regain a lost way of life.

13.26 Paterson, Katherine. **Lyddie.** Dutton/Lodestar Books, 1991. 182 pp. ISBN 0-525-67338-5. Fiction.

In the winter of 1843, Lyddie leaves her parents' debt-ridden farm for a factory job in Lowell, Massachusetts. There she will earn a wage that will enable her to pay off the farm debt and regain possession of the land. To do this, Lyddie must endure long hours, a crowded boardinghouse, and terrible working conditions under a cruel overseer. Will she jeopardize her job and future by becoming friends with the radical Diana, who is crusading for better working conditions?

ALA Best Books for Young Adults, 1992
ALA Notable Books for Children, 1992
Booklist Editors' Choice, 1991
IRA Teachers' Choices, 1992
Notable 1991 Children's Trade Books in the Field of Social Studies
School Library Journal Best Books, 1991

13.27 Paulsen, Gary. **Nightjohn.** Delacorte Press, 1993. 92 pp. ISBN 0-385-30838-8. Fiction.

Nightjohn is one of the few slaves to escape alive from the Waller plantation. Yet he returns to teach young Sarney and other slaves how to read. Those who learn to read and write risk horrible punishment, but Nightjohn brings them more than knowledge; in a world of brutality, he brings hope. Based on true events and told in vivid, living language, this novel is about a man of mythic proportions; it is a forceful story about unforgettable characters.

ALA Best Books for Young Adults, 1994
ALA Notable Books for Children, 1994
IRA Children's Choices, 1994
Notable 1994 Children's Trade Books in the Field of Social Studies
School Library Journal Best Books, 1992

13.28　Peck, Robert Newton. **Arly.** Scholastic/Point Books, 1991. 150 pp. ISBN 0-590-43469-1. Fiction.

Arly Poole is growing up poor in the rural South. The year is 1927, and the hardscrabble life of a farm worker, or picker, is the inevitable prospect of Arly's life. He and his friends face a life of continued poverty and despair, of being enslaved by the landowner. Arly finds hope when a schoolteacher arrives and begins to reveal a hitherto unknown world to the locals. In facing tragedy and hardship, Arly brings the life of a farm worker into focus.

13.29　Penman, Sharon Kay. **The Reckoning.** Henry Holt, 1991. 592 pp. ISBN 0-8050-1014-9. Fiction.

Prince Llewelyn ap Gruffydd dreams of a united, independent Wales. The inevitable confrontation between Llewelyn and Prince Edward of England is precipitated by Edward's kidnapping of Llewelyn's bride-to-be, Ellen de Montfort. Author Sharon Kay Penman has the unique gift of making the past as intensely immediate as the present. Thirteenth-century England is a time of political intrigues, incredible violence, passion, and change. In this book, the historical characters of the royal houses of England and Wales are fascinating, alive, and entirely human.

13.30　Rinaldi, Ann. **A Break with Charity: A Story about the Salem Witch Trials.** Harcourt Brace Jovanovich/Gulliver Books, 1992. 253 pp. ISBN 0-15-200353-3. Fiction.

It is 1692. Salem, Massachusetts, is gripped by a mass hysteria that turns life upside down for Susanna English, her family, and her community. Charges of witchcraft and subsequent trials lead to twenty-four deaths and many shattered lives. Susanna, aware of the origins of this tragedy, works to bring it to an end. Based on information about events and people that the author uncovered through research, *A Break with Charity* re-creates the life and language of a significant time in colonial America.

ALA Best Books for Young Adults, 1993
Notable 1992 Children's Trade Books in the Field of Social Studies

13.31　Rinaldi, Ann. **The Fifth of March: A Story of the Boston Massacre.** Harcourt Brace/Gulliver Books, 1993. 333 pp. ISBN 0-15-200343-6. Fiction.

Why should a fourteen-year-old indentured servant be interested in whether the colonists revolt against Britain? Rachel Marsh wishes to remain uninvolved. Her friend Jane, however, has actively sided with the Patriots, while Rachel's employer, John Adams, is conservative and unaligned. With the help of Mrs. Adams, Rachel learns to read. This new power, and her growing feelings for a British soldier, complicate her life in eighteenth-century Boston. Events around Rachel compel her to take a stand and live with the consequences.

13.32 Rinaldi, Ann. **In My Father's House.** Scholastic Hardcover Books, 1993. 304 pp. ISBN 0-590-44730-0. Fiction.

With humor and sensitivity, Ann Rinaldi tells the story of Oscie, a Virginia girl growing up during the Civil War. After the death of her father, Oscie feels responsible for running the plantation. She reluctantly surrenders some of her control when her mother remarries. As the war rages around her, Oscie battles her stepfather and one of the slave girls. Neither battle, however, keeps Oscie from experiencing her first love. Surprisingly, this family plays a part in the beginning and ending of the Civil War.

ALA Best Books for Young Adults, 1994.

13.33 Savin, Marcia. **The Moon Bridge.** Scholastic, 1992. 231 pp. ISBN 0-590-45873-6. Fiction.

Even as World War II rages around fifth-grader Ruthie Fox, life seems wonderful to her. But the war comes closer to home when the fiancé of Ruthie's teacher is killed. Then Mitzi Fujimoto arrives at school. Ruthie's best friend calls Mitzi a "Jap" and refuses to allow others to be Mitzi's friend. Ruthie takes a stand, and a friendship with Mitzi is formed. Then Mitzi's family is taken away to an internment camp for the rest of the war. Ruthie fears she will never see Mitzi again, but near the end of the war Mitzi writes, asking Ruthie to meet her at the Moon Bridge in San Francisco. Can their friendship survive all that has happened?

13.34 Temple, Frances. **Taste of Salt: A Story of Modern Haiti.** Orchard Books, 1992. 179 pp. ISBN 0-531-08609-7. Fiction.

Burned and disfigured, young Djo may not survive the terrorist attack on Lafanmi, a boys' shelter begun by Father Jean-Bertrand Aristide. Aristide assigns a young girl to tape-record Djo's story, and their friendship develops as Djo slowly and painfully recalls the events of his life—events closely linked with Haiti's struggle for democracy and Aristide's rise in political power in the 1980s. This sensitive and exciting story brings alive recent political events in Haiti and the sound of the Haitian language.

Jane Addams Award, 1993

13.35 Walsh, Jill Paton. **A Parcel of Patterns.** Farrar, Straus and Giroux/ Aerial Books, 1992. 137 pp. ISBN 0-374-45743-3. Fiction.

It is 1665 in a rural English village in Derbyshire. Normal life comes to an abrupt halt with the arrival of the plague and the resulting tragedy for the people of Eyam. Mall Percival recounts the events and the fear, superstition, and suffering of the villagers. Mall tells of the sacrifices people make in an effort to keep the disease from spreading, and she paints a vivid picture of life in seventeenth-century rural England. First published in Great Britain, 1983.

13.36 Weaver-Gelzer, Charlotte. **In the Time of Trouble.** E. P. Dutton, 1993. 275 pp. ISBN 0-525-44973-6. Fiction.

Fourteen-year-old Jessie goes to a missionary boarding school in the African country of Cameroon. She dreams of her upcoming journey to Egypt, where she will attend high school. However, in Cameroon in the 1950s, there is a struggle for national independence from France, and Jessie and her missionary parents are drawn into the conflict. Jessie learns to deal with the people around her during these times of trouble, and it deepens her belief in God and in herself.

13.37 Weems, David B. **Son of an Earl . . . Sold for a Slave.** Illustrated by Mauro Magellan. Pelican Books, 1993. 136 pp. ISBN 0-88289-921-X. Fiction.

James Gour, the fifteen-year-old son of a Scottish earl, is kidnapped, sent to North Carolina prior to the Revolutionary War, and sold as a bonded slave under the name of John Scot. He is drawn into the colonists' fight for freedom as he attempts to gain his own freedom. When James escapes his bondage, he tries to return to Scotland to claim what is rightfully his, only to discover that his only way back to Scotland is to book passage on a British freighter and become a Tory.

13.38 Whittaker, Dorothy Raymond. **Angels of the Swamp.** Walker, 1992. 209 pp. ISBN 0-8027-8129-2. Fiction.

It is the summer of 1932—in the depths of the Great Depression. Taffy, Jody, and Jeff, three young people who are alone on the Florida coast, meet and establish a life together. Though they face different kinds of problems, the three are able to team up and use their wits to make life work and to become a part of the society from which they had escaped.

13.39 Wisler, G. Clifton. **Red Cap.** Dutton/Lodestar Books, 1991. 160 pp. ISBN 0-525-67337-7. Fiction.

In 1862, at age thirteen, Ransom J. Powell joins the Union Army and becomes a drummer boy. Two years later he is captured and taken to Camp Sumter, a Confederate prison in Andersonville, Georgia. He remains loyal to the Union even though switching allegiances would have released him. Ransom makes friends with a Confederate guard, who looks out for him and gets him the job of camp drummer boy. This is a story of friendship, bravery, and the resilience of the human spirit.

ALA Best Books for Young Adults, 1992
IRA Teachers' Choices, 1992
Notable 1991 Children's Trade Books in the Field of Social Studies

14 History and Geography

14.1 Adams, Simon, John Briquebec, and Ann Kramer. **Illustrated Atlas of World History.** Random House, 1992. 155 pp. ISBN 0-679-92465-5. Nonfiction.

Take a journey from prehistoric times to the present by using maps and illustrations. This informative atlas, replete with marvelous photographs, "shows that history is not just about empires and civilizations, dates and events, but about ordinary people and how they lived." First published in Great Britain, 1991.

14.2 Ashabranner, Brent. **A Memorial for Mr. Lincoln.** Photographs by Jennifer Ashabranner. G. P. Putnam's Sons, 1992. 113 pp. ISBN 0-399-22273-1. Nonfiction.

What is the story behind the creation of the memorial to Abraham Lincoln, perhaps this country's most loved and admired president? How are memorials to presidents proposed? Who has to approve? Where does the money come from to build a memorial? How is a memorial designed and then built? Brent Ashabranner presents a vivid account responding to these questions. Through the text and the black-and-white photographs, readers learn much about this striking memorial's architect, Henry Bacon, and its sculptor, Daniel Chester French, and also a bit about the president himself and the special place he holds in the hearts and minds of many people.

14.3 Ashley, Beth. **Marin.** Photographs by Hal Lauritzen. Chronicle Books, 1993. 120 pp. ISBN 0-8118-0022-9. Nonfiction.

What lies on the other side of the Golden Gate Bridge from San Francisco? Marin County. Marin has a variety of geographic features—beaches and wildlands, mountains and redwood forests, farmlands and islands, all described in this intriguing pictorial guidebook.

14.4 Ayer, Eleanor H. **The Anasazi.** Walker, 1993. 124 pp. ISBN 0-8027-8184-5. Nonfiction.

Abandoned pueblos in the area generally including the Four Corners, where Arizona, Utah, Colorado, and New Mexico come together, reveal part of the history of the cliff dwellers—the Anasazi. This ancient civilization originated in Asia about 14,000 years ago; their descendants resided in the American Southwest between the years 100 and 1300. The Anasazi then vanished but gave rise to various Pueblo Indian tribes, including the Hopi and the Zuni. In text, illustrations, and photographs, Eleanor H. Ayer describes how the Anasazi changed from nomads to farmers and details their contributions as basket weavers, the ingenuity of their dwellings on cliffs, and their underground pit houses or kivas.

14.5   Beattie, Owen, and John Geiger. **Buried in Ice: The Mystery of a Lost Arctic Expedition.** Illustrated by Janet Wilson. Scholastic, 1992. 64 pp. ISBN 0-590-43848-4. Nonfiction.

Exploring the polar regions of the earth is always dangerous. What would it be like to be on a ship locked in ice, unable to escape? How would you cross miles of ice to reach dry land, food, and warmth? Owen Beattie and John Geiger investigate the story of selected sailors on a mid-1840s expedition to the Arctic, tracing events through subsequent rescue efforts. Photographs and illustrations are fascinating, including those of the preserved bodies of three sailors buried in ice for nearly 150 years.

ALA Best Books for Young Adults, 1993
ALA Quick Picks for Young Adults, 1993
Notable 1992 Children's Trade Books in the Field of Social Studies

14.6   Bubriski, Kevin. **Portrait of Nepal.** Chronicle Books, 1993. 150 pp. ISBN 0-8118-0205-1. Nonfiction.

Kevin Bubriski has spent considerable time in Nepal, first for four years in the late 1970s as a Peace Corps volunteer and then for three years in the mid-1980s, when he took the stirring portraits presented in this book. In four chapters, each focusing on a particular region and each containing about twenty portraits or landscapes, Bubriski celebrates the Nepali people and their culture in transition. The black-and-white photographs (taken with a view camera) are rich in detail, are provocative in their timelessness, and remind us of a way of life that is inexorably receding into the past.

14.7   Cousteau Society. **An Adventure in the Amazon.** Simon and Schuster, 1992. 45 pp. ISBN 0-671-77071-3. Nonfiction.

Great rivers are always fascinating, and when the world's longest river is explored by Jean Jacques Cousteau, readers are treated to some exciting pictures and interesting sights. See the tropical rainforest, the Ashanica tribal people, parrots, and large fish; see fishing with a bow and arrow, different uses of body paint, and an array of flora and fauna. The photos are magnificent.

14.8   Epler, Doris M. **The Berlin Wall: How It Rose and Why It Fell.** Millbrook Press, 1992. 128 pp. ISBN 1-56294-114-3. Nonfiction.

Why has so much been made in recent years of the tearing down of the Berlin Wall? To find out, read Doris M. Epler's review of the twenty-eight-year history of the Berlin Wall, the events leading to the wall's construction, efforts of the East Germans to escape to the West, the circumstances causing the wall's destruction, and the problems facing a reunified Germany. Epler relates factual information in a compelling manner in discussing the importance of the Berlin Wall.

14.9   Eyre, Ronald, Nadine Gordimer, Nigel Hamilton, Christopher Hitchens, Frederic Raphael, Richard Rodriguez, Jon Swain, and John Wells. **Frontiers.** BBC Books, 1991. 272 pp. ISBN 0-563-20701-9. Nonfiction.

Frontiers, based on the BBC television series, contains eight chapters, each telling a different story. Snapshots of man-made frontiers seek to discover "what it was like living under the shadow of a frontier at a particular moment in time." The snapshots include divided countries, such as Ireland and Cyprus, and examine the borders between Thailand and Cambodia, South Africa and Mozambique, Russia and Finland, France and Spain, and Mexico and the United States—lines that separate the rich and the poor, the free and the oppressed.

14.10   Faber, Harold. **From Sea to Sea: The Growth of the United States.** Charles Scribner's Sons, 1992. 246 pp. ISBN 0-684-19442-2. Nonfiction.

How did the United States acquire the land within its borders? What were the negotiations that led to specifying the boundaries for the thirteen original colonies? What territories were added through purchase, through war, or through other means? With what countries other than Great Britain did the United States need to negotiate? Harold Faber answers these questions about the geographical development of the country in a clear, direct, and informative manner. The map by Jackie Aher provides graphic illustration of the years and boundaries representing the territory acquired to make up the contiguous forty-eight states.

14.11   Feinberg, Barbara Silberdick. **American Political Scandals Past and Present.** Franklin Watts, 1992. 159 pp. ISBN 0-531-11126-1. Nonfiction.

Why would the vice president of the United States duel with the former secretary of the treasury? Why would the niece of a U.S. president refuse to be the president's hostess as long as the wife of one of his cabinet members continued to be invited to White House functions? Have there been instances when the winner of the popular vote was not elected president? Have deals been made to assure the election of one candidate over another? Why would a member of the U.S. House of Representatives beat a member of the Senate with a cane? Answers to these questions and many more can be found in this book.

14.12 Freedman, Russell. **An Indian Winter.** Illustrated by Karl Bodmer. Holiday House, 1992. 88 pp. ISBN 0-8234-0930-9. Nonfiction.

What might a German noble and a Swiss painter discover on a trip up the Missouri River in 1833? Russell Freedman draws upon the journal kept by Prince Alexander Philipp Maximilian and paintings by Karl Bodmer to recapture the winter they spent more than a century and a half ago in what probably is now North Dakota. Learn what everyday life was like for North Americans on the high plains, especially in winter, and gain insight into their customs and roles.

ALA Best Books for Young Adults, 1993
ALA Notable Books for Children, 1993
IRA Teachers' Choices, 1993
Notable 1992 Children's Trade Books in the Field of Social Studies

14.13 Gallant, Roy A. **Ancient Indians: The First Americans.** Enslow, 1989. 128 pp. ISBN 0-89490-187-7. Nonfiction.

Roy Gallant traces the coming of Native Americans to the Americas, describing artifacts and locations that document the migration of these peoples, their development as societies, and their cultures. At the same time, his work reveals how scientists study ancient cultures and how they interpret the artifacts discovered. A number of black-and-white photographs and illustrations support the text.

14.14 Grant, Neil. **The Great Atlas of Discovery.** Illustrated by Peter Morter. Alfred A. Knopf, 1992. 64 pp. ISBN 0-679-91660-1. Nonfiction.

Author Neil Grant announces his own purpose and scope: "This atlas tells the story of exploration from the earliest travelers of the ancient world to modern space voyages." Each topic (Ancient Explorers, Viking Voyages, Cook in the South Seas) is presented in a two-page section; the centerpiece of each is a clear, scaled map, with route(s) taken and places visited. Additionally, the map is flanked by portraits of the travelers, notes on significant events and findings, and occasional curios related to the voyage. There is also a short, useful section on navigation and navigational aids.

14.15 Greene, Melissa Fay. **Praying for Sheetrock.** Addison-Wesley, 1991. 335 pp. ISBN 0-499-90753-8. Nonfiction.

McIntosh County, Georgia, is the setting for this true account of a rural southern community in the 1970s. As African American citizens struggle to claim their civil rights, politics, lies, and power plays all come into focus. Both sides are never what they seem: black and white, the heroes often have feet of clay, and the villains are not always all that evil.

14.16 Grissom, Michael Andrew. **Southern by the Grace of God.** Pelican Books, 1992. 572 pp. ISBN 0-88289-761-6. Nonfiction.

Originally published in 1988 by the Rebel Press, this book venerates the Old South culture, traditions, and values that have made the American South distinctive. The book is replete with photographs and illustrations and contains some maps. The author unabashedly advocates preserving the southern heritage, striving to make his case by recounting changes he sees as eroding the attitudes and convictions of an earlier era.

14.17 Hall, B. C., and C. T. Wood. **Big Muddy: Down the Mississippi through America's Heartland.** Photographs by Clarence Hall and Rhonda Hall. E. P. Dutton, 1992. 290 pp. ISBN 0-525-93476-6. Nonfiction.

B. C. Hall and C. T. Wood have had a lifelong love affair with the Mississippi River. They recount their own travels from the Mississippi headwaters at Lake Itaska in Minnesota to the river's entry into the Gulf of Mexico at the Louisiana coast; they provide a history of early explorers looking for the Northwest Passage, pirates, riverboats, Mark Twain, and Native Americans; they discuss the influence of the Mississippi on travel, settlement, opening the West, politics, and the environment. Black-and-white photographs support the text in a powerful description of the importance of this river in the development of the United States.

14.18 Harris, Jacqueline L. **History and Achievement of the NAACP.** Franklin Watts, 1992. 159 pp. ISBN 0-531-11035-4. Nonfiction.

In this book in the African-American Experience series, Jacqueline Harris discusses the forces that led to the founding of the biracial

National Association for the Advancement of Colored People and the particular individuals involved. She relates the efforts of the NAACP to achieve civil rights for African Americans and examines the achievements, disappointments, and future directions for the organization and its mission.

14.19 Haskins, Jim. **Against All Opposition: Black Explorers in America.** Walker, 1992. 86 pp. ISBN 0-8027-8138-1. Nonfiction.

Have you ever thought about, or even heard about, explorers of African or African American heritage? Jim Haskins has. In chapters that are fast paced and informative, Haskins describes contributions by a number of black explorers in America from before Columbus to the present. Short chapters look at the lives of Estevanico (who traveled from Mexico into the American Southwest), Jean Baptiste Point du Sable (founder of Chicago), York (a key member of the Lewis and Clark expedition), James Beckwourth (mountain man), Matthew Henson (Arctic explorer), and astronauts Guion Bluford and Ronald McNair.

Notable 1992 Children's Trade Books in the Field of Social Studies

14.20 Haskins, Jim. **Get on Board: The Story of the Underground Railroad.** Scholastic, 1993. 152 pp. ISBN 0-590-45418-8. Nonfiction.

Discover how the Underground Railroad got its name, read about the heroic individuals—the conductors, station masters, and passengers—who risked death to escape or help others escape slavery. Learn about the "fugitive slave laws," about individuals such as Harriet Tubman, John Brown, Jarmain Wesley Loguen ("Underground Railroad King"), William Still, Josiah Henson (reputedly the inspiration for *Uncle Tom's Cabin*), William and Ellen Craft, Henry "Box" Brown (who escaped slavery by nailing himself in a box to be shipped to Pennsylvania), and many others. This book is informative, entertaining, and replete with pictures and illustrations. (Only the placement of Vicksburg in Virginia, instead of Mississippi, mars this book.)

Notable 1994 Children's Trade Books in the Field of Social Studies

14.21 Hayman, Leroy. **The Assassinations of John and Robert Kennedy.** Scholastic, 1992. 151 pp. ISBN 0-590-46539-2. Nonfiction.

Within five years in the 1960s, the president of the United States and his brother, then a U. S. senator campaigning for president, were assassinated. How did their families endure the loss? What was it like to have the murders "officially" solved but to have so many unanswered questions? Did the assassins act alone? Why were these brothers killed? Will the truth ever be revealed?

14.22 Jacques, Geoffrey. **The African-American Movement Today.** Franklin Watts, 1992. 144 pp. ISBN 0-531-11033-8. Nonfiction.

This is one of several books in the African-American Experience series devoted to an examination and recounting of black history and culture, providing additional information and reason to celebrate the diversity of the American people. In this book, Geoffrey Jacques focuses on a number of changes in the African American movement since the civil rights efforts of the 1950s and 1960s. He highlights the accomplishments of numerous African Americans in leadership roles in politics, corporations, literature, and the arts, and the particular contributions of women and of black churches. Jacques recounts as well areas where progress is slower and where economic disparity exists, and he suggests ways to remedy selected circumstances.

14.23 James, Simon. **Ancient Rome.** Illustrated by Bill Le Fever. Viking, 1992. 47 pp. ISBN 0-670-84493-4. Nonfiction.

Imagine what it was like to live in the Roman Empire. This See through History book builds on Simon James's experience as an archaeologist specializing in Roman collections at the British Museum. The book reveals life in town and country and provides an overview of trade, habits, government, work, religion, and entertainment in the ancient Mediterranean world.

Notable 1990 Children's Trade Books in the Field of Social Studies

14.24 Kort, Michael. **The Rise and Fall of the Soviet Union.** Franklin Watts, 1992. 128 pp. ISBN 0-531-11040-0. Nonfiction.

What led to the fall of the Union of Soviet Socialist Republics and the overthrow of Mikhail Gorbachev? What were the forces in 1917 that led to the Russian Revolution that overthrew the tsar? to the rise of the Bolshevik Party? to the Communist Party? What were the roles of Peter the Great, Lenin, Stalin, Khrushchev, Brezhnev, and Gorbachev? What were the policies of *glasnost* and *perestroika* designed to accomplish? Michael Kort discusses responses to these and other questions as he presents an interesting overview of several hundred years of Russian history. Black-and-white photographs of Soviet leaders and people are included.

14.25 Landsman, Susan. **Who Shot JFK? A History Mystery.** Avon/ Camelot Books, 1992. 90 pp. ISBN 0-380-77063-6. Nonfiction.

Avon's series of history mysteries presents intriguing aspects of true mysteries not solved to everyone's satisfaction. In this book, author Susan Landsman presents photographs, maps, facts, and questions about the assassination of President John F. Kennedy and lists other sources to consult for those readers who would like to study this case in more detail. Find out about the early 1960s; learn about Lee Harvey Oswald, Jack Ruby, the Warren Commission, and various theories about the assassination—who did it, how it was done, who else might have been involved. Decide for yourself, after examining the evidence, what you believe really happened.

14.26   Lerner Geography Department. **Armenia.** Lerner, 1993. 56 pp. ISBN 0-8225-2806-1. Nonfiction.

The Geography Department of Lerner Publications examines the individual republics that have emerged from the former Union of Soviet Socialist Republics in its Then and Now series. Using photographs, maps, charts, and text prepared by a number of researchers, the history, culture, geography, society, and challenges of the republics are described. This book on Armenia, the smallest of the fifteen former Soviet republics, focuses in part on the particular aspects of a landlocked nation with an ancient Southwest Asian influence. The republic borders the present-day nations of Turkey and Iran.

14.27   Lerner Geography Department. **Azerbaijan.** Lerner, 1993. 56 pp. ISBN 0-8225-2810-X. Nonfiction.

This Then and Now book on Azerbaijan details the influence that location has on this republic bordering the Caspian Sea, the world's largest lake. The republic sits on the traditional border between Europe and Asia and on the trade route between the Middle East and Russia. Also influential for the nation was the discovery of oil and other minerals.

14.28   Lerner Geography Department. **Belarus.** Lerner, 1993. 56 pp. ISBN 0-8225-2811-8. Nonfiction.

The republic of Belarus is the focus of this Then and Now book. It is a landlocked nation bordering Poland on the west and with close ties in language, culture, and history to Russia, its neighbor to the east.

14.29   Lerner Geography Department. **Cyprus in Pictures.** Lerner, 1992. 64 pp. ISBN 0-8225-1910-0. Nonfiction.

The book is one of several in the Lerner Visual Geography series. Each book combines text with maps and photos (both black-and-white and color). The island of Cyprus is presented visually and in words, with emphasis on its topography, history and government, economy, religion, culture, and people.

14.30 Lerner Geography Department. **Georgia.** Lerner, 1993. 56 pp. ISBN 0-8225-2807-X. Nonfiction.

This book in the Then and Now series discusses the geography, history, politics, economics, and ecology of the former Soviet republic of Georgia. This mountainous nation borders the Black Sea and is rich in minerals and coal.

14.31 Lerner Geography Department. **Lithuania.** Lerner, 1992. 56 pp. ISBN 0-8225-2804-5. Nonfiction.

The Then and Now book on Lithuania examines all aspects of this country bordering Poland and the Baltic Sea and reviews the long history of Lithuania's fight for freedom, most recently illustrated by its break from Soviet domination. Learn how Lithuanians are revamping education, agriculture, politics, economy, and society; enjoy the richly colored photographs, maps, and charts; and marvel at the resourcefulness of these courageous people.

14.32 Lerner Geography Department. **Moldova.** Lerner, 1993. 56 pp. ISBN 0-8225-2809-6. Nonfiction.

Moldova, the focus of this Then and Now book on former Soviet republics, borders the Black Sea and Romania. The book describes the nation's agriculture and industry; it examines the influences from Russia and Romania and the conflicts among descendants of these peoples and also the Gagauz (Ethnic Turks).

14.33 Lerner Geography Department. **Ukraine.** Lerner, 1993. 64 pp. ISBN 0-8225-2808-8. Nonfiction.

The former Soviet republic of Ukraine is a rich agricultural region bordering Poland, Romania, and the Black Sea. This Then and Now book charts the influence of the Cossacks on this populous republic and the efforts of its inhabitants to retain a distinctive culture in spite of Russian domination.

14.34 Lerner Geography Department. **Uzbekistan.** Lerner, 1993. 56 pp. ISBN 0-8225-2812-6. Nonfiction.

Uzbekistan, another former Soviet republic, is situated in Asia to the north of Afghanistan. This Then and Now book focuses in part on the agrarian economy and lifestyle of Uzbekistan and on the influence of the nation's deserts, dry plains, and fertile valleys.

14.35 Lester, Julius. **Long Journey Home: Stories from Black History.** Dial Books, 1993. 150 pp. ISBN 0-8037-4953-8. Nonfiction.

Julius Lester examines several little known "movers of history." The vignettes are based on historical fact and represent stories of typical individuals rather than the famous or the great. Some of the vignettes are set during the Civil War, others after that time. Read, for instance, about Bob Lemmons, a black cowboy who single-handedly rounded up herds of wild mustangs. Read about blues-playing Rambler; educated Ben, who escapes to Canada; and Jake, who seeks Mandy following emancipation. Read about Louis, who escapes and helps with the Underground Railroad, and the nameless parent who tells a child about slavery, about Africa, and about the "long journey home." First published in 1972.

Boston Globe–Horn Book Fanfare Honor Book, 1972
National Book Award finalist, 1972

14.36 Lindop, Edmund. **Assassinations That Shook America.** Franklin Watts, 1992. 142 pp. ISBN 0-531-11049-4. Nonfiction.

What is assassination? Is it different from murder? Why has America had so many assassinations of leaders in the history of the country? This book examines questions such as these as it focuses on the assassinations of four presidents and three other political leaders—Abraham Lincoln, James Garfield, William McKinley, John F. Kennedy, Huey Long, Martin Luther King Jr., and Robert Kennedy. Author Edmund Lindop explores the circumstances that led to each assassination and to the consequences of the event in the United States.

14.37 Manley, Deborah, editor. **The Guinness Book of Records, 1492: The World Five Hundred Years Ago.** Facts on File, 1992. 192 pp. ISBN 0-8160-2772-2. Nonfiction.

What was the world like in the year Columbus "discovered" America? This retrospective look at 1492 acknowledges controversial points of view regarding what Columbus accomplished. It presents demographics, geology, geography, astronomy, natural phenomena, and facts about the fifteenth-century world; it describes various accomplishments in transportation, exploration, commerce, science, construction, art, sport, religion, and rulers.

This book offers an intriguing means of learning more about the world at the beginning of global communication.

14.38 Matthiessen, Peter. **In the Spirit of Crazy Horse.** Penguin, 1992. 646 pp. ISBN 0-670-83617-6. Nonfiction.

History books tell of settlers from Europe bargaining with Native Americans for land, of acquiring such land by legal and illegal means, of broken treaties. Does such treatment of Native Americans continue? Read this book and judge for yourself whether the Federal Bureau of Investigation and the federal and state courts have been fair and just in their treatment of those individuals associated with the American Indian Movement (AIM). Examine the complex issues and events leading up to a June 1975 shootout near Wounded Knee, South Dakota, that resulted in the death of two FBI agents and one Native American; the subsequent conviction of Leonard Peltier on murder charges; and the efforts to prove his innocence. (This controversial book, first published in 1983, was kept out of the public's hands during an eight-year court battle.)

14.39 McFall, Christie. **America Underground.** Dutton/Cobblehill Books, 1992. 80 pp. ISBN 0-525-65079-2. Nonfiction.

Subterranean exploration is always fascinating. Christie McFall presents in words, black-and-white photographs, maps, and illustrations an array of passages beneath the earth's surface—from caves to tunnels, from pipelines to sewers.

14.40 McLaughlin, Jack. **To His Excellency Thomas Jefferson: Letters to a President.** Avon Books, 1993. 344 pp. ISBN 0-380-71964-9. Nonfiction.

What did the general public write to their president early in the nineteenth century? How much about a president of the United States is revealed in correspondence? What can we learn about the issues and concerns of citizens at a time when the United States was growing dramatically? Jack McLaughlin has examined letters written to Thomas Jefferson during his presidency, grouping them into the themes of politics, patronage, youth, women, debt and justice, literature, invention, health, lunatics, and lovers. This organizational strategy enables the reader to follow correspondence to Jefferson on a particular topic and his responses.

14.41 McLaurin, Melton A. **Celia, a Slave.** Avon Books, 1993. 178 pp. ISBN 0-380-71935-5. Nonfiction.

How were some female slaves treated by their American "owners" in the period up to the Civil War? Were slaves in the lower Midwest treated the same as those in the South? Why were laws arranged largely to protect slave owners? What rights did slaves have, including slaves who were raped? Read about Celia's trial, its causes and consequences, for a better understanding of the political economy of slavery and the relationships of race, gender, and power in the moral dilemma of slavery. This is carefully constructed description and analysis by a historian documenting the facts and the basis for interpretation.

14.42   Meltzer, Milton. **The Amazing Potato: A Story in Which the Incas, Conquistadors, Marie Antoinette, Thomas Jefferson, Wars, Famines, Immigrants, and French Fries All Play a Part.** HarperCollins, 1992. 117 pp. ISBN 0-06-020807-4. Nonfiction.

Milton Meltzer presents a concise history of the potato, from its origin in South America and its introduction in Europe in the 1500s to its impact in Ireland and the United States, and as a potential answer to world hunger. Did you know that the potato crop is worth far more than the gold that Europeans found in the Americas? That potatoes represent a multibillion-dollar industry? That they are considered to be virtually a perfect food? That there are so many ways to prepare potato dishes that it is difficult to list them all? Read Meltzer's book, and you will learn other fascinating information about this delicious tuber.

ALA Notable Books for Children, 1993
Booklist Editors' Choice, 1992
Notable 1992 Children's Trade Books in the Field of Social Studies
School Library Journal Best Books, 1992

14.43   Murphy, Jim. **Across America on an Emigrant Train.** Houghton Mifflin/Clarion Books, 1993. 150 pp. ISBN 0-395-63390-7. Nonfiction.

Imagine what it was like to travel by railroad across the United States in the 1870s. What would the journey be like for someone from another country? for a budding famous author? for someone in love visiting a very ill sweetheart? Jim Murphy combines all these elements as he traces poet and novelist Robert Louis Stevenson's journey from Scotland to America by ship and then from New Jersey to California by train. Drawing upon Stevenson's journals and employing numerous black-and-white illustrations, Murphy weaves an informative story of travel across the country more than 100 years ago and reveals a number of interesting aspects of frontier life and the hardships facing emigrants.

ALA Notable Books for Children, 1994
Booklist Editors' Choice, 1993
NCTE Orbis Pictus Award, 1994
Notable 1994 Children's Trade Books in the Field of Social Studies
School Library Journal Best Books, 1993

14.44 Myers, Walter Dean. **Now Is Your Time! The African-American Struggle for Freedom.** HarperCollins, 1991. 292 pp. ISBN 0-06-024371-6. Nonfiction.

From pre–Civil War America to the modern Civil Rights movement, Walter Dean Myers chronicles the history of African Americans in this concise and well-written book. Myers looks at a few significant events emblematic of their eras. His ultimate message is that "what we understand of our history is what we understand of ourselves." This is a particularly good source for an introduction to American history and to the struggle endured by African Americans.

ALA Best Books for Young Adults, 1992
ALA Notable Books for Children, 1992
Coretta Scott King Author Award, 1992
NCTE Orbis Pictus Honor Book, 1992

14.45 Ofosu-Appiah, L. H. **People in Bondage: African Slavery since the 15th Century.** Lerner/Runestone Press, 1993. 112 pp. ISBN 0-8225-3150-X. Nonfiction.

Have you ever wondered how slavery began and whether it was practiced anywhere else outside the United States? African scholar L. H. Ofosu-Appiah examines slavery from its ancient beginnings to its practice in the Americas and the West Indies. He compares slavery briefly with other forms of servitude where individuals or groups have kept others in systematic control—from labor camps to the feudal system of serfs to indentured servants. The text is accompanied by black-and-white photographs and illustrations.

14.46 Pringle, Laurence. **Antarctica: The Last Unspoiled Continent.** Simon and Schuster, 1992. 56 pp. ISBN 0-671-73850-X. Nonfiction.

This book provides a good introduction to Antarctica. In ten short chapters, the book contains a large number of vivid photographs of icebergs, penguins, exploration camps, whales, and other sea life. Learn about the human impact on this continent and the efforts necessary to keep it from being spoiled.

ALA Notable Books for Children, 1993
Notable 1992 Children's Trade Books in the Field of Social Studies

14.47 Rappaport, Doreen, editor. **American Women: Their Lives in Their Words.** HarperCollins/Harper Trophy Books, 1992. 318 pp. ISBN 0-690-04817-3. Nonfiction.

With a deft hand, editor Doreen Rappaport has drawn excerpts from diaries, letters, speeches, and other original documents to portray American history as experienced by American women. The selections span all periods of American history, from descriptions of women's struggles to survive in the New World to modern women's concerns. Running through these compelling first-person reports is one dominant thread: women's quest for equality in all areas of life—the right to vote, to own property, to attend college, to earn equal pay for equal work, and to determine their own futures. Useful as a research document, this book has the added feature of being easy reading.

ALA Best Books for Young Adults, 1992
Notable 1990 Children's Trade Books in the Field of Social Studies

14.48 Rowland-Warne, L. **Costume.** Alfred A. Knopf, 1992. 64 pp. ISBN 0-679-91680-6. Nonfiction.

See fashion trends come around—and around—in this examination of clothing styles from Adam and Eve to today's jeans and T-shirts. Between the time of the Romans and the twentieth century, women and men were often uncomfortable for the sake of fashion, which was often based on the latest political or religious movement. Colorful photographs and drawings allow this Eyewitness picture book to speak louder than words in presenting a broad representation of clothing through the ages.

Notable 1992 Children's Trade Books in the Field of Social Studies

14.49 Samuel, Ray, Leonard V. Huber, and Warren C. Ogden. **Tales of the Mississippi.** Pelican, 1992. 240 pp. ISBN 0-88289-930-9. Nonfiction.

Originally published in 1955 and now in paperback for the first time, this account is the combined effort of two New Orleans newspapermen and a collector of Mississippi River artifacts, pictures, and material. These engaging tales, with black-and-white illustrations, include the European discovery of the Mississippi by DeSoto, Mike Fink and the race of the steamboats *Rob't E. Lee* and *Natchez,* and women riverboat captains.

14.50   Shubert, Adrian. **The Land and People of Spain.** HarperCollins, 1992. 244 pp. ISBN 0-06-020218-1. Nonfiction.

The country of Spain has had considerable influence on world history and has played a prominent role in the discovery, exploration, and exploitation of the Americas. This book is one of many in the Land and People series exploring the history and culture of different countries. Read it to learn more about the people and dialects of the different Spanish regions, the influences of Catholic and Moslem traditions, the politics and the people, the industry and the culture, the Basques and the Conquistadores. The text is enriched by the inclusion of maps, black-and-white photographs, and illustrations.

14.51   Stanley, Jerry. **Children of the Dust Bowl: The True Story of the School at Weedpatch Camp.** Crown, 1992. 81 pp. ISBN 0-517-58782-3. Nonfiction.

What is it like to be driven from home by endless drought, to have a farm incapable of growing anything because of dust and lack of irrigation, to move across the country in hope of finding work and in search of education for your children, only to be rejected, called an "Okie," and looked down upon? This is an informative and interesting account of Oklahoma families who escaped the "dust bowl" drought of the 1930s and who settled in a community in southern California known as Weedpatch Camp. There they found a caring superintendent who helped build a school that others clamored to attend.

ALA Notable Books for Children, 1993
Booklist Editors' Choice, 1992
NCTE Orbis Pictus Award, 1993
Notable 1992 Children's Trade Books in the Field of Social Studies
School Library Journal Best Books, 1992

14.52   Stegner, Wallace. **Beyond the Hundredth Meridian: John Wesley Powell and the Second Opening of the West.** Penguin, 1992. 438 pp. ISBN 0-14-015994-0. Nonfiction.

In this biography of Major John Wesley Powell, Pulitzer Prize–winning author Wallace Stegner describes Powell's contributions to exploring and recording the western part of the United States in the era following the Civil War. Stegner includes a number of reproduced photographs from the period, artistic renderings, and maps to illustrate the West and Southwest, especially the Colorado River and Grand Canyon. Powell foresaw what exploitation would do to the West and warned against such abuse. This memorable book goes well beyond simple biography to present a true sense of the grandeur and the reality of nature in the American West. First published in 1954.

14.53   Strom, Yale. **Uncertain Roads: Searching for the Gypsies.** Macmillan/Four Winds Press, 1993. 112 pp. ISBN 0-02-788531-3. Nonfiction.

Who are the Rom? American author Yale Strom was able to gain access to Eastern European and European Rom (or gypsy) communities and to gain insight into an often misunderstood culture. Through interviews and photographs, Strom makes a significant effort to reveal this culture, its love of music, and the racism it has experienced.

14.54   Tchudi, Stephen. **Lock and Key: The Secrets of Locking Things Up, In, and Out.** Charles Scribner's Sons, 1993. 113 pp. ISBN 0-684-19363-9. Nonfiction.

Hold your keys in your hand for a moment and just consider what it is that they represent—access to home, work, or travel. Have you ever really considered the significance of the lock and key? In his latest book, Stephen Tchudi does just that, providing a wonderful and fascinating overview of the lock and key from ancient history to the present. Tchudi also looks at both legendary locks and keys and at the linguistic significance of the terms *lock* and *key* in our language. Don't miss this book; your relationship with locks and keys will never be the same.

14.55   Travis, David. **The Land and People of Italy.** HarperCollins, 1992. 244 pp. ISBN 0-06-022784-2. Nonfiction.

The book is one of many in the Land and People series exploring the history and culture of different countries. The informative, easy-to-read text of each book is enriched by the inclusion of maps, black-and-white photographs, and illustrations. In this book, David Travis presents several views of Italy, reflecting the customs and traditions evolving in different sections of the country due to geographic and historical influences. From the days of the Etruscans and the Roman Empire to the remarkable recovery from the devastation of World War II, Travis describes the importance of Italy and its people as they sit at a crossroads of the world.

14.56 Wakin, Edward, and Daniel Wakin. **Photos That Made U.S. History. Vol. 1: From the Civil War Era to the Atomic Age** and **Vol. 2: From the Cold War to the Space Age.** Walker, 1993. 50 pp. and 45 pp. ISBN 0-827-8231-0 and 0-8027-8272-8. Nonfiction.

This two-volume set is an interesting array of photographs from defined periods in U.S. history. Volume 1 concentrates on seven photographs. Edward and Daniel Wakins set the context for each photograph and describe the event—from Abraham Lincoln campaigning to the bombing of Hiroshima. Volume 2 focuses on another seven photographs, this time ranging from Richard Nixon confronting Khrushchev to a photograph of Earth taken from the moon.

Notable 1994 Children's Trade Books in the Field of Social Studies

14.57 Weston, Mark. **The Land and People of Pakistan.** HarperCollins, 1992. 242 pp. ISBN 0-06-022790-7. Nonfiction.

In this book in the Land and People series, Mark Weston effectively presents an overview of Pakistan. He examines the country's history, the difficulties it faces due to high illiteracy and a burgeoning population, the geography of its five regions, the influence of the Muslim religion, and the civilizations that have inhabited the land for 4,500 years.

Notable 1992 Children's Trade Books in the Field of Social Studies
School Library Journal Best Books, 1992

14.58 Wood, Tim. **The Aztecs.** Viking, 1992. 47 pp. ISBN 0-670-84492-6. Nonfiction.

Who were the Aztecs? Why are they important in history? Answers to these and other questions are presented in this compact overview of the Aztecs, with vivid illustrations and four see-through cutaways of Montezuma's palace, an Aztec house, a temple, and the Great Temple of Tenochtitlan. The book covers the Aztecs' encounters with other tribes, their civilization, and the coming of the Spanish in 1519. It provides an excellent introduction to the customs, beliefs, and culture of this interesting and productive people.

Notable 1992 Children's Trade Books in the Field of Social Studies

15 Hobbies and Travel

15.1   Brunhouse, Jay. **Adventuring on Eurail,** 2d ed. Pelican, 1991. 305 pp. ISBN 0-88289-834-5. Nonfiction.

If you are thinking of hitting the major stops between Greece and Scandinavia, take a look at this updated guidebook. Country by country, it tells you how to plan your itinerary and purchase Eurail passes, what sights to see, and even which side of the train to sit on for the best view. Among the strong points are timetables for major destinations in each country, tips on sleepers, concise sets of "vital tips" individualized for each country, and appendixes providing addresses of train and tourist offices and Eurail Aid offices. This comprehensive book even covers water crossings between England and Ireland and across the English Channel. You may want to purchase a more specialized book if you are limiting your travel to a single country, and if you are interested in side trips off the main routes, you will need to pick up information locally. If, however, you are planning to travel extensively in Europe, this book will take you a long way.

15.2   Emmet, E. R. **Brain Puzzler's Delight.** Sterling, 1993. 96 pp. ISBN 0-8069-8816-9. Nonfiction.

Divided by type and difficulty levels, the puzzles in this book offer a variety of logical reasoning problems reminiscent of whodunits and what's-missing situations. Good for many ages, this book is challenging and entertaining. Only elementary mathematical knowledge is required, and solutions are provided.

15.3   Englebert, Victor. **Wind, Sand and Silence: Travels with Africa's Last Nomads.** Chronicle Books, 1991. 181 pp. ISBN 0-8118-0010-5. Nonfiction.

At intervals over more than two decades, writer/photographer Victor Englebert lived and traveled with several of Africa's nomadic tribes, each of which gets its own chapter in this book. Judged by its outward appearance and price, this is a coffee-table book, but the text rises above that level and makes this a useful book for the serious student as well as the casual reader. Englebert provides not just beautiful photos but also extraordinary insights into the lives of these desert peoples who have survived for thousands of years in some of the world's harshest environments. Written in first-person, his narrative is lyrical and intimate. The carefully chosen photographs illustrate lifestyles, not just landscape.

15.4 Feenstra, Marcel, Philip J. Carter, and Christopher P. Harding. **The Ultimate IQ Book.** Ward Lock, 1993. 128 pp. ISBN 0-7063-7148-8. Nonfiction.

The authors have compiled original puzzles and tests from members of the world's leading high-IQ societies. Rated from moderately hard to fiendishly difficult, these puzzles run the gamut of word, number, and logic problems. Not only are solutions provided, but so are unsolved problems and three complete IQ tests. Good luck! First published in Great Britain, 1993.

15.5 Heafford, Philip. **Great Book of Math Puzzles.** Sterling, 1993. 96 pp. ISBN 0-8069-8814-2. Nonfiction.

Do you know what the number 1,760 represents? Or what the Romans used as an aid with calculations? These are only two examples of the many mathematical history and computation puzzles in this wonderfully fun book. Although a little algebra might help readers, this collection is good for many ages, in the classroom or at home. The solutions are provided.

15.6 Houston, Dick. **Safari Adventure.** Photographs by Dick Houston. Dutton/Cobblehill Books, 1991. 145 pp. ISBN 0-525-65051-2. Nonfiction.

For years Dick Houston dreamed of Africa as he had read about it and seen it in the old Martin and Osa Johnson movies. Finally he left Ohio and his classroom behind and headed to Africa to start his own safari company and to see firsthand what might be left of the older, wilder Africa, still untouched by civilization. This book chronicles Houston's initial expedition through Kenya and Tanzania, his close encounters with wild animals, and a thrilling climb up Mt. Kilimanjaro, the highest peak in Africa. Toward the end of the book he exclaims, "Oh, the wonders we had seen!" Thanks to his clear prose and fine photos, we see and enjoy the wonders with him. Houston contributes frequently to leading travel magazines.

15.7 Kesselheim, Alan S. **Silhouette on a Wide Land.** Fulcrum, 1992. 203 pp. ISBN 1-55591-092-0. Nonfiction.

Ostensibly an account of a year spent as a laborer/caretaker on a remote ranch on the Colorado plains, this book is much, much more. Alan S. Kesselheim began the job after he had finished college and "dabbled in a few jobs and some travel," and he considers it successful that he "learned enough about rural work to avoid looking foolish most of the time." However, he learned a great deal besides how to string a wire fence and deliver a calf. Kesselheim's acute sensitivity to the austere landscape, to nature, and to the strong and taciturn people whom he learned to respect teaches us much about both natural and social history of the high plains country. There can indeed be an odyssey in the meditations of the self-exiled writer, if his mind and eye are keen and his voice the voice of a poet.

Booklist Editors' Choice, 1992

15.8   Overstreet, Robert M. **The Overstreet Comic Book Companion: Identification and Price Guide.** Avon Books, 1992. 591 pp. ISBN 0-380-76911-5. Nonfiction.

This book provides an overview to comic book collecting. Comic book terminology, grading, handling, storage, and selling tips are given. The book also includes complete listings of the hardcover picture books published in the 1930s and a comprehensive section on "Comic Character Kings" from the 1930s to the 1990s.

16 The Holocaust

16.1 Atkinson, Linda. **In Kindling Flame: The Story of Hannah Senesh, 1921–1944.** William Morrow/Beech Tree Books, 1992. 214 pp. ISBN 0-688-11689-2. Nonfiction.

Hannah Senesh is brought to life in a compelling way through her diaries and poetry and through the words of those who knew her. This intense young woman embraced Zionism during the rise of Nazi Germany and moved to Palestine to help establish a Jewish homeland. She later returned to her native Hungary as a paratrooper in an attempt to liberate Jewish people. At the age of twenty-two, capture and execution awaited her.

16.2 Birger, Trudi, with Jeffrey M. Green. **A Daughter's Gift of Love: A Holocaust Memoir.** Jewish Publication Society, 1992. 218 pp. ISBN 0-8276-0420-3. Nonfiction.

Trudi Birger describes how a happy, secure childhood is cut short as she and her family flee Hitler's Germany. When flight is no longer possible, they are confined to the Slobodka ghetto in Kovna, Lithuania. Jews are used for slave labor, are slowly starved, and are rounded up and massacred. When Trudi and her mother are shipped out of the ghetto to Stutthof concentration camp, they find that it is only their selfless devotion to each other that keeps them alive.

16.3 Block, Gay, and Malka Drucker. **Rescuers: Portraits of Moral Courage in the Holocaust.** Holmes and Meier, 1992. 255 pp. ISBN 0-8419-1322-6. Nonfiction.

Skillful interviews and vivid, honest photographs form a portrait of seemingly ordinary people who risked their lives and the lives of their loved ones for otherwise doomed Jewish strangers during World War II. We learn what motivated these forty-nine rescuers as they talk to us in their own words. In just a few pages we get to know each rescuer, as well as those they saved. Each story is a generous, memorable gift, making this a unique, suspenseful, and inspirational book.

Booklist Editors' Choice, 1992

16.4 Frame, Veronica Foldes. **On Whom I Have Mercy.** Riverview, 1993. 271 pp. ISBN 0-9635160-0-0. Fiction.

Katalin takes her Christian beliefs for granted until she falls in love with and marries a Jewish man. As her beloved Istvan is sent to a concentration camp, Katalin, now Jewish under the law, must spend the remainder of World War II hiding in the homes of Christian friends. She sends their young son to live with a family in the countryside, and she can only pray for his and Istvan's well-being.

16.5   Greenfeld, Howard. **The Hidden Children.** Ticknor and Fields, 1993. 118 pp. ISBN 0-395-66074-2. Nonfiction.

Can you imagine what it would be like to lose your home and possessions and be separated from your parents? Imagine how it would feel to forget who your parents are, or to be tortured by fears that they might never again find you. Consider the burden of living a secret life in hiding, or a false life disguised as a Christian. The memories of thirteen Jews who were hidden children during World War II are woven together, along with photographs, in this revealing book.

Notable 1994 Children's Trade Books in the Field of Social Studies

16.6   Handler, Andrew, and Susan V. Meschel, editors. **Young People Speak: Surviving the Holocaust in Hungary.** Franklin Watts, 1993. 160 pp. ISBN 0-531-11044-3. Nonfiction.

A birthday party in the country brings Andre a first experience with horses, watermelons—and the military police. Eva, her Olympic goals interrupted, describes living in a Swiss "protected" house: although she is starving, each day Eva runs up and down five flights of stairs two hundred times to keep her legs strong. Ten-year-old Peter describes being saved by one of Raoul Wallenberg's famous Swedish passes after the deportation of his parents. Eight others, survivors of the Holocaust in Hungary, tell their stories in direct, sensitive prose.

Notable 1994 Children's Trade Books in the Field of Social Studies

16.7   Isaacman, Clara, as told to Joan Adess Grossman. **Clara's Story.** Jewish Publication Society, 1993. 119 pp. ISBN 0-8276-0243-X. Nonfiction.

As the Nazis enter Belgium, young Clara and her family make numerous attempts to escape but find land and sea avenues closed. They go into hiding in Antwerp, first in the basement of a bakery, later with different families for short periods of time. Then Clara's father is betrayed, and her brother Hershie is sent to

Auschwitz. Clara and her sister are dependent upon their mother's uncanny ability to sense when a house has become unsafe, or when the people around them are not trustworthy.

16.8   Kertész, Imre (translated by Christopher C. Wilson and Katharina M. Wilson). **Fateless.** Northwestern University Press, 1992. 191 pp. ISBN 0-8101-1049-0. Fiction.

George, the teenage narrator, is taken from the bus one day and finds himself on his way to Auschwitz with no premonition of what is to come. He gains his knowledge one horror at a time, unsuspecting of what lies ahead in yet another concentration camp. This book is as realistic as any autobiographical account: Kertész himself was imprisoned in Auschwitz, and his experience combined with his tremendous writing ability makes this an unforgettable and compelling book.

Booklist Editors' Choice, 1992

16.9   Landau, Elaine. **The Warsaw Ghetto Uprising.** Macmillan/New Discovery Books, 1992. 143 pp. ISBN 0-02-751392-0. Nonfiction.

This heroic story of World War II unfolds as the Nazis force more and more Jews into a small, walled-off part of Warsaw, Poland, where disease and starvation kill nearly 50,000 Jews each year. Faced with death or deportation to concentration camps, several underground groups emerge, alliances are formed, and meticulous plans are made to prepare for battle. In the ensuing siege, Jews battle the well-armed Nazi forces for twenty-eight days, killing large numbers of Nazis before the doomed Warsaw ghetto is destroyed.

16.10   Leitner, Isabella. **The Big Lie.** Scholastic, 1992. 48 pp. ISBN 0-590-45569-9. Nonfiction.

How would you feel about neighbors who gleefully cheer or close their eyes as you are herded through the city, crammed into cattle cars, and taken off to prison camp? Isabella Leitner and her family of seven confront the changes in their Hungarian homeland with strength and courage. Her straightforward view of the Nazi concentration camps provides a compelling account of a family's journey to freedom against the odds of Hitler's "Big Lie."

Notable 1992 Children's Trade Books in the Field of Social Studies

16.11   Linnéa, Sharon. **Raoul Wallenberg: The Man Who Stopped Death.** Jewish Publication Society, 1993. 151 pp. ISBN 0-8276-0440-8. Nonfiction.

A man of integrity and single-minded purpose, Raoul Wallenberg was the sole hope of thousands of Hungarian Jews. This Swedish diplomat assigned to Budapest during World War II was deeply hated by the Nazis for the brazen manner in which he saved Jews, often from trains destined for the death camps. Author Sharon Linnéa depicts Wallenberg as a complex and creative individual and includes photographs taken by Wallenberg's close associate, Tom Veres, who often used a concealed camera. This is a more in-depth treatment than Michael Nicholson and David Winner's book, *Raoul Wallenberg* (16.14); both are equally engrossing.

16.12   Matas, Carol. **Daniel's Story.** Scholastic, 1993. 136 pp. ISBN 0-590-46588-0. Fiction.

Daniel does not mind when he is forced to leave his public school and attend a school for Jews. What he does not realize is that this is just the beginning of the loss of freedom for Jewish people in Hitler's Germany. When Daniel and his family are forced from their home, they begin a long and harrowing journey to the Jewish ghetto in Lodz, Poland, and then to Auschwitz, the Nazi death camp. Surrounded by starvation, inhuman terrors, and death, Daniel keeps his courage with the help of his family and friends as they struggle to stay alive.

Notable 1994 Children's Trade Books in the Field of Social Studies

16.13   Matas, Carol. **Lisa's War.** Scholastic, 1991. 111 pp. ISBN 0-590-43517-5. Fiction.

It is the spring of 1940, and Hitler's German army is continuing a year-old occupation of most of Europe by invading Denmark and Norway. Lisa, the teenage daughter of a Jewish doctor, understands the grave danger her family is facing because of their religion. Her personal perspective on the Holocaust and her bravery in joining freedom fighters is reminiscent of the Anne Frank story. Lisa takes part in a daring flight from the German threat and the prospect of imprisonment and death.

IRA Young Adults' Choices, 1991

16.14   Nicholson, Michael, and David Winner. **Raoul Wallenberg: The Swedish Diplomat Who Saved 100,000 Jews from the Nazi Holocaust before Mysteriously Disappearing.** Gareth Stevens, 1989. 68 pp. ISBN 1-55532-820-2. Nonfiction.

This is a thrilling story of Raoul Wallenberg, a fascinating man who risked his own life countless times in order to secure freedom for Hungarian Jews during World War II. Manufacturing Swedish passes that looked authentic (but were fakes) was just one of the many ways in which Wallenberg and his associates saved over 100,000 individuals. This brief book is packed with photographs, maps, and drawings that provide further information about Wallenberg's life. His story is a strong testimony to the great things that can be accomplished by one person who cares.

16.15 Sender, Ruth Minsky. **The Holocaust Lady.** Macmillan, 1992. 192 pp. ISBN 0-02-781832-2. Nonfiction.

Ruth Minsky Sender's youth was spent in a Polish ghetto, a Nazi concentration camp, and a displaced persons camp (described in her books *The Cage* and *To Life*). Sender continues her autobiography with her move to America, where she raises a family, writes, and teaches. She also talks to students and answers their letters about her World War II experience. Why continue this painful "burden of remembering," as she calls it? It is, Sender feels, "the duty of passing on the agonizing memories so that the world will learn from them."

Notable 1992 Children's Trade Books in the Field of Social Studies

16.16 Toll, Nelly S. **Behind the Secret Window: A Memoir of a Hidden Childhood during World War Two.** Dial Books, 1993. 161 pp. ISBN 0-8037-1362-2. Nonfiction.

Nelly Toll was a child when the Germans invaded Poland. Her family was forced to move to the Jewish ghetto in Lwów, Ukraine, and unsuccessfully attempted to escape to Hungary. For thirteen months, Toll and her mother were hidden in a Gentile home in a small space behind a bricked-up window. During that time Troll painted over sixty watercolor pictures and kept a journal that was the basis for this book. Her beautiful and sensitive paintings (also reproduced in the book) convey her longing for friends, sunshine, and freedom.

IRA Children's Books Award, 1994
Notable 1994 Children's Trade Books in the Field of Social Studies

16.17 Voigt, Cynthia. **David and Jonathan.** Scholastic Hardcover Books, 1992. 256 pp. ISBN 0-590-45165-0. Fiction.

In a military hospital during the Vietnam War, surgeon Henry Marr examines a severely injured soldier, Jonathan Nafiche. The reunion with his teen buddy not only forces him to decide whether he should perform the lifesaving surgery but also triggers a flashback to when David, Jonathan's cousin and a Holocaust survivor, entered—and disrupted—their lives. Author Cynthia Voigt provides historical background on the Holocaust and provides an awareness of the distinctions in people and a sensitive story of the coming-of-age of two fifteen-year-olds.

16.18   Volavková, Hana, editor. **I Never Saw Another Butterfly: Children's Drawings and Poems from Terezin Concentration Camp, 1942–1944.** Schocken Books, 1993. 106 pp. ISBN 0-8052-4115-9. Nonfiction.

Nearly 15,000 children passed through the Czech ghetto of Terezin on their way to the death camps. Executions, hunger, and lack of medical care killed people daily, yet books, art, and music became weapons against despair. The children at Terezin were taught by talented Jewish teachers and were encouraged to write and draw. These drawings, paintings, and poems bring to life the children who created them. The end of the book contains biographical information about each of the young artists and authors.

ALA Best Books for Young Adults, 1994

16.19   Vos, Ida (translated by Terese Edelstem and Inez Smidt). **Anna Is Still Here.** Houghton Mifflin, 1993. 139 pp. ISBN 0-395-65368-1. Fiction.

The war is over. Anna no longer has to hide in an attic, and she is reunited with her parents. But she wonders why they don't hear from friends and relatives, why her parents whisper quietly at night, why they won't tell her what happened to them during the war when the Nazis occupied Holland. And Anna is deathly afraid of the white house that she must pass on her way to school. Does a Nazi live there? Is he lying in wait for her?

16.20   Walshaw, Rachela, and Sam Walshaw. **From out of the Firestorm: A Memoir of the Holocaust.** Shapolsky, 1991. 154 pp. ISBN 1-56171-021-0.

Rachela Walshaw tells the story of her devout Jewish family of ten. Their small Polish town, Wonchock, is burned to the ground by the German army. At age seventeen, Rachela is sent away to the Hasak labor camp. Her sister, Tobcia, joins her there, while other family members are lost to ghetto diseases, crematoria ovens, and senseless murder. Rachela and Tobcia survive Hasak, Leipzig, and unexpected dangers of liberation. The last chapter details the experiences of their brother Shmulek, the only other surviving family member.

16.21 Yolen, Jane. **Briar Rose.** Tor Books, 1992. 200 pp. ISBN 0-812-55862-6. Fiction.

Becca's favorite story has always been her "Gemma's" version of Sleeping Beauty. As Gemma nears the end of her life, she insists that she was the princess in the castle in the sleeping woods and that a prince rescued her. A deathbed promise takes Becca, a reporter by profession, on an investigative journey to Poland to one of the worst hells in Hitler's Europe: Chelmno, where 320,000 people, mainly Jews, died. This intriguing modern-day story, which alternates with chapters repeating Gemma's tale of Sleeping Beauty told to Becca in her childhood, brings to life the princess, the castle, the lifesaving kiss, and the horror of evil.

ALA Best Books for Young Adults, 1993

16.22 Zar, Rose. **In the Mouth of the Wolf.** Jewish Publication Society, 1992. 225 pp. ISBN 0-8276-0382-7. Nonfiction.

Resourcefulness and a keen sense of danger were all that stood between Ruszka (Rose) Guterman and death in Nazi-occupied Poland. Her father advised her that the safest place to hide was in the open, among the Nazis. After working in a shoe factory and a hospital, Rose obtained a job working for Kommandant Roemer as a maid and governess. Living under a false identity was a terrible strain as the years went by; loneliness and danger were a daily presence.

17 Horror, Witchcraft, and the Supernatural

17.1 Cooney, Caroline B. **The Cheerleader.** Scholastic/Point Books, 1991. 179 pp. ISBN 0-590-44316-X. Fiction.

The vampire suggests to Althea, in a "voice like antique silk, faded and slightly torn," that she could be popular. For sweet but lonely Althea, it is an offer too irresistible to refuse, and overnight the fifteen-year-old becomes one of the most popular girls at school—a girl with friends, dates, and party invitations, surrounded by smiles and attention, a girl who becomes a cheerleader. But it is all due to the vampire—who never gives without expecting return. What does he want from Althea? If he does not get what he wants, what will happen to the most popular girl in town? A spine tingler with a surprise ending.

ALA Quick Picks for Young Adults, 1992

17.2 Cooney, Caroline B. **Freeze Tag.** Scholastic/Point Books, 1992. 166 pp. ISBN 0-590-45681-4. Fiction.

Meghan grew up in a typical neighborhood, playing yard games, eating at friends' houses, sharing secrets, falling in love with the boy next door. In this typical neighborhood, though, is atypical, spooky, unloved Lannie, who seems to have the power to literally *freeze* people to death. The neighborhood kids keep Lannie's power a secret—who knows, anyway, if what they thought they saw her do is what happened? Years pass, and Lannie grows up to use her powers in a more adult—and terrifying—way. The game is Freeze Tag, and the stakes are life and death.

17.3 Cooney, Caroline B. **The Return of the Vampire.** Scholastic/Point Books, 1991. 166 pp. ISBN 0-590-44884-6. Fiction.

Plain Devnee, the new girl in town who has moved into the haunted house, encounters the vampire in this sequel to *The Cheerleader*. Like her predecessor, who made a contract with the vampire in order to be popular, Devnee wishes for Aryssa's beauty and Victoria's intelligence. Devnee's conscience hurts her when she gets her wishes and her two classmates are destroyed, but when the vampire threatens Devnee's mother, her unholy alliance with the evil creature changes. Will Devnee have the courage to turn her back on her new life—even to save her mother?

17.4 Cooney, Caroline B. **The Vampire's Promise.** Scholastic/Point Books, 1993. 166 pp. ISBN 0-590-45682-2. Fiction.

It started as a party in the old abandoned house—the one in which weird things have happened and that now is to be torn down for the new shopping mall. The six teenagers are having a great time in the empty, dark tower room until the only inhabitant returns—the vampire. Blocking the door with his powers, the hungry creature refuses to let anyone leave until the six voluntarily choose someone to be his next victim. Who will be chosen and how will the group decide? This is the last volume in Caroline Cooney's vampire trilogy.

17.5 Craig, Kit. **Gone.** Little, Brown, 1992. 278 pp. ISBN 0-316-15923-9. Fiction.

The Hale family, despite a serene exterior, is suffering. The father, a naval officer, disappeared in his nuclear submarine and has been declared missing in action. The mother, Clary, and the three kids, teens Michael and Teah and young Tommy, keep hoping for his return. To all outward appearances, the Hales are carrying on bravely, but suddenly Clary also vanishes, leaving no trace. Michael and Teah take Tommy and set off to find their mother, using whatever skills and knowledge they have. What they find is Clary's dark past, and murder and terror are part of it. Mature language and situations.

ALA Best Books for Young Adults, 1993

17.6 Davidson, Nicole. **The Stalker.** Avon/Flare Books, 1992. 170 pp. ISBN 0-380-76645-0. Fiction.

Jennifer likes her part-time job at Caramelbun, a bakery at the mall. The job gives her extra money and allows her to get away from her strict father. But closing up alone late one night, Jennifer is nearly killed, attacked by someone hiding in the dark, empty mall. Who would want to kill Jennifer? And is her attack related to another murder in the mall, unsolved for these many months? This is a well-written, suspenseful story with an unexpected ending.

17.7 Edwards, Nicholas. **Arachnophobia.** Scholastic/Point Books, 1990. 119 pp. ISBN 0-590-44228-7. Fiction.

If you are afraid of spiders—if you are an *arachnophobe*—you will want to stay away from this easy-reading yet frightening tale of deadly South American spiders who arrive in a small town in California to multiply . . . and kill.

17.8   Ellis, Carol. **The Window.** Scholastic/Point Books, 1992. 168 pp. ISBN 0-590-44916-8. Fiction.

Jody does not yet know everyone in the group, but the weeklong ski trip to a great resort gives her an opportunity to make new friends. The fun stops, though, when Jody falls on the slopes and has to spend the rest of the week nursing a sprained ankle. Bored and restless, she stares out her bedroom window at the lodge—and sees a murder. Unfortunately, the murderer sees Jody, too—and comes back to silence her.

17.9   Forrest, Elizabeth. **Phoenix Fire.** DAW Books, 1992. 364 pp. ISBN 0-88677-515-9. Fiction.

Into this complicated tale of Chinese myth and the reality of today's Los Angeles come two ancient beasts, the Phoenix and the Demon, who reemerge from centuries of slumber in order to fight to the death. Through Susan, a young widow, El, an amateur archaeologist, and others, the stage is set for a titanic—and deadly—confrontation.

17.10   Garth, G. G. **Nightmare Matinee.** Bantam Books, 1994. 134 pp. ISBN 0-553-56566-4. Fiction.

There's a new horror flick in town, and everyone at the high school is going to see it. Some devotees have already viewed it numerous times. A few things, however, are odd: not only does the film seem to change every time it is viewed, but the kids who watch it are changing, too. And when some kids grow fangs and an amazing amount of body hair, or have worms emerging from their pores, it is evident something about that film is terribly wrong.

17.11   Gilmore, Kate. **Enter Three Witches.** Scholastic/Point Books, 1992. 210 pp. ISBN 0-590-44494-8. Fiction.

In this funny, well-written book, Bren is an ordinary kid living in New York City. His parents are separated, he is falling in love with a girl in his class, and he is heavily involved in the school production of *Macbeth*. Bren, however, lives, literally, with three witches: both his mother and grandmother are witches, and their attic boarder also practices black magic. What is a normal kid to do?

Booklist Editors' Choice, 1990

17.12 Gorman, Carol. **Die for Me.** Avon/Flare Books, 1992. 138 pp. ISBN 0-380-76686-8. Fiction.

Holly Reynolds, a popular senior girl, is killed under mysterious circumstances, but that does not keep her best "friends" from having a party barely a month after her death. At the party, out comes the Ouija board—and it makes predictions of even more deaths. Everyone laughs, but a few threatening letters and still another murder later, the game turns serious. The question is not only *who* will be next—but *why*?

17.13 Guiley, Rosemary Ellen. **The Encyclopedia of Ghosts and Spirits.** Facts on File, 1992. 374 pp. ISBN 0-8160-2140-6. Nonfiction.

With over 400 entries and seventy illustrations, this reference book ranges from *All Hallow's Eve* to *Zombies,* including both famous and obscure stories of ghosts, witches, apparitions, and unexplained phenomena.

17.14 Hoh, Diane. **The Invitation.** Scholastic/Point Books, 1991. 169 pp. ISBN 0-590-44904-4. Fiction.

The spoiled and very rich Cass Rockingham always has an extravagant fall party at her family's mansion, to which only the most popular kids are invited. That is, until this fall, when Sarah Drew and her four "nobody" friends get invitations to Cass's bash. The five are puzzled, but they decide to go—after all, maybe Cass really likes them. Not! The evening is filled with surprises, including one death, and the center of the mystery turns out to be quite surprising.

17.15 Hoh, Diane. **The Train.** Scholastic, 1992. 164 pp. ISBN 0-590-45640-7. Fiction.

A group of high school friends is traveling cross-country by train to San Francisco for a class trip. The only downer is that in the baggage compartment is the coffin of another classmate, cruelly nicknamed Frog, whom everyone disliked and who recently died in a fiery car crash. Then one girl is nearly strangled to death, and a boy is stabbed. There is no place to hide on the train, and when Hannah is attacked and put in Frog's coffin, everyone is alarmed. Hannah lives—but why was the coffin empty? Where is Frog?

17.16 Huff, Tanya. **Blood Lines.** DAW Books, 1993. 271 pp. ISBN 0-88677-530-2. Fiction.

The Egyptology Department of Toronto's Royal Art Museum is thrilled to acquire an undisturbed sarcophagus, or ancient coffin. Carefully removing the mummy inside seems just the first step of exciting research and fame for the museum. But research must wait—the mummy is not really dead, and its liberation means death and domination. Ex-cop Vicki Nelson, detective Mike Culluci, and 450-year-old vampire Henry Fitzroy discard their differences and work together to destroy the evil. Violence, mature language and theme. Sequel to *Blood Price* and *Blood Trail.*

17.17 King, Stephen. **Dolores Claiborne.** Viking, 1993. 305 pp. ISBN 0-670-84452-7. Fiction.

Written in the voice of Dolores Claiborne, this novel tells of a hard-bitten woman who has led a difficult life and has survived. Unhappily married, working for a wealthy and impossibly demanding woman, Dolores has not had many good things happen to her during her life on Little Tall Island. Dolores Claiborne is a determined woman, however, and not afraid to fight—or kill—to protect what she cherishes.

17.18 King, Stephen. **Insomnia.** Viking, 1994. 787 pp. ISBN 0-670-85503-0. Fiction.

Ralph Roberts's wife has died, and now, as he deals with his grief, he is waking up earlier and earlier every morning. Soon Ralph is living on only a few hours of sleep a night—and then other odd things begin happening to him. Ralph notices strange behavior in some of his longtime neighbors and, without warning, begins to see incredible colors swirling around people's heads and bodies. Ralph wonders if he is losing his mind in grief but finds, however, he is not alone in his insomnia or in his intermittent ability to see brilliant colors—his neighbor Lois is having similar experiences. Together, they realize that sinister forces are at work. In a climactic scene, the two unite to confront an evil force that would destroy their community.

17.19 King, Stephen. **Nightmares and Dreamscapes.** Viking, 1993. 816 pp. ISBN 0-670-85108-6. Fiction.

Twenty-three short stories are in this latest collection from the prince of horror, Stephen King. Is the mysterious pilot of the small plane in "The Night Flier" really a vampire? Can "Dolan's

Cadillac" just disappear into the desert floor? Why do most of the townspeople in "You Know They Got a Hell of a Band" so closely resemble rock stars—that is, rock stars who are dead? The weird, the odd, and the macabre are all offered here.

17.20   Murphy, Jim. **Night Terrors.** Scholastic, 1993. 177 pp. ISBN 0-590-45341-6. Fiction.

Digger's name is appropriate: he is, literally, a grave digger. He is also a guide to horror, for he is the smart and witty narrator of these twelve tales of terror and fear. This unique collection links grisly and believable stories through Digger's voice. Watch for a big surprise at the end.

ALA Quick Picks for Young Adults, 1994

17.21   Oates, Joyce Carol. **Black Water.** Penguin/Plume Books, 1993. 154 pp. ISBN 0-452-26986-5. Fiction.

It is night, and Kitty Kelleher, twenty-six, is trapped in a car nearly submerged in black water. There has been an accident, and the car's driver, a dashing older man who is a U.S. senator, has freed himself and swum to the surface. Surely he is returning to rescue Kitty—after all, this is their first "date." He wouldn't just save himself and let her die—or would he? This suspense novel is loosely based on the Chappaquiddick incident involving Senator Ted Kennedy.

17.22   Pike, Christopher. **The Eternal Enemy.** Pocket Books/Archway Paperbacks, 1993. 180 pp. ISBN 0-671-74509-3. Fiction.

When Rela's new VCR records the evening news, something is a little different—the news Rela sees on the screen is for the *next* day. How can her machine know—and tape—the future? What are the strange dreams Rela keeps having? Can Christopher, Rela's new boyfriend, help? This is an unsettling, complicated time-travel tale with a satisfying twist at the end.

17.23   Pike, Christopher. **Road to Nowhere.** Pocket Books/Archway Paperbacks, 1992. 212 pp. ISBN 0-671-74508-5. Fiction.

Teresa is running away from home: her parents are indifferent to her, and she has just found out that her best friend and her boyfriend are in love. Sad and desperate, Teresa flees in the dark, only to pick up two mysterious hitchhikers in her flight from home. The three are roughly the same age, and to pass the time on the dark highway, they tell stories of people they know. But what is truth? What is fiction? And why does Teresa feel something deeply mysterious is happening to her as she drives into the night?

17.24 Posner, Richard. **Someone to Die For.** Pocket Books/Archway Paperbacks, 1993. 234 pp. ISBN 0-671-74940-4. Fiction.

Susyn is the family's good girl; she is responsible, trustworthy, dependable. Her younger sister, Traci, is just the opposite, and though Susyn loves her sister and feels responsible for her, she is sick of Traci's running away from home. Enter Gary, an attractive stranger on a motorcycle, who seems to bring to Susyn mystery and danger and romance—and a little bit of murder, too.

17.25 Posner, Richard. **Sweet Sixteen and Never Been Killed.** Pocket Books/Archway Paperbacks, 1993. 211 pp. ISBN 0-671-86506-4. Fiction.

Cara, editor of the school paper, is capable, smart, and efficient, three qualities that have not always brought her friends. When Cara plays reporter to provide background for a news story and visits a psychic, there are unexpected, disturbing predictions about her future. Cara's life changes: she meets and falls in love with the mysterious, red-headed Danny, and she is almost killed in a series of accidents, just as predicted. But *who* is trying to kill Cara, and *why* is her death so important? This is a suspenseful, taut, well-written tale.

17.26 Stine, R. L. **Beach House.** Scholastic/Point Books, 1992. 210 pp. ISBN 0-590-45386-6. Fiction.

Set on stilts at the ocean's edge, the beach house is the focus of this time-travel thriller. Two groups of teens, one in the summer of 1956, one in the present day, frolic and romance near and around the empty, mysterious beach house. Separated by the decades, the teens' stories intertwine—as does their danger—because someone, for some reason, is killing them one by one.

17.27 Westall, Robert. **Yaxley's Cat.** Scholastic, 1991. 147 pp. ISBN 0-590-45175-8. Fiction.

Rose is on vacation in England with her bored teenage children, Tim and June, when the three meander into a small village in the country. Walking near the sea, they encounter an intriguing cottage for rent; they change their plans and decide to stay for a week. Old Sipp Yaxley's cottage holds treasure, mysterious books, and a secret: it also holds the threat of murder and danger to the family. Yaxley's cat is one clue in this tightly written, suspenseful novel that ends all too soon. There are some British terms and dialogue, but most readers will catch on quickly.

ALA Best Books for Young Adults, 1993

17.28   Westwood, Chris. **Calling All Monsters.** HarperCollins, 1993. 218 pp. ISBN 0-06-022462-2. Fiction.

Joanne loves to read horror stories, and when she realizes that one of her favorite writers, the masterful Martin Wisemann, lives near her town, she has a perfect subject for her English project. However, Martin Wisemann has stopped publishing, and when Joanne talks with him, he appears haunted by inexplicable fears. Then those fears come to visit Joanne: it seems that the monsters in the pages of Wisemann's books are alive, real, and very deadly.

17.29   Westwood, Chris. **Shock Waves.** Houghton Mifflin/Clarion Books, 1992. 180 pp. ISBN 0-395-63111-4. Fiction.

Leigh is a promising but lonely art student in her first year of college. Through a dating service, Apollo Introductions, she meets and quickly falls in love with Stephen, who seems to be the answer to her dreams. It is just too good to be true—but then Leigh's friends start dying and Stephen's behavior becomes stranger and stranger. Leigh wonders if Stephen is the answer to her prayers, or the beginning of a nightmare.

17.30   Windsor, Patricia. **The Christmas Killer.** Scholastic/Point Books, 1991. 263 pp. ISBN 0-590-43310-5. Fiction.

In this tightly plotted tale that is both sardonic and scary, a dead girl seems to have the ability to predict when the killer will next strike. But who is the killer?

IRA Young Adults' Choices, 1993

17.31   Yolen, Jane, and Martin H. Greenberg, editors. **Vampires: A Collection of Original Stories.** HarperCollins/Harper Trophy Books, 1993. 225 pp. ISBN 0-06-026801-8. Fiction.

This is a comprehensive, entertaining collection of thirteen vampire tales. Especially recommended are the utterly surprising "There's No Such Thing" and the hysterical (yes, some vampire stories can be funny) "Blood-Ghoul of Scarsdale."

ALA Best Books for Young Adults, 1992

18 Human Rights

18.1   Archer, Jules. **They Had a Dream: The Civil Rights Struggle from Frederick Douglass to Marcus Garvey to Martin Luther King and Malcolm X.** Viking, 1993. 258 pp. ISBN 0-670-84494-2. Nonfiction.

In six chapters with subdivisions, historian Jules Archer records the struggle of black people in America. Black Americans will appreciate reading about their strong, rich heritage, while white Americans can gain a better understanding of the plight of African Americans in the confrontations for racial equality. This book traces the struggle from former slave Frederick Douglass to Marcus Garvey, Martin Luther King Jr., and Malcolm X, four remarkable leaders.

18.2   Atkin, S. Beth. **Voices from the Fields: Children of Migrant Farmworkers Tell Their Stories.** Little, Brown/Joy Street Books, 1993. 96 pp. ISBN 0-316-05633-2. Nonfiction.

Migrant workers' children living in the Salinas Valley of California recall stories of their families in difficult, painful, joyful, and sad situations. The experiences are presented in scenes in the field, in the home, in a gang, and with friends and parents. The hardships and hopes of these Mexican Americans are revealed in the children's own voices. Through poetry, first-person interviews, and photographs, the heartwarming revelations demonstrate their pride and strong zeal for a better life.

ALA Best Books for Young Adults, 1994
Booklist Editors' Choice, 1993
Notable 1994 Children's Trade Books in the Field of Social Studies
School Library Journal Best Books, 1993

18.3   Edelman, Marian Wright. **The Measure of Our Success: A Letter to My Children and Yours.** Beacon Press, 1992. 97 pp. ISBN 0-8070-3102-X. Nonfiction.

In a wise and thoughtful response to the crisis of moral conscience in our world, Marian Wright Edelman presents twenty-five short lessons of hope. Each lesson is elaborated through her own personal story. Edelman grew up as an African American woman in racially segregated South Carolina. The strength she received from that upbringing is inspirational, but she does not rest on inspiration. She challenges all of us to serve others as she has done and to be the best that we can be.

ALA Best Books for Young Adults, 1993

18.4 Gaines, Ernest. **A Lesson before Dying.** Alfred A. Knopf, 1993. 256 pp. ISBN 0-679-41477-0. Fiction.

The lesson that local teacher Grant Wiggins is supposed to impart to convicted robber Jefferson is one of dignity. Condemned to death for a murder in which he played an inadvertent part, Jefferson is ready to die in despair, disgrace, and ignorance. At the insistence of Grant's aunt and her best friend, Jefferson's mother, the reluctant teacher visits the condemned man every week before his imminent execution. Jefferson, however, is angry and unresponsive. Can Grant help him learn the most important lesson before dying?

18.5 Haskins, James. **The March on Washington.** HarperCollins, 1993. 144 pp. ISBN 0-06-021290-X. Nonfiction.

James Haskins provides a powerful, moving account of the 1963 March on Washington and the circumstances that led up to that momentous event. With an introduction by James Farmer, author and civil rights activist, this easy-to-read book shares details of actions behind the scenes that would be unknown to most people. Rich in historical fact, the text provides a more intimate view of the people and the preparation involved in this signal event in the African American struggle for equality.

Notable 1994 Children's Trade Books in the Field of Social Studies

18.6 Langone, John. **Spreading Poison: A Book about Racism and Prejudice.** Little, Brown, 1993. 178 pp. ISBN 0-316-51410-1. Nonfiction.

In today's society, prejudice and racism are evident daily: in the media, in our schools, and in our neighborhoods. Few people, however, understand the origin of these attitudes. John Langone discusses in detail the sources of racism and prejudice. He examines the various myths and stereotypes surrounding racial bigotry, religious persecution, and homosexuality, along with historical and social events that fostered them. Langone explores the significant contributions of several ethnic groups and presents a fact-filled argument against the prejudices that plague society. He advocates knowledge and understanding of individual differences and provides clear and easy-to-read information in a straightforward approach.

18.7 Levine, Ellen, editor. **Freedom's Children: Young Civil Rights Activists Tell Their Own Stories.** Avon/Flare Books, 1994. 189 pp. ISBN 0-380-72114-7. Nonfiction.

Ellen Levine records an accurate account of thirty African American voices as they struggle through the Civil Rights movement in the South. As these courageous young people share their stories, they do so in an uplifting way, though their experiences were often humiliating. Their ten-year involvement tells of frustrations, disappointments, triumph, and sense of pride.

Jane Addams Award, 1994
ALA Best Books for Young Adults, 1994
Booklist Editors' Choice, 1993
IRA Children's Book Award, 1994
Notable 1994 Children's Trade Books in the Field of Social Studies
School Library Journal Best Books, 1992

18.8 Lusane, Clarence. **The Struggle for Equal Education.** Franklin Watts, 1992. 144 pp. ISBN 0-531-11121-0. Nonfiction.

Clarence Lusane, an author, activist, and journalist, presents the history of the struggle for equal education in America. He traces the beginning of black education from the pre–Civil War period to Reconstruction through the Civil Rights movement to the present day. He examines a number of initiatives, legal battles, and political reforms relating to education. In-depth coverage is given to the resistance to desegregation in the 1960s and several contemporary affirmative action initiatives.

18.9 Mizell, Linda. **Think about Racism.** Walker, 1992. 230 pp. ISBN 0-8027-8113-6. Nonfiction.

This well-researched text provides historical accounts from early America and the African slave trade through the civil rights protests in the 1970s. Included are biographical profiles of significant individuals during each of the time periods. The chapters of the text, which cover such social issues as Jim Crow laws, slavery laws, and NAACP battles, end with review questions that can be useful in classroom discussions. The author focuses on the past and continued presence of racism in society and defines it in relation to prejudice. This easy-to-read reference provides information in a clear, succinct manner and includes photographs and illustrations.

18.10 Pascoe, Elaine. **South Africa: Troubled Land,** rev. ed. Franklin Watts, 1992. 139 pp. ISBN 0-531-11139-3. Nonfiction.

South Africa is among the wealthiest African countries, rich in minerals and other natural resources. This wealth is enjoyed, however, by a minority of people who control the country politically. As a result, South Africa is a country involved in racial and political turmoil. This thorough and interesting discussion of South African history covers the early history of the country: apartheid, resistance movements, leadership, and its complex economic, social, and educational system. Also included in the book are a historical time line and photographs.

18.11 Pohl, Constance, and Kathy Harris. **Transracial Adoption: Children and Parents Speak.** Franklin Watts, 1992. 137 pp. ISBN 0-531-11134-2. Nonfiction.

Should white parents be allowed to adopt a child of African American heritage? Or should any person of one race be allowed to raise a child of another race? Do the children of such adoptions lose their cultural identity? This book takes a candid look at racially mixed families. Through interviews with family members, a realistic picture is painted of the rewards and the heartbreaks of these adoptions, providing some answers to tough questions.

18.12 Powledge, Fred. **We Shall Overcome: Heroes of the Civil Rights Movement.** Charles Scribner's Sons, 1993. 201 pp. ISBN 0-684-19362-0. Nonfiction.

This exceptional coverage of the Civil Rights movement of the 1960s is documented in an interesting, simplified format designed for young readers. Thoroughly explained are the attitudes of the period, events such as the boycotts, marches, and legal battles, and the effects of the movement on American society. Terms are defined within the context of each chapter, a time line and photographs are provided, and coverage includes stories from activists of the period.

18.13 Senna, Carl. **The Black Press and the Struggle for Civil Rights.** Franklin Watts, 1993. 160 pp. ISBN 0-531-11036-2. Nonfiction.

Carl Senna reveals the significant role of the black press. In sixteen chapters, he carefully explains the varying styles that journalists use and the stories they pursue. The main purposes of the first black newspaper were to report aspects of the black experience and to abolish slavery. This book also documents the varied contributions that African American journalists make today.

18.14 Siegel, Beatrice. **Murder on the Highway: The Viola Liuzzo Story.** Four Winds Press, 1993. 125 pp. ISBN 0-02-782632-5. Nonfiction.

Is the United States "One nation, under God ... with liberty and justice for all"? Beatrice Siegel's account of Viola Liuzzo's tragic murder pierces the heart as the reader traces Liuzzo's life and her call to fight for civil rights in the 1960s. Members of the Ku Klux Klan gunned Liuzzo down as she gave support to the march from Selma, Alabama, to Montgomery. Because justice was not for all, Liuzzo was moved to act, which cost her her life.

18.15   Silver, Norman. **Python Dance.** E. P. Dutton, 1992. 230 pp. ISBN 0-525-45161-7. Fiction.

Set in Johannesburg, South Africa, this novel deals with Ruth's painful initiation into the world of adults—a world filled with prejudices, conflicts, and tough decisions about sex and relationships. Intrigued by the Python Dance, the Venda tribe's guided ritual initiation for girls, sixteen-year-old Ruth goes through a python dance of her own to reach maturity. She is forced to face the injustices and prejudices that surround her and to accept the part her own prejudices played in the death of her mother.

18.16   Taylor, Mildred D. **Mississippi Bridge.** Illustrated by Max Ginsburg. Bantam/Skylark Books, 1992. 62 pp. ISBN 0-553-15992-5. Fiction.

The authentic events of this poignant story are narrated by ten-year-old Jeremy Sims, a white boy who lives in Mississippi in the 1930s. Jeremy is at the general store when the weekly bus to Jackson arrives. Several black passengers are waiting to ride the bus, including the grandmother of Stacey Logan, his neighbor. Throughout the day, Jeremy has witnessed many segregation practices that have puzzled and sometimes embarrassed him. When several white passengers arrive late, the black passengers, who have been waiting all day, are forced to give up their seats. In a twist of fate, a tragic accident takes place, and the bus never makes it to Jackson.

Notable 1990 Children's Trade Books in the Field of Social Studies

18.17   Terkel, Susan Neiburg. **Ethics.** Dutton/Lodestar Books, 1992. 134 pp. ISBN 0-525-67371-7. Nonfiction.

Susan Neiburg Terkel provides a well-balanced view of ethics and morals in society and discusses the various historical influences, such as religion and tradition, that guide our Western approach to making ethical decisions. *Ethics* is an easy-to-read source of factual information when looking for accounts of moral issues in the court system, including school prayer, abortion, and other issues.

Terkel provides many examples of situations that today's youth might encounter. A sense of right and wrong brings about a fair resolution and helps individuals make the right decision.

18.18 Williams, Michael. **Crocodile Burning.** Dutton/Lodestar Books, 1992. 198 pp. ISBN 0-525-67401-2. Fiction.

Seraki Mandindi is a high school student growing up in Soweto, South Africa. Through him we learn how unrest in the 1980s affects his community and family. Seraki's brother has been imprisoned, there is strife among his mother, father, and uncle, and there are gangs controlling the streets. In the midst of this, Seraki gets a part in a South African play that depicts the injustices suffered by South Africans and that calls for a deliverance from the old ways that hinder them. To Seraki's surprise, the play is taken to Broadway. Even though he leaves South Africa for New York, Seraki does not escape many of the old practices that faced him in his homeland. The novel contains historically correct incidents that add to the realism of the plot. It is rich in symbolism and the vernacular of South Africa.

ALA Best Books for Young Adults, 1993
Notable 1992 Children's Trade Books in the Field of Social Studies

19 Humor and Satire

19.1   Barreca, Regina. **They Used to Call Me Snow White . . . But I Drifted: Women's Strategic Use of Humor.** Penguin, 1991. 223 pp. ISBN 0-14-016835-4. Nonfiction.

Making a fairly thorough examination of and comparison between male and female humor, Regina Barreca probes the reasons why some comedians' jokes provoke laughter from audiences and others do not. Further, she offers suggestions to women about how to respond to comments that hint at both overt and covert sexual harassment. The sometimes frank, "earthy" language of this book makes it more suitable for mature readers.

19.2   Bauer, Joan. **Squashed.** Delacorte Press, 1992. 194 pp. ISBN 0-385-30793-1. Fiction.

Abounding in humor, this novel captures a young girl's ability to recognize her own flaws while setting no limitations on the possibilities for achieving what often seems to be against all odds. Ellie, about twenty pounds overweight, has two goals: to shed pounds in order to attract Wes, a newcomer in town, and to grow a giant pumpkin to dethrone the pompous Cyril Pool, who has always captured the top prize for his pumpkins at the Rock River Pumpkin Weigh-In. With Wes's help, Ellie is able to accomplish at least one of her goals despite numerous obstacles (including the weather and pumpkin thieves) and to discover that people are not always judged by outward appearances.

ALA Quick Picks for Young Adults, 1993
School Library Journal Best Books, 1992

19.3   Breathed, Berkeley. **Politically, Fashionably, and Aerodynamically Incorrect: The First Outland Collection.** Little, Brown, 1992. 120 pp. ISBN 0-316-10701-8. Nonfiction.

This book gathers the Outland cartoons of Berkeley Breathed into a compilation that ranges from his earliest drawings to his more mature creations. Unlike his continuing strip Bloom County, each Outland cartoon segment is complete unto itself and offers satirical commentary on a variety of ordinary aspects of society. Because of the maturity of its themes, the cartoon segments would probably best be appreciated by older readers.

19.4   Brooks, Charles, editor. **Best Editorial Cartoons of the Year: 1992 Edition.** Pelican Books, 1992. 172 pp. ISBN 0-88289-910-4. Nonfiction.

The bold caricatures and the brief explanations preceding each section of cartoons help readers understand the current problems facing this country and the world. The collection includes almost every aspect of life that touched the American people in 1991—from homelessness to hunger, from economics to politics, from education to environment, from war to peace initiatives, plus much, much more. Charles Brooks's presentation of these editorial cartoons could be a boon to high school students' knowledge of the world in which they live.

19.5   Dahl, Roald. **The Vicar of Nibbleswicke.** Illustrated by Quentin Blake. Viking, 1991. 22 pp. ISBN 0-670-84384-9. Fiction.

Delightfully witty, this brief narrative packs a big punch as it tackles the serious problem of dyslexia, or reading disabilities. In the story, the vicar seems doomed forever after a long bout with dyslexic blunders before his congregation; however, he eventually finds the help he needs. Roald Dahl's simple and humorous approach to the subject makes this an appealing story, while readers also become aware of dyslexia in our society and the assistance that is available. Quentin Blake's humorous illustrations further attract the reader to this tale of a disorder that has hindered so many.

19.6   Koertge, Ron. **The Harmony Arms.** Little, Brown/Joy Street Books, 1992. 177 pp. ISBN 0-316-50104-2. Fiction.

Despite wanting to remain in Bradleyville with his mother and his friends, young Gabriel agrees to go to California when his father lands a month-long job with a movie studio. His father writes and illustrates children's books; now, after many years of trying, he has a chance to prove his worth. Initially, fourteen-year-old Gabriel is embarrassed by his father's work, but with the help of a new friend, he gradually begins to see his life, and his father, in a different light.

ALA Best Books for Young Adults, 1993
ALA Notable Books for Children, 1993
School Library Journal Best Books, 1992

19.7   Lodge, David. **Paradise News.** Viking, 1992. 293 pp. ISBN 0-670-84228-1. Fiction.

Moving from a quiet, rather obscure life into a world that borders on paradise, an Englishman finds himself reveling in newfound pleasure. Bernard, who began his trip to Hawaii out of a sense of obligation, learns that he can do and be anything that he wants, a discovery that comes to him later in life than it does to most. Nonetheless, this revelation opens up a wide range of possibilities for Bernard—a chance to really live life in all its aspects and possibly even to love in a way that his old life in England did not afford him.

19.8   Peck, Richard. **Bel-Air Bambi and the Mall Rats.** Delacorte Press, 1993. 181 pp. ISBN 0-385-30823-X. Fiction.

When Mr. Babcock's poor financial planning causes his family to lose everything, the Babcocks are forced to give up their fashionable Bel-Air home and luxurious life. They set off with little money and no possessions and end up in the father's hometown of Hickory Fork, where they are forced to live with Mr. Babcock's mother. Life takes a drastic turn immediately as they find that life in this small town is far from peaceful and simple. Using their show business background, the Babcocks try to turn the citizens around and restore the simplicity of small-town life for everyone.

School Library Journal Best Books, 1993

19.9   Reidelbach, Maria. **Completely Mad: A History of the Comic Book and Magazine.** Little, Brown, 1993. 208 pp. ISBN 0-316-73890-5. Nonfiction.

This pictorial account of the history of the comic book and comic strip predecessors of *Mad* magazine, including criticisms and humorous accounts, traces Max Gaines's creation of the dime comic book in the 1930s to the evolution of *Mad* magazine. Simple humor, sophisticated wit, and subtle satire have all found a place in the magazine, always with the intent of being unobtrusive to the public. The author not only presents the favorable comments that have been made about *Mad*, but also relates stories of outraged and disgruntled readers. *Completely Mad* includes illustrations of political and social concerns of the country à la Alfred E. Neuman and also contains an appendix.

ALA Best Books for Young Adults, 1993

19.10   Wood, A. J. **Errata: A Book of Historical Errors.** Illustrated by Hemesh Alles. Simon and Schuster/Green Tiger Press, 1992. 32 pp. ISBN 0-671-77569-3. Nonfiction.

Would an Inca warrior have ridden a camel? Would a Viking have listened to the radio? Readers of this book need to recall their knowledge of history. Twelve bold, colorful illustrations depict scenes from cultures as diverse as Aztec to Zulu and from places as distant as Australia to the Arctic. Each picture contains ten objects erroneously tucked away. The trick is to find the items that do not belong to each civilization. Answers are provided at the back of the book, as is additional information about the twelve civilizations.

19.11   Zindel, Paul. **The Pigman and Me.** HarperCollins/Charlotte Zolotow Books, 1992. 168 pp. ISBN 0-06-020858-9. Nonfiction.

Future writer Paul Zindel, his sister, Betty, and their mom move into a home of their own on Staten Island with another single mother and her twin sons. The house comes with cockroaches, a cemetery next door, and an airport behind it, but each family gets a floor of the house and half of the backyard. Paul meets Nonno Frankie Vivona, who becomes his mentor, or pigman, and helps him discover the secret of life. Paul remembers a significant year in his teenage life when he becomes best friends with Jennifer Wolupopski, gets into a fight with John Quinn, and recounts other experiences during his year in Travis, New York.

ALA Best Books for Young Adults, 1993
ALA Notable Books for Children, 1993
Notable 1992 Children's Trade Books in the Field of Social Studies
School Library Journal Best Books, 1992

20 Inspiration and Religion

20.1   Barrett, Timothy Hugh (introduction by). **Tao: To Know and Not Be Knowing.** Chronicle/Labyrinth Books, 1993. 57 pp. ISBN 0-8118-0420-8. Nonfiction.

A beautifully illustrated book, *Tao: To Know and Not Be Knowing* directs one toward the Taoist way of thinking. It comments on the single comprehensive symbol, the legend, natural law, and living in harmony with nature. The text clearly explains the underlying principles of this Eastern philosophy. Other titles in the Eastern Wisdom series are *Sufism* and *Zen.*

20.2   Barrett, Timothy Hugh (introduction by). **Zen: The Reason of Unreason.** Chronicle/Labyrinth Books, 1993. 57 pp. ISBN 0-8118-0403-8. Nonfiction.

Zen: The Reason of Unreason, a colorful, pictorial production, establishes the seriousness of concentration or meditation. This book begins with an explanation of the origin of Zen doctrine and continues to the perception of reality and self. In addition, teachings of essential qualities of Bodhidharma, Shakyamuni, and Mahakashyapa enlighten the reader. Through representative haikus, dialogues, stories, and koans, the Zen experience is explained. This volume is one of three in the Eastern Wisdom series.

20.3   Eisler, Colin, editor. **David's Songs: His Psalms and Their Story.** Illustrated by Jerry Pinkney. Dial Books, 1992. 58 pp. ISBN 0-8037-1059-3. Nonfiction.

Do you want to know the thoughts of the Biblical hero David at various stages of his life? Colin Eisler records forty-six of David's psalms, and Jerry Pinkney, an award-winning artist, illustrates the book in full-color paintings. Key ideas of David's life as a shepherd boy, a bandit, a Hebrew king, and a lonely, bitter man are shared at the beginning of the book. Each psalm is preceded by an explanation of David's view of his life.

20.4   Goleman, Daniel, Paul Kaufman, and Michael Ray. **The Creative Spirit.** Penguin/Plume Books, 1993. 185 pp. ISBN 0-452-26879-6. Nonfiction.

This examination of the stages of the creative process explores the wisdom of one's inner spirit. It is a thorough study, citing firsthand experiences that take one from place to place and that involve various actions. The book promises that beauty is everywhere; one just has to find it.

20.5   Schaeffer, Frank. **Portofino.** Macmillan, 1992. 248 pp. ISBN 0-02-607051-0. Fiction.

Growing up is not easy when you are the son of fundamentalist missionaries. Calvin is often embarrassed by his parents as they vacation on the Mediterranean because they openly pray for, criticize, or attempt to lead others to Christ, no matter where they happen to be. The reader experiences Calvin's journey to adulthood as he struggles to find his identity, falls in love, and begins to define his set of morals. He learns to accept people as they are—especially his parents.

Booklist Editors' Choice Award, 1992

20.6   Thomas, Joyce Carol. **When the Nightingale Sings.** HarperCollins, 1992. 148 pp. ISBN 0-06-020295-5. Fiction.

Marigold, an orphan girl who was born in a southern swamp, wonders why she is constantly mistreated. Living with a mean woman and her twin daughters, Marigold has to clean the house, take care of Arlita and Carita, and respond to all of Ruby's whims. The ever-present song in strong-willed Marigold's heart changes her life, and she eventually finds her family and her place.

20.7   Waley, M. I. (introduction by). **Sufism: The Alchemy of the Heart.** Chronicle/Labyrinth Books, 1993. 57 pp. ISBN 0-8118-0410-0. Nonfiction.

Text and striking illustrations recount and depict the principles and features of the Eastern philosophy of Sufism. One of three volumes in the Eastern Wisdom series, the book presents the history and development of Sufism and identifies its attributes and essential elements. Developing a pure heart and ultimately absorbing spiritual music are also presented to the reader.

20.8   Wilson, Terry P. (introduction by). **Hopi: Following the Path of Peace.** Chronicle/Labyrinth Books, 1994. 57 pp. ISBN 0-8118-0430-5. Nonfiction.

Part of the Native American Wisdom series, *Hopi* is an account of this Indian tribe of the Southwest, their philosophy, and their wisdom, from the creation of the Four Worlds to the annual Hopi ceremonial cycle, which is timed to correspond with the change of seasons and with the harvest of crops. This colorful book presents a description of Hopi principles, rituals, ceremonies, teachings, and life journey, as these Native Americans aim to live in harmony with each other and with nature.

20.9   Wilson, Terry P. (introduction by). **Lakota: Seeking the Great Spirit.** Chronicle/Labyrinth Books, 1994. 57 pp. ISBN 0-8118-0450-X. Nonfiction.

In a small, picture-filled volume in the Native American Wisdom series, the life of the Lakota, also called the Sioux, and their wisdom, rites, and rituals are described. The three main subgroups of these Plains Indians are the Eastern or Santee group, the Central group, and the Western or Teton group. Their interaction with the environment is shown as their main source of wisdom and the basis for seeking Wakan-Tanka, the Great Spirit. The book also explains the legend of the White Buffalo Woman and the seven sacred rites of the Lakota.

20.10   Wilson, Terry P. (introduction by). **Navajo: Walking in Beauty.** Chronicle/Labyrinth Books, 1994. 57 pp. ISBN 0-8118-0442-9. Nonfiction.

The Navajo tribe is an Indian nation that has adapted over and over again, causing its members to endure through their troubles. Their enchanted land, their unique emergence, and their healing ceremonies have led to their ability to walk in beauty. Each time this tribal group meets to sing and chant, the members are renewed. The Navajo life, wisdom, and rituals are described in this volume in the Native American Wisdom series.

21 Language and Literature

21.1 Ammer, Christine. **Seeing Red or Tickled Pink: Color Terms in Everyday Language.** E. P. Dutton, 1992. 215 pp. ISBN 0-525-93462-6. Nonfiction.

What's your favorite color? Orange for *Agent Orange, A Clockwork Orange,* or the *Orangemen*? Pink for a *pink slip* or a *rosy future*? What about *deep purple*? Have you ever been caught *red-handed*? What's a *white elephant*? This book gives the origins of these and nearly 850 other colorful terms. Remember the yellow ribbons on homes honoring the soldiers in the Gulf War? This book proposes a few origins, including a 1973 song. Another suggestion traces the origin back to the Civil War, when Union soldiers would leave yellow kerchiefs for their sweethearts as a remembrance.

21.2 Freeman, Morton S. **Hue and Cry and Humble Pie: The Stories behind the Words.** Penguin/Plume Books, 1993. 292 pp. ISBN 0-452-26924-5. Nonfiction.

In this book you can learn the fascinating origins of terms. What's a brand-new *bikini*? How might a *bikini* be fresh from the fire, as in glowing metal, newly fired? Perhaps the fire is from the 1947 atomic tests in the Marshall Islands? Or might the effect of a brand-new *bikini* be that of an atomic blast? To learn more about the origins of such words as *bikini, gringo, gossip,* or even *book,* read this one.

21.3 Grambs, David. **Did I Say Something Wrong?** Illustrated by Mary Kornblum. Penguin/Plume Books, 1993. 244 pp. ISBN 0-452-26831-1. Nonfiction.

This book tells about terms that sound taboo but are completely acceptable. Its twenty-six chapters with glossaries and intermittent quizzes point out the remarkable number of double entendres, or words with a double meaning, in our English language. Covering different fields, each chapter is an essay using the specialized vocabularies and jargon. Even a *spermophobe* (one who fears germs) can enjoy this clean book.

21.4 Killens, John Oliver, and Jerry W. Ward Jr., editors. **Black Southern Voices: An Anthology of Fiction, Poetry, Drama, Nonfiction,**

and Critical Essays. Penguin/Meridian Books, 1992. 608 pp. ISBN 0-452-01096-9.

When many persons think of the southern literary tradition, they think first of William Faulkner, Eudora Welty, Flannery O'Connor, Tennessee Williams, and other white writers. There are, however, other southern writers equally distinct, vibrant, and authentic—the black southern voices. This collection of works by twentieth-century black writers includes both established authors, such as Richard Wright, John Killens, Maya Angelou, and Alice Childress, and many emerging writers. The selections cover a broad spectrum, but the central theme throughout is the struggle for freedom, equality, and humaneness. This volume provides readers with a clearer vision of the total southern literary tradition.

21.5   Kohl, Herbert, Erica Kohl, Dee Garner, Antonia Kohl, Joshua Kohl, and Megan Marsnik. **From Archetype to Zeitgeist: Powerful Ideas for Powerful Thinking.** Illustrated by Deborah Hohenberg, Madeline Kibbe, Antonia Kohl, Joshua Kohl, Haruko Nishimura, and William Zindel. Little, Brown, 1992. 246 pp. ISBN 0-316-50138-7. Nonfiction.

Recognizing the need for students to have the appropriate vocabulary to express their complex ideas, Herbert Kohl and others have written a collection of short essays defining such words as *subliminal*, *aesthetics*, and *irony*. The explanations help put ideas into words and define difficult concepts. Because the language of ideas is often connected by topic, the book is structured by the following chapters: the arts, literature, religion, philosophy, logic and reasoning, critical thinking, anthropology and linguistics, sociology, psychology, economics, and political science.

21.6   Pearson, Michael. **Imagined Places: Journeys into Literary America.** Photographs by John Lawrence and Joel Mednik. University Press of Mississippi, 1991. 323 pp. ISBN 0-87805-526-6. Nonfiction.

The title of this book is only partially accurate in that Michael Pearson travels to six locales that are real enough: the regions most closely associated with writers Robert Frost, William Faulkner, Flannery O'Connor, Ernest Hemingway, John Steinbeck, and Mark Twain. Twain's Hannibal today is not that much like the St. Joe of the novels, but the other places—despite some unavoidable changes and occasional commercialization—strongly remind Pearson (and us) of the places we have come to know through the works of their most famous residents; and the people Pearson finds along the way bear strong resemblances to the characters that each writer made familiar to his or her readers. Overall, this literary odyssey shows us how real are the worlds of our most powerful literature and how firmly grounded in truth and observation is our best regional literature. A strong secondary theme is that America's classic literature is regional, yet universal.

21.7 Ryan, Elizabeth A. **How to Be a Better Writer.** Troll Associates, 1992. 95 pp. ISBN 0-8167-2462-8. Nonfiction.

This brief book in the Troll Survival series covers report and essay writing in a helpful manner. Student writers are taken through the steps in the writing process with many examples and helpful questions used to prompt and guide. The material is presented in a clear and nonthreatening style, and students can follow the ideas on their own. The book includes ideas on writing openers, transitions, and closings. The chapters on "Creative Writing" and "News Writing" are short overviews.

21.8 Ryan, Elizabeth A. **How to Build a Better Vocabulary.** Troll Associates, 1992. 111 pp. ISBN 0-8167-2460-1. Nonfiction.

Another in the Troll Survival series, this handbook begins with some self-assessment tests. After a brief chapter on aids to building a better vocabulary (such as mnemonic devices and different kinds of dictionaries), more extensive chapters cover prefixes, roots, synonyms and antonyms, word histories, and foreign words. The book concludes with short chapters on "Words Often Confused," a pronunciation guide, and spelling hints.

21.9 Ryan, Elizabeth A. **How to Make Grammar Fun—(and Easy!).** Troll Associates, 1992. 111 pp. ISBN 0-8167-2456-3. Nonfiction.

This brief book in the Troll Survival series is patterned after other grammar handbooks or reference manuals. The chapters cover the parts of speech and the parts of a sentence, a few common problems (such as when to use *who/which/that* and *them/these/those*), tricky verbs, "words that are often confused," punctuation, and capitalization.

21.10 Ryan, Steve. **Test Your Word Play IQ.** Sterling, 1993. 96 pp. ISBN 0-8069-0412-7. Nonfiction.

The wordsmith will love this collection of assorted word puzzles. With names like *Bamboozle, Word World,* and *Divide and Conjure,* who can resist? Rated on levels of difficulty from one to three pencils, these puzzles require reason and logic. A word to the daring—although all the words exist in the English language, you might not find them in the dictionary. Solutions are provided.

21.11   Schloff, Laurie, and Marcia Yudkin. **Smart Speaking: Sixty-Second Strategies for More Than 100 Speaking Problems and Fears.** Penguin/Plume Books, 1992. 238 pp. ISBN 0-452-26777-3. Nonfiction.

Do various speaking situations make you nervous? These sixty-second pointers cover "Conversational Blocks," "Telephone Hang Ups," and "Nerves." Quick tips on doing formal presentations, leading meetings, or meeting new people are covered as well, plus other strategies that will help in social, school, and work situations. Each of the more than 100 problem situations is brief, and the strategies give specific steps to improvement.

22 Multicultural Themes

22.1 Alvarez, Julia. **How the García Girls Lost Their Accents.** Penguin/Plume Books, 1992. 290 pp. ISBN 0-452-26806-0. Fiction.

Four sisters from the Dominican Republic move with their parents to New York City in the 1960s and find their new life a struggle. For Carla, Sandra, Yolanda, and Sofia, the questions about their new life in America—and the solutions—are all different. When they visit home, they are no longer Dominican; when they return to America, they feel alien. Yet the García girls prevail in this warm and wise story of two cultures colliding.

22.2 Andrews, William L., editor. **The African-American Novel in the Age of Reaction: Three Classics.** Penguin/Mentor Books, 1992. 587 pp. ISBN 0-451-62849-7. Fiction.

These three classics are protest novels against the South's doctrine of "separate but equal," which governed race relations following the Civil War. *Iola Leroy,* by Frances E. W. Harper, is the story of a light-skinned young woman who discovers at the death of her southern planter father that her mother was a former slave. Charles W. Chesnutt's *The Marrow of Tradition* portrays the devastating effects of white supremacist politics on a small southern town. *The Sport of the Gods* by Paul Lawrence Dunbar tells the grim story of a southern black mother, son, and daughter who migrate to New York City to escape disgrace when the father of the family is falsely charged with robbery and sent to the state penitentiary. The themes of these novels are still timely today.

22.3 Archer, Chalmers, Jr. **Growing Up Black in Rural Mississippi: Memories of a Family, Heritage of a Place.** Walker, 1992. 147 pp. ISBN 0-8027-1175-8. Nonfiction.

Chalmers Archer Jr. shares with the reader his life as an African American child growing up in the Deep South during the 1940s and 1950s. Although he mentions some of the discrimination his family faced, he does not dwell upon it. Instead, he focuses on his close-knit family and the rich heritage passed on to him. The book is filled with family history, legends, and descriptions of a lifestyle that has all but disappeared.

22.4 Archer, Jules. **They Had a Dream: The Civil Rights Struggle from Frederick Douglass to Marcus Garvey to Martin Luther King**

and Malcolm X. Viking, 1993. 258 pp. ISBN 0-670-84494-2. Nonfiction.

In six chapters with subdivisions, historian Jules Archer records the struggle of black people in America. Black Americans will appreciate reading about their strong, rich heritage, while white Americans can gain a better understanding of the plight of African Americans in the confrontations for racial equality. This book traces the struggle from former slave Frederick Douglass to Marcus Garvey, Martin Luther King Jr., and Malcolm X, four remarkable leaders.

22.5   Armstrong, Jennifer. **Steal Away.** Orchard Books, 1992. 207 pp. ISBN 0-531-08583-X. Fiction.

It is 1896, and thirteen-year-old Mary finds herself on a surprising journey with her grandmother: a train trip to Canada to visit a sick friend. Mary's comfortable convictions are challenged as she learns that the woman they are going to visit, Bethlehem, is a former slave. Gran and Bethlehem recount their escape together to freedom some forty years previously. Bethlehem's adopted daughter, Free, helps Mary record the event, and in the process the story becomes Mary's and Free's story as well.

ALA Best Books for Young Adults, 1993
ALA Notable Books for Children, 1993
IRA Teachers' Choices, 1993

22.6   Atkin, S. Beth. **Voices from the Fields: Children of Migrant Farmworkers Tell Their Stories.** Little, Brown/Joy Street Books, 1993. 96 pp. ISBN 0-316-05633-2. Nonfiction.

Migrant workers' children living in the Salinas Valley of California recall stories of their families in difficult, painful, joyful, and sad situations. The experiences are presented in scenes in the field, in the home, in a gang, and with friends and parents. The hardships and hopes of these Mexican Americans are revealed in the children's own voices. Through poetry, first-person interviews, and photographs, the heartwarming revelations demonstrate their pride and strong zeal for a better life.

ALA Best Books for Young Adults, 1994
Booklist Editors' Choice, 1993
Notable 1994 Children's Trade Books in the Field of Social Studies
School Library Journal Best Books, 1993

22.7   Ayer, Eleanor H. **The Anasazi.** Walker, 1993. 124 pp. ISBN 0-8027-8184-5. Nonfiction.

Abandoned pueblos in the area generally including the Four Corners, where Arizona, Utah, Colorado, and New Mexico come together, reveal part of the history of the cliff dwellers—the Anasazi. This ancient civilization originated in Asia about 14,000 years ago; their descendants resided in the American Southwest between the years 100 and 1300. The Anasazi then vanished but gave rise to various Pueblo Indian tribes, including the Hopi and the Zuni. In text, illustrations, and photographs, Eleanor H. Ayer describes how the Anasazi changed from nomads to farmers and details their contributions as basket weavers, the ingenuity of their dwellings on cliffs, and their underground pit houses or kivas.

22.8   Banks, Lynne Reid. **One More River,** rev. ed. Morrow Junior Books, 1992. 243 pp. ISBN 0-688-10893-8. Fiction.

Lesley is an intelligent, wealthy, pretty, and popular Jewish girl living a comfortable life in Canada. But after an extravagant party celebrating her fourteenth birthday, her life takes some dramatic turns. It all starts when Lesley's father tells her the family is moving to Israel, a country at war with its Arab neighbors. Lesley at first refuses to go, but she has no choice. Relations with her parents become strained when she has to leave her friends and home, learn a new and difficult language, adjust to living in a kibbutz with other Israeli teenagers, and survive the Six-Day War of 1967. First published in 1973.

22.9   Beatty, Patricia. **Lupita Mañana.** William Morrow/Beech Tree Books, 1992. 190 pp. ISBN 0-688-11497-0. Fiction.

Lupita's nickname is "Mañana" because she always thinks life will be better *tomorrow.* After their father dies in a fishing accident, Lupita's brother mocks her optimism when their family must take desperate steps to survive. The only way to get money is for Lupita and her brother to leave Mexico and work in the United States. Sneaking across the border, however, is dangerous and difficult, and they risk imprisonment or death in trying.

22.10 Berry, James. **Ajeemah and His Son.** HarperCollins/Willa Perlman Books, 1992. 83 pp. ISBN 0-06-021044-3. Fiction.

In this story set in the early 1800s, Ajeemah, a native of Ghana, and his eighteen-year-old son, Atu, are abducted by fellow Africans as they walk to a neighboring village with a dowry for Atu's bride-to-be. They soon find themselves on a slave ship bound for Jamaica. Sold to different sugar plantations and separated forever, one finds freedom in death, the other in life.

22.11   Berry, James. **The Future-Telling Lady, and Other Stories.** HarperCollins, 1993. 139 pp. ISBN 0-06-021435-X. Fiction.

Born and raised in Jamaica, James Berry has chosen that setting for the seven stories in this collection. Ghosts, magic, and the future-telling lady, subjects prominent in the culture of the West Indies, serve as excellent vehicles for Berry to explore such concerns as lying, stealing, and sibling rivalry. Of particular interest is the title story, "The Future-Telling Lady," which focuses on parent-child relationships and efforts made to improve those relationships. First published in Great Britain, 1991.

22.12   Bezine, Ching Yun. **On Wings of Destiny.** Penguin/Signet Books, 1992. 396 pp. ISBN 0-451-17320-1. Fiction.

Qing, Sumiko, and Te fight their individual struggles, growing up in oppression and fear. Qing's wealthy family loses its power and possessions when the Communists take over China in the late 1940s; her parents and her brother Te leave her behind when they flee to Taiwan. There Te learns painfully that the Nationalist Chinese and the Taiwanese hate and fight each other. In Hawaii, Sumiko opposes her mother's desire for her to marry into wealth and success. The three end up in America struggling to achieve their dreams together. Mature language and situations.

22.13   Buss, Fran Leeper (with Daisy Cubias). **Journey of the Sparrows.** Dutton/Lodestar Books, 1991. 155 pp. ISBN 0-525-67362-8. Fiction.

Nailed into a crate and loaded into the back of a truck, Maria, her younger brother, and her pregnant sister make their escape to the United States. Even in Chicago they still must be "invisible," or the immigration officials will return them to their brutal existence in El Salvador. Maria is the best hope for her family. Her father and brother-in-law were murdered, and she must help her mother and baby sister make an escape soon from their hiding place in Mexico.

22.14 Campbell, Bebe Moore. **Your Blues Ain't like Mine.** Ballantine Books, 1993. 332 pp. ISBN 0-345-38395-8. Fiction.

Written for a mature audience, this novel contains graphic descriptions of sensitive situations and explicit sexual references. Based loosely on a historic case from the 1950s, the novel tells the story of the Deep South, its social injustices, and its codes of behavior. One of the characters, Armstrong Todd, a fifteen-year-old Chicago-born black, does not fully understand these codes. It is his murder that opens the story and allows the reader to learn about the black and white families of the Delta region of Mississippi. A best-seller, Bebe Moore Campbell's novel spans the years from 1955 to 1988 and shows how one act of racist violence destroys the lives of several black and white families for three generations.

22.15 Campbell, Eric. **The Year of the Leopard Song.** Harcourt Brace Jovanovich, 1992. 160 pp. ISBN 0-15-299806-3. Fiction.

When Alan returns to his Tanzanian home after a year of schooling in England, he senses tension in the air. His good friend, Kimathi, disappears, the native workers on his father's coffee plantation leave the fields, and a bloody message is scrawled on the barn wall. A strange feeling drives Alan to search for his friend on the slopes of Mt. Kilimanjaro, where Kimathi has gone to fulfill a tribal ritual. The two boys are drawn to an encounter that changes their lives forever.

22.16 Cannon, A. E. **The Shadow Brothers.** Dell/Laurel-Leaf Library, 1992. 179 pp. ISBN 0-440-21167-0. Fiction.

When Marcus Jenkins and his foster brother and running teammate, Henry, turn sixteen, they confront both the bonds and conflicts of brotherhood. Henry demonstrates his Navajo heritage and turns toward a world to which Marcus will never belong. Marcus is forced to discover his own strengths and passions, which include his feelings for Henry's former girlfriend, Celia. This story blends the traditional elements of a coming-of-age novel with realistic situations about prejudice, self-acceptance, and winning the race.

22.17   Carter, Steven R. **Hansberry's Drama: Commitment and Complexity.** Penguin/Meridian Books, 1993. 199 pp. ISBN 0-452-01105-1. Nonfiction.

After giving a brief overview of the life, writings, and literary style of African American dramatist Lorraine Hansberry, author Steven R. Carter provides an in-depth analysis of five of her most famous plays. He also looks at two of her works (one complete, one not) as well as the influence of the theater of the absurd. Although Hansberry died at age thirty-four, she left a rich literary legacy, as clearly defined in each of these essays. For further reference and study, Carter includes an extensive list of works cited at the end of each chapter.

American Book Award, 1992

22.18   Choi, Sook Nyul. **Echoes of the White Giraffe.** Houghton Mifflin, 1993. 137 pp. ISBN 0-395-64721-5. Fiction.

Sookan, her mother, and her younger brother flee south from Seoul to Pusan, in American-occupied Korea. They end up living in a paper shack on the mountain along with many other refugee families. The war with Japan is over, but now civil war has erupted in Korea. During this period of her life, without her father and three older brothers, Sookan works hard to keep her goal of going to an American university. Sequel to *Year of Impossible Goodbyes.*

22.19   Colchie, Thomas, editor. **A Hammock beneath the Mangoes: Stories from Latin America.** Penguin/Plume Books, 1992. 430 pp. ISBN 0-452-26866-4. Fiction.

The twenty-six stories included in this collection provide an excellent introduction to the works of Hispanic writers such as Gabriel García Márquez, Carlos Fuentes, Isabel Allende, and Jorge Amado. Although set in Latin America, the stories transcend geographical boundaries because of the universal truths the authors address. Some stories are amusing, while others like "The Doll Queen" and "Love" are haunting and thought provoking.

22.20   Cooper, Michael L. **Playing America's Game: The Story of Negro League Baseball.** Dutton/Lodestar Books, 1993. 96 pp. ISBN 0-525-67407-1. Nonfiction.

With verve and clarity, Michael Cooper tells the exciting story of the Negro baseball league. Because racism kept blacks out of the major leagues for nearly half a century, Negroes played a separate version of America's favorite pastime. Nevertheless, the Negro leagues lifted the spirits of countless black people throughout segregated America and gave them hope. Here is the informative, inspiring story of such exceptional athletes as Andrew "Rube" Foster, John Henry Lloyd, and James "Cool Papa" Bell. It details the hardships they faced as well as the accomplishments they achieved. When Jackie Robinson and other great athletes broke into the major leagues in the late 1940s, the Negro leagues collapsed, but their place in history will be remembered and admired.

22.21   Cox, Clinton. **The Forgotten Heroes: The Story of the Buffalo Soldiers.** Scholastic, 1993. 180 pp. ISBN 0-590-45121-9. Nonfiction.

Even though the Civil War ended slavery in the United States, acceptance of and opportunities for black people were limited. Thus many headed west, including the thousands who joined the calvary and became known as Buffalo Soldiers. It is ironic that those who had recently won freedom contributed to restricting the freedom of Native Americans; in the process, they helped to open land for white settlement but to close it to African Americans and Native Americans. This book reveals the "incredible heroism and an integrity that deserves our honor," an integrity and heroism belonging to the Buffalo Soldiers and to the Native Americans they fought.

Notable 1994 Children's Trade Books in the Field of Social Studies

22.22   Cox, Clinton. **Undying Glory: The Story of the Massachusetts 54th Regiment.** Scholastic, 1991. 159 pp. ISBN 0-590-44170-1. Nonfiction.

If you have seen the movie *Glory*, then you know the subject of this book—the bravery, determination, and success of the first regiment of African American soldiers. The Massachusetts 54th infantry regiment, led by a young white officer, proved its mettle at the Battle of Charleston and subsequently in the Civil War. As a result, the first black officers came from the 54th regiment. The success of these first black soldiers in the U.S. Army and their 180,000 African American comrades is inspirational to blacks and whites alike.

22.23   Cromartie, Warren, with Robert Whiting. **Slugging It Out in Japan: An American Major Leaguer in the Tokyo Outfield.** Penguin/Signet Books, 1992. 336 pp. ISBN 0-451-17076-8. Nonfiction.

Welcome to the world of Japanese baseball, where a black ballplayer fresh from the Montreal Expos needed all his baseball skills, street smarts, and native pride to give as much as he took on his way to becoming a star in the land of the rising sun. Warren Cromartie, a top National League outfielder, was an African American playing baseball in a land where to be only half-Japanese made one an object of contempt. He tells his story with pride, a story of bad calls, bad vibes, bad-mouthing, and bad feelings. This first-person account of a skilled professional is the frankest, most painful, yet most revealing, look at the way Japanese play ball and other games of life.

22.24   Cronyn, George W., editor. **American Indian Poetry: An Anthology of Songs and Chants.** Fawcett/Columbine Books, 1991. 294 pp. ISBN 0-449-90670-1.

This book, first published in 1918, remains one of the most complete collections of Native American poetry. It contains both *translations* (more literal renderings) and *interpretations* in separate sections. The translations, which occupy more than half the book, are arranged by region, then by type; the interpretations are arranged by collector's name. Kenneth Lincoln's foreword is difficult going but says some interesting things about the history of America's interest in Native American literature. Mary Austin's new introduction argues that the songs and chants demand to be sung and danced and are not really intended for nor suitable for "eye" reading.

22.25   Davis, Ossie. **Just like Martin.** Simon and Schuster, 1992. 215 pp. ISBN 0-671-73202-1. Fiction.

In the fall of 1963, a young man growing up in Alabama comes face to face with the reality of racial inequality in America. Issac Stone confronts the tragedy of the racially motivated bombing of his church and then has to find a way to respond. Influenced by Dr. Martin Luther King Jr. and his doctrine of nonviolence, Issac tries to face the attitudes of others and to change them. The objections of his father make Issac's struggle personal as well as political.

Notable 1992 Children's Trade Books in the Field of Social Studies

22.26   Dickinson, Peter. **Tulku.** Dell/Laurel-Leaf Library, 1993. 286 pp. ISBN 0-440-21489-0. Fiction.

After his father's mission in China is destroyed, Theodore is on his own, fleeing from the rebels of the Boxer Uprising of 1898–1900. When he encounters Mrs. Jones, a strong, kind botanist, he hears and sees things that are startling because of his religious background. Mrs. Jones takes Theodore along, escaping from the rebels and bandits and traveling to Tibet and the Lama. Yet once again they are into trouble because the Lama thinks they hold magical powers that will lead to Tulku. First published in Great Britain, 1979.

22.27 Dubois, Muriel L. **Abenaki Captive.** Illustrated by Susan Fair Lieber. Carolrhoda/Adventure in Time Books, 1994. 180 pp. ISBN 0-87614-753-8. Fiction.

As the members of the St. Francis Abenaki tribe embark on their annual trapping and hunting expedition, Ogistin takes the place of his older brother Simi, who was recently killed by the English. When the Abenaki hunters encounter John Stark and his companions trapping on Indian lands, they capture the white men. During the time that the English captives live with the Abenaki, Ogistin experiences conflicting feelings of revenge and respect, while Stark comes to appreciate the ways of the Abenaki.

22.28 Duong Thu Huong (translated by Phan Huy Duong and Nina McPherson). **Paradise of the Blind.** William Morrow, 1993. 270 pp. ISBN 0-688-11445-8. Fiction.

The first Vietnamese novel to be translated and published in North America, this book traces the lives of three women striving to maintain "dignity in a society that expects ever greater sacrifices from them." This haunting story, set in what was then the Soviet Union, appeals to the senses with its vivid imagery and also explores the politics and culture of the 1980s. Follow Hang as she begins her reflections from a dormitory as an "exported worker" at a Russian textile factory—reflections on her childhood in Vietnam, on her family history, and on the events that led her to leave her country. The novel includes a glossary of Vietnamese food and cultural terms. First published in Vietnam, 1988.

22.29 Eckert, Allan W. **A Sorrow in Our Heart: The Life of Tecumseh.** Bantam Books, 1992. 862 pp. ISBN 0-553-08023-7. Nonfiction.

The Shawnee chief Tecumseh proved himself a valiant leader early in his life. Skilled as a hunter and a warrior, he nevertheless opposed cruel torture of other humans, even captives, and demonstrated that disdain by taking a strong stand against such brutal acts that the Shawnee customarily inflicted. He was able to influence other Native Americans because of his eloquence and the high esteem in which he was held. Respect for Tecumseh was not confined merely to the tribes of the midwestern area but extended to the white villages as well. As a result of his reputation for decency, he was able to gather and to provide information that would lead to victory over American military forces who intended to annihilate the Native American population in the late 1700s and early 1800s.

22.30   Edelman, Marian Wright. **The Measure of Our Success: A Letter to My Children and Yours.** Beacon Press, 1992. 97 pp. ISBN 0-8070-3102-X. Nonfiction.

In a wise and thoughtful response to the crisis of moral conscience in our world, Marian Wright Edelman presents twenty-five short lessons of hope. Each lesson is elaborated through her own personal story. Edelman grew up as an African American woman in racially segregated South Carolina. The strength she received from that upbringing is inspirational, but she does not rest on inspiration. She challenges all of us to serve others as she has done and to be the best that we can be.

ALA Best Books for Young Adults, 1993

22.31   Feelings, Tom. **Soul Looks Back in Wonder.** Illustrated by Tom Feelings. Dial Books, 1993. 33 pp. ISBN 0-8037-1001-1.

This is an interesting and beautiful book, emphasizing the beauty and creativity of blackness in both painting and poetry. Tom Feelings first did a series of strong paintings of young African Americans, then called upon writers such as Margaret Walker, Maya Angelou, and Walter Dean Myers to contribute short poems to accompany each painting. One poem by Langston Hughes, done years ago for a Feelings poster, appears here for the first time in a book. The illustrations are uniformly superb, the poems a little less so, but a number of them are of high merit and could well stand alone. This volume should appeal to readers spanning many years, reaching well down into the grades.

ALA Best Books for Young Adults, 1994
ALA Quick Picks for Young Adults, 1994
Coretta Scott King Illustrator Award, 1994

22.32   Fergus, Charles. **Shadow Catcher.** Soho Press, 1991. 308 pp. ISBN 0-939149-55-9. Fiction.

Most photographs of Native Americans taken at the turn of the century were posed and were often resisted by the Indians, who believed their souls were stolen by the photographers, or "shadow catchers." In 1913, wealthy Rodman Wanamaker funded an expedition to bring words of peace to Native Americans and to obtain their allegiance to the United States. One member of the expedition was Joseph Dixon, who had built his photographic reputation on the posed, idealized Indian photos. But to the dismay of the Bureau of Indian Affairs, someone else on the expedition was recording more accurate portrayals that showed Native American poverty, shabby living conditions, and affinity for alcohol, and was sending these photographs to an eastern newspaper. Two views of Native Americans are presented in this book, one based on their actual situation and the other based on an idealized fiction the government wanted shown.

22.33   Forkner, Ben, editor. **Louisiana Stories.** Pelican, 1990. 399 pp. ISBN 0-88289-784-5. Fiction.

This collection of sixteen stories provides an excellent view of life in Louisiana over the years, while at the same time it presents a variety of characters and universal experiences and emotions. Native Louisiana writers George Washington Cable and Ernest Gaines write of the Creole and African American experiences respectively. William Faulkner and Robb Forman Dew, writers who spent only a portion of their lives in Louisiana, capture the feeling of the South, specifically New Orleans, but their focus is more on the emotions of their characters than on the setting itself.

22.34   Gaines, Ernest. **A Lesson before Dying.** Alfred A. Knopf, 1993. 256 pp. ISBN 0-679-41477-0. Fiction.

The lesson that local teacher Grant Wiggins is supposed to impart to convicted robber Jefferson is one of dignity. Condemned to death for a murder in which he played an inadvertent part, Jefferson is ready to die in despair, disgrace, and ignorance. At the insistence of Grant's aunt and her best friend, Jefferson's mother, the reluctant teacher visits the condemned man every week before his imminent execution. Jefferson, however, is angry and unresponsive. Can Grant help him learn the most important lesson before dying?

22.35   Gallant, Roy A. **Ancient Indians: The First Americans.** Enslow, 1989. 128 pp. ISBN 0-89490-187-7. Nonfiction.

Roy Gallant traces the coming of Native Americans to the Americas, describing artifacts and locations that document the migration of these peoples, their development as societies, and their cultures. At the same time, his work reveals how scientists study ancient cultures and how they interpret the artifacts discovered. A number of black-and-white photographs and illustrations support the text.

22.36   Gardner, Robert, and Dennis Shortelle. **The Forgotten Players: The Story of Black Baseball in America.** Walker, 1993. 120 pp. ISBN 0-8027-8248-5. Nonfiction.

This is the story of hundreds of black baseball players who played thousands of exciting games before sellout crowds prior to the integration of major league baseball. Robert Gardner and Dennis Shortelle report on what life was like in the Negro baseball leagues that flourished before Jackie Robinson broke the color barrier in the late 1940s. This book is not about how many games were won by Satchel Paige or how many home runs were slammed by Josh Gibson. Rather, it is about baseball players who were banned from major league baseball because of the color of their skin. They played because they loved the game and wanted to keep the path open for those who eventually broke the barrier that had divided professional baseball into black and white leagues for half a century.

22.37   Garland, Sherry. **Shadow of the Dragon.** Harcourt Brace, 1993. 314 pp. ISBN 0-15-273530-5. Fiction.

Danny Vo faces many problems caused by his Vietnamese heritage. At age sixteen, he wants to fit in with his American friends, but his grandmother tries to raise him in a traditional Vietnamese home. When his cousin, Sang Le, joins the family, many problems arise both inside and outside the home. This book reveals the difficulties and prejudices faced by a family trying to survive in a foreign culture.

ALA Best Books for Young Adults, 1994
Booklist Editors' Choice, 1993

22.38   Greene, Melissa Fay. **Praying for Sheetrock.** Addison-Wesley, 1991. 335 pp. ISBN 0-499-90753-8. Nonfiction.

McIntosh County, Georgia, is the setting for this true account of a rural southern community in the 1970s. As African American citizens struggle to claim their civil rights, politics, lies, and power plays all come into focus. Both sides are never what they seem: black and white, the heroes often have feet of clay, and the villains are not always all that evil.

22.39   Greene, Patricia Baird. **The Sabbath Garden.** Dutton/Lodestar Books, 1993. 212 pp. ISBN 0-525-67430-6. Fiction.

In an ethnically mixed Lower East Side neighborhood in Manhattan, Opie Tyler, a fourteen-year-old basketball star, and Conchita, a beautiful Puerto Rican girl, make an effort to be friends as they deal with their frustrations. Opie, feeling a sadness that "stretched to the farthest end of her life," befriends Mr. Leshko, the only remaining Jew in the tenement, and becomes instrumental in giving the community a reason for working together.

22.40   Grover, Wayne. **Ali and the Golden Eagle.** Greenwillow Books, 1993. 150 pp. ISBN 0-688-11385-0. Fiction.

Ali and his family live in a remote Saudi Arabian village that lies at the bottom of a deep valley. Wayne is an American working in the area. Ali's family are great falconers, training and competing with other villages. One day Wayne uses his skills to catch a young eagle, which Ali and his father carefully train to hunt. Through the fame and attention Ali gains with his eagle, the lives of Ali and his entire village are changed dramatically.

22.41   Guy, Rosa. **Edith Jackson.** Dell/Laurel-Leaf Library, 1992. 179 pp. ISBN 0-440-21137-9. Fiction.

Edith Jackson, seventeen, is the oldest child of six. After the death of her mother and abandonment by her father, Edith and her sisters are moved from one foster home to another. Edith tries to keep the girls together, but eventually social workers break up the family. Edith runs away, only to be ostracized because of her dark complexion and her unstable home environment. A provocative story of a young black girl who is faced with challenging decisions and tragedies in her life, this novel tells of Edith Jackson's struggle to survive. Mature situations.

22.42   Guy, Rosa. **The Music of Summer.** Delacorte Press, 1992. 180 pp. ISBN 0-385-30599-0. Fiction.

Sarah Richardson's eighteenth summer changes her life. She has always lived in a small apartment with her mother, who has worked hard to provide Sarah with the means to become successful—a good education and musical training. Even though Sarah has graduated from high school and is attending music classes at the famous Juilliard School, she has not broken her ties with her childhood friend, Cathy Johnson. Cathy, on the other hand, seems eager to rid herself of Sarah and makes cruel and demeaning remarks about Sarah, especially her dark-skinned complexion. Cathy's mother invites Sarah to join them on a trip to Cape Cod, where Sarah meets Jean Pierre.

ALA Best Books for Young Adults, 1993

22.43   Hamilton, Virginia. **Paul Robeson: The Life and Times of a Free Black Man.** HarperCollins, 1992. 105 pp. ISBN 0-06-022189-5. Nonfiction.

A multitalented African American man born in the late nineteenth century, Paul Robeson overcame innumerable odds to become a successful athlete, singer, and actor. His accomplishments did not come easily, but his outspoken nature enabled him to express a keen belief in his own ability in a society that did not recognize equality for all. Through his father's encouragement and his personal drive, Paul Robeson was able to attend college and law school. Later he expanded his careers to include the theater and the concert circuit. For a time he enjoyed fame and respect, but when he voiced opinions that many in this country viewed as "un-American," he was branded as a Communist. When Robeson would not soften his position, his passport was canceled, preventing him from traveling outside the United States. Years later the Supreme Court reversed the passport decision, and Robeson continued his foreign concerts.

22.44   Hansberry, Lorraine (edited by Robert Nemiroff). **A Raisin in the Sun: The Unfilmed Original Screenplay.** Penguin/Plume Books, 1992. 206 pp. ISBN 0-452-26776-5. Fiction.

The Younger family, a microcosm of the African American family of the 1950s, has lived in an apartment on Chicago's South Side for the last thirty-five years. When the father dies and leaves the family a substantial sum of money, the survivors' dreams may finally be realized: a house for the mother, a store for the son, and a college education for the daughter. But then an unexpected twist of events changes all three of their lives.

22.45   Hansen, Joyce. **Between Two Fires: Black Soldiers in the Civil War.** Franklin Watts, 1993. 160 pp. ISBN 0-531-11151-2. Nonfiction.

Part of a series entitled the African-American Experience, this book traces the efforts of 180,000 blacks who saw the American Civil War as a chance to earn their freedom and to prove their bravery and loyalty as well. Told through the accounts of journalists, the letters and diaries of soldiers, and reports by officers, the stories are vividly presented, accompanied by black-and-white illustrations, engravings, and photographs.

Notable 1994 Children's Trade Books in the Field of Social Studies

22.46   Hansen, Joyce. **The Captive.** Scholastic, 1994. 195 pp. ISBN 0-590-41625-1. Fiction.

Kofi lives a life of privilege as the son of an Ashanti chief on the Ivory Coast of Africa. When a family slave betrays and kills Kofi's father, Kofi himself is sold into slavery. A "waterhouse" (slave ship) takes him to America, where he is purchased by a Puritan farmer. Kofi learns how to survive in a new land and attempts to gain his freedom, eventually dedicating his life to helping free other slaves.

Notable 1995 Children's Trade Books in the Field of Social Studies

22.47   Harris, Jacqueline L. **History and Achievement of the NAACP.** Franklin Watts, 1992. 159 pp. ISBN 0-531-11035-4. Nonfiction.

In this book in the African-American Experience series, Jacqueline Harris discusses the forces that led to the founding of the biracial National Association for the Advancement of Colored People and the particular individuals involved. She relates the efforts of the NAACP to achieve civil rights for African Americans and examines the achievements, disappointments, and future directions for the organization and its mission.

22.48   Haskins, James. **Black Music in America: A History through Its People.** HarperCollins/Harper Trophy Books, 1993. 198 pp. ISBN 0-690-04462-3. Nonfiction.

James Haskins gives us a picture of black music by providing interviews with famous artists such as Louis Armstrong, Jelly Roll Morton, W. C. Handy, and Scott Joplin. He explores the early music of slaves, songs and spirituals, the birth of ragtime and the blues through classic jazz, bop, soul, disco, and modern jazz. Haskins also discusses the classical black musicians: William Grant Still, Samuel Coleridge-Taylor, and Marian Anderson. A comprehensive index is included.

22.49   Haskins, James. **The Life and Death of Martin Luther King, Jr.** William Morrow/Beech Tree Books, 1992. 182 pp. ISBN 0-688-11690-6. Nonfiction.

Divided into two distinct parts, this biography represents yet another author's research into the life and times of Martin Luther King Jr. James Haskins reports the usual events of King's birth in 1929, his youth, and his manhood; his interest in and study of the teachings of Christ, Gandhi, and Thoreau; and his desire for a life better than the one that he and other African Americans in the South had come to despise. Biographer James Haskins covers King's preparation for the ministry, his leadership in the early Civil Rights movement, the zenith of his power and influence, and his assassination in 1968. Part two deals with the aftermath of his assassination and the unanswered questions regarding both King's presumed killer, James Earl Ray, and the possibility of a conspiracy.

22.50   Haskins, James. **The March on Washington.** HarperCollins, 1993. 144 pp. ISBN 0-06-021290-X. Nonfiction.

James Haskins provides a powerful, moving account of the 1963 March on Washington and the circumstances that led up to that momentous event. With an introduction by James Farmer, author and civil rights activist, this easy-to-read book shares details of actions behind the scenes that would be unknown to most people. Rich in historical fact, the text provides a more intimate view of the people and the preparation involved in this signal event in the African American struggle for equality.

Notable 1994 Children's Trade Books in the Field of Social Studies

22.51   Haskins, Jim. **Against All Opposition: Black Explorers in America.** Walker, 1992. 86 pp. ISBN 0-8027-8138-1. Nonfiction.

Have you ever thought about, or even heard about, explorers of African or African American heritage? Jim Haskins has. In chapters that are fast paced and informative, Haskins describes contributions by a number of black explorers in America from before Columbus to the present. Short chapters look at the lives of Estevanico (who traveled from Mexico into the American Southwest), Jean Baptiste Point du Sable (founder of Chicago), York (a key member of the Lewis and Clark expedition), James Beckwourth (mountain man), Matthew Henson (Arctic explorer), and astronauts Guion Bluford and Ronald McNair.

Notable 1992 Children's Trade Books in the Field of Social Studies

22.52   Haskins, Jim. **Get on Board: The Story of the Underground Railroad.** Scholastic, 1993. 152 pp. ISBN 0-590-45418-8. Nonfiction.

Discover how the Underground Railroad got its name, read about the heroic individuals—the conductors, station masters, and passengers—who risked death to escape or help others escape slavery. Learn about the "fugitive slave laws," about individuals such as Harriet Tubman, John Brown, Jarmain Wesley Loguen ("Underground Railroad King"), William Still, Josiah Henson (reputedly the inspiration for *Uncle Tom's Cabin*), William and Ellen Craft, Henry "Box" Brown (who escaped slavery by nailing himself in a box to be shipped to Pennsylvania), and many others. This book is informative, entertaining, and replete with pictures and illustrations. (Only the placement of Vicksburg in Virginia, instead of Mississippi, mars this book.)

Notable 1994 Children's Trade Books in the Field of Social Studies

22.53   Haskins, Jim. **One More River to Cross: The Stories of Twelve Black Americans.** Scholastic, 1992. 200 pp. ISBN 0-590-42896-9. Nonfiction.

This book chronicles the lives of twelve African Americans, eight men and four women, who have made major contributions to American life. Beginning with Crispus Attucks and ending with Ronald McNair, the author writes of the great difficulties these individuals faced and their determination to succeed. Their life stories serve as role models for today's youth.

ALA Best Books for Young Adults, 1993
Notable 1992 Children's Trade Books in the Field of Social Studies

22.54   Hesse, Karen. **Letters from Rifka.** Henry Holt, 1992. 148 pp. ISBN 0-8050-1964-2. Fiction.

Through letters written to her cousin Tovah in Russia, young Rifka tells of her family's dramatic escape from persecution in Russia in 1919 and their immigration to America. The journey entails numerous setbacks: humiliating physical examinations, typhus, separation from her family, and a year's delay in Belgium when she contracts the skin disease ringworm and is not allowed to board the ship for America. Bright and determined, Rifka finds comfort in her one book, a volume of Pushkin's poetry, and faces each setback with renewed courage. This story is based on the immigrant experiences of the author's grandparents.

ALA Best Books for Young Adults, 1993
ALA Notable Books for Children, 1993
IRA Children's Book Award, 1993
School Library Journal Best Books, 1992

22.55   Higginsen, Vy, with Tonya Bolden. **Mama, I Want to Sing.** Scholastic, 1992. 183 pp. ISBN 0-590-44201-5. Fiction.

Doris Winter had to sing! From the time she was a little girl sitting in the back row while her mother attended choir rehearsals, she knew she had to sing. Winter was taken into the adult choir at Mount Calvary Baptist Church in Harlem, and from that beginning, her career took off. Against her mother's wishes, Winter moved from church music into jazz and became one of the most popular black singers of the 1960s. The play *Mama, I Want to Sing*—the story of this young black woman with the wonderful musical career—played off-Broadway for seven years and toured the United States and abroad.

22.56   Highwater, Jamake. **Anpao: An American Indian Odyssey.** Illustrated by Fritz Scholder. HarperCollins/Harper Trophy Books, 1992. 256 pp. ISBN 0-397-31750-6. Fiction.

In this retelling of the Blackfoot Indian legend of the young brave who travels to the Sun to have his scar removed, Anpao journeys to get the Sun's permission to marry the beautiful Ko-Ko-mik-e-is. As in other stories based on Native American oral tradition, Anpao meets Coyote, Raven, Grandmother Spider, and the Mouse People. When he returns, Anpao has earned the love and trust of Ko-Ko-mik-e-is.

22.57   Hillerman, Tony. **Sacred Clowns.** HarperCollins, 1993. 305 pp. ISBN 0-06-016767-X. Fiction.

Lieutenant Joe Leaphorn and Officer Jim Chee, well-known Navajo Tribal Policemen, team up to solve two seemingly unrelated murders. First, an art teacher is killed at a mission school on the Navajo reservation. The next day, and many miles away, a sacred clown completes his role in a tribal ceremony and is killed. The only link between the two murders is a runaway student from the mission school whose uncle is the dead sacred clown, but no one can locate this student. Leaphorn and Chee once again fall back on their patience, careful questioning, and understanding of the Navajo culture to solve the murders.

22.58   Hobbs, Will. **Beardance.** Atheneum, 1993. 197 pp. ISBN 0-689-31867-7. Fiction.

When Cloyd learns that grizzly bears have been spotted in his Colorado mountains, he heads off in search of them. He feels responsible for the death of a male grizzly the previous summer, and helping these endangered bears may give him the chance to right things. His Native American grandmother taught him, "To live right, give something back." With dangers from weather and men threatening Cloyd and the bears, he must decide how much of himself to give in order to save the grizzlies.

ALA Best Books for Young Adults, 1994

22.59   Hoig, Stan. **People of the Sacred Arrows: The Southern Cheyenne Today.** Dutton/Cobblehill Books, 1992. 130 pp. ISBN 0-525-65088-1. Nonfiction.

The Sacred Arrow Renewal ceremonies and the annual Sun Dance bring Oklahoma's Southern Cheyenne back to the lands where their tribes once roamed freely, before the white man's prejudices and restrictions separated their communal nation. The struggle to retain old values and customs while adjusting to conditions brought on by the settlement of the West are told with personal insight by a native Oklahoman who grew up near the Cheyenne territories. Photographs and old prints add to the telling.

22.60 Hudson, Jan. **Sweetgrass.** Scholastic/Point Books, 1991. 157 pp. ISBN 0-590-43486-1. Fiction.

Sweetgrass is a fifteen-year-old Native American of the Blackfoot tribe, who live on the prairies of western Canada in what is now Alberta. It is 1837. Her primary concern is her prospect of marriage, but Sweetgrass also faces violence and confronts a devastating outbreak of smallpox. The difficulty of the unsettled and demanding life of the Blackfoot is vividly portrayed. Sweetgrass exhibits courage, demonstrating the power of the human spirit to face such adversities as loneliness, fear, and even death, and she emerges with new strength.

IRA Young Adults' Choices, 1991

22.61 Hyde, Margaret O. **Peace and Friendship: Russian and American Teens Meet.** Dutton/Cobblehill Books, 1992. 96 pp. ISBN 0-525-65107-1. Fiction.

American and Russian teens get to know each other and make changes in their thinking and their feelings through pen pals, organizations, and exchange programs. The characters realize the necessity of expressing themselves and working together. Samantha, Igor, Jessica, and Ben make a special effort to relate to others. The novel offers suggestions for becoming pen pals and provides a list of exchange programs.

22.62 Ione, Carole. **Pride of Family: Four Generations of American Women of Color.** Avon Books, 1993. 217 pp. ISBN 0-380-71934-7. Nonfiction.

Carole Ione begins her memoir by telling the reader about her childhood and the three strong women of color who raised her. There was her mother, a journalist and composer; her straight-laced great-aunt Sistonie, a doctor; and her fun-loving grandmother Be-Be, an entertainer and restaurateur. The author shares her travels, her two failed marriages, and her discovery of her great-grandmother's diary. It is through this search of the past that

Carole Ione gains a deeper understanding of herself and the women who raised her.

22.63 Jacques, Geoffrey. **The African-American Movement Today.** Franklin Watts, 1992. 144 pp. ISBN 0-531-11033-8. Nonfiction.

This is one of several books in the African-American Experience series devoted to an examination and recounting of black history and culture, providing additional information and reason to celebrate the diversity of the American people. In this book, Geoffrey Jacques focuses on a number of changes in the African American movement since the civil rights efforts of the 1950s and 1960s. He highlights the accomplishments of numerous African Americans in leadership roles in politics, corporations, literature, and the arts, and the particular contributions of women and of black churches. Jacques recounts as well areas where progress is slower and where economic disparity exists, and he suggests ways to remedy selected circumstances.

22.64 Jen, Gish. **Typical American.** Penguin/Plume Books, 1992. 296 pp. ISBN 0-452-26774-9. Fiction.

In five distinctly titled parts, Gish Jen tells a story of an immigrant Asian man and his sister, who think and behave like Americans. In a world full of obstacles, Ralph Chang works on his Ph.D. in engineering, becomes an American citizen, marries Helen, has two children, takes driving lessons, and buys a car and a house. Then adultery enters the picture, and Ralph's life changes.

22.65 Jenkins, Lyll Becerra de. **Celebrating the Hero.** Dutton/Lodestar Books, 1993. 179 pp. ISBN 0-525-67399-7. Fiction.

Camilla Draper, a young American girl of Hispanic descent, must come to grips with the death of her mother. After receiving a letter asking her to come to her mother's hometown in Colombia to a ceremony honoring her grandfather, Camilla decides that the best way to remember her mother would be to attend this event. In the process, she learns much about her mother and her culture—complete with political repression. The story portrays the Hispanic culture, including family traditions and storytelling.

22.66 Jin, Ha. **Between Silences: A Voice from China.** University of Chicago Press, 1990. 79 pp. ISBN 0-226-39986-9.

Between the ages of fourteen and nineteen, Ha Jin (real name, Xuefei Jin) served in the People's Army of China during the Cultural Revolution of the 1960s. These poems, written originally in

English and published while Ha Jin was a graduate student in the United States, personalize and reveal that turmoil through a variety of personae and voices. A few speak of love and friendship; more speak of heartbreak and horror. We meet children going off to war, such as the young volunteer (perhaps the poet himself) who feared the Russians: "We decided to go to the army / for we did not want to be roasted at home / like little pigs." We hear the voice of the calloused general calmly telling how he took care of possible enemy agents in his squad: "I did not bother to find them out. / I just shot the few persons I suspected." Once or twice the language is mature, but all of the poems are crystal-clear, understated, and very, very powerful.

22.67   Johnson, James Weldon. **Lift Every Voice and Sing.** Illustrated by Elizabeth Catlett. Walker, 1993. 34 pp. ISBN 0-8027-8250-7.

This is a short book of many parts. It opens with two pages of introductory material by author Jim Haskins on the composition of the anthem by African American poet James Weldon Johnson, plus biographical notes on the Johnson brothers and illustrator Elizabeth Catlett. The complete text of the song follows, spread over twelve pages facing Catlett's dramatic linocuts, which were created as a totally separate project more than forty years after the song. Closing the book is a page reproducing Catlett's original caption for each linocut and the complete sheet music. The heart of the book, Johnson's words and Catlett's powerful images, so completely complement each other that they seem to have been created simultaneously.

Booklist Editors' Choice, 1993
Notable 1994 Children's Trade Books in the Field of Social Studies

22.68   Jones, Edward P. **Lost in the City.** Photographs by Amos Chan. William Morrow, 1992. 249 pp. ISBN 0-688-11526-8. Nonfiction.

A collection of portraits set in Washington, D.C., *Lost in the City* presents short sketches about everyday city people who struggle to maintain a sense of purpose despite the inherent difficulties they face. The subjects of Jones's sketches are African American men and women who go about their daily routines, immersing themselves in their tasks in the belief that they can somehow become an integral part of their society. Jones has created a series of mini-novels about characters who, in their battle to be a part of life, are forced to relegate their losses to a secondary position.

22.69   Killens, John Oliver, and Jerry W. Ward Jr., editors. **Black Southern Voices: An Anthology of Fiction, Poetry, Drama, Nonfiction,**

and Critical Essays. Penguin/Meridian Books, 1992. 608 pp. ISBN 0-452-01096-9.

When many persons think of the southern literary tradition, they think first of William Faulkner, Eudora Welty, Flannery O'Connor, Tennessee Williams, and other white writers. There are, however, other southern writers equally distinct, vibrant, and authentic—the black southern voices. This collection of works by twentieth-century black writers includes both established authors, such as Richard Wright, John Killens, Maya Angelou, and Alice Childress, and many emerging writers. The selections cover a broad spectrum, but the central theme throughout is the struggle for freedom, equality, and humaneness. This volume provides readers with a clearer vision of the total southern literary tradition.

22.70   King, Coretta Scott. **My Life with Martin Luther King, Jr.,** rev. ed. Penguin/Puffin Books, 1993. 315 pp. ISBN 0-14-036805-1. Nonfiction.

Written as a tribute to her husband and as an inspiration to young African Americans of today, *My Life with Martin Luther King, Jr.* deals with the trials and the successes of the civil rights leader. In this biography, Coretta Scott King gives detailed accounts of the threats, the marches, the sit-ins, and the numerous jailings that her husband endured, along with the personal fears and other emotions that she and the family suffered. A lengthy description of the preparations for and the execution of the 1963 March on Washington, D.C., is given, as is attention to the King family and friends who assisted in the gallant effort to end racial discrimination and oppression in the United States. King's account is a commendable effort to recall her husband's accomplishments, but her narrative frequently becomes rather verbose and tiring, especially for young readers.

22.71   King, Woodie, and Ron Milner, editors. **Black Drama Anthology.** Penguin/Meridian Books, 1986. 671 pp. ISBN 0-452-00902-2. Fiction.

The African American experiences of the 1960s and 1970s are graphically illustrated in this collection of twenty-three plays by both famous (Imamu Amiri Baraka, Langston Hughes) and less well known (Errol Hill, Ron Zuber) playwrights. Drawing from personal experience, the playwrights convey with harsh realism the voices of anger, pride, oppression, confrontation, honesty, and sometimes even humor. The plays vary in length, and several can be read in one sitting.

22.72 Kissinger, Rosemary K. **Quanah Parker: Comanche Chief.** Pelican, 1991. 129 pp. ISBN 0-88289-785-3. Nonfiction.

A daring story of a brave young Comanche chief who vowed to fight the white man for Indian land, this tale of valor and stark determination is a classic example of the struggle between the Native American's love for the land and the white man's desire for expansion. Born to a white mother and an Indian father and reared in the ways of the Comanche, Quanah Parker pledged to uphold the Comanche lifestyle and traditions and to resist the government's plan to confine his people to reservations. For a time, he was able to keep his pledge, but when he recognized the imminent danger of starvation and death for the Comanches, he realized he had to comply with the government. Parker did so, but on his own terms, and he became a liaison between his people and the white man.

22.73 Koller, Jackie French. **The Primrose Way.** Harcourt Brace Jovanovich, 1992. 271 pp. ISBN 0-15-256745-3. Fiction.

In 1633, sixteen-year-old Rebekah joins her missionary father in the newly established Puritan settlement in New England. She befriends the niece of the chief of the local Pawtucket Indian tribe and begins to learn about Indian culture. As time passes, Rebekah begins to question whether the "savages" she has been sent to save need to be saved at all. This book addresses the important question of whether one group has the right to judge others and force them to conform to a different way of life.

ALA Best Books for Young Adults, 1993

22.74 Kuklin, Susan. **Speaking Out: Teenagers Take on Race, Sex, and Identity.** G. P. Putnam Sons, 1993. 165 pp. ISBN 0-399-22532-3. Nonfiction.

What happens when you make a high school racially balanced: 25 percent Asian, 25 percent African American, 25 percent Hispanic, and 25 percent white? Does it improve or worsen prejudice? Susan Kuklin asked a group of people to discuss prejudice, race, sexuality, and being different. When the students were given the chance to talk for themselves, they clearly showed that their feelings are the same—it hurts to be labeled. Further discussion showed they learned valuable lessons about self-esteem, compatibility, and respect.

ALA Quick Picks for Young Adults, 1994
Booklist Editors' Choice, 1993

22.75 La Puma, Salvatore. **A Time for Wedding Cake.** Penguin/Plume Books, 1992. 256 pp. ISBN 0-452-26814-1. Fiction.

Using provocative, controversial situations and mature language, *A Time for Wedding Cake* effectively conveys the story of Gene Leone, a World War II veteran who returns to Bensonhurst, Brooklyn. As Gene, the second son of a Sicilian family, tells his story, he reveals how he is controlled by lust and molded by family traditions, philosophies, and relationships. The reader's attention is held as Gene becomes both a victim and a perpetrator of marred, decadent relationships.

22.76 Laird, Elizabeth. **Kiss the Dust.** Dutton Children's Books, 1992. 279 pp. ISBN 0-525-44893-4. Fiction.

First Tara sees a teenage boy shot at close range by the Iraqi secret police; then her father has to escape in the middle of the night because of his involvement with the Kurdish resistance movement. Finally, Tara and her mother must leave their home and seek sanctuary in the hills of Kurdistan, giving up the comforts Tara has known for thirteen years and becoming fugitives from the Iraqis. It is 1984, and the family's flight takes them from one refugee camp to another, one frightening situation to the next, while Tara wonders if they will ever find a safe place to live. First published in Great Britain, 1991.

ALA Best Books for Young Adults, 1993
Notable 1992 Children's Trade Books in the Field of Social Studies

22.77 Lamar, Jake. **Bourgeois Blues: An American Memoir.** Penguin/Plume Books, 1992. 174 pp. ISBN 0-452-26911-3. Nonfiction.

On first glance, *Bourgeois Blues* seems to be simply a story of how easily success came to a young man who had privileges few other African Americans enjoy. But this description is deceptive. Jake Lamar's private school education seemed an almost natural prelude to his enrollment in and eventual graduation from Harvard, where, to his father's chagrin, he displayed his journalistic talent by working on the staff of a school newspaper. It is his father, in fact, who produces the conflict in young Jake's life. Despite this conflict, Lamar succeeds in becoming the youngest writer for *Time* magazine, where he does a reputable job and also learns what it means to be a black man in middle-class America.

22.78 Langone, John. **Spreading Poison: A Book about Racism and Prejudice.** Little, Brown, 1993. 178 pp. ISBN 0-316-51410-1. Nonfiction.

In today's society, prejudice and racism are evident daily: in the media, in our schools, and in our neighborhoods. Few people, however, understand the origin of these attitudes. John Langone discusses in detail the sources of racism and prejudice. He examines the various myths and stereotypes surrounding racial bigotry, religious persecution, and homosexuality, along with historical and social events that fostered them. Langone explores the significant contributions of several ethnic groups and presents a fact-filled argument against the prejudices that plague society. He advocates knowledge and understanding of individual differences and provides clear and easy-to-read information in a straightforward approach.

22.79 Lee, Gus. **China Boy.** Penguin/Signet Books, 1992. 394 pp. ISBN 0-451-17434-8. Fiction.

Kai Ting is the first American-born member of his Mandarin Chinese family living in San Francisco. Respecting his mother deeply, he spends much time with her. Her death and his father's remarriage to an intolerant American leave Kai torn between the culture he was taught to respect and the culture in which he has to survive. Kai turns to the YMCA to learn how to defend himself and opens up a new world of people and self-respect.

Booklist Editors' Choice, 1991

22.80 Lee, Marie G. **Finding My Voice.** Houghton Mifflin, 1992. 165 pp. ISBN 0-395-62134-8. Fiction.

Ellen Sung's senior year serves as her final chance to stage the best year ever in making friends, attaining excellent grades, and being accepted in college. In the process, Ellen encounters pressure from her parents, pressure as the only Asian student in school, and unkind comments from her peers. Through it all, she "finds her voice."

ALA Quick Picks for Young Adults, 1993
IRA Young Adults' Choices, 1994

22.81 Lester, Julius. **Long Journey Home: Stories from Black History.** Dial Books, 1993. 150 pp. ISBN 0-8037-4953-8. Nonfiction.

Julius Lester examines several little known "movers of history." The vignettes are based on historical fact and represent stories of typical individuals rather than the famous or the great. Some of the vignettes are set during the Civil War, others after that time. Read, for instance, about Bob Lemmons, a black cowboy who single-handedly rounded up herds of wild mustangs. Read about blues-playing Rambler; educated Ben, who escapes to Canada; and Jake, who seeks Mandy following emancipation. Read about Louis, who escapes and helps with the Underground Railroad, and the nameless parent who tells a child about slavery, about Africa, and about the "long journey home." First published in 1972.

Boston Globe–Horn Book Fanfare Honor Book, 1972
National Book Award finalist, 1972

22.82   Levine, Ellen, editor. **Freedom's Children: Young Civil Rights Activists Tell Their Own Stories.** Avon/Flare Books, 1994. 189 pp. ISBN 0-380-72114-7. Nonfiction.

Ellen Levine records an accurate account of thirty African American voices as they struggle through the Civil Rights movement in the South. As these courageous young people share their stories, they do so in an uplifting way, though their experiences were often humiliating. Their ten-year involvement tells of frustrations, disappointments, triumph, and sense of pride.

Jane Addams Award, 1994
ALA Best Books for Young Adults, 1994
Booklist Editors' Choice, 1993
IRA Children's Book Award, 1994
Notable 1994 Children's Trade Books in the Field of Social Studies
School Library Journal Best Books, 1992

22.83   Lipsyte, Robert. **The Brave.** HarperCollins/Harper Keypoint/Charlotte Zolotow Books, 1991. 195 pp. ISBN 0-06-023916-6. Fiction.

The Brave proves again why Robert Lipsyte is a master of the young adult sports novel. Lipsyte has an unfailing gift for portraying troubled teenagers, and seventeen-year-old Sonny Bear is no exception. Leaving the Moscondagas Indian reservation for the streets of New York, boxer Sonny Bear tries to harness his inner rage by training with Alfred Brooks, a former boxer turned policeman. Brooks thinks that Sonny has the talent to make it to the top, to be a contender. But first Sonny has to learn to act smart, take control of his life, and beat "the monster"—the anger he brought with him from the reservation. Fans of *The Contender* will not be disappointed by this long-awaited sequel and will be eager to read the next book about Sonny Bear, *The Chief.*

ALA Best Books for Young Adults, 1992
ALA Quick Picks for Young Adults, 1992
School Library Journal Best Books, 1991

22.84 Lipsyte, Robert. **The Chief.** HarperCollins, 1993. 226 pp. ISBN 0-06-021068-0. Fiction.

On the verge of having a shot at the heavyweight boxing championship, nineteen-year-old Sonny Bear finds himself with conflicting loyalties when trouble erupts on his reservation over the construction of a new gambling casino. Martin Malcolm Witherspoon, who calls himself "the only Black in America who can't jump," comes to save Sonny Bear and Alfred Brooks and tell their story of a wild and dangerous ride as they try to rescue the reservation and win the title. *The Chief*, a sequel to *The Brave*, will continue to satisfy young adult readers who search for tough action and sports appeal.

22.85 Lipsyte, Robert. **Jim Thorpe: 20th-Century Jock.** HarperCollins, 1993. 95 pp. ISBN 0-06-022989-6. Nonfiction.

Jim Thorpe was America's first great all-around athlete. A Native American who was stripped of his own language, clothing, and culture and drilled in the ways of whites, Thorpe is remembered for his accomplishments as an Olympic decathlon winner in 1912 and as an outstanding professional football and baseball player. Thorpe's baseball skills were major league, but he was hired by the New York Giants more for his fame than his hitting. However, his greatest athletic love was football, and he played the game into middle age. As a member of the Canton, Ohio, Bulldogs, he was an early player, owner, and official of what would become the National Football League. Perhaps his daughter, Charlotte, described him best: "Young and old loved him for what he was—a big, warm, fun-loving boy-man."

22.86 Louie, David Wong. **Pangs of Love.** Penguin/Plume Books, 1992. 225 pp. ISBN 0-452-26888-5. Fiction.

Many of the characters in this collection of eleven short stories by David Wong Louie are Chinese American. His stories deal with modern-day issues in American life, such as abortion, dating, and gay lifestyles. They are witty, surprising, sometimes surreal, and meant for the mature reader.

22.87 Lusane, Clarence. **The Struggle for Equal Education.** Franklin Watts, 1992. 144 pp. ISBN 0-531-11121-0. Nonfiction.

Clarence Lusane, an author, activist, and journalist, presents the history of the struggle for equal education in America. He traces the beginning of black education from the pre–Civil War period to Reconstruction through the Civil Rights movement to the present day. He examines a number of initiatives, legal battles, and political reforms relating to education. In-depth coverage is given to the resistance to desegregation in the 1960s and several contemporary affirmative action initiatives.

22.88   Lyons, Mary E. **Sorrow's Kitchen: The Life and Folklore of Zora Neale Hurston.** Charles Scribner's Sons, 1990. 125 pp. ISBN 0-684-19198-9. Nonfiction.

This illustrated biography of one of America's often forgotten female authors is simply and tastefully written. *Sorrow's Kitchen* takes the reader from the rather unhappy childhood of Zora Neale Hurston as she grew up in Florida to her determination to obtain an education and her migration from the South to New York City during the height of the Harlem Renaissance in the 1920s. Hurston made frequent trips to her native Florida and the West Indies in search of folklore, and eventually returned to Florida, where she died in poverty in 1960. Excerpts from Hurston's works and photographs taken throughout her life are included.

ALA Best Books for Young Adults, 1992
IRA Teachers' Choices, 1991
School Library Journal Best Books, 1991

22.89   Margolies, Jacob. **The Negro Leagues: The Story of Black Baseball.** Franklin Watts, 1993. 128 pp. ISBN 0-531-11130-X. Nonfiction.

The Negro Leagues: The Story of Black Baseball looks at a part of baseball history that is seldom examined. It follows African Americans in baseball from the game's beginnings nearly 150 years ago through the years immediately following the integration of major league baseball. It is a story of great ballplayers who played in obscurity because of the color of their skin: their very existence was ignored by major newspapers and radio. Jacob Margolies profiles some of the leading figures in black baseball—including Rube Foster, Satchel Paige, and Josh Gibson—and describes some of black baseball's greatest games. This history of the Negro leagues not only reveals the discrimination against black baseball players but also highlights the outstanding achievements of talented African Americans.

Notable 1994 Children's Trade Books in the Field of Social Studies

22.90   Matthiessen, Peter. **In the Spirit of Crazy Horse.** Penguin, 1992. 646 pp. ISBN 0-670-83617-6. Nonfiction.

History books tell of settlers from Europe bargaining with Native Americans for land, of acquiring such land by legal and illegal means, of broken treaties. Does such treatment of Native Americans continue? Read this book and judge for yourself whether the Federal Bureau of Investigation and the federal and state courts have been fair and just in their treatment of those individuals associated with the American Indian Movement (AIM). Examine the complex issues and events leading up to a June 1975 shootout near Wounded Knee, South Dakota, that resulted in the death of two FBI agents and one Native American; the subsequent conviction of Leonard Peltier on murder charges; and the efforts to prove his innocence. (This controversial book, first published in 1983, was kept out of the public's hands during an eight-year court battle.)

22.91   Mazer, Anne, editor. **America Street: A Multicultural Anthology of Stories.** Persea Books, 1993. 150 pp. ISBN 0-89255-190-9. Fiction.

Gary Soto, Langston Hughes, Grace Paley, and others offer insight into the cultural differences of many youth growing up in America. While readers can learn something about what it means to be Latino, Asian, African American, or Jewish in America, they are also likely to be struck by the universal needs of the characters—the need to belong, to have friends, and to achieve goals.

22.92   McClintock, Norah. **The Stepfather Game.** Scholastic/Point Books, 1991. 190 pp. ISBN 0-590-43971-5. Fiction.

How can three half-sisters be so different? There is Brynn, the beautiful, studious, and responsible one who tries to take care of Chloe, the wild Chinese American child, and Phoebe, the youngest and plumpest. Each has obstacles to overcome. Brynn almost loses her best friend over a boy; Chloe, never dateless, finds herself without one when her boyfriend shuns her because of her mixed heritage; and Phoebe goes on a starvation diet that lands her in the hospital. Together they learn to help each other through their obstacles.

22.93   McKissack, Patricia C., and Fredrick McKissack. **Sojourner Truth: Ain't I a Woman?** Scholastic, 1992. 178 pp. ISBN 0-590-44690-8. Nonfiction.

Drawing upon history, this inspirational biography is ideal for teens. For the many who are unaware of the contributions of the early American slave population, this book provides insight into one woman's quest for equal rights for her race in general and for women in particular. Sojourner Truth, born a slave in 1797, traveled across the country, spreading the truth to all who wanted to hear, and left in her wake many enlightened individuals who came to realize that being a woman did not mean being weak and ineffectual. Despite her inability to read, Sojourner Truth demonstrated that she could learn, and she tapped every resource at hand to convey her message. Her determination to be regarded as a person entitled to all the privileges afforded others comes through clearly and elevates Sojourner Truth to the rank of a truly great American pioneer.

ALA Best Books for Young Adults, 1993
ALA Notable Books for Children, 1993
Boston Globe–Horn Book Nonfiction Award, 1993
IRA Teachers' Choice, 1993

22.94 McLaurin, Melton A. **Celia, a Slave.** Avon Books, 1993. 178 pp. ISBN 0-380-71935-5. Nonfiction.

How were some female slaves treated by their American "owners" in the period up to the Civil War? Were slaves in the lower Midwest treated the same as those in the South? Why were laws arranged largely to protect slave owners? What rights did slaves have, including slaves who were raped? Read about Celia's trial, its causes and consequences, for a better understanding of the political economy of slavery and the relationships of race, gender, and power in the moral dilemma of slavery. This is carefully constructed description and analysis by a historian documenting the facts and the basis for interpretation.

22.95 Means, Florence Crannell. **The Moved-Outers.** Walker, 1992. 156 pp. ISBN 0-8027-7386-9. Fiction.

Sumiko (Sue) Ohara spends the fall of 1941 doing what most high school seniors do—singing in the church choir, having fun with her lifelong best friend, Emily, dreaming about college and "the real world." But the "real world" intrudes with the bombing of Pearl Harbor on December 7, 1941, and Sue and her Japanese American family are faced with racial prejudice and overzealous patriots. The family is forced to move to an internment camp for the remainder of the war. Originally published in 1945, *The Moved-Outers* was the first book for young adults to deal with the forced internment of Japanese Americans during World War II.

Newbery Honor Book, 1946

22.96 Meyer, Carolyn. **Where the Broken Heart Still Beats: The Story of Cynthia Ann Parker.** Harcourt Brace Jovanovich, 1992. 196 pp. ISBN 0-15-200639-7. Nonfiction.

Carolyn Meyer has taken "the key facts of the history of Cynthia Ann Parker and used them as a framework on which to fashion the story of her life, as it could have been." Historians of the American West agree that Parker was captured by Comanche warriors in the mid-1800s and lived among her captors for twenty-five years before being "rescued" by Texas Rangers and returned to her relatives. These well-meaning rescuers failed to realize that Parker was no longer a member of the white man's culture. Her heart and soul belonged to the Comanches, and she and her small daughter longed to return to her Comanche husband and two sons in their Indian settlement.

ALA Best Books for Young Adults, 1993
IRA Teachers' Choices, 1993
Notable 1992 Children's Trade Books in the Field of Social Studies

22.97 Meyer, Carolyn. **White Lilacs.** Harcourt Brace/Gulliver Books, 1993. 242 pp. ISBN 0-15-200641-9. Fiction.

White Lilacs, written in the first person and based on factual events, tells a tale of segregation and violence. Rose Lee is a young black girl growing up in Dillon, Texas, in the 1920s, and her family and friends are moved from their homes so that the white citizens of Dillon may have a park to beautify the town. Rose Lee has been given the responsibility of recording the buildings before they are torn down or moved to a less fertile area. She slowly grows to realize that some of her white neighbors and employers are not concerned with her welfare or her well-being. The white lilac, a symbol of hope, flourishes throughout the story.

ALA Best Books for Young Adults, 1994

22.98 Miller, David Humphreys. **Custer's Fall: The Native American Side of the Story.** Penguin/Meridian Books, 1992. 271 pp. ISBN 0-452-01095-0. Nonfiction.

This reissue of David Humphreys Miller's 1957 book is fascinating reading. Basing his book on interviews with more than seventy Native American participants, the author brings an immediacy to the Battle of the Little Bighorn through the perspective of Native Americans—the other side of the "winning" of the West. With the exception of one chapter, "White Man's World," which describes other events in 1876, the book focuses on the day that

Native Americans defeated General George Custer and inflicted their worst defeat on the U.S. Army.

22.99   Mizell, Linda. **Think about Racism.** Walker, 1992. 230 pp. ISBN 0-8027-8113-6. Nonfiction.

This well-researched text provides historical accounts from early America and the African slave trade through the civil rights protests in the 1970s. Included are biographical profiles of significant individuals during each of the time periods. The chapters of the text, which cover such social issues as Jim Crow laws, slavery laws, and NAACP battles, end with review questions that can be useful in classroom discussions. The author focuses on the past and continued presence of racism in society and defines it in relation to prejudice. This easy-to-read reference provides information in a clear, succinct manner and includes photographs and illustrations.

22.100   Mohr, Nicholasa. **El Bronx Remembered: A Novella and Stories.** HarperCollins/Harper Keypoint Books, 1993. 263 pp. ISBN 0-06-024314-7. Fiction.

This collection of twelve stories captures the lives and spirit of the Puerto Rican immigrants who came to New York in search of the American dream. From Hector, who must wear his uncle's orange, pointed-toed shoes to graduation, to the Fernandez family, who keep a hen tied to the leg of the kitchen table, the characters are real, as is their fight to survive.

National Book Award for Children's Literature finalist, 1976

22.101   Mori, Kyoko. **Shizuko's Daughter.** Henry Holt, 1993. 220 pp. ISBN 0-8050-2557-X. Fiction.

Twelve-year-old Yuki and her mother, Shizuko, are true friends, exploring and capturing nature's beauty in words and drawings. The two find comfort in one another since Hideki, Yuki's father, is seldom home and shows little interest in his wife and daughter. Hideki's behavior eventually drives Shizuko to suicide, which devastates Yuki. Her new, critical stepmother creates a cold, distant home in which Yuki can never do anything right. Yuki learns to bear this new life by relying on memories of her mother and the way life used to be. Notes on the setting describe the Japanese cities in which the story takes place, and a glossary provides additional information.

ALA Best Books for Young Adults, 1994
Notable 1994 Children's Trade Books in the Field of Social Studies

22.102 Myers, Walter Dean. **Brown Angels: An Album of Pictures and Verse.** HarperCollins, 1993. 36 pp. ISBN 0-06-022918-7.

Utterly unique, this book is an album of turn-of-the-century photos of African American children plus evocative, supportive poetry. Walter Dean Myers writes in a variety of styles—some poems are reminiscent of jump-rope chants, others of blues stanzas, still others are supple, delicate lyrics—styles chosen to complement the moods of the subjects in the photographs. The result is a delightful blend, at times amusing, at times moving, a real lesson in artistic judgment.

ALA Notable Books for Children, 1994

22.103 Myers, Walter Dean. **Malcolm X: By Any Means Necessary.** Scholastic, 1993. 200 pp. ISBN 0-590-46484-1. Nonfiction.

Walter Dean Myers gives an objective account of Malcolm X (1925–65), one of the most influential civil rights leaders of the twentieth century. By seeing Malcolm as a child in Nebraska, Wisconsin, and Michigan and a young man in Boston and Harlem, one can better understand Malcolm as an adult—how he was able to use his talents to promote the growth of the Nation of Islam and why he sought changes, "by any means necessary," in the way African Americans were treated.

ALA Best Books for Young Adults, 1994
IRA Teachers' Choices, 1994
Coretta Scott King Author Honor Book, 1994

22.104 Myers, Walter Dean. **The Mouse Rap.** HarperCollins/Harper Trophy Books, 1992. 186 pp. ISBN 0-06-024344-9. Fiction.

In this tale of summer adventure in Harlem, fourteen-year-old Mouse and Styx remain friends through basketball, a dance contest, and a search for treasure left in an abandoned building. Mouse's life is complicated when his absent father reappears and seems interested in rejoining the family. Each chapter opens with an introductory rap by Mouse, and author Walter Dean Myers uses African American dialect to tell his story.

IRA Children's Choices, 1991

22.105 Myers, Walter Dean. **Now Is Your Time! The African-American Struggle for Freedom.** HarperCollins, 1991. 292 pp. ISBN 0-06-024371-6. Nonfiction.

From pre–Civil War America to the modern Civil Rights movement, Walter Dean Myers chronicles the history of African

Americans in this concise and well-written book. Myers looks at a few significant events emblematic of their eras. His ultimate message is that "what we understand of our history is what we understand of ourselves." This is a particularly good source for an introduction to American history and to the struggle endured by African Americans.

ALA Best Books for Young Adults, 1992
ALA Notable Books for Children, 1992
Coretta Scott King Author Award, 1992
NCTE Orbis Pictus Honor Book, 1992

22.106 Myers, Walter Dean. **Somewhere in the Darkness.** Scholastic Hardcover Books, 1992. 168 pp. ISBN 0-590-42411-4. Fiction.

Jimmy cannot decide what to do with his life. He knows he should stay in school but finds that some days it is easier to stay home. One afternoon a stranger calls out to him from the darkness of his Harlem tenement hallway. The voice belongs to Crab, his father, who has escaped from prison and who wants Jimmy to know who his father really is. Crab takes Jimmy from New York and his "Mamma Jean" on a trip across the country to visit his own boyhood town.

ALA Best Books for Young Adults, 1993
ALA Notable Books for Children, 1993
ALA Quick Picks for Young Adults, 1993
Booklist Editors' Choice, 1992
Boston Globe–Horn Book Fiction Honor Book, 1992
Coretta Scott King Author Honor Book, 1993
Newbery Honor Book, 1993

22.107 Myers, Walter Dean, creator (written by Stacie Johnson). **The Party.** Bantam Books, 1992. 150 pp. ISBN 0-553-29720-1. Fiction.

Murphy High friends find a need to make decisions regarding class events, dating, and friendship. Questions of whether to go to college and what to do with their lives and their bodies precipitate the actions of the group of friends at 18 Pine Street. Jennifer Wilson, in competition with the senior party, throws a big junior party at her home—without telling her mother. The party gets wild, and a few expensive items are broken. Sarah Gordon remains the caring, concerned friend throughout in this book about a group of teenagers from varying racial backgrounds. Second book in the 18 Pine St. series.

22.108 Myers, Walter Dean, creator (written by Stacie Johnson). **Sort of Sisters.** Bantam Books, 1992. 149 pp. ISBN 0-553-29719-8. Fiction.

This novel is the first in the continuing story of Sarah Gordon and her gang from Murphy High, who meet regularly at the new hangout, the pizzeria at 18 Pine Street. In this story centering on friends of different racial backgrounds, Sarah is looking forward to her junior year, especially when her cousin, Tasha, comes to live with her family. Sarah intends to introduce Tasha to her friends and to include her in their circle, but Tasha has other plans. When she arrives, she soon manages to win the friendship of the group and even seems to gain the attention of Dave Hunter, the boy that Sarah likes. Tension grows between the two girls, and Tasha and Sarah attempt to find a way to mend their relationship. First book in the 18 Pine St. series.

22.109 Namioka, Lensey. **The Coming of the Bear.** HarperCollins, 1992. 230 pp. ISBN 0-06-020289-0. Fiction.

Zenta and Matsuzo, two young Japanese samurai, find themselves stranded on an island inhabited by the primitive Ainu people. The Ainu take them to their *kotan* (village) and feed them. Eventually the two warriors realize that they must leave the island, but soon they find themselves trying to prevent conflict between the Ainu and nearby Japanese settlers. This story of cultural difference and prejudice in sixteenth-century Japan presents a timeless theme in a unique setting.

22.110 Nixon, Joan Lowery. **Land of Dreams.** Delacorte Press, 1994. 152 pp. ISBN 0-385-31170-2. Fiction.

When Kristin Swenson and her parents emigrate to Minnesota in 1902, she looks forward to the new freedoms that her life in America offers. She wants to speak English, live and work in a city, and make choices for herself. She does not want to continue living the way she did in Sweden. However, that is not the way of her parents and their community. Everyone keeps telling Kristin that change must be gradual, but she wants it immediately. She wonders if she will realize her dream of independence. Third book in the Ellis Island series.

22.111 Nixon, Joan Lowery. **Land of Promise.** Bantam/Skylark Books, 1993. 169 pp. ISBN 0-553-08111-X. Fiction.

This Ellis Island novel follows Rose Carney, a fifteen-year-old Irish farm girl who immigrates to Chicago in 1902. Rose works as a store clerk to help her father and brother raise enough money to bring her mother and sister to America. Rose's attempts are constantly thwarted by her father's drinking and her brother's obsession with giving financial support to a radical group dedicated to freeing Ireland by violent means. At Jane Addams's Hull House, Rose finds a peaceful way of social reform. Second book in the Ellis Island series.

22.112 Nye, Naomi Shihab, editor. **This Same Sky: A Collection of Poems from around the World.** Macmillan/Four Winds Press, 1992. 212 pp. ISBN 0-02-768440-7.

If you have ever wanted to see modern poetry from outside the Anglo-American mainstream, this collection will show you what is going on in poetry around the world. While a handful of the poems come from Canada, New Zealand, and Wales and were written in English, the others (approximately 120 of them) come from more than sixty nations as diverse as Bangladesh, Japan, Angola, Syria, Sweden, and Peru. Other than Octavio Paz and Pablo Neruda, most contributors are younger poets who are virtually unknown in the United States. Naomi Shihab Nye includes several pages of notes on contributors and a one-page bibliography of contemporary anthologies, many of which will interest younger readers.

ALA Notable Books for Children, 1993

22.113 O'Dell, Scott. **Sing Down the Moon.** Dell/Yearling Books, 1992. 137 pp. ISBN 0-440-40673-0. Fiction.

In 1863, the government of the United States sent Colonel Kit Carson west to Arizona to destroy the lives of the Navajo people. Bright Morning, a young girl tending sheep in a Navajo village, lives through this ordeal, the fleeing of her people, and the Long Walk of the Navajo people into imprisonment. Growing into adulthood and gaining independence are a part of this story of Bright Morning's struggle to return home and regain a lost way of life.

22.114 Otfinoski, Steven. **Nelson Mandela: The Fight against Apartheid.** Millbrook Press, 1992. 118 pp. ISBN 1-56294-067-8. Nonfiction.

In 1990, Nelson Mandela was freed from prison after serving twenty-seven years for leading the fight in South Africa against apartheid. Author Steven Otfinoski begins the book by giving a brief history of the country and by describing Mandela's childhood as the son of a Thembu chief. He then traces Mandela's lifelong struggle for black rights and gives a detailed account of the world events that led to Mandela's release from prison.

22.115 Parks, Rosa, with Jim Haskins. **Rosa Parks: My Story.** Dial Books, 1992. 189 pp. ISBN 0-8037-0673-1. Nonfiction.

On December 1, 1955, Rosa Parks refused to give up a seat to a white man on a segregated bus in Montgomery, Alabama. With this act of defiance, the Civil Rights movement became a national cause. But long before that day, Rosa Parks had been fighting against injustice. She begins her story by describing the many forms of discrimination she and her family faced living in the South and ends with a discussion of the years since 1955.

ALA Best Books for Young Adults, 1993
ALA Notable Books for Children, 1993
ALA Quick Picks for Young Adults, 1993
IRA Children's Choices, 1993
IRA Young Adults' Choices, 1994

22.116 Paulsen, Gary. **Nightjohn.** Delacorte Press, 1993. 92 pp. ISBN 0-385-30838-8. Fiction.

Nightjohn is one of the few slaves to escape alive from the Waller plantation. Yet he returns to teach young Sarney and other slaves how to read. Those who learn to read and write risk horrible punishment, but Nightjohn brings them more than knowledge; in a world of brutality, he brings hope. Based on true events and told in vivid, living language, this novel is about a man of mythic proportions; it is a forceful story about unforgettable characters.

ALA Best Books for Young Adults, 1994
ALA Notable Books for Children, 1994
IRA Children's Choices, 1994
School Library Journal Best Books, 1992

22.117 Paulsen, Gary (translated into Spanish by Gloria De Aragón Andújar). **Sisters/Hermanas.** Harcourt Brace, 1993. 127 pp. ISBN 0-15-275323-0. Fiction.

This is the story of two girls who live in entirely different worlds. Rosa, a young Mexican girl, struggles against the chains of poverty in order to survive in a highly materialistic United States. Traci, a product of a wealthy American family, contends with the pressures of family and society and the interpretation of success. These two girls are different, yet similar; they are in a sense sisters in a difficult world. This bilingual book has text in both English and Spanish.

22.118 Perry, Bruce. **Malcolm: The Life of a Man Who Changed Black America.** Station Hill Press, 1992. 380 pp. ISBN 0-88268-103-6. Nonfiction.

Malcolm tells the story behind what motivated Malcolm Little, the young boy who became Malcolm X, the civil rights activist who inspired some and infuriated others. As a child, Malcolm learned to persuade others in order to get his way, and he later developed the talent to influence thinking with his orations. His hardships and struggles during his youth are explored, including his prison term in the mid-1940s, when he made the decision to leave behind his drug addiction and devote his life to being a Muslim and to speaking for the oppressed in America.

22.119 Pettit, Jayne. **My Name Is San Ho.** Scholastic, 1992. 149 pp. ISBN 0-590-44172-8. Fiction.

San Ho has lived with the terrors of war since his first breath. When his father is taken away to fight and die for the Vietcong and the bombings and killings get too close to home, San Ho's mother sends him to Saigon to live. Then his mother marries an American soldier, moves to the United States, and sends for San Ho. Another frightening time begins as he makes the journey to a new life with a confusing language, a stepfather, strange foods, and racism. San Ho must overcome his fears in order to experience happiness in his new home.

22.120 Pohl, Constance, and Kathy Harris. **Transracial Adoption: Children and Parents Speak.** Franklin Watts, 1992. 137 pp. ISBN 0-531-11134-2. Nonfiction.

Should white parents be allowed to adopt a child of African American heritage? Or should any person of one race be allowed to raise a child of another race? Do the children of such adoptions lose their cultural identity? This book takes a candid look at racially mixed families. Through interviews with family members, a realistic picture is painted of the rewards and the heartbreaks of these adoptions, providing some answers to tough questions.

22.121 Powledge, Fred. **We Shall Overcome: Heroes of the Civil Rights Movement.** Charles Scribner's Sons, 1993. 201 pp. ISBN 0-684-19362-0. Nonfiction.

This exceptional coverage of the Civil Rights movement of the 1960s is documented in an interesting, simplified format designed for young readers. Thoroughly explained are the attitudes of the period, events such as the boycotts, marches, and legal battles, and the effects of the movement on American society. Terms are defined within the context of each chapter, a time line and photographs are provided, and coverage includes stories from activists of the period.

22.122 Pullman, Philip. **The Broken Bridge.** Alfred A. Knopf/Borzoi Books, 1992. 218 pp. ISBN 0-679-91972-4. Fiction.

Ginny and her father have a close relationship. She believes that her mother, a black Haitian artist, is dead. Then, at age sixteen, Ginny learns some disturbing things about her father's past. Angry that he has not been totally honest, Ginny decides to find out the truth. Her search leads her to an art gallery in Liverpool where she comes face to face with the truth, only to realize that the truth is sometimes very hard to live with.

ALA Best Books for Young Adults, 1993

22.123 Qualey, Marsha. **Revolutions of the Heart.** Houghton Mifflin, 1993. 184 pp. ISBN 0-395-64168-3. Fiction.

Revolutions of the Heart is a touching story covering topics that today's teenagers might have to deal with in their lives. Cory Knutson is Summer High School's senior sweetheart, but she has to endure hardships in her senior year: racial bias associated with her boyfriend, Mac, and the death of her mother. Author Marsha Qualey shows how a young heart survives in tough times.

ALA Best Books for Young Adults, 1994
ALA Quick Picks for Young Adults, 1994
School Library Journal Best Books, 1992

22.124 Rana, Indi. **The Roller Birds of Rampur.** Henry Holt, 1993. 298 pp. ISBN 0-8050-2670-3. Fiction.

Born in India and raised in England, seventeen-year-old Shelia Mehta struggles to find a balance between the Eastern philosophy that is her heritage and the Western influences that are so familiar to her. Indi Rana presents a story of a young woman who is confused about who she really is. With a trip to India and her grandparents' help, Shelia begins to understand her relationship to an ancient culture that is complex, compelling, and full of contradictions. Then, she must discover her karma, or life force.

22.125 Rodriguez, Richard. **Days of Obligation: An Argument with My Mexican Father.** Penguin Books, 1993. 230 pp. ISBN 0-670-81396-6. Nonfiction.

In this collection of autobiographical essays, Richard Rodriguez explores his own cultural identity. The son of immigrants from Mexico, he is a native Californian, but his complexion and features clearly mark his Mexican heritage. Rodriguez feels keenly the tug of two cultures within him—what he calls the tragic vision of Mexico versus the comic, or optimistic, vision of California.

Meditative, frank, poetic, these essays deal with what it means to be an American.

22.126 Roth-Hano, Renée. **Safe Harbors.** Macmillan/Four Winds Press, 1993. 214 pp. ISBN 0-02-777795-2. Fiction.

Renée Roth-Hano begins her story, written in journal style, on January 15, 1951, and continues through May 16 of that year. She recalls her memory as an unhappy Jewish girl, coming to New York to begin a new life where no one knows her. Roth-Hano struggles with her painful and pleasant memories of France before her life is able to slowly take a new form.

22.127 Roy, Jacqueline. **Soul Daddy.** Harcourt Brace Jovanovich/ Gulliver Books, 1992. 235 pp. ISBN 0-15-277193-X. Fiction.

Who am I? Where do I come from? How do I fit in? Fifteen-year-old Hannah Curren asks herself these questions daily. She and her twin sister, Rosie, live in a white suburb of London with their white mother. Suddenly, their father, a famous black reggae musician, and their half-sister, Nicola, appear on the scene. Hannah's life drastically changes as she finds a new extended family and begins to realize what it really means to be black. First published in Great Britain, 1990.

22.128 Rushdie, Salman. **Imaginary Homelands: Essays and Criticism, 1981–1991.** Penguin Books, 1991. 439 pp. ISBN 0-670-83952-3. Nonfiction.

This collection of essays by a British Indian, now living in London, provides a fresh perspective on the international scene in politics and literature during the 1980s. The seventy-five brief essays cover a broad range of topics—politics of India, Pakistan, Great Britain, and the United States, particularly the effects of race and religion on politics; the migrant experience; contemporary literature, movies, and television; and censorship of his novel *The Satanic Verses*. In drawing on his roots in India for his art, Salman Rushdie is forced to recognize that the imaginative vision is always fractured, distorted by personal memory, and that it is impossible to capture the real past, thus his title *Imaginary Homelands*.

22.129 Savin, Marcia. **The Moon Bridge.** Scholastic, 1992. 231 pp. ISBN 0-590-45873-6. Fiction.

Even as World War II rages around fifth-grader Ruthie Fox, life seems wonderful to her. But the war comes closer to home when the fiancé of Ruthie's teacher is killed. Then Mitzi Fujimoto arrives at school. Ruthie's best friend calls Mitzi a "Jap" and refuses to allow others to be Mitzi's friend. Ruthie takes a stand, and a friendship with Mitzi is formed. Then Mitzi's family is taken away to an internment camp for the rest of the war. Ruthie fears she will never see Mitzi again, but near the end of the war Mitzi writes, asking Ruthie to meet her at the Moon Bridge in San Francisco. Can their friendship survive all that has happened?

22.130 Seabrooke, Brenda. **The Bridges of Summer.** Dutton/Cobblehill Books, 1992. 143 pp. ISBN 0-525-65094-6. Fiction.

Zarah suffers from culture shock when her mother sends her from New York City to Domingo Island, South Carolina, to spend the summer with her grandmother, Quanamina, and her little cousin Loomis. How is she ever going to become Princess Zarah the dancer on this isolated island that does not even have running water or electricity? It is a remote place where the people speak Gullah, an unusual African American dialect, and where many folk traditions are still a way of life. Yet, fourteen-year-old Zarah learns many things about herself and her rich Gullah heritage from this proud, strong woman who rules her island just as her family before her.

22.131 Senna, Carl. **The Black Press and the Struggle for Civil Rights.** Franklin Watts, 1993. 160 pp. ISBN 0-531-11036-2. Nonfiction.

Carl Senna reveals the significant role of the black press. In sixteen chapters, he carefully explains the varying styles that journalists use and the stories they pursue. The main purposes of the first black newspaper were to report aspects of the black experience and to abolish slavery. This book also documents the varied contributions that African American journalists make today.

22.132 Simmen, Edward, editor. **North of the Rio Grande: The Mexican-American Experience in Short Fiction.** Penguin/Mentor Books, 1992. 428 pp. ISBN 0-415-62834-9. Fiction.

Included in this anthology are stories by Anglos and Mexican American writers, with each group presenting a different perspective on the culture and daily lives of Mexican Americans. Sandra Cisneros, Stephen Crane, Carlos Flores, Willa Cather, Maria Cristina Meña, and other talented writers portray the struggle and racial prejudice Mexican Americans have faced in this country. This collection showcases Chicano writers and promotes a deeper appreciation for the twelve million Americans of Mexican descent.

22.133 Solomon, Barbara H., editor. **Other Voices, Other Vistas: Short Stories from Africa, China, India, Japan, and Latin America.**

Penguin/Mentor Books, 1992. 476 pp. ISBN 0-451-62845-4. Fiction.

This collection of twenty-five stories from Africa, China, India, Japan, and Latin America not only provides information about these cultures but also offers insight into universal experiences and relationships as well. Facing economic hardships, trying to relate to and understand one's parents, and wrestling with political issues are but three of the kinds of struggles the characters face.

22.134 Soto, Gary. **Living up the Street**. Dell, 1992. 167 pp. ISBN 0-440-21170-0. Nonfiction.

To read *Living up the Street* is to come to know poet and novelist Gary Soto, at least in part. From his early childhood days, when he and his siblings took delight in teaching their friends to fight, to his adult struggles to become a writer, Soto gives the reader an honest look at what it was like to grow up as a Mexican American in the barrio of Fresno. Although it would have been easy to focus on the negative, Soto chooses instead to recall incidents and relationships that reveal a broad range of emotions—courage, jealousy, humor, love, loyalty, deceit, and determination.

22.135 Soto, Gary. **Pacific Crossing.** Harcourt Brace Jovanovich, 1992. 144 pp. ISBN 0-15-259187-7. Fiction.

Lincoln Mendoza, a fourteen-year-old Mexican American, and his friend Tony accept an invitation to study in Japan. As participants in a student-exchange program, Lincoln stays with the Ono family and Tony with the Inaba family. During their six-week stay, Lincoln becomes close friends with the Onos' son, Mitsuo, and the two learn to appreciate one another's heritage. The book includes a glossary of Spanish and Japanese phrases.

22.136 Soto, Gary. **Small Faces.** Dell/Laurel-Leaf Library, 1993. 137 pp. ISBN 0-440-21553-6. Nonfiction.

Whether Mexican American novelist and poet Gary Soto is recalling how he met and fell in love with his wife, attending a concert, speculating on his role in society, or lamenting the destruction of the rain forests, he is an engaging writer. His willingness to reveal himself as one who laughs, cries, and cares deeply about family, friends, and the world around him is likely to appeal to most readers.

22.137 Soto, Gary, editor. **Pieces of the Heart: New Chicano Fiction.** Chronicle Books, 1993. 171 pp. ISBN 0-8118-0068-7. Fiction.

Gary Soto, a well-known Latino poet and novelist, has compiled sixteen short stories written by Americans of Mexican descent. "The Waltz of the Fat Man," "Summer League," "La Loco Santa," and "The Jumping Bean" are four of the stories in this diverse collection. The stories vary greatly in plot, setting, and style, but the characters are Chicanos—not the stereotypes found in much literature, but real people dealing with life's struggles. Each is a "piece of the heart."

22.138 Spinelli, Jerry. **Maniac Magee.** HarperCollins/Harper Trophy Books, 1992. 184 pp. ISBN 0-06-440424-2. Fiction.

Jerry Lionell "Maniac" Magee is orphaned at age three and becomes homeless eight years later when he runs away from his uncaring aunt and uncle. He is still running the following year when he arrives in Two Mills, Pennsylvania. The first person he meets there is Amanda Beale, and soon he is taken in by her African American family, becoming the only white person to live in the town's East End. The scraggly little kid with the tattered shoes amazes all with his running speed and an inside-the-park "frog" home run; he teaches an old man how to read and in return learns about the man's baseball career in the minor leagues; and he helps remove the color barrier between the East End and the West End. First published in 1990.

ALA Notable Books for Children, 1991
Booklist Editors' Choice, 1990
Boston Globe–Horn Book Fiction Award, 1990
Newbery Medal, 1991

22.139 Staples, Suzanne Fisher. **Haveli.** Alfred A. Knopf, 1993. 259 pp. ISBN 0-679-84157-1. Fiction.

In this magnificent sequel to *Shabanu: Daughter of the Wind,* Shabanu, a Pakistani young woman, is now married to the elderly Rahim and struggles to find acceptance for herself and her daughter, Mumtaz, among the other wives of the household. Shabanu works in subtle ways to assure a better future for Mumtaz, but just when Shabanu's goals seem in sight, violence, love, and betrayal separate her from everything she holds dear. Shabanu must choose between her own dreams and her responsibilities in this mesmerizing and evocative book.

ALA Best Books for Young Adults, 1994
Booklist Editors' Choice, 1993
School Library Journal Best Books, 1993

22.140 Strom, Yale. **Uncertain Roads: Searching for the Gypsies.** Macmillan/Four Winds Press, 1993. 112 pp. ISBN 0-02-788531-3. Nonfiction.

Who are the Rom? American author Yale Strom was able to gain access to Eastern European and European Rom (or gypsy) communities and to gain insight into an often misunderstood culture. Through interviews and photographs, Strom makes a significant effort to reveal this culture, its love of music, and the racism it has experienced.

22.141 Taylor, Mildred D. **Mississippi Bridge.** Illustrated by Max Ginsburg. Bantam/Skylark Books, 1992. 62 pp. ISBN 0-553-15992-5. Fiction.

The authentic events of this poignant story are narrated by ten-year-old Jeremy Sims, a white boy who lives in Mississippi in the 1930s. Jeremy is at the general store when the weekly bus to Jackson arrives. Several black passengers are waiting to ride the bus, including the grandmother of Stacey Logan, his neighbor. Throughout the day, Jeremy has witnessed many segregation practices that have puzzled and sometimes embarrassed him. When several white passengers arrive late, the black passengers, who have been waiting all day, are forced to give up their seats. In a twist of fate, a tragic accident takes place, and the bus never makes it to Jackson.

Notable 1990 Children's Trade Books in the Field of Social Studies

22.142 Taylor, Theodore. **Timothy of the Cay.** Harcourt Brace, 1993. 161 pp. ISBN 0-15-288358-4. Fiction.

In April 1942, Phillip Enright, an eleven-year-old white boy, and Timothy Gumbs, a black man of seventy, are shipwrecked in the Caribbean when their ship is torpedoed. Phillip is blinded by the blast. He and Timothy survive for three months on a tiny island, but when a hurricane strikes, Timothy dies. Phillip must manage alone for two months before he is rescued. Years later, remembering and recalling Timothy's wisdom, Phillip returns to Timothy's burial site. Sequel to *The Cay.*

ALA Best Books for Young Adults, 1994
Notable 1994 Children's Trade Books in the Field of Social Studies

22.143 Temple, Frances. **Taste of Salt: A Story of Modern Haiti.** Orchard Books, 1992. 179 pp. ISBN 0-531-08609-7. Fiction.

Burned and disfigured, young Djo may not survive the terrorist attack on Lafanmi, a boys' shelter begun by Father Jean-Bertrand

Aristide. Aristide assigns a young girl to tape-record Djo's story, and their friendship develops as Djo slowly and painfully recalls the events of his life—events closely linked with Haiti's struggle for democracy and Aristide's rise in political power in the 1980s. This sensitive and exciting story brings alive recent political events in Haiti and the sound of the Haitian language.

Jane Addams Award, 1993
Booklist Editors' Choice, 1992
IRA Children's Book Award, 1993
School Library Journal Best Books, 1992

22.144 Thomas, Joyce Carol, editor. **A Gathering of Flowers: Stories about Being Young in America.** Harper and Row/Harper Keypoint Books, 1990. 232 pp. ISBN 0-06-026174-9. Nonfiction.

To read these stories is to gain a better understanding of oneself as well as others. Gary Soto, Maxine Hong Kingston, and the other writers represented in this book show that love, fear, success, failure, joy, pain, and sorrow are universal emotions and experiences. In entertaining and thought-provoking ways, the authors present young adults from a variety of ethnic backgrounds wrestling with such issues as religious faith, first love, and the treatment of those society considers misfits.

22.145 Uchida, Yoshiko. **The Invisible Thread.** Simon and Schuster/ Julian Messner, 1991. 136 pp. ISBN 0-671-74164-0. Nonfiction.

In this book, award-winning author Yoshiko Uchida recounts not only her own life but a terrible chapter in American history, the imprisonment of thousands of Japanese Americans during World War II. Without bitterness, Uchida tells of her family's losses, both material possessions and respect. She says she writes of this horrible experience because "I want each new generation of Americans to know what once happened in our democracy. I want them to love and cherish the freedom that can be snatched away so quickly, even by their own country."

ALA Best Books for Young Adults, 1993

22.146 Walter, Mildred Pitts. **Mississippi Challenge.** Macmillan/ Bradbury Press, 1992. 205 pp. ISBN 0-02-792301-0. Nonfiction.

Mildred Pitts Walter traces the history and struggles of African Americans in the state of Mississippi, from slavery to the civil rights era. Readers can learn much about the Freedman's Bureau, the Mississippi Freedom Democratic Party, and the Student Nonviolent Coordinating Committee. The book is compelling in story and includes black-and-white photographs.

22.147 Warner, Lucille Schulberg. **From Slave to Abolitionist: The Life of William Wells Brown.** Dial Books, 1993. 135 pp. ISBN 0-8037-2743-7. Nonfiction.

William Wells Brown is not a well-known name, but his life story is amazing. He began as a slave on a Missouri farm and died at age sixty-nine as a free man, an antislavery lecturer, a world traveler, and the first black American novelist. The author adapted Brown's writings to a first-person narrative that vividly describes the horrors of slavery and Brown's personal struggles to become a free man.

22.148 Weaver-Gelzer, Charlotte. **In the Time of Trouble.** E. P. Dutton, 1993. 275 pp. ISBN 0-525-44973-6. Fiction.

Fourteen-year-old Jessie goes to a missionary boarding school in the African country of Cameroon. She dreams of her upcoming journey to Egypt, where she will attend high school. However, in Cameroon in the 1950s, there is a struggle for national independence from France, and Jessie and her missionary parents are drawn into the conflict. Jessie learns to deal with the people around her during these times of trouble, and it deepens her belief in God and in herself.

22.149 Weidhorn, Manfred. **Jackie Robinson.** Atheneum, 1993. 207 pp. ISBN 0-689-31644-5. Nonfiction.

Jack Roosevelt Robinson started life deep in poverty and surrounded by prejudice, but through a rare combination of athletic skill, intelligence, leadership, and courage, he went on to become a national hero, cheered by baseball fans, admired by his peers, and courted by politicians. When Robinson was chosen by the Brooklyn Dodgers in 1947 to be the first black man to play major league baseball, he had to perform a delicate balancing act while silently withstanding insults and threats to himself and his family. Despite these pressures, Robinson emerged from his first season as rookie of the year. Largely because of his talent and courage, baseball was integrated without violence or legislation. After his ten-year baseball career ended, Jackie Robinson remained an ardent supporter of the Civil Rights movement, and through his involvement in business and politics, he continued to fight against racial injustice despite the criticism he received.

Notable 1994 Children's Trade Books in the Field of Social Studies

22.150 Wesley, Valerie Wilson. **Where Do I Go from Here?** Scholastic, 1993. 138 pp. ISBN 0-590-45606-7. Fiction.

Two young African Americans manage to plot their own course in a predominately white environment. Marcus and Nia have the opportunity of a lifetime when they each receive a scholarship to Endicott, the best prep school in the United States. They almost lose their way, however, as they struggle to maintain their own identity and culture in a sometimes insensitive and unaware climate. This is a good read for any young person who wants to understand what it is like to be in the minority.

ALA Quick Picks for Young Adults, 1994

22.151 Williams, Michael. **Into the Valley.** Putnam/Philomel, 1993. 191 pp. ISBN 0-399-22516-1. Fiction.

At age seventeen, Walter does not understand what is happening in his South African country. Then he reads about a seventeen-year-old general who is responsible for saving his village. When his brother dies, Walter begins a search for the youthful general whom no one claims to know. He wants to understand his country's problem and his part in it—but first he must fight for his life. First published in South Africa, 1990.

22.152 Williams-Garcia, Rita. **Fast Talk on a Slow Track.** Dutton/Lodestar Books, 1991. 182 pp. ISBN 0-525-67334-2. Fiction.

Denzel Watson, a young black man and dedicated student, has difficulty deciding how to tell his parents that he is not going to attend Princeton, which is their great desire for him. Denzel becomes a door-to-door salesman during the summer, and in a deliberate effort to compete, he discovers himself.

ALA Best Books for Young Adults, 1992
ALA Quick Picks for Young Adults, 1992
School Library Journal Best Books, 1991

22.153 Wilson, August. **Two Trains Running.** Penguin/Plume Books, 1993. 110 pp. ISBN 0-452-26929-6. Fiction.

This play is set in Pittsburgh in 1969, where several patrons of Memphis Lee's restaurant sit around the counter and discuss the ills of the world. Through these characters, we see portraits of black America and the African American experience. The restaurant regulars are struggling to cope with the turbulence of their changing world: the diner is scheduled to be torn down, an ex-con is looking for a job, and various others are being affected by the economy. Using vivid characters, Pulitzer Prize–winning dramatist August Wilson paints the events of everyday life of ordinary people in a culturally rich and authentic portrait.

22.154 Witkin, Zara (edited by Michael Gelb). **An American Engineer in Stalin's Russia: The Memoirs of Zara Witkin, 1932–1934.** University of California Press, 1991. 363 pp. ISBN 0-520-07134-4. Nonfiction.

Not only was Zara Witkin a brilliant engineer; he also was an idealist. It was his idealism that took him to Stalin's Russia in 1932 with the hope that he could be a part of the great experiment called Communism. The corruption of the bureaucrats, their lack of sensitivity to the suffering of the masses, and his failure to win the heart of Russian actress Emma Tsesarskaia disappointed Witkin and led to his return to California in 1934.

22.155 Wood, Tim. **The Aztecs.** Viking, 1992. 47 pp. ISBN 0-670-84492-6. Nonfiction.

Who were the Aztecs? Why are they important in history? Answers to these and other questions are presented in this compact overview of the Aztecs, with vivid illustrations and four see-through cutaways of Montezuma's palace, an Aztec house, a temple, and the Great Temple of Tenochtitlan. The book covers the Aztecs' encounters with other tribes, their civilization, and the coming of the Spanish in 1519. It provides an excellent introduction to the customs, beliefs, and culture of this interesting and productive people.

Notable 1992 Children's Trade Books in the Field of Social Studies

22.156 Wyman, Carolyn. **Ella Fitzgerald: Jazz Singer Supreme.** Franklin Watts/Impact Books, 1993. 117 pp. ISBN 0-531-13031-2. Nonfiction.

Despite her shy nature, Ella Fitzgerald managed to overcome tremendous stumbling blocks to become one of the greatest jazz vocalists in the world. Starting out by winning a small sum of money in a Harlem music competition, Fitzgerald has since sung with top bands and renowned musicians in the United States and other countries. This straightforward, simply written biography outlines the difficulties Fitzgerald experienced with segregation when she was on tour, her failed marriages, and the weight problem that she has battled since childhood, but it also relates the happier times in her life. Source notes and a discography are included in the book for those interested in the chronology of her career.

22.157 Yep, Laurence, editor. **American Dragons: Twenty-Five Asian American Voices.** HarperCollins, 1993. 234 pp. ISBN 0-06-021495-3.

While Laurence Yep taught creative writing in Asian American studies, he collected twenty-five short stories, poems, and excerpts from plays—all written by Asian Americans. The contributors include well-known authors, such as Maxine Hong Kingston, and new writers. They explore all the questions immigrants must face: Who am I? How do I fit in? What is the American dream? Each contributor shows a fresh, new perspective of life as an Asian American.

ALA Best Books for Young Adults, 1994

23 Mysteries, Spies, and Crime

23.1 Brown, Rosellen. **Before and After.** Farrar, Straus and Giroux, 1992. 354 pp. ISBN 0-374-10999-0. Fiction.

This story centers on Carolyn, who is a pediatrician, her husband, Ben, who is a sculptor, and their two children, seventeen-year-old Jacob and his younger sister, Judith. The family has moved to a small New England town to enjoy the comforts of rural life, but Jacob disappears when the police come to question him about the death of his girlfriend. The story of a brutal crime of passion unfolds as Carolyn, Ben, and Judith alternately tell how their lives are changed forever and how they struggle to survive as they are pitted against each other, the community, and the law. Mature language and situations.

Booklist Editors' Choice, 1992

23.2 Cadnum, Michael. **Calling Home.** Viking, 1991. 138 pp. ISBN 0-670-83556-8. Fiction.

Peter, his girlfriend Angela, his best friend Mead, and their friend Lani, all high school seniors, always hang out together in their small California town. When Mead disappears, Peter knows that Mead is dead and that he is to blame. Because Mead's mother is so worried and Mead's father is ill, Peter calls them and impersonates Mead. As Mead's mother becomes more frantic and his father's condition worsens, Peter is tortured with guilt. Peter drinks and takes pills to make it through each day and wonders if anything could be worse than confessing.

ALA Quick Picks for Young Adults, 1992

23.3 Collins, Wilkie. **The Woman in White.** Bantam Books, 1990. 564 pp. ISBN 0-553-21186-2. Fiction.

Young Walter Hartright first sees the mysterious lady in white while walking to London. When he accepts a position as a drawing master at Limmeridge House in Cumberland, he meets the beautiful Laura and finds himself caught up in a series of events involving mistaken identities, locked rooms, and locked asylums. To save Laura, Walter must find the woman in white and uncover the secret of an unscrupulous nobleman. Victorian England is the setting for this classic novel of mystery and suspense originally published in 1860.

23.4 Crew, Gary. **Strange Objects.** Simon and Schuster, 1993. 216 pp. ISBN 0-671-79759-X. Fiction.

On a school field trip in Australia, sixteen-year-old Steven Mesenger discovers an old iron pot containing a diary and a mummified hand, relics from a seventeenth-century shipwreck. The story is told through Steven's notes, newspaper accounts, and the diary of Wouter Loos, a convicted murderer who was cast adrift off the coast of Australia along with a seventeen-year-old psychopath. Steven's life is dominated by the discovery and the visions he begins to have involving the characters in Loos's diary, and then Steven suddenly disappears. First published in Australia, 1990.

23.5 Dhondy, Farrukh. **Black Swan.** Houghton Mifflin, 1993. 217 pp. ISBN 0-395-66076-9. Fiction.

Rose earns a scholarship to attend one of the drama colleges in or near London, but she must find a holiday job. When her mother becomes ill, Rose takes her place caring for the elderly, eccentric Mr. Bernier. Mr. B. sets her to work transcribing the diary of a black man, a contemporary of Shakespeare and Marlowe. Through her work, Rose discovers the manuscript holds a secret that could shock the literary world and that Mr. B.'s true identity could get them both killed. First published in Great Britain, 1992.

23.6 Doyle, Sir Arthur Conan. **The Adventures of Sherlock Holmes.** Illustrated by Barry Moser. William Morrow/Books of Wonder, 1992. 342 pp. ISBN 0-688-10782-6. Fiction.

This collection of Sir Arthur Conan Doyle's first twelve stories, originally published a century ago, is an excellent introduction to the famous English detective Sherlock Holmes and his comrade Dr. Watson. Included are such famous cases as "The Red-headed League," illustrating Doyle's mastery of the original plot; "The Five Orange Pips" and "The Adventure of the Blue Carbuncle," suspenseful stories representative of Doyle's powers of deduction; and "The Adventure of the Speckled Band," illustrating Doyle's ability to create atmosphere.

23.7 Duncan, Lois. **Who Killed My Daughter?** Delacorte Press, 1992. 289 pp. ISBN 0-385-30781-0. Nonfiction.

In 1989 in Albuquerque, New Mexico, eighteen-year-old Kaitlyn Duncan was shot to death while driving home from a girlfriend's house. This is the true story of Lois Duncan's search for the murderer of her daughter. Faced with insufficient evidence provided by the police, who decide that Kaitlyn's death is the result of a random killing, Lois Duncan enlists the aid of a newspaper reporter and several known psychics. The author hopes that reading the book will motivate potential informants to come forward.

ALA Best Books for Young Adults, 1993
Margaret A. Edwards Award, 1991

23.8 Dunning, John. **Booked to Die.** Avon Books, 1993. 321 pp. ISBN 0-380-71883-9. Fiction.

Cliff Janeway, a Denver homicide detective, is a book lover and book collector. When a down-and-out book scout is murdered, Cliff is sure that he can solve the case. He believes that the murderer is Jackie Newton, a suspected psychopath, and he also suspects that Newton is guilty of a series of vagrant killings. When Cliff's overzealous pursuit of Newton costs him his badge, he follows his true passion and becomes a book dealer, buying and selling valuable first editions. Cliff now has time to get to the bottom of the slayings and to bring the killer to justice. Mature language and situations.

23.9 Ferguson, Alane. **Overkill.** Macmillan/Bradbury Press, 1992. 168 pp. ISBN 0-02-734523-8. Fiction.

Seventeen-year-old Lacey is trying to cope with problems at school and in her relationship with her lawyer sister. When Lacey's friend Celeste is murdered, Lacey's recurring nightmares lead the police to believe that she knows more than she is telling. Lacey is charged with Celeste's murder. With the help of her therapist, Lacey hopes her dreams will reveal the murderer's identity.

ALA Quick Picks for Young Adults, 1993

23.10 Guerard, Albert. **Gabrielle: An Entertainment.** Donald I. Fine, 1992. 224 pp. ISBN 1-55611-288-2. Fiction.

Thomas Randall, an American diplomat who is in Paris to attend a conference on Latin America, is tired of the constant presence of security men. He longs for one night to wander the streets he knew when, as a young boy, he attended school in Paris. The captivating Gabrielle helps Thomas escape from the hotel, but then her taxi-driver boyfriend kidnaps him. Thomas's night out becomes a nightmare as he and Gabrielle are caught up in the European underground and become victims of a succession of captors and causes. Mature situations.

23.11 Henry, Sue. **Murder on the Iditarod Trail.** Avon Books, 1993. 246 pp. ISBN 0-380-71758-1. Fiction.

"Iditarod: A grueling eleven-hundred-mile dog sled race across a frigid Arctic wilderness—a torturous test of endurance, skill and courage for a $250,000 reward." Jessie Arnold, Alaska's female "musher," realizes that some of the top Iditarod mushers contending for this year's award are being murdered in gruesome ways. State trooper Sergeant Alex Jensen fears that Jessie may be the next victim and is determined to solve the mystery in a race against time.

ALA Best Books for Young Adults, 1992

23.12 Hoobler, Dorothy, and Thomas Hoobler. **Vanished!** Walker, 1991. 104 pp. ISBN 0-8027-8149-7. Nonfiction.

This book in the Fact or Fiction Files series examines the facts and controversies about the disappearances of several famous people. Readers are encouraged to make up their own minds about the mysterious events. Included are mystery writer Agatha Christie; D. B. Cooper, who hijacked an airliner; aviator Amelia Earhart, who disappeared in 1937 on a flight around the world; and Raoul Wallenberg, the Swedish diplomat who saved thousands of Jews from the Nazis during World War II.

23.13 Kerr, M. E. **Fell Down.** HarperCollins/Harper Keypoint/Charlotte Zolotow Books, 1991. 191 pp. ISBN 0-06-021764-2. Fiction.

When his best friend is killed in a car crash, seventeen-year-old Fell drops out of his fancy prep school, determined to investigate his friend's death. In his search for the truth, he is drawn back to his school. What Fell learns there leads him to a ventriloquists' convention and to the solution of a mysterious disappearance and murder that happened twenty years earlier. Sequel to *Fell.*

Booklist Editors' Choice, 1991

23.14 Kirkpatrick, Sidney D., and Peter Abrahams. **Turning the Tide: One Man against the Medellin Cartel.** Penguin/Onyx Books, 1992. 317 pp. ISBN 0-451-40317-7. Fiction.

Richard Novak, a father of five and a professor at Concordia College near New York City, is also a lover of the sea. He goes to Norman's Cay in the Bahamas, hoping to set up a diving facility to study hammerhead sharks. Soon Novak finds himself in the nerve center of the Medellin Cartel and in combat with the kingpin of Colombia's cocaine empire. The events of this novel are based on actual court transcripts, court testimony, and interviews with the participants. The dialogue, however, has been re-created, based on these sources.

23.15   Landau, Elaine. **Big Brother Is Watching: Secret Police and Intelligence Services.** Walker, 1992. 144 pp. ISBN 0-8027-8161-6. Nonfiction.

Author Elaine Landau gives an insightful look at what happens when governments begin to fear other countries, or even their own people, and call into action the secret police, whose techniques include intimidation, suppression of dissent among their own citizens, and spying on other countries. The author also examines some of the organizations that work to counter international human rights abuses and to prevent human rights injustices.

23.16   Masters, Anthony. **A Watching Silence.** Simon and Schuster, 1992. 153 pp. ISBN 0-671-79173-7. Fiction.

Martin is lonely on Scotland's Shetland Islands, where his parents have come to write a book. He often visits the ruined village called Settler, five old stone cottages facing the water. When Martin finds a silver knife in one of the cottages, he is attacked by a catlike creature. Then an African factory ship is wrecked off the coast, and Martin is caught up in a series of dangerous events. Eventually he uncovers the mystery of Settler and the mystery surrounding the disappearance of valuable antiquities. First published as *Klondyker* in Great Britain, 1991.

23.17   Nixon, Joan Lowery. **A Candidate for Murder.** Dell/Laurel-Leaf Library, 1992. 210 pp. ISBN 0-440-21212-X. Fiction.

When Cary Amberson's father decides to run for governor of Texas, Cary's life changes, but not in ways she expects. Her friends treat her differently, and even her relationship with her boyfriend becomes strained. Cary receives frightening phone calls in the night and believes that someone is following her. With the help of Sally Jo Wilson, a new friend who is a newspaper reporter, Cary delves into a political conspiracy surrounding the election, only to discover that she herself is in mortal danger.

23.18   Nixon, Joan Lowery. **The Dark and Deadly Pool.** Dell/Laurel-Leaf Library, 1992. 179 pp. ISBN 0-440-20348-1. Fiction.

Liz Rafferty is glad to get a summer job at the Ridley Hotel health club. Suddenly, however, strange things are happening. Liz sees a dark shadow in the pool one night, guests' wallets are stolen, and valuable hotel items disappear. She is determined to find out who is behind the trouble, but when a hotel guest is murdered, Liz discovers her own life is in danger.

23.19 Nixon, Joan Lowery. **The Name of the Game Was Murder.** Delacorte Press, 1993. 192 pp. ISBN 0-385-30864-7. Fiction.

Samantha, an aspiring fifteen-year-old writer, visits her great-uncle Augustus, a noted author, at his mansion on Catalina Island off the coast of California. Augustus invites his guests to participate in a game, but the game leads to murder. Samantha discovers that she may become another victim when, in a race against time, she searches for a manuscript and a killer.

23.20 Pfoutz, Sally. **Missing Person.** Viking, 1993. 177 pp. ISBN 0-670-84663-5. Fiction.

Carrie, a high school senior in a small town in Maryland, finds her life completely disrupted when her mother disappears. Carrie's father seems preoccupied with his work, her older sister still feels the pain of growing up with an alcoholic mother, and even friends and neighbors do not seem to care. When even the handsome detective who is the brother of Carrie's boyfriend shows little interest in her mother's disappearance, Carrie is determined to discover the truth, but she wonders if there is anyone she can trust.

23.21 Prather, Ray. **Fish and Bones.** HarperCollins, 1992. 255 pp. ISBN 0-06-025122-0. Fiction.

After the Bank of Sun City, Florida, is robbed, stolen money begins to appear in many unlikely places. Thirteen-year-old Bones hopes to collect a reward for finding the robber, but as he searches for clues, he discovers that some of the townspeople have a secret. It is only when Bones learns the secret that he realizes he knows the identity of the robber.

School Library Journal Best Books, 1992

23.22 Pullman, Philip. **The White Mercedes.** Alfred A. Knopf, 1993. 170 pp. ISBN 0-679-93198-8. Fiction.

When seventeen-year-old Chris Marshall's parents divorce, he finds it difficult to accept the changes in his life. But in his small English town, he enjoys his summer job working for Oxford Entertainment Systems because it allows him to spend a lot of time out of the house. Then Chris meets Jenny, who is unlike anyone he has ever known. Chris becomes caught up in a web of deceit as a criminal seeks revenge. Through a series of tragic events, Chris achieves a wisdom beyond his years and experiences a loss that will affect his life, perhaps forever. Mature situations. First published in Great Britain, 1992.

23.23   Rappaport, Doreen. **The Alger Hiss Trial.** HarperCollins, 1993. 184 pp. ISBN 0-06-025120-4. Nonfiction.

In August 1948, Whittaker Chambers, an ex-Communist, accuses Alger Hiss, a highly respected government official, of having been a Communist spy. In December, Hiss is indicted by a federal grand jury; however, the trial results in a hung jury and no verdict. In November 1949, a second trial begins. The author reconstructs that trial, using testimony from edited transcripts of the trial. As you examine the facts in this Be the Judge, Be the Jury book, you can reach your own conclusions. Do you think Alger Hiss was guilty?

23.24   Rappaport, Doreen. **The Lizzie Borden Trial.** HarperCollins/ Harper Trophy Books, 1993. 175 pp. ISBN 0-06-025114-X. Nonfiction.

On August 4, 1892, in Fall River, Massachusetts, Andrew Borden, a wealthy businessman, and his second wife, Abby, are brutally murdered. Andrew's daughter Lizzie is arrested and tried for the murders. Doreen Rappaport uses testimony from edited transcripts of the trial to reconstruct the murder. Readers of this Be the Judge, Be the Jury book read the testimony of the witnesses, examine the evidence, and serve as a juror to determine whether Lizzie is guilty—or not guilty.

23.25   Reaver, Chap. **M.O.T.E.** Dell/Laurel-Leaf Library, 1992. 217 pp. ISBN 0-440-21173-5. Fiction.

While seventeen-year-old Chris Miller and his best friend Bill are building a clubhouse, they meet Mote, a mysterious Vietnam vet. The boys befriend Mote and in return benefit from his wise guidance. Then Mote is accused of murdering a sadistic teacher, and Chris finds himself in the hospital because someone thinks he knows too much. The boys and two very unusual policemen attempt to solve the crime. Mature situations.

23.26   Rose, Malcolm. **The Highest Form of Killing.** Harcourt Brace Jovanovich, 1992. 240 pp. ISBN 0-15-234270-2. Fiction.

Chemist Derek Thorn, his friend Sylvia, and her former boyfriend Mark discover that the Ministry of Defense is researching chemical warfare soon after Sylvia and Mark find the body of a MOD worker along with a vial of deadly T42. As they become caught up in a web of conspiracy and Mark takes matters into his own hands, events take a strange twist beyond their control.

23.27 Shreve, Anita. **Strange Fits of Passion.** Penguin/Onyx Books, 1992. 380 pp. ISBN 0-451-40300-2. Fiction.

Maureen English flees with her baby from New York City to the small town of St. Hilaire, Maine. To those who befriend this young woman with the horribly beaten face, she gives her name as Mary Amesbury. But she has not run far enough, for soon there is a charge of rape, a murder, and a suicide. One final betrayal, an article written by an ambitious journalist, haunts Maureen for the rest of her life.

23.28 Wells, Rosemary. **The Man in the Woods.** Scholastic/Point Books, 1991. 231 pp. ISBN 0-590-43826-3. Fiction.

Helen's first days in the large high school are a real challenge. On her way home the second day, Helen sees an automobile accident caused by the "Punk Rock Thrower." Without thinking, she follows a man up the hill into the woods. Though she does not catch him, he sees her, and from that moment on Helen is in danger. The police make an arrest, but Helen knows the real criminal is still out there somewhere. When she receives several threats, she and her friend Pinky must discover the man's secret before it is too late.

23.29 Wells, Rosemary. **When No One Was Looking.** Scholastic/Point Books, 1991. 218 pp. ISBN 0-590-43514-0. Fiction.

Young Kathy Bardy wants to be the New England tennis champion. Her coach Marty, her parents, and her best friend Julia offer her constant encouragement and support. Only Kathy's sister, Jody, seems unimpressed by her talent. The one person standing between Kathy and the title is Ruth Grimm, a big, strong player, until Ruth is found in the bottom of the club pool. Marty and even Kathy become suspects before the police decide Ruth's death is an accident. But then Kathy learns the terrible truth.

23.30 Wersba, Barbara. **You'll Never Guess the End.** HarperCollins/ Charlotte Zolotow Books, 1992. 132 pp. ISBN 0-06-020449-4. Fiction.

Fifteen-year-old New Yorker Joel Greenberg attempts to cope with feelings of neglect when his older brother J. J. publishes his first novel and becomes an overnight success. Unexpectedly, Joel and his devoted dog Sherlock become involved in a funny but nearly tragic adventure. Encouraged by one of the many homeless people he helps, Joel, with Sherlock's help, finds J. J.'s former girl-friend—who has been kidnapped—and in doing so, Joel learns much about himself.

23.31   Westall, Robert. **Stormsearch.** Farrar, Straus and Giroux, 1992. 124 pp. ISBN 0-374-37272-1. Fiction.

Tim Vaux and his little sister, Tracy, spend summer vacations with their aunt and uncle on the harsh English seacoast while their parents work with Third World governments for the United Nations. The summers have always been exciting for Tim, but never as much as the summer when he discovers an antique model ship on the beach after a stormy night. While Uncle Geoff is restoring the model, he and Tim discover a hidden letter that leads them to an unsolved family mystery and the story of a doomed Victorian love.

24 Myths, Legends, and Folklore

24.1 Geras, Adèle. **The Tower Room.** Harcourt Brace Jovanovich, 1992. 150 pp. ISBN 0-15-289627-9. Fiction.

This story is the first in a trilogy based on fairy tales. Like Rapunzel, Megan falls in love, but in this tale the "prince" is Simon Findlay, the male lab assistant in an all-girls' boarding school in London. Megan has come to the school to live with a foster mother, the head mistress, after her parents are killed. Then Megan discovers that her foster mother has chosen Simon for herself.

24.2 Geras, Adèle. **Watching the Roses.** Harcourt Brace Jovanovich, 1992. 152 pp. ISBN 0-15-294816-3. Fiction.

In this modern-day version of the Sleeping Beauty fairy tale, Alice, Bella, and Megan look forward to Alice's eighteenth birthday. But Alice's family dreads this day because Aunt Violette placed a curse on Alice at her christening—death at the age of eighteen. On the night of her birthday party, the curse appears to have come true, except Alice lies in a coma-like state following a horrible experience. Sequel to *The Tower Room* and second book of the trilogy. First published in Great Britain, 1991.

24.3 Highwater, Jamake. **Anpao: An American Indian Odyssey.** Illustrated by Fritz Scholder. HarperCollins/Harper Trophy Books, 1992. 256 pp. ISBN 0-397-31750-6. Fiction.

In this retelling of the Blackfoot Indian legend of the young brave who travels to the Sun to have his scar removed, Anpao journeys to get the Sun's permission to marry the beautiful Ko-Ko-mik-e-is. As in other stories based on Native American oral tradition, Anpao meets Coyote, Raven, Grandmother Spider, and the Mouse People. When he returns, Anpao has earned the love and trust of Ko-Ko-mik-e-is.

24.4 Nimmo, Jenny. **Ultramarine.** Dutton Children's Books, 1992. 199 pp. ISBN 0-525-44869-1. Fiction.

Ned and his sister Nellie live by the sea and feel very unconnected to any humans, including their mother. When she remarries and they are left with their odd grandmother and aunt, strange occurrences begin. They meet an unusual man from the sea who asks for their help saving endangered birds and who helps them unravel the secrets of their family in this ecological fantasy and mystery. First published in Great Britain, 1990.

24.5   Racine, Jean (translated by Margaret Rawlings). **Phèdre.** Penguin Books, 1991. 180 pp. ISBN 0-14-044591-9. Nonfiction.

Shakespeare is known for his great heroes, Racine for his great heroines. One such is Phèdre, the central character in a story based on Greek legend. Phèdre is the wife of Theseus, king of Athens and Trozene. Against her will, she falls passionately in love with her stepson, Hippolytus. Horrified over this illicit passion, Phèdre feigns hatred of Hippolytus and nearly starves herself to death. When word comes of the death of Theseus, she is persuaded by her nurse, Oenone, to confess her love to Hippolytus, only to learn immediately afterward that Theseus is alive. In Greek mythology, even the idea of a crime is severely punished, but no one punishes Phèdre more than she does herself. This edition gives the English translation and the French version on opposite pages.

24.6   Rhyne, Nancy. **The South Carolina Lizard Man.** Illustrated by Mauro Magellan. Pelican, 1992. 139 pp. ISBN 0-88289-907-4. Fiction.

Before they leave their beloved South Carolina home, twins Josh and Matt are determined to explore Hell Hole Swamp, home of the seven-foot-tall lizard. When they find the monster, they become involved in adventure and solve the mystery of the sphinx in this unusual and satisfying tale.

24.7   Rice, Robert. **The Last Pendragon: A Novel.** Walker, 1992. 209 pp. ISBN 0-8027-1180-4. Fiction.

King Arthur is dead, and his kingdom is decaying. Irion is elected tribune of a band of warriors who are preparing to fight the Saxons and regain their land. To succeed, Irion must reconcile two opposing aspects of his heritage: he is the grandson of Arthur and son of Medraut, Arthur's murderer. With the help of Irion's long lost mother and the last remaining knight of the Round Table, Camelot may yet be regained and the Britons freed from a reign of terror.

ALA Best Books for Young Adults, 1993

24.8   Sutcliff, Rosemary. **The Shining Company.** Farrar, Straus and Giroux, 1992. 296 pp. ISBN 0-374-46616-5. Fiction.

In this story of true friends and an epic tragedy set in Britain in the year 600, three hundred warriors—the Shining Company—follow the example of Arthur Pendragon and the hero Cuchulainn in order to push the Saxon invaders from their land. Poet Aneirin rides with them to tell the story for Mynyddog, King of the Gododdin. First published in Great Britain, 1990.

ALA Notable Books for Children, 1991
Booklist Editors' Choice, 1990
IRA Young Adults' Choices, 1992
School Library Journal Best Books, 1990

24.9 Wein, Elizabeth E. **The Winter Prince.** Atheneum, 1993. 202 pp. ISBN 0-689-31747-6. Fiction.

Medraut, eldest son of King Arthur, lives in the shadow of Lleu, Arthur's legitimate son and heir to the throne. Medraut's responsibility is to protect Lleu, and often the half-brothers are in daring life-threatening situations against Arthur's enemies. But Medraut also thinks of what would happen if Lleu were not alive. *The Winter Prince* is a new look at Medraut, who, in league with his mother, Morgause, is usually cast as the villain in Arthurian tales.

24.10 Young, Richard Alan, and Judy Dockrey Young, editors. **Outlaw Tales: Legends, Myths, and Folklore from America's Middle Border.** August House, 1992. 224 pp. ISBN 0-87483-195-4. Nonfiction.

In this collection of tales about the lives of famous, infamous, and lesser-known outlaws, the editors make an attempt to differentiate among folktales, legends, myths, and family stories. Only documented accounts are presented, although some examples of commonly told but false tales are provided. The notorious exploits of female outlaw Belle Starr, from the first time she eluded the law through a clever disguise up to her ambush and death by an unknown person, are recounted. Accounts of other infamous outlaws, such as Wild Bill Hickok, Frank and Jesse James, and the "Hanging Judge," are also included in this informative and entertaining book. The lack of an index limits *Outlaw Tales* as a research tool, although the table of contents might prove adequate.

25 Performing Arts

25.1   Arnold, Sandra Martín. **Alicia Alonso: First Lady of the Ballet.** Walker, 1993. 90 pp. ISBN 0-8027-8243-4. Nonfiction.

"First Lady of the Ballet" is how Alicia Alonso is thought of in ballet circles. Alonso wanted to dance, and nothing was going to stop her. Then, when she was twenty years old, she was confined to bed for two years after eye surgery to correct two detached retinas. During those years she used her fingers as legs and practiced with them. After she and her husband, Fernando, left Cuba for the United States, their first opportunity came with the Mordkin Ballet, the forerunner of the American Ballet Theatre. From then on, the two were in great demand in the ballet world and in Broadway musicals. Alicia Alonso is known as one of the great interpreters of the ballet *Giselle;* in her seventies, she still practices every day and still performs short works. Ballet lovers will enjoy this story of a great woman's life.

25.2   Betancourt, Jeanne. **Kate's Turn.** Scholastic, 1992. 133 pp. ISBN 0-590-43103-X. Fiction.

It is a dream come true! Kate wins a scholarship to a famous ballet school and moves from Oregon to New York City to join in the world of dance. While students in the company are able to take part in professional performances, the strain of rehearsing and performing is great. Kate must decide if this life is worth the struggle and separation from her family.

25.3   Carter, Steven R. **Hansberry's Drama: Commitment and Complexity.** Penguin/Meridian Books, 1993. 199 pp. ISBN 0-452-01105-1. Nonfiction.

After giving a brief overview of the life, writings, and literary style of African American dramatist Lorraine Hansberry, author Steven R. Carter provides an in-depth analysis of five of her most famous plays. He also looks at two of her works (one complete, one not) as well as the influence of the theater of the absurd. Although Hansberry died at age thirty-four, she left a rich literary legacy, as clearly defined in each of these essays. For further reference and study, Carter includes an extensive list of works cited at the end of each chapter.

American Book Award, 1992

25.4 Catalano, Grace. **Joey Forever: A Biography of Joey Lawrence.** Bantam Books, 1993. 119 pp. ISBN 0-553-56611-3. Nonfiction.

Joey Lawrence or Joey Russo? Fans of the television series *Blossom* will find answers as we take an inside look into the private life of Joey Lawrence. Since the age of five, Joey has managed to work within the television and recording industries and still remain the kid next door, even while being pursued by adoring fans. Photos follow Joey from an adorable child in television commercials to the teen heartthrob rock star he has become.

25.5 Hansberry, Lorraine (edited by Robert Nemiroff). **A Raisin in the Sun: The Unfilmed Original Screenplay.** Penguin/Plume Books, 1992. 206 pp. ISBN 0-452-26776-5. Fiction.

The Younger family, a microcosm of the African American family of the 1950s, has lived in an apartment on Chicago's South Side for the last thirty-five years. When the father dies and leaves the family a substantial sum of money, the survivors' dreams may finally be realized: a house for the mother, a store for the son, and a college education for the daughter. But then an unexpected twist of events changes all three of their lives.

25.6 Haskins, James. **Black Music in America: A History through Its People.** HarperCollins/Harper Trophy Books, 1993. 198 pp. ISBN 0-690-04462-3. Nonfiction.

James Haskins gives us a picture of black music by providing interviews with famous artists such as Louis Armstrong, Jelly Roll Morton, W. C. Handy, and Scott Joplin. He explores the early music of slaves, songs and spirituals, the birth of ragtime and the blues through classic jazz, bop, soul, disco, and modern jazz. Haskins also discusses the classical black musicians: William Grant Still, Samuel Coleridge-Taylor, and Marian Anderson. A comprehensive index is included.

25.7 Hautzig, David. **DJs, Ratings, and Hook Tapes: Pop Music Broadcasting.** Macmillan, 1993. 44 pp. ISBN 0-02-743471-0. Nonfiction.

Radio music fills our lives, but getting that music out is complicated. David Hautzig took his camera to two popular radio stations to explain this process: the disc jockey, the selection and scheduling of songs, the sale of on-air advertising, the role of ratings, the expertise of the engineering department, and how the general manager ties it all together.

25.8   Higginsen, Vy, with Tonya Bolden. **Mama, I Want to Sing.** Scholastic, 1992. 183 pp. ISBN 0-590-44201-5. Fiction.

Doris Winter had to sing! From the time she was a little girl sitting in the back row while her mother attended choir rehearsals, she knew she had to sing. Winter was taken into the adult choir at Mount Calvary Baptist Church in Harlem, and from that beginning, her career took off. Against her mother's wishes, Winter moved from church music into jazz and became one of the most popular black singers of the 1960s. The play *Mama, I Want to Sing*—the story of this young black woman with the wonderful musical career—played off-Broadway for seven years and toured the United States and abroad.

25.9   King, Woodie, and Ron Milner, editors. **Black Drama Anthology.** Penguin/Meridian Books, 1986. 671 pp. ISBN 0-452-00902-2. Fiction.

The African American experiences of the 1960s and 1970s are graphically illustrated in this collection of twenty-three plays by both famous (Imamu Amiri Baraka, Langston Hughes) and less well known (Errol Hill, Ron Zuber) playwrights. Drawing from personal experience, the playwrights convey with harsh realism the voices of anger, pride, oppression, confrontation, honesty, and sometimes even humor. The plays vary in length, and several can be read in one sitting.

25.10   Kingman, Lee. **Break a Leg, Betsy Maybe!** William Morrow/Beech Tree Books, 1993. 250 pp. ISBN 0-688-11789-9. Fiction.

Break a Leg, Betsy Maybe! is written in the form of a play script, telling about Betsy's favorite class, drama, and its relation to her life. Betsy gets involved in the high school drama club in an effort to get to know her classmates. She has recently moved from a small private school to a large high school and feels timid about making friends. While involved in the school play, she discovers how hard it is to grow up and be in love. Readers with a love for the theater will understand Betsy's problems.

25.11   Kosser, Mike. **Hot Country.** Avon Books, 1993. 262 pp. ISBN 0-380-77061-X. Nonfiction.

Country music has become a national passion in the past few years. In *Hot Country*, several introductory chapters explain this musical explosion that has surprised everyone. The rest of the book provides biographical sketches of singers Garth Brooks, Billy

Ray Cyrus, Vince Gill, Alan Jackson, George Strait, Randy Travis, Travis Tritt, and Ricky Van Shelton.

25.12 Lamb, Wendy, editor. **Ten out of Ten: Ten Winning Plays Selected from the Young Playwrights Festival, 1982–1991.** Delacorte Press, 1992. 296 pp. ISBN 0-385-30811-6. Fiction.

Written by young adults under the age of nineteen, the plays in this collection deal with friendship, dating, street life, as well as alcoholism and drugs, suicide, murder, and romance. For example, "Women and Wallace" traces the boyhood of the title character as he deals with his mother's suicide, his relocation to his grandmother's house, and his attempts to feel fully accepted and loved by female students in his classes.

25.13 Meyerowitz, Joel. **George Balanchine's *The Nutcracker*.** Little, Brown, 1993. 105 pp. ISBN 0-316-56921-6. Nonfiction.

Peter Tchaikovsky made the world aware of the story of *The Nutcracker*. Joel Meyerowitz has photographed the New York City Ballet company's production of this ballet and produced a gorgeous, full-color book. He has included a list of the dancers so that they may be identified. The book also contains a warning that the purchase of this book gives no right to the copying of choreography, sets, or costumes.

25.14 Perlman, Marc. **Youth Rebellion Movies.** Lerner, 1993. 80 pp. ISBN 0-8225-1640-3. Nonfiction.

Rebellion against authority has always played a part in growing up, but in the 1950s the juvenile delinquent became a buzzword and a new kind of "hero" for Hollywood filmmakers. From Elvis, Brando, and James Dean to the 1989 movie *Heathers,* these easy-to-read synopses of the most successful rebellion movies let you decide if films are true reflections of the problems arising when troubled youths thwart authority.

25.15 Platt, Richard. **Film.** Alfred A. Knopf/Dorling Kindersley Books, 1992. 64 pp. ISBN 0-679-91679-2. Nonfiction.

What do a movie camera and a sewing machine have in common? The answer is found in this abundantly illustrated history of film and the film industry, from the first "moving picture" to today's special effects and animatronics. In its heyday, the industry spawned "picture palaces" which accommodated up to 6,200 moviegoers, and Hollywood stars found themselves the subjects of collectors cards. Sound film was created *without* electronic amplification. Much succinct information about film is provided in this brief overview. Part of the Eyewitness Books series.

Notable 1992 Children's Trade Books in the Field of Social Studies

25.16   Pritikin, Karin. **The King and I: A Little Gallery Book of Elvis Impersonators.** Photographs by Kent Barker. Chronicle Books, 1992. 95 pp. ISBN 0-8118-0244-2. Nonfiction.

Elvis Presley impersonators reveal their inspirations for becoming re-creators of various phases in the entertainer's career. Personal comments and photos allow us to see each impersonator as he or she gives reasons for wanting to carry on the spirit of Elvis and perform for demanding audiences. All have been touched in some way by the singer and have developed essential techniques that they think best represent the King and his music.

25.17   Sansweet, Stephen J. **Star Wars: From Concept to Screen to Collectible.** Photographs by Steve Essig and David Tucker. Chronicle Books, 1992. 131 pp. ISBN 0-8118-0101-2. Nonfiction.

Star Wars, The Empire Strikes Back, and *The Return of the Jedi* caught the imagination of the American public and quickly became some of the most successfully marketed science fiction movies of the century. Collecting memorabilia from these movies has become popular. This encyclopedia-like book containing over 150 pictures traces the success of these state-of-the-art movies that combine animation and special effects with the classic theme of good versus evil. This book is a must for *Star Wars* collectors.

25.18   Schwartzman, Arnold. **Phono-Graphics: The Visual Paraphernalia of the Talking Machine.** Photographs by Garry Brod. Chronicle Books, 1993. 120 pp. ISBN 0-8118-0302-3. Nonfiction.

Everyone interested in collecting will find *Phono-Graphics* a fascinating history of the ads and labels accompanying the phonograph. Art of the 1920s, 1930s, and 1940s is reflected in the record jackets, record labels, tins that held phonograph needles, and advertising. The book contains full-color reproductions.

25.19   Staskowski, Andréa. **Movie Musicals.** Lerner, 1992. 80 pp. ISBN 0-8225-1639-X. Nonfiction.

Movie musicals from Fred Astaire to Patrick Swayze: What common threads do they share? How have they changed? This easy-to-read reference provides background information about the featured performers and a synopsis of each screenplay. Author Andréa Staskowski presents a history of movie musicals, from the introduction of *The Jazz Singer* in 1927 to musicals of the 1970s, that parallels the general trends found in society during this period. For those interested in further viewing, a brief listing of musical films available on home video is given.

25.20   Voigt, Cynthia. **Orfe.** Atheneum, 1992. 120 pp. ISBN 0-689-31771-9. Fiction.

Living in the world of commercial music is tough, and Orfe shows us just how tough it is. She starts out life after high school using her musical talent playing on street corners for money thrown into a hat. After she puts together her band, the group begins playing real club dates. All of Orfe's dreams are put into the songs she writes—including her dream of marrying Yuri, a drug addict.

25.21   Werner, Vivian. **Petrouchka: The Story of the Ballet.** Illustrated by John Collier. Viking, 1992. 29 pp. ISBN 0-670-83607-9. Fiction.

Petrouchka, the Russian version of the English Punch, was chosen by Igor Stravinsky to retell the story of the Butter Week Fairs in St. Petersburg that occur before Lent. Petrouchka is symbolic of the turmoil in Russia and the problems of being a human being. This story of the puppet's love for the ballerina features compelling paintings by John Collier.

26 Poetry

26.1 Behn, Robin, and Chase Twichell, editors. **The Practice of Poetry: Writing Exercises from Poets Who Teach.** HarperCollins/Harper Perennial Books, 1992. 299 pp. ISBN 0-06-271507-0.

So you are a would-be poet who has run dry. Pick up this book and discover nearly a hundred detailed and highly helpful exercises suggested and explained by professional poets who are also teachers (Rita Dove, Theodore Weiss, Daniel Halpern, and Stanley Plumly, among others). The exercises are arranged topically: getting started, using the unconscious, developing image and metaphor, voice, technical matters (such as sound, rhythm, structure), revision, and writer's block. The contributors frequently refer to or provide sample poems, and a twenty-one-page appendix gives a generous bibliographical guide to published works referred to in the text. A second appendix gives both sources of poetry books and extensive contributors' notes. This sophisticated book is best used by advanced students, but some of the exercises can be adapted for the beginner.

26.2 Bernos de Gasztold, Carmen (translated by Rumer Godden). **Prayers from the Ark.** Illustrated by Barry Moser. Viking, 1992. 71 pp. ISBN 0-670-84496-9.

This is a newly published selection from the original best-seller of the same name. Written by a French nun almost fifty years ago, these poems are "Catholic in origin but catholic also in the sense that they are for everyone." In these thirteen short monologues, Noah and twelve creatures address self-revelatory prayers to God that are unique, unsentimental, and totally honest. The color illustrations by Barry Moser are equally bold complements to the poems themselves.

26.3 Bierhorst, John, editor. **Lightning inside You, and Other Native American Riddles.** Illustrated by Louise Brierley. William Morrow, 1992. 104 pp. ISBN 0-688-09582-8.

John Bierhorst's collection of 120 riddles—plus an eleven-page introductory essay—gives us quite an insight into the Native American mind and into the subjects that Native Americans considered important enough for riddles. We are accustomed to treating Anglo Saxon riddles as literature; these examples from North, Central, and South American tribes are equally intriguing. And for those who do not consider riddles as poetry, remember that most riddles are pure metaphor.

26.4 Birmingham Museums and Art Gallery. **A Little Book of English Verse.** Chronicle Books, 1993. 59 pp. ISBN 0-8118-0532-8.

One-half of this pocket-sized book consists of twenty-seven sonnets and brief lyrics, almost all among the most quoted and most memorized in the English language. The authors range from Michael Drayton to W. H. Davies and Edward Thomas, with a heavy emphasis on the Romantics. The other half of the book consists of poems and facing-page illustrations from the Birmingham Museums and Art Gallery. The illustrations, generally lush and romantic, are beautifully apropos of the poems with which they are matched.

26.5 Chappell, Fred. **C: Poems.** Louisiana State University Press, 1993. 52 pp. ISBN 0-8071-1784-6.

The title *C* signifies that the volume contains 100 poems, and yes, they are short ones. A very few are translations; most are original marvels of compression and poetic ease with highly varied subjects. Fred Chappell mingles bits of wit in epigram form with prayers and dinnertime graces with pithy advice from an imaginary sex manual. The variety of tones is equally wide-ranging. Whichever poem you read, you will find a blend of wit and intellect with accomplished use of language and meter. This is some of the most disciplined writing of recent years.

26.6 Cronyn, George W., editor. **American Indian Poetry: An Anthology of Songs and Chants.** Fawcett/Columbine Books, 1991. 294 pp. ISBN 0-449-90670-1.

This book, first published in 1918, remains one of the most complete collections of Native American poetry. It contains both *translations* (more literal renderings) and *interpretations* in separate sections. The translations, which occupy more than half the book, are arranged by region, then by type; the interpretations are arranged by collector's name. Kenneth Lincoln's foreword is difficult going but says some interesting things about the history of America's interest in Native American literature. Mary Austin's new introduction argues that the songs and chants demand to be sung and danced and are not really intended for nor suitable for "eye" reading.

26.7 Day, Aidan, editor. **Alfred Lord Tennyson: Selected Poems.** Penguin Books, 1991. 376 pp. ISBN 0-14-044545-5.

Anyone who has lost a talented friend in youth will find "In Memoriam," Tennyson's elegy on the death of Arthur Hallam, a deeply comforting and cathartic experience. In addition, this volume contains one other long work, "Maud," and many very readable short poems. The clear, smooth, melodious lines of Tennyson's poetry make it ideal for oral reading. Well-known poems in this collection also include "The Lady of Shalott," "Ulysses," "Break, Break, Break," "The Charge of the Light Brigade," and "Crossing the Bar." Tennyson's deft portrayals of the deeply human traits of both heroes and common folk make him a poet for all ages.

26.8   Dove, Rita. **Thomas and Beulah.** Carnegie-Mellon University Press, 1986. 79 pp. ISBN 0-88748-020-9.

One is tempted to call this book one long poem in many parts, rather than a collection of poems. Individually, the poems focus on moments in the lives of Rita Dove's grandparents; collectively, they narrate and highlight those two lives, and it is collectively that they gain a strength and richness that they would lack as short individual poems. Sometimes a later poem recalls an image or line from an earlier one; sometimes the earlier piece is not even fully understood until the later piece clarifies it. To aid the reader, Dove includes a short chronology of key events in her grandparents' lives.

26.9   Dunn, Sara, and Alan Scholefield, editors. **Poetry for the Earth.** Fawcett/Columbine Books, 1992. 247 pp. ISBN 0-449-90559-3.

This is a rich and broad collection: from the Roman poet Horace to Amy Clampitt; from Japan to the United States; from haiku to three-page lyrics; from rhapsodic elegy to poems of fear and despair. The more than 200 poems are grouped by mood and attitude into sections, such as Celebration, Loss, Anger. It is not a political collection per se; rather, the editors chose "to re-emphasize the concept of environment as constant and contiguous, not a 'bundle of issues' but something all of us experience." The lengthy introduction explains the selection criteria and offers brief, valuable comments on the history of nature poetry—comments that often add fruitful insights into both individual poems and poetic movements. The volume also includes brief biographical notes on the poets included.

26.10 Feelings, Tom. **Soul Looks Back in Wonder.** Illustrated by Tom Feelings. Dial Books, 1993. 33 pp. ISBN 0-8037-1001-1.

This is an interesting and beautiful book, emphasizing the beauty and creativity of blackness in both painting and poetry. Tom Feelings first did a series of strong paintings of young African Americans, then called upon writers such as Margaret Walker, Maya Angelou, and Walter Dean Myers to contribute short poems to accompany each painting. One poem by Langston Hughes, done years ago for a Feelings poster, appears here for the first time in a book. The illustrations are uniformly superb, the poems a little less so, but a number of them are of high merit and could well stand alone. This volume should appeal to readers spanning many years, reaching well down into the grades.

ALA Best Books for Young Adults, 1994
ALA Quick Picks for Young Adults, 1994
Coretta Scott King Illustrator Award, 1994

26.11 Fleischman, Paul. **Joyful Noise: Poems for Two Voices.** Illustrated by Eric Beddows. HarperCollins/Harper Trophy/Charlotte Zolotow Books, 1992. 44 pp. ISBN 0-06-021853-3.

Paul Fleischman's earlier *I Am Phoenix: Poems for Two Voices* gave us two-voice poems about birds, spoken by birds. This new volume provides duets about insects, spoken by insects. Subjects range from grasshoppers to a chrysalis becoming a butterfly; moods vary from joyous to sad, from meditative to whimsical.

Boston Globe–Horn Book Honor Book, 1988
Newbery Medal, 1989

26.12 Groves, Ruth V., editor. **301 Favorite Poems: Old and New.** Ruth V. Groves, 1992. 322 pp. ISBN 0-9634199-0-0.

If you have ever wanted a one-volume collection of the old standards, or if you have ever had a line of poetry running around in your head and have been unable to find its source, then this may be the book for you. The editor (as well as publisher), a former teacher with decades of experience, has put together an anthology of poems that worked for her—not so much the "great" poems as the "useful." Her taste leans toward poems with pronounced moral or patriotic themes, with rhyme, and with meter. Appendixes include a brief glossary of poetic terms and short biographies of the poets.

26.13 Harvey, Anne, editor. **Shades of Green.** Illustrated by John Lawrence. Greenwillow Books, 1991. 192 pp. ISBN 0-688-10890-3.

Sometimes we need to be reminded of how our own roots are sunk deep in nature, and this is the book to do it. Anne Harvey's rich collection of nature-related poems takes us on a journey through the countryside and celebrates every green and growing thing. Almost 200 poems—most of them British, with a smattering from the United States, Asia, and other locales—capture varied moods and visions of nature, but in the main, their tones are hopeful and optimistic. You will find many traditional friends among these poems and a few modern surprises as well. First published in Great Britain, 1991.

26.14 Jin, Ha. **Between Silences: A Voice from China.** University of Chicago Press, 1990. 79 pp. ISBN 0-226-39986-9.

Between the ages of fourteen and nineteen, Ha Jin (real name, Xuefei Jin) served in the People's Army of China during the Cultural Revolution of the 1960s. These poems, written originally in English and published while Ha Jin was a graduate student in the United States, personalize and reveal that turmoil through a variety of personae and voices. A few speak of love and friendship; more speak of heartbreak and horror. We meet children going off to war, such as the young volunteer (perhaps the poet himself) who feared the Russians: "We decided to go to the army / for we did not want to be roasted at home / like little pigs." We hear the voice of the calloused general calmly telling how he took care of possible enemy agents in his squad: "I did not bother to find them out. / I just shot the few persons I suspected." Once or twice the language is mature, but all of the poems are crystal-clear, understated, and very, very powerful.

26.15 Johnson, James Weldon. **Lift Every Voice and Sing.** Illustrated by Elizabeth Catlett. Walker, 1993. 34 pp. ISBN 0-8027-8250-7.

This is a short book of many parts. It opens with two pages of introductory material by author Jim Haskins on the composition of the anthem by African American poet James Weldon Johnson, plus biographical notes on the Johnson brothers and illustrator Elizabeth Catlett. The complete text of the song follows, spread over twelve pages facing Catlett's dramatic linocuts, which were created as a totally separate project more than forty years after the song. Closing the book is a page reproducing Catlett's original caption for each linocut and the complete sheet music. The heart of the book, Johnson's words and Catlett's powerful images, so completely complement each other that they seem to have been created simultaneously.

Booklist Editors' Choice, 1993
Notable 1994 Children's Trade Books in the Field of Social Studies

26.16 Kumin, Maxine. **Looking for Luck.** W. W. Norton, 1992. 94 pp. ISBN 0-393-03085-7.

By now we know what to expect when we begin a new book by Maxine Kumin: open, honest, accessible poems; poems with a strong narrative quality leading to a twist of insight; poems whose difficulties (and they are few) are "experiential rather than textual." Kumin's poems speak to the average, nonbookish reader without the assistance of a critic with a double handful of theories. This collection, her tenth, connects us to her life on her New Hampshire farm, her travels, and people she finds interesting. Her prefatory poem, "Credo," both announces her subjects and affirms her belief in their importance: "I believe in magic . . . in living on grateful terms with the earth . . . the thrust to go on." By the time we finish this book, we have experienced (to borrow another line) the "known astonishment of what has been."

26.17 Livingston, Myra Cohn, editor. **A Time to Talk: Poems of Friendship.** Macmillan/Margaret K. McElderry Books, 1992. 115 pp. ISBN 0-689-50558-2.

Eighty poems, representing several centuries and a variety of cultures, show the varied faces of friendship. Many of the selections are themselves old friends ("We Real Cool," "The Telephone," "To Lou Gehrig," and "On the Death of Friends in Childhood"), while other, less familiar choices add their own charm and wisdom. Occasionally the editor chooses passages on friendship from a longer work: excerpts from *Christabel*, *Medea*, *The Prelude*, and *As You Like It*, among others, add unique perspectives to the theme. The middle section (of five thematically arranged sections), entitled "Strange Friends, False Friends," really lifts this collection out of the ordinary as it surprises the reader with whimsical, unexpected, and even embittered looks at friendships strained and broken.

26.18 Longley, Judy. **My Journey toward You.** Helicon Nine Editions, 1993. 58 pp. ISBN 0-9627460-5-3.

Judy Longley shows us that the stuff of real life is the stuff of poetry. She opens with "Gauguin and Bonnard" in which French painter Pierre Bonnard, unlike his countryman Paul Gauguin, stays home and paints pictures of his own wife. She ends with a poem about holding a child as they ride a circus elephant: "his small body trusts my arm,/ the wide maternal rocking/ toward nowhere we've ever been." In between these two, we are at home with Longley: with her past, her family, her garden, and especially her dying husband. Most of the pieces, then, are about memory that "requires an impulse only the living/ possess," but the last two, "Witness/Clearing Your Study" and "Riding a Circus Elephant," ease toward affirmation and toward the unknown.

26.19 Marsh, James. **From the Heart.** Dial Books, 1993. 32 pp. ISBN 0-8037-1449-1.

Think of this book as a collection of offbeat valentines, and you won't be far wrong. Fifteen short rhyming poems about love face fifteen corresponding illustrations. The verses usually contain puns ("happiness . . . has brought me down to sighs"), while the bright illustrations of animals and plants always manifest a perfect stylized heart.

26.20 Matthews, William. **Selected Poems and Translations, 1969–1991.** Houghton Mifflin, 1992. 200 pp. ISBN 0-395-63121-1.

Perhaps because he is less mannered, less flamboyant, less eccentric than many of his contemporaries, William Matthews is a less well known poet, and that's our loss. This collection shows him to be a marvelously witty, intelligent, and skilled writer, highly accessible, yet full of quirks and turns that make him unique. His translations (from Fallon, the Roman poet Martial, and various Bulgarian poets) sound so sure and firm that they seem more like originals than the usual translations. And his original poems, both early and recent, take us on unhurried meditations about our world: they are indeed leisurely, narrative, full of rewarding side trips, yet always wrapping themselves up with a finely tied knot at the end. His language is a heightened vernacular, sometimes mature, always right.

26.21 Meredith, William. **Partial Accounts: New and Selected Poems.** Alfred A. Knopf, 1987. 194 pp. ISBN 0-394-55993-2.

This book, William Meredith's eighth, won him the Pulitzer Prize in 1988, yet he remains curiously unknown. While his first books from the 1940s (represented here by ten poems) come across as mannered and overly concerned with form, the work of his middle and later years is far more interesting and complex, far-ranging in subject matter, clear in voice and tone. During those decades when so many poets seemed angry and negative, Meredith remained refreshingly calm and optimistic, not just about the world but about poetry itself: "Poetry makes such things happen/ sometimes, as certain people do/ at the right juncture of our lives./ Don't knock it; it has called across/ the enchanted chasm of love/ resemblances like rescue gear."

26.22 Minczeski, John. **Gravity.** Texas Tech University Press, 1991. 67 pp. ISBN 0-89672-267-8.

Gravity—sometimes you escape it, sometimes you cannot. For poet John Minczeski, gravity obviously figures in a number of poems dealing with flying and with his father, a flight instructor. Sometimes, though, it figures in metaphors for other kinds of freedom: iced-up wings suddenly thaw, a venomous snake moves away, a trapped bat escapes. More often, gravity is a metaphor for what holds the poet to his family, to events and conflicts he could not escape, even to his lost Polish heritage. Minczeski's range of topics is wide: grade school book reports, an Elvis impersonator, columbines, men plummeting from a dirigible. Always, his clear, highly intelligible free verse illuminates both the strange and the familiar in our lives.

26.23 Moon, Pat. **Earth Lines: Poems for the Green Age.** Greenwillow Books, 1991. 63 pp. ISBN 0-688-11853-4.

At the outset, a book of fifty poems about ecology, vanishing wildlife, pollution, hunger, and similar social concerns sounds very unappetizing, but Pat Moon is skilled enough and witty enough to pull off an acceptable, even entertaining book. Some of the poems are good as serious poetry; some are funny; some work with ironic, mind-pleasing twists; some are good light-verse pieces that can stand comparison with anyone's light verse.

26.24 Morgan, Robert. **Green River: New and Selected Poems.** Wesleyan University Press, 1991. 88 pp. ISBN 0-8195-1181-1.

If you think only of novelists and short-story writers when you think "southern," think again. The South is producing an increasing number of fine poets, and Robert Morgan is among them. This book pulls together poems from his previous seven books (1969–90) plus a number of new poems. His writing is firmly grounded in the land and mountains of the South; in its people, their work and lore; and in the inner lives of us all. He uses free verse and a language that is clear and accessible, yet rich in metaphor and craftily turned phrases.

26.25 Myers, Walter Dean. **Brown Angels: An Album of Pictures and Verse.** HarperCollins, 1993. 36 pp. ISBN 0-06-022918-7.

Utterly unique, this book is an album of turn-of-the-century photos of African American children plus evocative, supportive poetry. Walter Dean Myers writes in a variety of styles—some poems are reminiscent of jump-rope chants, others of blues stanzas, still others are supple, delicate lyrics—styles chosen to complement the moods of the subjects in the photographs. The result is a delightful blend, at times amusing, at times moving, a real lesson in artistic judgment.

ALA Notable Books for Children, 1994

26.26 Neruda, Pablo (translated by W. S. Merwin). **Twenty Love Poems and a Song of Despair.** Illustrated by Jan Thompson Dicks. Chronicle Books, 1993. 79 pp. ISBN 0-8118-0320-1.

Like Kahlil Gibran's *The Prophet*, Pablo Neruda's love poems are the favorites of youthful admirers, though Neruda's work has achieved much higher critical status (including the Nobel Prize in 1971). *Twenty Love Poems* originally appeared in 1924 after censorship problems over its sometimes explicit sexuality. This fine new translation by W. S. Merwin does not read like the generic translation: stilted and wooden, as if done by a computer with a thesaurus. The lines are supple, the metaphors genuine, the surreal as off-key as we have any right to expect. The poems are sensual and earthy; the illustrations likewise are fully revealing at times. First published in Chile, 1924.

26.27 Norris, Pamela, editor. **Sound the Deep Waters: Women's Romantic Poetry in the Victorian Age.** Little, Brown/Bulfinch Press, 1992. 120 pp. ISBN 0-8212-1895-6.

The "angel of the hearth" is a popular term for the Victorian woman. According to editor Pamela Norris's introduction, "for some women at least the reality was rather different from the stereotype." All the poems in this anthology are by women, which shows that some indeed escaped the hearth. However, the subjects and attitudes seen in the poems do little to dispel the stereotype. The forty-eight poems (somewhat arbitrarily divided into four exactly equal sections) seldom surprise; rather, almost all are mannered, sentimental verse, typically Victorian and Pre-Raphaelite. Aside from a few poems by Emily Dickinson and Emily Brontë, there is little here of freedom and rebellion. The poems deal more with romantic yearnings, love requited and unrequited, happy and sad moments amid nature. The facing-page illustrations are well-known Pre-Raphaelite paintings—and here, too, there is little to show liberated womanhood. First published in Great Britian, 1991.

26.28 Nye, Naomi Shihab, editor. **This Same Sky: A Collection of Poems from around the World.** Macmillan/Four Winds Press, 1992. 212 pp. ISBN 0-02-768440-7.

If you have ever wanted to see modern poetry from outside the Anglo-American mainstream, this collection will show you what is going on in poetry around the world. While a handful of the poems come from Canada, New Zealand, and Wales and were written in English, the others (approximately 120 of them) come from more than sixty nations as diverse as Bangladesh, Japan, Angola, Syria, Sweden, and Peru. Other than Octavio Paz and Pablo Neruda, most contributors are younger poets who are virtually unknown in the United States. Naomi Shihab Nye includes several pages of notes on contributors and a one-page bibliography of contemporary anthologies, many of which will interest younger readers.

ALA Notable Books for Children, 1993

26.29 O'Grady, Tom, editor. **The Hampden-Sydney Poetry Review Anthology, 1975–1990.** Hampden-Sydney College, 1990. 309 pp. ISBN 0-940975-91-X.

Almost all poetry published today appears in journals with small circulations and is seldom seen by students and teachers. Though its name may not be widely known, *The Hampden-Sydney Poetry Review* is considered a prestige market by working poets. Contributions by such notables as May Sarton, A. R. Ammons, Marge Piercy, Henry Taylor, X. J. Kennedy, and Howard Moss testify to its quality. The more than 250 poems in this collection come from all parts of the United States and (in translation) from Europe. Tom O'Grady has selected clear, structured free verse that is accessible to most readers and that shows a strong interest in idea and sound. These are good poems to study, to teach, or just to read for pleasure.

26.30 Paulos, Martha, editor. **Felines: Great Poets on Notorious Cats.** Illustrated by Martha Paulos. Chronicle Books, 1992. 64 pp. ISBN 0-8118-0103-9.

This collection (a sequel to Martha Paulos's *Doggerel*) reads like a "Who's Who" of great poets: from Baudelaire to Dickinson and Wilde, from Eliot to Neruda and Tolkien. The poetry—high quality and as varied as the poets—ranges from the whimsical to the fantastic, from the flattering portrait by Thomas Morley to Don Marquis's terrifying tomcat, who "chants the hate of a million years / As he swings his snaky tale." Paulos herself provides twenty-five linocut illustrations that show her playful imagination.

26.31 Seay, James. **The Light as They Found It.** William Morrow/Quill Paperbacks, 1990. 70 pp. ISBN 0-688-08932-1.

Henry Taylor once said of his own poetry, "I look long and hard at something that doesn't move much." The same is not quite true of James Seay. The things he looks at—near accidents, postcards from his grandparents, Chuck Berry, Elvis, cheese, and an old bed that causes strange dreams—these things hold still, but the poet's mind never does. In an unique blend of narrative mediation and occasionally mature language, Seay explores not just the things themselves but their associations and implications, and how he relates to it all. When he recalls the combination of a cottonmouth, an Angus bull, a redwing blackbird, and himself, he asks what is his "possible distinction" from the others. That's what this book is about.

26.32 Simic, Charles. **The World Doesn't End: Prose Poems.** Harcourt Brace Jovanovich, 1989. 74 pp. ISBN 0-15-198575-8.

The short short story and the prose poem are both growing fads of the past several years. That Charles Simic won the Pulitzer Prize for this collection of very short prose pieces (few are more than half a page) may indicate that the movement has surprising strength, though Simic's work is virtually unique in several respects. His poems are surreal and quite obscure at times, yet occasionally some strike the reader as funny, poignant, or ironic. Even so, their obscurity makes it difficult to see their relationship, how one poem in the collection plays off against another. The opening section seems to have more unity and appears to be based on Simic's childhood experiences in wartime Yugoslavia. After this section, however, the poems grow more and more obscure, and analysis becomes more difficult.

Pulitzer Prize for American Poetry, 1990

26.33 Stephens, Mariflo, editor. **Some Say Tomato.** Northwood Press, 1993. 70 pp. ISBN 0-9638892-0-6.

There are collections of love poems, sports poems, and nature poems—why not a collection of tomato poems? All the poems collected here are about tomatoes or refer to tomatoes or celebrate tomatoes, or ever so slightly allude to tomatoes. The resulting harvest is richer than you might imagine. Contributors range from the editor's children to Rita Dove, William Stafford, and Maxine Kumin. There is even a song lyric by John McCutcheon and Si Kahn. Readers will be amused by tomatoes seen as "harlots/

flaunting their bulging roundness/ in skin-tight bright covers," stricken by lines like "on freezer shelves ice crystals form, pink as froth on the lips of the drowned," and surprised at how such an unlikely premise has yielded such good results overall.

26.34 Strand, Mark. **Selected Poems.** Alfred A. Knopf, 1990. 152 pp. ISBN 0-679-73301-9.

Culled from his first six books, these poems form a solid, broad introduction to the work of our fourth poet laureate, Mark Strand. He is an original: he likes to tease, to play games with your mind, to show you a paradox and then take it away, or show you simplicity and then prove it is a paradox. He writes with deceptive clarity and a quirky personal sense of the strange, the absurd, the ironic, and the humorous in his life. You will find some poems difficult, others with mature language, but keep reading—Strand will make you look at your own life in new and startling ways and show you that poetry is not all physical detail and description: for him, it's the thought that counts.

26.35 Strand, Mark, editor. **The Best American Poetry, 1991.** Macmillan/Collier Books, 1991. 326 pp. ISBN 0-02-069844-5.

What is modern poetry? This anthology provides an answer. Mark Strand, former poet laureate, collected seventy-five poems from leading magazines and journals across the country and supplemented them with nearly fifty pages of "Contributors' Notes and Comments." The result is both an interesting sampling of very contemporary poetry and a "Who's Who" of modern poets. The poems themselves do not represent a true cross section of what is being published today. Reflecting Strand's personal taste, they lean toward the academic tradition, and their style, language, and allusions make them less than accessible to the general reader. However, the serious, mature student or teacher of poetry will find them rewarding.

26.36 Tate, James. **Selected Poems.** Wesleyan University Press, 1991. 239 pp. ISBN 0-8195-1192-7.

For thirty years, James Tate has been writing poems in an almost patented style: short, puzzling lyrics that dare you to understand them. His images are frequently highly personal, sometimes bizarre, and even surrealistic at times. Tate is fond of the vignette and epiphany, but usually gives his reader only the bare-bones moment without developing it for emotion or clarification. His real strength is sound—even the most obscure poems have a haunting musicality that encourages rereading.

Pulitzer Prize for American Poetry, 1992
W. D. Williams Award of the Poetry Society of America, 1992

26.37   Taylor, Henry. **Compulsory Figures: Essays on Recent American Poets.** Louisiana State University Press, 1993. 318 pp. ISBN 0-8071-1755-2.

Henry Taylor, himself a superb poet with a Pulitzer Prize to his credit, is also a fine critic, what colleague Dana Gioia calls a "practical critic"—that is, he has no special theoretical ax to grind, no hard-to-understand literary theory to explain. Rather, he takes us to the poem itself and shows us what is good and likable about it, and why we should find it good and likable. This collection examines the key poems of seventeen modern poets, including May Sarton, William Stafford, Gwendolyn Brooks, and James Wright. Discussions of theme are there, but Taylor's special gift in these essays is his focus on the "how"—the technical accomplishments of each writer.

26.38   Turner, Ann. **Grass Songs.** Illustrated by Barry Moser. Harcourt Brace Jovanovich, 1993. 52 pp. ISBN 0-15-136788-4.

Each year we learn more about the hardships of the westward-moving pioneers from the diaries and letters of women who made that arduous journey. Ann Turner's intense, gritty poems let us hear these women's voices in a very direct, emotional way as they meet the many trials and few pleasures of the pioneer experience. Most of the seventeen personae are anonymous, but a few named speakers are based on real women. Olive Oatman, who preferred life with her Indian captors to the world of her Anglo rescuers, is an especially memorable character. Barry Moser's pencil illustrations, based on real photographs, have an antique feel and beautifully complement the text.

26.39   Van Duyn, Mona. **Near Changes: Poems.** Alfred A. Knopf, 1990. 70 pp. ISBN 0-394-58444-9.

Mona Van Duyn is not exactly a household name, nor is she often included in high school anthologies. Yet when she won the Pulitzer Prize in 1991, she added the last major award to an already overwhelming collection. Van Duyn writes about everything—car washes, genetic experiments on pigs, zinnias—yet every poem shows she cares about the world and what happens in it. As she says in one meditative poem, "The Accusation," "no

lie can conceal the truth/ That our kind was built to be caring."
Of the thirty-two poems in this collection, eleven originally appeared in the *New Yorker* or *Poetry*, major publications for the best contemporary poetry.

Pulitzer Prize for American Poetry, 1991

26.40   Wagner, Shelly. **The Andrew Poems.** Texas Tech University Press, 1994. 86 pp. ISBN 0-89672-319-4.

What to say about a book that has one gripping, knockout poem after another and whose total effect is more powerful than *any* other book of poetry you are likely to find? Andrew was five when he drowned, and his mother eventually turned to writing to cope with his death. She has produced not a group of maudlin, carelessly sentimental poems but a superbly crafted ensemble that communicates with immediate and total clarity. Be warned: Shelly Wagner will move you. Beneath the extraordinarily simple and concrete language is grief enough to crush, such terrible beauty as we can hardly bear, and yet a wise and transcendent healing. Like Samuel Taylor Coleridge's Ancient Mariner, she compels us to listen: "Do not walk away from me./ I am a mother./ Come closer, sit down/ and listen." And her final message is for us to grieve and share: "Fear of loss/ and walls of self-protection/ will kill me/ long before a broken heart./ I pray,/ let every death/ break me so."

26.41   Wilbur, Richard. **New and Collected Poems.** Harcourt Brace Jovanovich, 1988. 393 pp. ISBN 0-15-165206-6.

This book won the 1989 Pulitzer Prize, and deservedly so. More than any other American poet of the past forty years, Richard Wilbur demonstrates the excitement and varied possibilities in highly formal verse. This volume (containing his life's poetic work excluding the verse translations and his lyrics for the musical *Candide*) shows us poetry in a potato, in "Wyeth's Milk Cans," in his objections to the McCarran-Walter Act allowing deportation of immigrants and naturalized citizens, in riddles from Symphosius, and in the Gaderene swine. Wilbur is not to be gulped in large doses but rather sipped and appreciated, a poem, or even a stanza or a line, at a time. He is wise, funny, humane—and one of the best craftsmen of our time.

Pulitzer Prize for American Poetry, 1989

27 Politics and Law

27.1 Bowe, Frank. **Equal Rights for Americans with Disabilities.** Franklin Watts/Impact Books, 1992. 144 pp. ISBN 0-531-13030-4. Nonfiction.

Only recently have Americans with disabilities—sensory, mental, or emotional—been afforded the equal rights purportedly guaranteed by the U.S. Constitution, primarily due to the 1990 Americans with Disabilities Act. What it is like to have a disability and the evolution of legislation to assure equal rights are addressed in a readable manner. Black-and-white photographs are included.

27.2 Carter, Jimmy. **Talking Peace: A Vision for the Next Generation.** Dutton Children's Books, 1993. 192 pp. ISBN 0-525-44959-0. Nonfiction.

Former President Jimmy Carter has devoted his adult life to public service, and in particular toward building understandings for peace. This book vividly examines causes and effects of conflicts and explains the need for nonviolent resolution. Accompanied by black-and-white photographs and by quotations from letters, President Carter's writing reveals his "fearless idealism" and his tenacity.

Notable 1994 Children's Trade Books in the Field of Social Studies
School Library Journal Best Books, 1993

27.3 Cooney, James A. **Think about Foreign Policy: The United States and the World,** 3d ed. Walker, 1993. 166 pp. ISBN 0-8027-7368-0. Nonfiction.

This is one of fourteen books in the Think series examining important issues. James A. Cooney discusses what foreign policy is and who makes it. He describes the history of U.S. foreign policy and the role of government agencies and institutions in developing such policy. Black-and-white illustrations and photographs tracing policy from the American Revolution to the Reagan years provide perspective for the reader wishing to be informed.

27.4 Davis, Bertha. **Gambling in America: A Growth Industry.** Franklin Watts/Impact Books, 1992. 112 pp. ISBN 0-531-13021-5. Nonfiction.

What is the phenomenon of gambling? What forms does gambling take? What help is available to the compulsive gambler? What are the differing opinions on the dangers and the merits of gambling in legalized form? What, for instance, are the implications for society of state lotteries? Bertha Davis examines these questions in a thoughtful manner. Black-and-white photographs augment the text.

27.5 Dolan, Edward F. **Child Abuse,** rev. ed. Franklin Watts, 1992. 127 pp. ISBN 0-531-11042-7. Nonfiction.

This revised edition treats the problem of child abuse with respect for the victims, calling upon facts and informed observers to convey the magnitude of this behavior. Edward F. Dolan describes the forms that abuse takes—physical abuse, neglect, and emotional abuse; sexual abuse; incest; exploitation of the child in pornography. Chapters on reasons behind abuse, history of child abuse, taking action against child abuse, and what individuals and groups can do to prevent abuse are also included.

27.6 Fitzmorris, James E., Jr. and Kenneth D. Myers. **Frankly, Fitz!** Pelican, 1992. 336 pp. ISBN 0-88289-915-5. Nonfiction.

This biography presents James E. Fitzmorris, a man of integrity who resisted temptations to compromise his values in order to win elections. It is a remarkable story of what Lindy Boggs, former representative to the U.S. Congress, describes as "positive leadership." Through Fitzmorris's reflections on his years in local and state politics (including his election as lieutenant governor of Louisiana, his two-time defeat as a candidate for mayor of New Orleans, and his candidacy as nominee for governor), one sees the development of Louisiana in the years following World War I.

27.7 Gardner, Sandra. **Street Gangs in America.** Photographs by Cary Herz. Franklin Watts, 1992. 112 pp. ISBN 0-531-11037-0. Nonfiction.

What causes gangs to form? How do they operate? What is their impact on society? Why are so many young persons caught up in gangs? Why are there so many senseless killings? Sandra Gardner explores these questions through interviews with members of several Los Angeles gangs. Black-and-white photographs support the text.

27.8 Greene, Laura Offenhartz. **Child Labor: Then and Now.** Franklin Watts, 1992. 144 pp. ISBN 0-531-13008-8. Nonfiction.

When is youth employment considered child labor? Why should children be allowed to work? What kinds of labor have children and youth been employed to do historically? Laura Offenhartz Greene examines that history, reform efforts, governmental regulation, and a series of contemporary child labor activities in the United States and abroad.

27.9   Guernsey, JoAnn Bren. **Should We Have Capital Punishment?** Lerner, 1993. 96 pp. ISBN 0-8225-2602-6. Nonfiction.

What should society do with people who commit murder? Should all murderers be treated the same, including children or mentally retarded individuals? Should those convicted of murder be executed? Just what are the responsibilities of government with respect to human life? JoAnn Bren Guernsey probes questions like these, citing real cases. The text is accompanied by black-and-white photos, charts, and graphs.

27.10   Kronenwetter, Michael. **United They Hate: White Supremacist Groups in America.** Walker, 1992. 133 pp. ISBN 0-8027-8162-4. Nonfiction.

While ethnic diversity is and has been a central aspect of American society for 300 years, white supremacist groups have existed from the Supreme Order of the Star Spangled Banner in 1845 to the recent emergence of David Duke as a political figure. This book documents some of the more notable activities of these divisive organizations and examines the efforts of law enforcement groups opposing them. Complete chapter notes and a bibliography make this book particularly useful for research.

27.11   Landau, Elaine. **Teens and the Death Penalty.** Enslow, 1992. 112 pp. ISBN 0-89490-297-0. Nonfiction.

Most states in America allow the death penalty, and in some states there is no minimum age for execution. Case histories of young people who have been executed for crimes bring into focus both sides of this controversial issue. History of the use of the death penalty and statistics about the relationship between race, poverty, and capital punishment are presented, as are sources for further research.

27.12   Landau, Elaine. **Terrorism: America's Growing Threat.** Dutton/Lodestar Books, 1992. 100 pp. ISBN 0-525-67382-2. Nonfiction.

The United States faces the threat of terrorism from organizations worldwide. As the world's sole remaining superpower, we have great strength but are vulnerable to the tactics of well-trained groups of terrorists. Author Elaine Landau examines these groups, giving a description of what is known about them. A number of notable terrorist attacks are chronicled, including the downing of Flight 103 over Lockerbie, Scotland, in December 1988. Potential threats for the future are outlined, and further readings on the topic are suggested. A complete bibliography and index make this work useful for reference.

27.13 Madsen, Peter, and Jay M. Shafritz. **Essentials of Government Ethics.** Penguin/Meridian Books, 1992. 468 pp. ISBN 0-452-01091-8. Nonfiction.

The authors have collected a series of essays by contemporary and historical figures regarding those who make the laws and the conflicts that arise regarding their responsibilities to uphold or circumvent such laws. Two contemporary ethical voids, Watergate and the bailouts of savings and loan associations, are examined, as are the philosophical positions of such historical figures as Plato and Niccolo Machiavelli, resulting in intriguing and informed debate.

27.14 Newton, David E. **Gun Control: An Issue for the Nineties.** Enslow, 1992. 128 pp. ISBN 0-89490-296-2. Nonfiction.

Firearms are made more effective and more deadly every year. Gun-related deaths continue to rise. The debate over how to control the violence continues, with powerful organizations on both sides of the debate. David E. Newton presents the arguments for both sides, along with the statistics that show why this is such a significant issue. This well-documented book is a comprehensive source on the issue of gun control.

27.15 Owens, Lois Smith, and Vivian Verdell Gordon. **Think about Prisons and the Criminal Justice System.** Illustrated by Peter Zale. Walker, 1992. 142 pp. ISBN 0-8027-8121-7. Nonfiction.

The experience of a juvenile offender illustrates this examination of our prison system. The authors present a history of American prisons and detail current issues concerning how the penal system serves the needs of society. A thorough glossary, appendix, and source list make this volume in the Think series particularly informative and useful for research.

27.16 Rushdie, Salman. **Imaginary Homelands: Essays and Criticism, 1981–1991.** Penguin Books, 1991. 439 pp. ISBN 0-670-83952-3. Nonfiction.

This collection of essays by a British Indian, now living in London, provides a fresh perspective on the international scene in politics and literature during the 1980s. The seventy-five brief essays cover a broad range of topics—politics of India, Pakistan, Great Britain, and the United States, particularly the effects of race and religion on politics; the migrant experience; contemporary literature, movies, and television; and censorship of his novel *The Satanic Verses*. In drawing on his roots in India for his art, Salman Rushdie is forced to recognize that the imaginative vision is always fractured, distorted by personal memory, and that it is impossible to capture the real past, thus his title *Imaginary Homelands*.

27.17 Shogan, Robert. **The Riddle of Power: Presidential Leadership from Truman to Bush.** Penguin/Plume Books, 1992. 358 pp. ISBN 0-452-26771-4. Nonfiction.

What can be done to assure effective leadership? Why do presidents have to struggle to assert their authority? Robert Shogan examines the interplay of character, ideology, and values as it affects the extent of success for the occupant of the White House. He devotes a chapter each to Harry Truman, Dwight Eisenhower, John Kennedy, Lyndon Johnson, Richard Nixon, Gerald Ford, Jimmy Carter, Ronald Reagan, and George Bush.

27.18 Steffan, Joseph. **Honor Bound: A Gay American Fights for the Right to Serve His Country.** Random House/Villard Books, 1992. 245 pp. ISBN 0-697-41660-9. Nonfiction.

This book not only addresses the author's struggle to serve his country but also presents a vivid account of the experiences of a midshipman during four years at the U.S. Naval Academy. Joseph Steffan describes his experiences growing up in Minnesota, his accomplishments in the classroom and on the track, his discovery as a 1980s adolescent that he developed good friendships with girls but no strong attachments, and his academic and training success in Annapolis. Steffan also reveals how abiding by the honor code—refusing to deny a rumor about his sexuality—led to dismissal from the Naval Academy weeks before he was to graduate, and he describes his subsequent efforts to gain justice through the legal system.

ALA Best Books for Young Adults, 1993

27.19 Strahinich, Helen. **Think about Guns in America.** Walker, 1992. 114 pp. ISBN 0-8027-8104-7. Nonfiction.

Helen Strahinich presents both sides of the gun control debate in this look at the facts about guns and their effect on our society. A history of guns and information about various kinds of guns are included. The appendix details gun laws in each of the fifty states and presents the major arguments of supporters and opponents of gun control laws. Part of the Think series.

27.20 Walter, Mildred Pitts. **Mississippi Challenge.** Macmillan/ Bradbury Press, 1992. 205 pp. ISBN 0-02-792301-0. Nonfiction.

Mildred Pitts Walter traces the history and struggles of African Americans in the state of Mississippi, from slavery to the civil rights era. Readers can learn much about the Freedman's Bureau, the Mississippi Freedom Democratic Party, and the Student Nonviolent Coordinating Committee. The book is compelling in story and includes black-and-white photographs.

27.21 Wilson, Reginald. **Think about Our Rights: Civil Liberties in the United States,** rev. ed. Walker, 1993. 113 pp. ISBN 0-8027-8127-6. Nonfiction.

This is one of fourteen books in the Think series examining important contemporary issues. Reginald Wilson, a civil rights expert, examines the individuals and events that have "determined the rights that we all possess as citizens in today's society." He asks and responds to questions such as these: "How does the Constitution protect our rights? What is the role of the Supreme Court? Who was Linda Brown?" Organized in four sections (introduction, historical background, contemporary debate, future outlook), the text is accompanied by black-and-white photographs and illustrations in this revision of the 1988 edition.

28 Romance

28.1 Berry, Liz. **Mel.** Viking, 1991. 214 pp. ISBN 0-670-83925-6. Fiction.

Mel, short for Melody, suddenly finds herself alone—her mother is in a mental hospital, and her father is gone. School becomes the most important thing in her life. While working on her art project and the renovation of her dingy apartment in preparation for her mother's return, Mel feels that she has found a real friend in her art teacher. Yet a crisis on her street proves her wrong. Mel finds help in others and learns the true value of friendship.

IRA Young Adults' Choices, 1993

28.2 Clapp, Patricia. **Jane-Emily.** William Morrow/Beech Tree Books, 1993. 153 pp. ISBN 0-688-04592-8. Fiction.

Louisa Amory is not looking forward to spending the summer of 1912 in a quiet New England town with Jane Canfield, her orphaned nine-year-old niece, and with elderly Mrs. Canfield, Jane's other grandmother. When Jane finds a silver reflecting ball in the garden, she is able to "see" her late father's sister, Emily, who died when she was Jane's age. Jane's obsession with Emily, Louisa's growing friendship with Mrs. Canfield's young doctor, and unexplained events result in a love story with a different twist.

28.3 Garden, Nancy. **Annie on My Mind.** Farrar, Straus and Giroux/Aerial Books, 1992. 234 pp. ISBN 0-374-404140-3. Fiction.

Falling in love is always a little scary, but for Liza it is more than scary—it is terrifying. When Liza meets Annie, she realizes that she has never before felt like this about anyone and probably will never do so again. That this sensitive portrayal of the growing friendship between two young women is troubling is no understatement, but the author handles her material gently, showing the reader what it feels like to love another woman.

28.4 Graham-Barber, Lynda. **Mushy! The Complete Book of Valentine Words.** Illustrated by Betsy Lewin. Avon/Camelot Books, 1993. 146 pp. ISBN 0-380-71650-X. Nonfiction.

Here is a catchy book that tells you everything you want to know about Valentine's Day. It explains how we have come to associate certain words with the day (such as *roses*, *chocolate*, and *kissing*). A historical table—with a country-by-country listing of the characteristics of the holiday—is provided, as is a complete index.

28.5   Harper, Karen. **Circle of Gold.** Penguin/Signet Books, 1993. 438 pp. ISBN 0-451-40381-9. Fiction.

Two small children from a poor Kentucky mountain farm are left in a community of Shakers, a religious group that founded several communities in nineteenth-century America. Life in the Shaker village is detailed in the story of Rebecca Blake, who grows up to marry a wealthy Englishman, moves to England, but returns to Kentucky.

28.6   Levoy, Myron. **Pictures of Adam.** William Morrow/Beech Tree Books, 1993. 218 pp. ISBN 0-688-11941-7. Fiction.

Fourteen-year-old Lisa Daniels's main interest in life is photography, and she is very good at it. When shy Adam Bates is put in her science class, she realizes that he is something special—a weird, special ed. kid from the hills who claims to be an alien from another planet. Lisa befriends Adam and sets out to prove to all (her parents included) that he is worth knowing. Her photojournalism entry of Adam's home, a shack in the hills, wakes up the town to conditions nobody should have to endure. Along the way, Lisa finds herself in love with Adam.

28.7   Magorian, Michelle. **Not a Swan.** HarperCollins/Laura Geringer Books, 1992. 404 pp. ISBN 0-06-024215-9. Fiction.

Not a Swan, set in England during World War II, is the story of three sisters who are evacuated to a small coastal town for the summer while their mother goes abroad with an entertainment troop. The sisters end up staying alone when their chaperone is drafted. Seventeen-year-old Rose, who is considered an ugly duckling compared with her beautiful older sisters, blossoms in her new setting. The freedom she has in the little town of Salmouth and the mystery of a locked room in their cottage help her to achieve independence and gain a feeling of self-worth. And in addition to finding herself, Rose discovers love. Mature situations. First published in Great Britain, 1991.

ALA Best Books for Young Adults, 1993

28.8   Pascal, Francine, creator (story by Laurie John). **Love, Lies, and Jessica Wakefield.** Bantam Books, 1993. 231 pp. ISBN 0-553-56306-8. Fiction.

The twins from Sweet Valley High are off to college—Sweet Valley University. Jessica, the spirited twin, is up to her usual tricks, and Elizabeth, the quiet one, is once again the victim. Since being a sorority member is so important to Jessica, she will do anything to be accepted—including impersonating Elizabeth. In this freshman year, Jessica meets wealthy, good-looking Mike, and Elizabeth uncovers a major scandal in the athletic department. Sequel to *College Girls* and a book in the Sweet Valley University series.

28.9   Pascal, Francine, creator (story by Kate William). **A Night to Remember.** Bantam Books, 1993. 345 pp. ISBN 0-553-29309-5. Fiction.

Sweet Valley High School is a typical high school—complete with competitive athletics, school clubs, and cheerleaders. One night, Prom Night, changes it forever. Identical twins Jessica, the social one, and Elizabeth, the studious one, dream up the most perfect prom with a "Save the Rain Forest" theme. The prize for the young woman chosen prom queen is a trip to Brazil and speaking engagements for Project Environmental Alert. Both twins want to win, and this causes a split in their closeness. While Elizabeth works to make the prom a success, Jessica pulls tricks to ensure that she becomes prom queen, but her tricks bring disastrous results on Prom Night. Part of the Sweet Valley High series.

28.10   Pearson, Kit. **Looking at the Moon.** Viking, 1991. 212 pp. ISBN 0-670-84097-1. Fiction.

Being thirteen is often a cross between wanting to be treated like an adult and feeling like a child. For Norah, a British girl far from her war-torn country, life during World War II is definitely not easy. A summer at the home of her guardian should be fun, but Norah's hopes for a carefree time quickly dampen when she finds herself falling in love with nineteen-year-old Andrew. That summer Norah discovers the fears that young adults face, and she realizes that being a gangly teenager is perhaps not so bad after all. The author gently touches on the decisions that young people are forced to make in order to survive, decisions that are often made alone.

28.11   Peyton, K. M. **Darkling.** Dell/Laurel-Leaf Library, 1992. 245 pp. ISBN 0-440-21211-1. Fiction.

A girl and a horse—a race horse—make an unbeatable Irish combination. Darkling will only allow Jenny to handle him, and what Jenny must go through to get this scruffy little horse to the winner's circle is marvelously told by K. M. Peyton. Jenny must turn into a jockey in order for Darkling to do his best and win. Jenny's love for a rival jockey adds romance to the story. First published in Great Britain, 1989.

IRA Young Adults' Choices, 1992

28.12 Powell, Randy. **Is Kissing a Girl Who Smokes Like Licking an Ashtray?** Farrar, Straus and Giroux, 1992. 198 pp. ISBN 0-374-33632-6. Fiction.

This novel is funny and real and touching. It is funny because life is funny, and it is real because young readers will see themselves in Biff, who is eighteen and awkward around girls. It is touching because Biff learns through Heidi, an offbeat young woman, that it is okay to talk to girls, even if they are weird and do stupid stuff like smoke. Heidi learns, too, that you do not always have to fight the system—once you learn to like yourself, things are okay.

ALA Best Books for Young Adults, 1993

28.13 Rodowsky, Colby. **Lucy Peale.** Farrar, Straus and Giroux, 1992. 163 pp. ISBN 0-374-36381-1. Fiction.

Lucy Peale is a heartwarming story about two young people brought together by chance in a time when both need someone for support. After Lucy, seventeen, becomes pregnant, her evangelist father tells her to leave home. With nowhere to go, she heads toward Ocean City, where she meets Jake, a young man struggling to be on his own. Their relationship grows as each helps the other through their independence and Lucy's pregnancy. This book is for the mature young adult who wants to read a poignant story about growing up and the problems that go along with it.

IRA Young Adults' Choices, 1994

28.14 Shura, Mary Francis. **Winter Dreams, Christmas Love.** Scholastic/Point Books, 1992. 343 pp. ISBN 0-590-44672-X. Fiction.

On Ellen Marlowe's first day in high school, her orientation upper classman turns out to be one of the most popular guys in the school. But Michael sees Ellen only as her brother's little sister. Nothing Ellen does—her classes, her running, her talent in art, or her involvement in the drama club—can shake her thoughts about Michael and her love for him. They share some wonderful moments together as they walk in the snow and work together on school plays, but Ellen knows that Michael will never accept her as anything but a young kid. Her fight with herself to find someone besides Michael gives readers a good picture of life in high school and the pain of first love.

28.15 Sonnenmark, Laura. **The Lie.** Scholastic Hardcover Books, 1992. 176 pp. ISBN 0-590-44740-8. Fiction.

Norrie's plan was to get a summer job as a beach photographer. Not only would she have fun and an excuse for wandering on the beach all day during her summer vacation, but she would be seeing and working with the guy she has decided is "the one." Just one little lie is all it takes to change a lot of things. This fast-moving story is set in places familiar to East Coast beachgoers.

28.16 Stanley, Carol. **The Last Great Summer.** Scholastic/Point Books, 1992. 216 pp. ISBN 0-590-45705-5. Fiction.

When a group of friends graduate from Rio Rojo High School, they have no idea that the summer will test their relationships in unexpected ways. Caitlin will fall in love, Jennifer will make a heart-breaking discovery and a wrenching decision, Patti will feel left out, and Leah and Danny will learn that reality is infinitely better than illusion. In the end, they all realize that while they have deep roots in River Bend, Texas, they must separate—if only for a time.

28.17 Thesman, Jean. **The Rain Catchers.** Avon/Flare Books, 1992. 182 pp. ISBN 0-380-71711-5. Fiction.

Fourteen-year-old Grayling lives with her grandmother and aunts near Seattle in a world of love and gentility. Every afternoon they drink their tea and tell their stories. But Grayling does not have a story. No one knows why her mother left her with her grand-mother after her father's death and went to San Francisco alone. During a special summer that brings a new friendship with Aaron, Gray learns about her own story for the first time. Hers is finally a story with a beginning, a middle, and an end, just as Grand-mother said every story should be.

ALA Best Books for Young Adults, 1992
Booklist Editors' Choice, 1991
School Library Journal Best Books, 1991
IRA Young Adults' Choices, 1993

28.18 Winton, Tim. **Lockie Leonard, Human Torpedo.** Little, Brown/Joy Street Books, 1991. 148 pp. ISBN 0-316-94753-9. Fiction.

Lockie Leonard is in high school when he moves to a new town in the south of Australia. His true passion is surfing, and before long he finds himself riding the waves of the local beach, where he first meets his new schoolmates—and they give him less than a warm reception. After he starts school, the only person in whom he can confide is his guidance counselor, who suggests he start a surfing club. Then Lockie meets Vicki, and the trouble begins. First published in Australia, 1990.

ALA Best Books for Young Adults, 1993

28.19 Wolfe, Anne Herron. **Wings of Love.** Bantam Books, 1993. 121 pp. ISBN 0-553-29978-6. Fiction.

Raising exotic birds provides Kalia with a way to occupy her time away from school and to contribute to the family's income. She has not had the opportunity to make friends due to frequent moves by her family. The friendship of two boys—one whom Kalia likes and one who likes her—helps her to feel more a part of her school. We learn of the Romany, or gypsy, culture through Kalia, who always measures what she does with thoughts of her deceased grandmother's spirit. A lost bird, Kalia's temper, and Tom's pride make this a very real story.

28.20 Wyss, Thelma Hatch. **A Stranger Here.** HarperCollins, 1993. 129 pp. ISBN 0-06-021439-2. Fiction.

Jada Sinclair spends the summer with her Aunt May, who enjoys being an invalid. One boring afternoon while Jada is dusting in the attic, she puts a record on the old Victrola, and the ghost of Starr Freeman appears. Starr, a soldier who was to have married Jada's cousin, was killed when his plane was shot down over the Pacific in World War II—on the same day that Jada was born. He knows Jada's thoughts and secrets and appears to her many times that summer—in the attic, in the cemetery, under the "Kissing Tree." When summer ends, and Jada is preparing to return home, Starr appears one more time to urge Jada to enjoy life and never forget him.

29 School and Social Situations

29.1   Amis, Kingsley. **We Are All Guilty.** Viking/Reinhardt Books, 1991. 92 pp. ISBN 0-670-84268-0. Fiction.

A psychological tale about high school student Clive Rayner, this short novel focuses on the guilt Clive feels about his role in a tragic mishap. In spite of Clive's mother and stepfather's efforts to teach him responsibility, he makes some poor choices, and as a result, he is left to reflect on his role in society and the responsibilities that he must accept.

29.2   Block, Francesca Lia. **Cherokee Bat and the Goat Guys.** HarperCollins/Harper Keypoint/Charlotte Zolotow Books, 1992. 121 pp. ISBN 0-06-447095-4. Fiction.

Cherokee Bat, her half-sister Witch Baby, and her friends Raphael and Angel Juan form a band called the Goat Guys. They sing and dance, and the drums, guitar, and bass make powerful music. At first the audience is small, but Cherokee feels the Goat Guys will soon win a wider audience. Lyrics, letters, and songs by Cherokee and the others are included.

ALA Best Books for Young Adults, 1992
ALA Quick Picks for Young Adults, 1993

29.3   Bunting, Eve. **Jumping the Nail.** Harcourt Brace Jovanovich, 1991. 148 pp. ISBN 0-15-241357-X. Fiction.

La Paloma, along the cliffs of southern California, is about to host its first big event in ten years. Mike Navarro, a risk taker, and Elisa Fratello share the danger in jumping the Nail, a place deemed bottomless because it is ninety feet from the top of the cliff to the ocean. It is peer pressure that causes many to make the dangerous jump into the water.

ALA Best Books for Young Adults, 1993
ALA Quick Picks for Young Adults, 1992

29.4   Cadnum, Michael. **Breaking the Fall.** Viking, 1992. 132 pp. ISBN 0-670-84687-2. Fiction.

To Jared, stealing into people's homes at night without anyone knowing about it is just a game. However, for Stanley, the fear and the rush of adrenaline is more like a drug. Stanley, who allows himself to be led and controlled by Jared, is seeking to understand himself and how to make his own choices, but first he must manage to overcome his fascination with Jared's quest to find the ultimate high.

ALA Quick Picks for Young Adults, 1993

29.5 Calvert, Patricia. **When Morning Comes.** Avon/Flare Books, 1992. 153 pp. ISBN 0-380-71186-9. Fiction.

Cat Kincaid, a fifteen-year-old school dropout, is bounced from one foster home to another because of her difficulty adapting to rules. Then Cat, the troubled pretender, moves to a third foster home to live with Annie Bowen, a beekeeper. There she meets Hooter Lewis, a seventeen-year-old farm boy, and attempts to subject him to her ways. From the very beginning of her new situation, she plans to leave "when morning comes."

29.6 Cormier, Robert. **Tunes for Bears to Dance To.** Delacorte Press, 1992. 112 pp. ISBN 0-385-30818-3. Fiction.

Henry has tremendous pressures on him: his beloved brother is dead, his father is overcome with depression, and his mother works all the time to support the family. The family has recently moved to a new town, where Henry makes friends with Mr. Levine, a survivor of a World War II concentration camp. Henry also finds a job working for a local grocer, Mr. Hairston, and his earnings are important to the family. Mr. Hairston, however, is one of writer Robert Cormier's great evil characters, and Henry must confront a series of impossible choices and somehow do the right thing.

ALA Best Books for Young Adults, 1993
ALA Quick Picks for Young Adults, 1993

29.7 Cormier, Robert. **We All Fall Down.** Delacorte Press, 1991. 193 pp. ISBN 0-385-30501-X. Fiction.

Jane Jerome and her family return home one night to find their home totally trashed—vomit, human feces, and urine cover the walls, furniture and glass are upended and shattered, empty liquor bottles are scattered throughout—and Karen, Jane's younger sister, lies barely alive at the foot of the basement stairs. As this disturbing novel unfolds, The Avenger seeks revenge on the trashers, who actually are middle-class youths from the neighboring town. And Buddy, one of the trashers with a drinking problem, becomes increasingly attracted to Jane, even in the midst of his own troubled life. In this book, Robert Cormier explores the impact of random violence and makes us look a little closer at what we would rather avoid.

ALA Best Books for Young Adults, 1992
IRA Young Adults' Choices, 1993
School Library Journal Best Books, 1991

29.8   Davis, Terry. **If Rock and Roll Were a Machine.** Delacorte Press, 1992. 209 pp. ISBN 0-385-30762-4. Fiction.

Bert Bowden stopped being academic, athletic, and well liked and became withdrawn when he was humiliated by an elementary school teacher. Now he is a sixteen-year-old junior at Thompson High and wants to own a Harley-Davidson Sportster more than anything else. Through his interest in writing, racquetball, and motorcycles, and because of two caring, understanding adults, Bert discovers what he has lost. Mature language.

ALA Best Books for Young Adults, 1993
ALA Quick Picks for Young Adults, 1993

29.9   Deaver, Julie Reece. **First Wedding, Once Removed.** HarperCollins/Harper Trophy/Charlotte Zolotow Books, 1993. 216 pp. ISBN 0-06-021427-9. Fiction.

Alwilda and Gib, brother and sister, are thoughtful of each other and enjoy each other's company in spite of the mischievous acts they play on each other. When Gib goes off to college and falls in love, Alwilda feels left behind. At the most important time in her life, Gib is no longer there for her.

29.10   Deaver, Julie Reece. **You Bet Your Life.** HarperCollins, 1993. 209 pp. ISBN 0-06-021517-8. Fiction.

Elizabeth (Bess) Milligan, seventeen, has to come to grips with the death of her mother, who committed suicide. She begins an internship at the Les Komack Show six months after the death and begins to communicate with her dad, a businessman. In the healing process, she writes letters to her mother to convey her accomplishments and to question her mother's act of destruction. Finally, she is able to get on with her own life once again.

29.11   Feiler, Bruce S. **Learning to Bow: An American Teacher in a Japanese School.** Ticknor and Fields, 1991. 321 pp. ISBN 0-395-58521-X. Nonfiction.

This is a different sort of travel book. Bruce Feiler leaves his thoroughly American roots (Georgia, Yale University) to teach English and the American culture to junior high students in Sano, Japan. As his opening epigraph puts it, "Half of teaching is learning," and Feiler tells a humorous, candid story of his own learning during his year abroad. A strong major theme is his depiction of the role Japanese schools play in a systematic, state-guided indoctrination in those values the state prizes: patriotism, group identity, and a strong work ethic. Along the way we also get a warm, very human story of Feiler's own adjustments, of teaching Japanese students to do high-fives, and of learning about himself as a human.

29.12 Gabhart, Ann. **Bridge to Courage.** Avon/Flare Books, 1993. 147 pp. ISBN 0-380-76051-7. Fiction.

Luke and his friend Jacob are being initiated into the Truelanders and must pass the test of courage. To Jacob's disappointment, Luke backs out, and Jacob becomes a Truelander alone. Throughout the story, Luke tries to reckon with his fear, a fear that his father has never understood and his mother has never known. Only Shea, who befriends Luke when he is being harassed by the Truelanders, tries to help him overcome his terror. Nothing helps until a near disaster forces Luke to cross "his own bridge to courage."

29.13 Greene, Patricia Baird. **The Sabbath Garden.** Dutton/Lodestar Books, 1993. 212 pp. ISBN 0-525-67430-6. Fiction.

In an ethnically mixed Lower East Side neighborhood in Manhattan, Opie Tyler, a fourteen-year-old basketball star, and Conchita, a beautiful Puerto Rican girl, make an effort to be friends as they deal with their frustrations. Opie, feeling a sadness that "stretched to the farthest end of her life," befriends Mr. Leshko, the only remaining Jew in the tenement, and becomes instrumental in giving the community a reason for working together.

29.14 Guy, Rosa. **Edith Jackson.** Dell/Laurel-Leaf Library, 1992. 179 pp. ISBN 0-440-21137-9. Fiction.

Edith Jackson, seventeen, is the oldest child of six. After the death of her mother and abandonment by her father, Edith and her sisters are moved from one foster home to another. Edith tries to keep the girls together, but eventually social workers break up the family. Edith runs away, only to be ostracized because of her dark complexion and her unstable home environment. A provocative story of a young black girl who is faced with challenging decisions and tragedies in her life, this novel tells of Edith Jackson's struggle to survive. Mature situations.

29.15   Guy, Rosa. **The Music of Summer.** Delacorte Press, 1992. 180 pp. ISBN 0-385-30599-0. Fiction.

Sarah Richardson's eighteenth summer changes her life. She has always lived in a small apartment with her mother, who has worked hard to provide Sarah with the means to become successful—a good education and musical training. Even though Sarah has graduated from high school and is attending music classes at the famous Juilliard School, she has not broken her ties with her childhood friend, Cathy Johnson. Cathy, on the other hand, seems eager to rid herself of Sarah and makes cruel and demeaning remarks about Sarah, especially her dark-skinned complexion. Cathy's mother invites Sarah to join them on a trip to Cape Cod, where Sarah meets Jean Pierre.

ALA Best Books for Young Adults, 1993

29.16   Hahn, Mary Downing. **The Wind Blows Backward.** Houghton Mifflin/Clarion Books, 1993. 263 pp. ISBN 0-395-62975-6. Fiction.

In the eighth grade, Spencer and Lauren were best friends; but when they entered high school, Spencer surrounded himself with new friends, friends who were more acceptable to his mother. In their senior year, a chance meeting rekindles their relationship, and Lauren and Spencer find their need for each other growing intensely. Lauren learns that Spencer is a troubled person and discovers the secret that has haunted him since his childhood. Together, they realize that Spencer must face his past before they can plan for a future together. Mary Downing Hahn's novel is an easy-to-read, well-written, and interesting account of eighteen-year-olds who must learn to cope with the issues of life and death.

ALA Quick Picks for Young Adults, 1993

29.17   Harrell, Janice. **Dusty Brannigan.** Avon/Flare Books, 1993. 152 pp. ISBN 0-380-76113-0. Fiction.

Deborah Susan Brannigan, one of five children, is awarded a scholarship to attend college. There she becomes *Dusty* Brannigan; she steps out of squalor and takes on a new life. Dusty spends her time trying to represent her new name and makes every effort to forget her family. The irony is that when campus closes for Christmas, Dusty's family forgets to pick her up.

29.18   Hayden, Torey L. **Ghost Girl: The True Story of a Child in Peril and the Teacher Who Saved Her.** Little, Brown, 1991. 307 pp. ISBN 0-316-35167-9. Nonfiction.

This is a moving and sometimes frightening account of a teacher's struggle to uncover the depth of abuse that has rendered a young girl speechless, a virtual walking ghost. Torey L. Hayden, a psychologist and special education teacher, tells her own story of helping "Jadie" to come to understand her own reality. Satanic cultism and ritual abuse are explored.

ALA Best Books for Young Adults, 1992
Booklist Editors' Choice, 1991

29.19 Hopper, Nancy J. **The Interrupted Education of Huey B.** Dutton/Lodestar Books, 1991. 129 pp. ISBN 0-525-67336-9. Fiction.

Huey is a senior who is in danger of failing English because of excessive tardiness and absences. He is spending the time trying to help an old man by watching the birds for him. This novel shows how Huey's teachers and administrators work to help him to pass and still be able to help watch the birds. Huey learns some lessons along the way, one of which is not to go with two girls at once.

29.20 Hyde, Margaret O. **Peace and Friendship: Russian and American Teens Meet.** Dutton/Cobblehill Books, 1992. 96 pp. ISBN 0-525-65107-1. Fiction.

American and Russian teens get to know each other and make changes in their thinking and their feelings through pen pals, organizations, and exchange programs. The characters realize the necessity of expressing themselves and working together. Samantha, Igor, Jessica, and Ben make a special effort to relate to others. The novel offers suggestions for becoming pen pals and provides a list of exchange programs.

29.21 Jen, Gish. **Typical American.** Penguin/Plume Books, 1992. 296 pp. ISBN 0-452-26774-9. Fiction.

In five distinctly titled parts, Gish Jen tells a story of an immigrant Asian man and his sister, who think and behave like Americans. In a world full of obstacles, Ralph Chang works on his Ph.D. in engineering, becomes an American citizen, marries Helen, has two children, takes driving lessons, and buys a car and a house. Then adultery enters the picture, and Ralph's life changes.

29.22 Johnson, Scott. **One of the Boys.** Atheneum, 1992. 246 pp. ISBN 0-689-31520-1. Fiction.

Eric Atwater, in search of himself and a sense of belonging, becomes attached to Marty Benbow, an aggressive, controlling, and intimidating new student at Emerson High School. Assigned to be Marty's guide, Eric learns that Marty is a born leader, immediately forming a group that cuts class, participates in pranks and schemes, and takes risks. Lacking confidence to pull away, Eric is caught up in the group's activities. He gets in trouble trying to help Ole, a homeless former musician.

ALA Best Books for Young Adults, 1993

29.23   Jones, Robin D. **The Beginning of Unbelief.** Atheneum, 1993. 153 pp. ISBN 0-689-31781-6. Fiction.

Fifteen-year-old Hal has been keeping a journal since he was six. One night when he and his father are camping, Hal cannot sleep because he is afraid of the dark. His father suggests that he give the little voice in his mind a name, and at that point Zach is born. Zach becomes Hal's alter ego. Hal discusses problems with Zach that he cannot share with anyone. Eventually Hal creates a story for Zach, and Zach becomes the commander in a spaceship. Consequently, within Hal's diary grows a science fiction story; Zach becomes so much a part of Hal's life that he wonders if he can live without him.

29.24   Kaplow, Robert. **Alessandra in Between.** HarperCollins, 1992. 202 pp. ISBN 0-06-023298-6. Fiction.

Alessandra struggles to exist without a boyfriend while her best friend is already dating. Her need for acceptance and her vulnerability are evident, but by the end of the novel Alessandra begins to overcome these feelings with her newfound love.

29.25   Kassem, Lou. **Odd One Out.** Fawcett/Juniper Books, 1994. 119 pp. ISBN 0-449-70432-7. Fiction.

Alison Grey is one of the most popular girls at Chandler High School, but she is unsure of herself as she tries to make the right decisions about her future. Like many teenagers in school today, Alison must learn to trust her instincts and have faith that she will do what is right.

29.26   King, Buzz. **Silicon Songs.** Dell/Laurel-Leaf Library, 1992. 164 pp. ISBN 0-440-21164-6. Fiction.

Seventeen-year-old Max is suddenly homeless. He was living with his Uncle Pete after his mother committed suicide, but Uncle Pete is now dying from cancer. Max spends his days wandering the beach and his nights working as a computer programmer. Desperate, Max considers selling computer time to South Africa, a plan that could land him in jail. But with some help from others, Max figures out what to do with his life.

29.27 Lee, Marie G. **Finding My Voice.** Houghton Mifflin, 1992. 165 pp. ISBN 0-395-62134-8. Fiction.

Ellen Sung's senior year serves as her final chance to stage the best year ever in making friends, attaining excellent grades, and being accepted in college. In the process, Ellen encounters pressure from her parents, pressure as the only Asian student in school, and unkind comments from her peers. Through it all, she "finds her voice."

ALA Quick Picks for Young Adults, 1993
IRA Young Adults' Choices, 1994

29.28 LeMieux, A. C. **The TV Guidance Counselor.** William Morrow/ Tambourine Books, 1993. 239 pp. ISBN 0-688-12402-X. Fiction.

When Jack Madden and his wife divorce, the family of four is devastated, with behaviors ranging from an identity crisis to a weird driving habit to becoming a miniature bag lady to landing in a psychiatric ward. The story opens with Michael in the hospital as a result of attempting suicide by jumping off the bridge into the Mohegan River. His treatments are completed, and his mother takes him home, to return to familiar things and people.

29.29 Levoy, Myron. **Kelly 'n' Me.** HarperCollins/Charlotte Zolotow Books, 1992. 202 pp. ISBN 0-06-020839-2. Fiction.

Anthony Milano, a poor boy and a real theater kid, encourages his mother to think positively about her ability to act. She is lonely and having difficulty adjusting to her divorce. Anthony has to be his mother's companion, cheerleader, and shrink. Then he meets Kelly Callahan, a rich girl with a confident glow, and the two perform music together on the streets of New York.

29.30 Lipsyte, Robert. **The Chemo Kid.** HarperCollins, 1992. 167 pp. ISBN 0-06-020285-8. Fiction.

Fred Bauer becomes the center of attention after he is diagnosed with cancer. Even more surprisingly, Fred's chemotherapy gives him the necessary superhuman powers to clean up his small town of Nearmont. With the help of the new friends he acquires while in group therapy and his old friends from Nearmont High, Fred is going to become a real-life superhero.

ALA Quick Picks for Young Adults, 1992

29.31 Lipsyte, Robert. **Summer Rules.** HarperCollins/Harper Keypoint/Ursula Nordstrom Books, 1992. 198 pp. ISBN 0-06-023898-4. Fiction.

Bobby Marks's father tells him about a summer job at Happy Valley Camp, but Bobby dreads the idea of spending his summer working with bratty rich kids and his big sister Michelle. He has other ideas about how to spend his summer but ends up at the camp. While it does not take him long to tire of the antics of campers like Harley Bell, Bobby meets Sheila, and she becomes his first love. His troubles are not over, however. His assignment as special counselor to a group of troublemakers soon keeps him busy. One night a fire starts, and before the culprits are identified, Bobby learns a lesson about society's idea of justice.

29.32 Lipsyte, Robert. **The Summerboy.** HarperCollins/Harper Keypoint/Charlotte Zolotow Books, 1992. 199 pp. ISBN 0-06-023889-5. Fiction.

Bobby Marks, a college student, takes a summer job as a laundry boy. He finds that he must deal with a foreman who hates him and employees who are forced to work in hazardous situations. He also has to prove himself in order to be accepted among his co-workers. In spite of the difficulties, Bobby sticks out the summer job and even manages to make things a little better for everyone else in the process.

29.33 Manes, Stephen. **Comedy High.** Scholastic Hardcover Books, 1992. 217 pp. ISBN 0-590-44436-0. Fiction.

We see the gambling town of Carmody, Nevada, through the eyes of a teenager named Ivan. The cheap, noisy, bright environment provides the backdrop for naked women and mature dialogue. Ivan's new high school is located in a hotel and offers courses in gambling, comedy, and performing. It's a shock, and Ivan goes through a major adjustment to his new environment.

29.34 Mango, Karin N. **Portrait of Miranda.** HarperCollins/Charlotte Zolotow Books, 1993. 232 pp. ISBN 0-06-021778-2. Fiction.

Miranda has spent her life under the shadow of the deceased aunt after whom she was named. In addition to having to live up to the legacy left to her, Miranda is fearful that she will lose her hearing just as her mother and aunt did. Her self-concept is poor, and so she tries hard to behave in the expected manner and not as she really feels. Her boyfriend helps her to see that she is special in her own right. Miranda also discovers that the hearing loss is not hereditary, and her life changes as a result.

29.35 Marino, Jan. **Like Some Kind of Hero.** Little, Brown, 1992. 216 pp. ISBN 0-316-54626-7. Fiction.

Ted Bradford, a bright, talented young man, wants to become a lifeguard and have girls falling at his feet as if he were some kind of a hero. His mom, however, wants Ted to cultivate independent thinking. In the process of accepting his responsibilities, Ted has difficulty trying to put his priorities in order. Mature language.

29.36 Mazer, Norma Fox, and Harry Mazer. **Bright Days, Stupid Nights.** Bantam Books, 1992. 195 pp. ISBN 0-553-08126-8. Fiction.

Extra! Extra! Read all about it! Chris, Faith, Elizabeth, and Vicki are all chosen from among hundreds of applicants to be summer interns at the Scottsville *Courier*. These four young people from different backgrounds establish a strong bond of friendship as they work and live together in very close quarters. They each discover new things about themselves and about one another as they struggle for independence and control in their own lives. Mature language.

29.37 McFann, Jane. **Free the Conroy Seven.** Avon/Flare Books, 1993. 152 pp. ISBN 0-380-76401-6. Fiction.

Seven students who have nothing in common are called to the assistant principal's office and accused of a crime. By playing a revealing game of true confessions during their lengthy stay in the office, these students unanimously and secretly protect one student who seems to be the likely culprit. After all of their anxiety, the students are amazed when the true culprit confesses.

ALA Quick Picks for Young Adults, 1994

29.38 McKenna, Colleen O'Shaughnessy. **The Brightest Light.** Scholastic Hardcover Books, 1992. 191 pp. ISBN 0-590-45347-5. Fiction.

Living in Romney, West Virginia, and employed at Jake's, Kitty Lee also keeps house for the Curtis family. She baby-sits for Mr. Curtis's three children when Mrs. Curtis is confined to her bedroom due to problems with alcohol. Kitty, an only child reared by Gramma and Pop, realizes that she is becoming too involved in her attempt to help the family solve their problems. As she becomes less involved with the Curtis family, Kitty falls in love.

29.39 Mowry, Jess. **Way Past Cool.** Farrar, Straus and Giroux, 1992. 310 pp. ISBN 0-374-28669-8. Fiction.

The Friends and the Crew, two street gangs in Oakland, California, share a common reality in a world of tension, love, and unjustified hatred. In an effort to secure their turf, they face dangerous challenges. Problems mount when Deek, a drug dealer, and his bodyguard, Ty, attempt to set the two gangs at odds. The novel is authentic in portraying the brutal activities of gangs. Mature language.

ALA Best Books for Young Adults, 1993
Booklist Editors' Choice, 1992

29.40 Myers, Walter Dean. **The Mouse Rap.** HarperCollins/Harper Trophy Books, 1992. 186 pp. ISBN 0-06-024344-9. Fiction.

In this tale of summer adventure in Harlem, fourteen-year-old Mouse and Styx remain friends through basketball, a dance contest, and a search for treasure left in an abandoned building. Mouse's life is complicated when his absent father reappears and seems interested in rejoining the family. Each chapter opens with an introductory rap by Mouse, and author Walter Dean Myers uses African American dialect to tell his story.

IRA Children's Choices, 1991

29.41 Myers, Walter Dean, creator (written by Stacie Johnson). **The Party.** Bantam Books, 1992. 150 pp. ISBN 0-553-29720-1. Fiction.

Murphy High friends find a need to make decisions regarding class events, dating, and friendship. Questions of whether to go to college and what to do with their lives and their bodies precipitate the actions of the group of friends at 18 Pine Street. Jennifer Wilson, in competition with the senior party, throws a big junior party at her home—without telling her mother. The party gets wild, and a few expensive items are broken. Sarah Gordon remains the caring, concerned friend throughout in this book about a group of teenagers from varying racial backgrounds. Second book in the 18 Pine St. series.

29.42 Myers, Walter Dean, creator (written by Stacie Johnson). **Sort of Sisters.** Bantam Books, 1992. 149 pp. ISBN 0-553-29719-8. Fiction.

This novel is the first in the continuing story of Sarah Gordon and her gang from Murphy High, who meet regularly at the new hangout, the pizzeria at 18 Pine Street. In this story centering on friends of different racial backgrounds, Sarah is looking forward to her junior year, especially when her cousin, Tasha, comes to live with her family. Sarah intends to introduce Tasha to her friends and to include her in their circle, but Tasha has other plans. When she arrives, she soon manages to win the friendship of the group and even seems to gain the attention of Dave Hunter, the boy that Sarah likes. Tension grows between the two girls, and Tasha and Sarah attempt to find a way to mend their relationship. First book in the 18 Pine St. series.

29.43 Naylor, Phyllis Reynolds. **Send No Blessings.** Penguin/Puffin Books/Jean Karl Books, 1992. 231 pp. ISBN 0-14-034859-X. Fiction.

Beth is determined to finish high school. She is also determined to find a way to get out of the trailer in which she lives with her father and mother and her nine younger brothers and sisters. Her parents are both hard-working, but because they lack high school diplomas, their jobs do not pay enough money for their large family. Beth's success in her business classes provides her with a dream to leave her small West Virginia town, but when she meets Harless, she has to decide if she wants to marry him and trade her dreams of independence for a life like her mother's.

29.44 Nelson, Peter. **Sylvia Smith-Smith.** Pocket Books/Archway Paperbacks, 1993. 180 pp. ISBN 0-671-70586-5. Fiction.

A fun, light novel, *Sylvia Smith-Smith* is titled after its main character, a senior high school student who thrives on challenge and intrigue. The novel, written in nonsequential chapters, chronicles the variety of situations in which Sylvia finds herself. In recounting such events as prom night or the time she challenged the school board's ruling on the school attendance policy, Sylvia shares stories of her family, her friends, and her exploits.

29.45 Pascal, Francine, creator (story by Laurie John). **College Girls.** Bantam Books, 1993. 235 pp. ISBN 0-553-56308-4. Fiction.

Twins Elizabeth and Jessica start Sweet Valley University with their best friends from high school. The tables turn for Elizabeth, however; she had been popular in high school but becomes an outcast in college. The novel follows the twins as they go through the mental, physical, and attitudinal stresses of the first year. Though friendships seem to be threatened by new challenges, valued relationships survive the ordeals. First book in the Sweet Valley University series.

29.46 Paulsen, Gary (translated into Spanish by Gloria De Aragón Andújar). **Sisters/Hermanas.** Harcourt Brace, 1993. 127 pp. ISBN 0-15-275323-0. Fiction.

This is the story of two girls who live in entirely different worlds. Rosa, a young Mexican girl, struggles against the chains of poverty in order to survive in a highly materialistic United States.

Traci, a product of a wealthy American family, contends with the pressures of family and society and the interpretation of success. These two girls are different, yet similar; they are in a sense sisters in a difficult world. This bilingual book has text in both English and Spanish.

29.47 Pfeffer, Susan Beth. **The Ring of Truth.** Bantam Books, 1993. 180 pp. ISBN 0-553-09224-3. Fiction.

Orphaned at a young age, sixteen-year-old Sloan Fredericks lives with her politically powerful grandmother. The only granddaughter in a wealthy family with a line of governors, Sloan has learned that appearance and association are important in her world. It is only after one of her grandmother's grand society parties that Sloan realizes the length to which her family will go to maintain the desired image and status. When Sloan shares with a group of friends that she was kissed by a prominent government official at the party, rumors soon spread about additional offenses that this official may have committed with other underaged girls. A media scandal evolves, and Sloan is pressured by her grandmother to keep quiet. In the midst of all the upheaval, Sloan learns that her grandmother has covered up a family secret for years.

29.48 Roth-Hano, Renée. **Safe Harbors.** Macmillan/Four Winds Press, 1993. 214 pp. ISBN 0-02-777795-2. Fiction.

Renée Roth-Hano begins her story, written in journal style, on January 15, 1951, and continues through May 16 of that year. She recalls her memory as an unhappy Jewish girl, coming to New York to begin a new life where no one knows her. Roth-Hano struggles with her painful and pleasant memories of France before her life is able to slowly take a new form.

29.49 Rubin, Susan Goldman. **Emily Good as Gold.** Harcourt Brace, 1993. 180 pp. ISBN 0-15-276633-2. Fiction.

Thirteen-year-old Emily Gold, a pretty girl who is developmentally disabled, struggles to feel good about herself. She knows that she is different from others her age and begins to feel lonely and rejected when her brother, Tom, marries Phyllis. Emily goes through a series of incidents, turns fourteen, sees her friend Donny again, and faces a decision that could change her life.

29.50 Sillitoe, Alan. **Saturday Night and Sunday Morning.** Penguin/Plume Books, 1992. 239 pp. ISBN 0-452-26909-1. Fiction.

In two parts and sixteen chapters, Arthur Seaton reveals his resentful, rebellious attitude by drinking excessively, exploiting other men's wives, and brawling at the local pubs. Though he works hard at the factory during the week, he lives to "blow" his wages on the weekend. Arthur's routine hangovers fail to dull his life or to inspire him to change. He shows determination and persistence in fighting to the end. Mature language and situations. First published in 1958.

29.51 Silver, Norman. **No Tigers in Africa.** Dutton Children's Books, 1992. 138 pp. ISBN 0-525-44733-4. Fiction.

When Selwyn Lewis was growing up in Cape Town, South Africa, he often dreamed of being chased by tigers. His parents were there to reassure him that there were no tigers in Africa. Later, when the family moves to England, his parents cannot help him overcome his problems. At fifteen, Selwyn is trying to adjust to life in a new country. Even though he is against apartheid, many of his opinions are considered racist in England, so his schoolmates make fun of him. At home, Selwyn's parents are having problems. His mother is away much of the time, and his father is sad and angry. In addition, Selwyn has to cope with his guilt over being involved in a death back home. Finally, Selwyn finds the stress too difficult to overcome.

Notable 1992 Children's Trade Books in the Field of Social Studies

29.52 Singer, Isaac Bashevis (translated by Rosaline Dukalsky Schwartz). **Scum.** Penguin/Plume Books, 1992. 218 pp. ISBN 0-452-26786-2. Fiction.

Does the childlike desire to seek thrills ever go away? When Max Barabander's only son dies in 1906, Max's wife, a former Argentine prostitute, mourns deeply. Fighting her loss, she sends Max to other women. However, his impotence leads him from Buenos Aires to Poland, the land of his virile youth. In turn-of-the-century Warsaw, he becomes immersed in the lives of five different women, including the daughter of a rabbi. His inability to tell them the truth leads eventually to violence.

29.53 Sirof, Harriet. **Because She's My Friend.** Atheneum, 1993. 184 pp. ISBN 0-689-31844-8. Fiction.

Two girls, Valerie Ross and Teri D'Angelo, meet and become friends though they are very different in personality. Valerie suffers an accident that paralyzes her leg, and she becomes a patient at the hospital where Teri does volunteer work. Their friendship persists through a series of encounters, realizations, and misunderstandings, and even as they drift apart, Valerie and Teri are able to share their good-byes.

29.54   Soto, Gary. **Pacific Crossing.** Harcourt Brace Jovanovich, 1992. 144 pp. ISBN 0-15-259187-7. Fiction.

Lincoln Mendoza, a fourteen-year-old Mexican American, and his friend Tony accept an invitation to study in Japan. As participants in a student-exchange program, Lincoln stays with the Ono family and Tony with the Inaba family. During their six-week stay, Lincoln becomes close friends with the Onos' son, Mitsuo, and the two learn to appreciate one another's heritage. The book includes a glossary of Spanish and Japanese phrases.

29.55   Spinelli, Jerry. **Maniac Magee.** HarperCollins/Harper Trophy Books, 1992. 184 pp. ISBN 0-06-440424-2. Fiction.

Jerry Lionell "Maniac" Magee is orphaned at age three and becomes homeless eight years later when he runs away from his uncaring aunt and uncle. He is still running the following year when he arrives in Two Mills, Pennsylvania. The first person Maniac meets there is Amanda Beale, and soon he is taken in by her African American family, becoming the only white person to live in the town's East End. The scraggly little kid with the tattered shoes amazes all with his running speed and an inside-the-park "frog" home run; he teaches an old man how to read and in return learns about the man's baseball career in the minor leagues; and he helps remove the color barrier between the East End and the West End. First published in 1990.

ALA Notable Books for Children, 1991
Booklist Editors' Choice, 1990
Boston Globe–Horn Book Fiction Award, 1990
Newbery Medal, 1991

29.56   Tamar, Erika. **Fair Game.** Harcourt Brace, 1993. 293 pp. ISBN 0-15-278537-X. Fiction.

Laura Jean Kettering, an outspoken high school senior, refutes an accusation of gang rape in Shorehaven, an affluent suburb. Cara Snowden, a teenage girl with mild mental disabilities, says that she has been raped by popular athletes and that Laura's boyfriend, Scott Delaney, was involved. In a letter to the editor, Laura lashes out at Cara because she feels Cara got the boys in trouble. Who is telling the truth? Mature language.

ALA Best Books for Young Adults, 1994

29.57   Thesman, Jean. **When the Road Ends.** Houghton Mifflin, 1992. 184 pp. ISBN 0-395-59507-X. Fiction.

Three young children and an ailing woman form an unlikely family when they are put together by fate and forced to fend for themselves. Mary Jack, the responsible one, and Adam, the distant one, are active members of this exceptional family. The other two, Jane and Mrs. Bradshaw, learn to let go of the ghosts from their past and come closer to each other. This is a compelling and heartwarming story for anyone who has felt alone and out of place.

ALA Best Books for Young Adults, 1993
ALA Notable Books for Children, 1993

29.58 Wartski, Maureen. **Dark Silence.** Fawcett/Juniper Books, 1994. 186 pp. ISBN 0-449-70418-1. Fiction.

After her mother's death, Randy feels lost and alone. Furthermore, when her father remarries and decides to move to another house, Randy has difficulty coping. Her focus is soon taken off her own problems, however, as she learns some unsettling secrets about her new neighbor, Delia Abbot. Eventually, Randy will learn that accepting her father's new wife does not mean that she is betraying her mother's memory.

29.59 Wesley, Valerie Wilson. **Where Do I Go from Here?** Scholastic, 1993. 138 pp. ISBN 0-590-45606-7. Fiction.

Two young African Americans manage to plot their own course in a predominately white environment. Marcus and Nia have the opportunity of a lifetime when they each receive a scholarship to Endicott, the best prep school in the United States. They almost lose their way, however, as they struggle to maintain their own identity and culture in a sometimes insensitive and unaware climate. This is a good read for any young person who wants to understand what it is like to be in the minority.

ALA Quick Picks for Young Adults, 1994

29.60 Williams-Garcia, Rita. **Fast Talk on a Slow Track.** Dutton/Lodestar Books, 1991. 182 pp. ISBN 0-525-67334-2. Fiction.

Denzel Watson, a young black man and dedicated student, has difficulty deciding how to tell his parents that he is not going to attend Princeton, which is their great desire for him. Denzel becomes a door-to-door salesman during the summer, and in a deliberate effort to compete, he discovers himself.

ALA Best Books for Young Adults, 1992
ALA Quick Picks for Young Adults, 1992
School Library Journal Best Books, 1991

29.61 Wilson, August. **Two Trains Running.** Penguin/Plume Books, 1993. 110 pp. ISBN 0-452-26929-6. Fiction.

This play is set in Pittsburgh in 1969, where several patrons of Memphis Lee's restaurant sit around the counter and discuss the ills of the world. Through these characters, we see portraits of black America and the African American experience. The restaurant regulars are struggling to cope with the turbulence of their changing world: the diner is scheduled to be torn down, an ex-con is looking for a job, and various others are being affected by the economy. Using vivid characters, Pulitzer Prize–winning dramatist August Wilson paints the events of everyday life of ordinary people in a culturally rich and authentic portrait.

29.62 Wood, June Rae. **The Man Who Loved Clowns.** G. P. Putnam's Sons, 1992. 224 pp. ISBN 0-399-21888-2. Fiction.

Thirteen-year-old Delrita Jensen, an only child, encounters a series of disappointments, hurt, and even death. Caring for Punky, an uncle with Down's syndrome, Delrita suffers mixed emotions. She loves Punky but feels ashamed when others are involved, especially now that they have moved to town. Punky develops self-esteem through a sheltered workshop, and Delrita learns from him that she must "spread her wings and fly." She realizes that people reach out to her in spite of her attempts to isolate herself from the world and remain invisible.

Notable 1992 Children's Trade Books in the Field of Social Studies
School Library Journal Best Books, 1992

30 Science and Technology

30.1 Asimov, Isaac, and Frederik Pohl. **Our Angry Earth.** Tor Books, 1993. 429 pp. ISBN 0-812-52096-3. Nonfiction.

Isaac Asimov and Frederik Pohl have laid out the vast variety of ways in which the activities of people are damaging the health of our planet. The first section covers the authors' ideas about hope for the Earth (which they term *Gaia,* the name for the ancient goddess of the Earth) and hope for the future. In the second section, the authors discuss alternatives to our present machines, power plants, and energy resources as well as alternatives in our daily lives. The authors then cover some of the social and economic changes that environmental problems will bring, and in conclusion they examine the political aspects of change: why real changes will be difficult and what political actions must be taken in order to bring change.

30.2 Bortz, Fred. **Mind Tools: The Science of Artificial Intelligence.** Franklin Watts/Venture Books, 1992. 108 pp. ISBN 0-531-12515-7. Nonfiction.

Will computers one day be able to identify a disease, read aloud, write music, or play chess—and win? They already can with the help of AI-based technology—artificial intelligence, or the capability of a machine to imitate intelligent human behavior. This book traces the AI research and interviews Alan Newell and Herbert Simon, known as the fathers of artificial intelligence. Explore these fascinating programs that imitate and enhance human mental capabilities, and discover what the future may hold.

30.3 Carson, Rachel L. **Under the Sea Wind.** Illustrated by Bob Hines. Penguin/Plume/Truman Talley Books, 1992. 304 pp. ISBN 0-452-26918-0. Nonfiction.

This fiftieth anniversary edition of Rachel Carson's *Under the Sea Wind* is both an introduction to nature writing and an introduction to the inhabitants and workings of the sea as told through the stories of Rynchops, a black skimmer; Scomber, a mackerel; and Anguilla, an eel. Although Carson's knowledge was that of a marine biologist, her writing is poetic. Illustrations by Bob Hines and a glossary provide additional information about the sea. First published in 1942.

30.4   Cohen, Daniel, and Susan Cohen. **Where to Find Dinosaurs Today.** Dutton/Cobblehill Books, 1992. 209 pp. ISBN 0-525-65098-9. Nonfiction.

The bones of dinosaurs and other extinct prehistoric creatures—or reconstructed models of them—can be found in nearly every one of the fifty states and in most Canadian provinces. The authors provide an extensive list of dinosaur locations, ranging from the totally scientific, such as the Museum of Comparative Zoology at Harvard University, to a whimsical double-life-sized brontosaurus with a gift shop in its belly. The authors have arranged these listings by regions and by state or province within each region and include location, hours, admission, and telephone numbers for each listing.

30.5   Dolan, Edward F. **Our Poisoned Sky.** Dutton/Cobblehill Books, 1991. 121 pp. ISBN 0-525-65056-3. Nonfiction.

This book is an excellent overview of the Earth's pollution problems. Edward F. Dolan clearly explains the pollutants, their effects on the ozone layer, and the consequences of acid rain and the greenhouse effect. He also reports on efforts to curb pollution and ways in which we can all contribute to a healthy environment.

30.6   Hecht, Jeff. **Vanishing Life: The Mystery of Mass Extinctions.** Charles Scribner's Sons, 1993. 149 pp. ISBN 0-684-19331-0. Nonfiction.

In this fascinating book, Jeff Hecht explores the phenomenon of mass extinctions in the Earth's past. He discusses not only the dinosaurs but what came before and after them, and he explores what we can learn about potential future happenings from these mass dyings. A glossary is provided.

30.7   Herbst, Judith. **Star Crossing: How to Get Around in the Universe.** Atheneum, 1993. 187 pp. ISBN 0-689-31523-6. Nonfiction.

Through a series of well-planned essays, Judith Herbst provides the reader with matter-of-fact, yet simple, explanations of how space travel happens, from the workings of the rocket engines to the question of physics. Each chapter begins with an intriguing hypothetical scenario. Even the most scientific reader will enjoy reading this book.

30.8   Madama, John. **Desktop Publishing: The Art of Communication.** Lerner, 1993. 61 pp. ISBN 0-8225-2303-5. Nonfiction.

You do not need to be a whiz to produce attractive, professional-looking newsletters, posters, or brochures. In this age of the computer, a publishing system will help you become an author and an illustrator. This book guides you through all aspects of desktop publishing, with chapters on planning, writing, illustrating, and layout techniques. All you need to add is your imagination.

30.9   Palfreman, Jon, and Doron Swade. **The Dream Machine: Exploring the Computer Age.** BBC Books, 1991. 205 pp. ISBN 0-563-36221-9. Nonfiction.

Did you know that forty years ago the first computers were as big as a room and cost millions of dollars? Today's computers are lap-sized, affordable, and available to most people. What a change! *The Dream Machine* provides an in-depth look at the development of the computer, beginning with the earliest physical aids people used to compute and ending with the exciting possibilities for tomorrow's computers.

30.10 Van Rose, Susanna. **Volcano and Earthquake.** Photographs by James Stevenson. Alfred A. Knopf, 1992. 63 pp. ISBN 0-679-91685-7. Nonfiction.

Humans have been curious about volcanic eruptions and earthquakes for as long as they have lived on Earth. This book explains how and why volcanoes and earthquakes occur and provides numerous color photographs that illustrate their devastating effects. It also describes how volcanoes and earthquakes are measured and how to prepare for such disasters.

31 Science Fiction

31.1 Aikin, Jim. **The Wall at the Edge of the World.** Ace Books, 1993. 309 pp. ISBN 0-441-87140-2. Fiction.

It was a distant future society that built the wall boundary to keep out the savage unknown. The Body was a society of telepaths who all *kenned,* or read each other's thoughts and feelings, and who were monitored by the priest figures with more and stronger telephathic gifts that could control anyone who might be slipping from the *ktess,* or group. At intervals, ceremonial "Cleansings" (which were actually beheadings) purified the ktess of *nulls,* any adolescents who had not become telepathic. Into this society come "wild women" in search of men captives to replace their dead husbands. In the raid, Danlo Ree is captured. She tries to survive in the world on the other side and stop the killing of the nulls. Danlo, "wild woman" Linne, two null boys, and a gifted but unhappy young telepath named Ainne struggle with impossible situations and overwhelming odds.

31.2 Allen, Roger MacBride. **Isaac Asimov's Caliban.** Ace Books, 1993. 312 pp. ISBN 0-441-09079-6. Fiction.

Violent crime, although rare, still makes Sheriff Alvar Kresh angry. Dr. Fredda Leving, robot scientist of renown, is attacked and left bleeding in her lab, and an experimental robot is missing. It is the kind of situation that could ignite the uneasy peace on Inferno between the Spacers, descendents of those who fled Earth with their robots, and the Settlers, descendents of those who stayed behind to live underground with advanced technology—but no robots. It is a situation that Simcor Beddle, leader of the Ironheads, could use to unleash violence, which could determine not just the political life or death of Governor Chanto Grieg but actual life or death of the entire planet. Sheriff Kresh has to work quickly to capture Caliban, an experimental robot who is loose and thinking for himself.

31.3 Anthony, Piers. **Hard Sell.** Ace Books, 1993. 268 pp. ISBN 0-441-31748-0. Fiction.

When Fisk Centers loses his three million dollars in one quick Mars land swindle, he is suddenly a broke and unemployed fifty-year-old. Bungling his first attempt at a new job, he finds himself an adoptive parent of an incorrigible eleven-year-old former ward of the state. Yola is a street-smart black girl with a mind and a mouth of her own. When she begins scouting out employment for Fisk, he finds himself driving a supersonic car in a suicide race, selling burial plots in Perpetual Laser Memorial Gardens, investigating misuse of live brains for the Death Insurance Agency, and making ads endorsing matter transporters. But these experiences do not totally prepare Fisk for dealing with Yola and the big business network of advertising.

31.4 Anthony, Piers. **Killobyte.** Ace Books, 1994. 312 pp. ISBN 0-441-44425-3. Fiction.

When disabled police officer Walter Toland gets his virtual reality equipment and logs onto the game "Killobyte," he can walk once again and have feeling where he had lost it. Baal Curran, a diabetic teen with a broken heart, also plays the game and likes to "flirt" with death. The two players find their new game with all of its different settings—ranging from medieval and magical to modern-day Beirut—to be an escape from their confining lives. But then a deranged teenage hacker puts a virus on Walter and Baal that will not allow them to exit from the game. If they cannot get back to their normal lives, Baal may die from insulin shock or both may starve to death. Baal and Walter have little choice: they give the hacker a similar virus and chase him throughout the game settings in an attempt to get the antivenin before they die.

Booklist Editors' Choice, 1992

31.5 Anthony, Piers, and Philip José Farmer. **The Caterpillar's Question.** Ace Books, 1992. 264 pp. ISBN 0-441-09488-0. Fiction.

Seven years ago, when she was six, Tappy Concord became blinded, scarred, mute, and crippled. Now Jack, a struggling college art student, is hired to drive her across the country to a clinic. In a strange tangle of feelings, Jack finds himself following Tappy through a portal into an alien world that desperately needs the Imago, an immortal spirit capable of evolving into a being of great power. The Imago was born into Tappy, and the Gaol empire is in a ruthless search to find the Imago's receptacle and contain it. Jack, Tappy, and those aliens who would aid the Imago are in a race against time and the Gaol to save themselves and their worlds. Mature themes and language.

31.6 Ashwell, Pauline. **Unwillingly to Earth.** Tor Books, 1992. 280 pp. ISBN 0-812-51929-9. Fiction.

Lizzie Lee has been raised on a mining planet, Excenus 23. She is one of the few women on the planet, and she is not very smart, a characteristic she gets from her father. When she unwillingly accepts a scholarship to a university on the planet Earth, it really is the last thing she wants to do, but she goes anyway. School on Earth is only the beginning of her new life, however. Soon there is murder, hostage taking, and a potential war to challenge her.

31.7   Asimov, Janet, and Issac Asimov. **Norby and the Oldest Dragon.** Ace Books, 1993. 152 pp. ISBN 0-441-58632-5. Fiction.

Cadet Jeff Wells and his personal robot, Norby, are invited to the greatest birthday party of the galaxy, the royal party of the Grand Dragon of Jamya. Jeff is to be accompanied by his handsome brother Fargo and by Albany, Fargo's fiancée. As a birthday favor, Jeff and Norby go to extend the Queen's personal invitation to her mother, the Grand Dowager, who retired fifty years ago and became a hermit on a distant island. When Jeff returns with the Grand Dowager, he finds that a mysterious yellow fog cloud has enveloped the entire planet of Jamya. The energy field cloud called Monos has come in search of something—knowledge? experience? life? death? control? No one knows what Monos is after, but suddenly everyone is in danger.

31.8   Asprin, Robert. **The Bug Wars.** Ace Books, 1993. 217 pp. ISBN 0-441-07373-5. Fiction.

Rahm, a Tzen of the warrior caste, flexes his talons as he returns to consciousness and prepares for combat. He is duty bound to preserve the empire. The Tzen had masked their existence from the enemy for over a million years while developing highly specialized castes of technicians, scientists, and warriors. Now Rahm and the other Tzen are ready for combat, and the first stage in reclaiming this planet is to defeat the huge wasplike creatures. Soon Rahm will be in combat with the Leapers, the Ants, and the weaponry the enemy has developed. Adjusting to different battle plans and different enemy targets is usual for a Tzen warrior; Rahm's biggest adjustment is his changing role as the battle for the planet continues.

31.9   Baird, Wilhelmina. **Crashcourse.** Ace Books, 1993. 277 pp. ISBN 0-441-12163-2. Fiction.

They are a strange trio, Cassie thinks: she, Mokey, and Dosh—a burglar, an artist, and a prostitute. In this polluted future world, she is Cat, a cat burglar stealing from the Aris class, who are too rich or too stoned to care. Mokey, actually Martin Faber, is the sculptor welding his gigantic visions, and Dosh is the Greek god, bodybuilder, would-be actor who is hooking while waiting for his movie break. They live in the seamy underside of societal rejects, criminals, mutants, and surgically created aberrations of humans. The only way to survive is to leave the planet, and the only way to earn that kind of money is to agree to be in the new cyber-cinema, where the movie is the character's experience, filmed as it happens. What the trio does not know, however, is that the moviemakers are really trying to kill them; their costar likes to end her movies with everyone but herself dead. Mature language and situations.

31.10 Barron, T. A. **The Ancient One.** Putnam/Philomel Books, 1992. 367 pp. ISBN 0-399-21899-8. Fiction.

Thirteen-year-old Kate goes to Oregon to visit her Aunt Melanie for the summer and is caught up in the struggle between loggers and her aunt. The center of the controversy is the crater, an area that is the remnant of a volcanic explosion resulting in the summit's collapse. The huge crater, a caldera, contains a lake surrounded by dense forest, and the loggers are desperate to cut the timber. Aunt Melanie, however, wants to protect the crater's resources. In a strange thunderstorm, Kate and a young logger, Jody, are transported 500 years into the past. Kate fights strange enemies, makes a friend, and meets mysterious creatures while struggling to solve the riddle that will allow them to return to the present.

IRA Young Adults' Choices, 1994

31.11 bes Shahar, Eluki. **Archangel Blues.** DAW Books, 1993. 252 pp. ISBN 0-88677-543-4. Fiction.

A half-woman, half-machine hellflower mercenary named Butterfly St. Cyr and her partner, Tiggy, are faced with a bigger task than in the two previous books in the series. Now they are out to destroy Governor-General Mallorum Archangel. With their highly illegal Old Federal Tech Library, known as Paladin, they must stop the war that could end any hope of peace in the Phoenix Empire. At the same time, Butterfly is fighting to keep control of her own body because another library is trying to take it over. She could be trapped in virtual reality and never escape. Violence. Third book in the Hellflower series.

31.12 Bradley, Marion Zimmer, and Mercedes Lackey. **Rediscovery: A Novel of Darkover.** DAW Books, 1993. 307 pp. ISBN 0-88677-561-2. Fiction.

A starship searching the universe for habitable planets is shocked to find a planet already inhabited by descendants of a starship lost centuries ago. The colonists have stopped using almost all forms of machinery. Most have mind abilities or *laran*, powers that include telepathy and more. Leonie Hastur, the beautiful daughter of one of the most powerful families, and her twin brother, Lorill, are to be trained in the use of their laran. Already Leonie's abilities are so strong that she has been able to use them somewhat without training, and she senses with terror that something huge and destructive is about to happen to planet Darkover.

31.13   Bredenberg, Jeff. **The Man in the Moon Must Die.** Avon Books, 1993. 215 pp. ISBN 0-380-76914-X. Fiction.

Chief executive officer Benito Funcitti is the only one in the company approved by the Interplanetary Commerce Commission for TeleComp travel, the human equivalent of faxing—a new body is assembled at the destination, molecule by molecule, according to the specifications fed the machine. Not only does TeleComping allow Benito immediate access to his empire branching out on the moon, but it also allows him to rid his body of the cancer that attempts to consume it from time to time. In TeleComping, the old body is vaporized as the new body arrives at its destination, but this time an accident creates a duplicate Benito without destroying the old. Now Benito I has to save himself from Benito II, who has legitimate control of his business empire and all personal assets—except Elvis, his Cyber wife of forty-three years. Benito I goes underground with Elvis into a strange network of electronic pirates, and his survival depends on his out-thinking . . . himself.

31.14   Busby, F. M. **The Singularity Project.** Tor Books, 1993. 350 pp. ISBN 0-312-85443-9. Fiction.

Mitch Banning, a young part-time engineer and freelance writer, hopes an anonymous story tip about a local businessman and millionaire, Elihu Coogan, might turn into a lucrative writing project. Elihu has been paying a local scientist, George Detweiler, to create a matter transmitter. George is not unknown to Mitch; he was a school bully when the two were kids. Mitch discovers that the millionaire is a longtime crook, and soon there is a missing scientist and ransom demands. Mitch thinks it sounds like an old con game, except for one nagging possibility—the matter transmitter might be real.

31.15   Card, Orson Scott, editor. **Future on Fire.** Tor Books, 1991. 376 pp. ISBN 0-812-51183-2. Fiction.

Here are fifteen short stories about everything from suspense thrillers to poems. In "Rachel in Love," a chimpanzee named Rachel has the memory of a teenage girl implanted into her brain, and she struggles to balance her human thoughts with her animal behavior. Meet Pretty Boy, a sixteen-year-old who is considering "going over" to the other side of the video screen and becoming "distilled information," a computer-disk blip that never grows any older. Mature language.

31.16 Card, Orson Scott. **The Memory of Earth.** Tor Books, 1992. 332 pp. ISBN 0-812-53259-7. Fiction.

The Oversoul, a master computer that watches over the planet Earth, has lost its memory banks. It was built millions of years ago, and its purpose was to save Earth's humans from being destroyed by their greatest enemies, other humans. Since the Oversoul lost its memory and has been unable to regulate the thoughts of all the people, humans are trying to achieve great power and fortune for themselves and have even started to kill each other in quest of their goals. But Elemak Mabbekew, Issib, Nafi, and the rest of the family have been chosen to help the Oversoul, if only it is not too late. Mature situations. First book in the Homecoming Saga series.

31.17 Card, Orson Scott. **Xenocide.** Tor Books, 1992. 592 pp. ISBN 0-812-50925-0. Fiction.

Before Jiang-qing dies, she issues one directive to be followed: Qing-jao is to follow her path and obey the Gods. Qing-jao is a God-spoken child and the most brilliant of the superintelligent, so to her falls the task of discovering what happened to the Fleet sent to destroy the planet Lusitania, the home of three different intelligent species: the Hive Queen, the pequininos, and humans. Also on Lusitania is the deadly virus descolada. The pequininos require it, the humans are killed by it, and the Starways Congress is so frightened by it that the planet is again targeted for destruction.

31.18 Chalker, Jack L. **Downtiming the Night Side.** Baen Books, 1993. 288 pp. ISBN 0-671-72170-4. Fiction.

It should have been a simple first day on the job for Ronald Moosic as security director for what appeared to be a government nuclear power plant. Instead, terrorists attempt to take over the installation; they steal two time-travel suits and exit into the past. Ron becomes the logical choice to pursue and perhaps undo whatever the pair do. But if Ron does not return from his time travel within the prescribed limitations, he will be absorbed by the person he has become. Thus begins Ron's entry into the time loops that replay through variations of events. The grand prize in the struggle turns out to be the fate of Earth.

31.19 Chalker, Jack L. **The Ninety Trillion Fausts.** Ace Books, 1992. 360 pp. ISBN 0-441-58103-X. Fiction.

The Ninety Trillion Fausts begins with the Exchange, a group of uneasily allied creatures from mutually distrustful planets in the alternate universe of the demons. In a series of strange events, demons imprisoned in amber for centuries are released. They immediately resume their efforts to magnify the evil in the individual and to take control of all the races in the universe. Only the five Exchange survivors working together might possibly reseal the Prince of Darkness away from the three alien races' ninety trillion souls that the prince wants to enslave. Third book in the Quintara Marathon.

31.20 David, Peter. **Starfleet Academy #3: Survival.** Pocket/Minstrel Books, 1993. 111 pp. ISBN 0-671-87086-6. Fiction.

Five Starfleet Academy cadets and three from Klingon volunteer to stay behind when the colonists evacuate the Dantar IV colony after the surprise attack. Tensions between the groups are growing, and they begin to fear they have been forgotten when the Vulcan Soleta captures one of the enemy attackers. The cadets find they must work as one team to find and dismantle an enemy base hidden somewhere on the planet. The Klingon female K'Ehleyr and the Starfleet Cadet Worf try to maintain peace and cooperation between their groups so they can disable the base before the enemy returns. Third book in the Starfleet Academy series of Star Trek: The Next Generation.

31.21 Dietz, William C. **Drifter's War.** Ace Books, 1992. 230 pp. ISBN 0-441-16815-9. Fiction.

They could have sold the ancient, alien, high-tech drift ship for a billion credits or so if Cap had not gotten drunk and given the space tabloid TV some information about the find. Suddenly every bounty hunter is after them! Pik Lando, a smuggler who is wanted for murder, Cap, an alcoholic former ship's captain, Melissa, Cap's daughter, bounty hunter Della Dee, and Cy, a cyborg electronic whiz, make a strange family, but family they are. Now they are running for their lives in an ancient ship that takes them to a distant world where the II Ronnians are enslaving the planet. But Pik's group has no other place to go.

31.22 Drake, David (edited by Bill Fawcett). **Battlestation.** Ace Books, 1993. 264 pp. ISBN 0-441-86032-X. Fiction.

The Fleet Battlestation *Stephen Hawking* is in a constant, lonely battle with the predatory insectlike Ichtons, who are moving through the galaxy, destroying every habitable planet and any species they find on those worlds. The Battlestation is the setting for the stories told from the varying perspectives of people on the ship: the cargo mover in the loading and storage decks, a nurse, a former space pirate, and the ne'er-do-well son of a crime family who turned respectable in the ship's service. The action portrayed in the stories includes individual selfishness, battles, espionage, rescues in space, and heroic sacrifice as the *Stephen Hawking* struggles far, far away from help and against great odds. Second book in the Vanguard series.

31.23 Elliott, Kate. **An Earthly Crown.** DAW Books, 1993. 500 pp. ISBN 0-88677-546-9. Fiction.

The alien race Chapalii has taken control of Earth, and all humans are under their rule. Only one human, Charles Soerensen, holds a position in the Chapalii Empire. A duke, Charles is granted a more primitive planet called Rhui as a gift. Four years after his last visit to Rhui, Charles returns for his sister, Tess, who has stayed behind to study the people of Rhui and who has married Ilya Bakhliian, the leader of the Jaran tribes, who are now fighting for their independence from the Habahkar king. Tess inadvertently risks Ilya's life and sends him into a coma. Although Charles realizes that Tess may not want to leave Rhui at this time, he needs her to help him reclaim Earth. But first he hopes to discover on Rhui some information that may help him free Earth from the alien Chapalii. Mature situations. First book in the Sword of Heaven series.

31.24 Elliott, Kate. **His Conquering Sword.** DAW Books, 1993. 495 pp. ISBN 0-88677-551-5. Fiction.

Charles Soerensen has come from Earth to the planet Rhui for two things: to find and reclaim his sister, Tess, and to try to discover additional information about fighting the alien Chapalii Empire now controlling Earth. Charles believes information about Mushai, once a rebel leader against the Chapalii, will help him in his attempt to overthrow them. Charles soon finds that he, Tess, and her husband, Ilya Bakhliian, who is the leader of the Jaran tribes on Rhui, agree on almost nothing. Each is a determined fighter, but they must make peace with one another before they can fight an outside enemy. Mature themes. Second book in the Sword of Heaven series.

31.25   Forward, Robert L. **Timemaster.** Tor Books, 1992. 306 pp. ISBN 0-812-51644-3. Fiction.

Randy Hunter became a billionaire when he inherited his father's company, but Randy does not like sitting behind a desk or running the company from his mansion on Earth. When an alien is discovered at the company's Hygiea mining base, Randy decides to go there immediately. The alien, Silverhair, is a warpgate to the future and back to the present. Randy decides not to return to Earth immediately, but to venture out and explore the universe with his own personal warpgate.

31.26   Harrison, Harry. **Stainless Steel Visions.** Illustrated by Bryn Barnard. Tor Books, 1993. 254 pp. ISBN 0-312-85245-2. Fiction.

Thirteen of Harry Harrison's stories are in this collection. In "The Streets of Ashkelon," a trader lives with aliens to harness their talents, but then a missionary invades their lives and changes them forever. In "Brave Newer World," the human race has mastered test-tube birth. The babies are to live in a complex that will grow into a town of genetically engineered humans, but it seems that someone has started killing the babies. Also included in this collection are an all-new Stainless Steel Rat story, in which the police have finally caught an aging Jimmy diGriz, and "Roommates," the basis for the movie *Soylent Green*.

31.27   Kagan, Janet. **Mirabile.** Tor Books, 1992. 278 pp. ISBN 0-812-50993-5. Fiction.

Annie is a scientist on the planet Earth trying to find the answers to everything. When she learns about the Loch Moose monster, she goes immediately to planet Mirabile. It seems that while the animals inhabiting Mirabile were specifically designed to proliferate and populate, they have begun producing dangerous and often carnivorous mutants. Some on Mirabile think Annie is a quack; Annie herself wonders if the stories are just made up. But there is no denying the Loch Moose monster, the flesh-eating kangaroo, known as Kangaroo Rex, or the voracious Frankenswine, all of which pose a threat to the planet.

31.28   Knight, Damon. **Why Do Birds.** Tor Books, 1992. 272 pp. ISBN 0-312-85174-X. Fiction.

Life in the twenty-first century is built upon high-tech mechanisms and communications, all of which seem very strange to a man from the 1930s who claims he was kidnapped by aliens and held in suspended animation. Ed Stone says that he was sent to the next century to put the human race in a box and save it from future destruction. Not only does he need a builder for the box, but he needs people to put faith in it. Is Earth actually going to be destroyed in twelve years? Or are the aliens really saving the human race? Mature language.

31.29 Kube-McDowell, Michael P. **Exile.** Ace Books, 1993. 289 pp. ISBN 0-441-22212-9. Fiction.

Meer Fastet has been trying for the last seventeen years to forget about the drowning and his part in it. Now the exiled traitor Kedar Nanchen has sent Meer a messenger with his last request: Meer is to bring Kedar's body back to be buried in Ana. The exarch, Oran Anadon, sends Meer to the outside, where exiles hide and are hunted, in order to fetch the body. The journey is full of the unknown, the water, the land outside the city, the exiles, and the truth about that terrible event. Finally Meer knows what he must do.

31.30 Laumer, Keith. **Retief and the Rascals.** Baen Books, 1993. 241 pp. ISBN 0-671-72168-2. Fiction.

Fortunately for Ben Magnan, Econ Officer of the Terran Mission, experienced and strong Jame Retief is assigned as his junior officer. Magnan and Retief have work to do: the ceremonial event on Bloor is turning into a riot between rival gangs and a hijacking power grab for illegal activities, commodities, and control. Everyone—from the Undesirables, the Objectionables, and the Filthies and Viles to the Groaci "diplomats"—wants a share, regardless of what they have to do to whom.

31.31 Leigh, Stephen. **Ray Bradbury Presents Dinosaur Planet.** Illustrated by John Paul Genzo. Avon Books, 1993. 280 pp. ISBN 0-380-76278-1. Fiction.

This is book two in a series based on the Bradbury short story "A Sound of Thunder." To the main characters, Travis and Eckels, this series adds three new teenagers: Aaron, Jennifer, and Peter, who are struggling with worlds from different times and realities and are bumping into each other because of disruptions from the shattered time-travel path. Mysterious time storms now carry things, people, and monsters from different worlds into each other's realities. Peter, Jennifer, and Eckels are captives on the dinosaur planet, looking for any piece of the path on which to escape. Travis and Aaron use the time machine to search for the correct current version of reality. Aaron also looks for Grandpa Carl while hiding from the current oppressive martial law and the monsters unleashed by the time storms. In addition, they all search for each other.

31.32   Leigh, Stephen. **Ray Bradbury Presents Dinosaur World.** Illustrated by Wayne Barlowe. Avon Books, 1992. 274 pp. ISBN 0-380-76277-3. Fiction.

Eighteen-year-old Aaron Cofield and his new girlfriend, Jennifer Mason, are enjoying a perfect August day in Green Town when a dinosaur appears in the woods behind Aaron's house. When they ask Peter Finnigan, Jennifer's former boyfriend, to take pictures of the dinosaur eggs to document the anomaly, they find much more—Travis, a safari guide from the future, a time machine, pieces of the floating time-path highway, and worlds from other realities. Through an accident, Aaron finds himself transported back in time alone. Jennifer and Peter follow in search of him but soon find themselves in a strange, dangerous world. They are taken prisoners by intelligent dinosaur creatures, some of whom want to sacrifice the two to their gods to stop the disturbances occurring in their world.

31.33   Levin, Betty. **Mercy's Mill.** Greenwillow Books, 1992. 241 pp. ISBN 0-688-11122-X. Fiction.

A move to the country from the city, a new stepfather, a mother immersed in restoring an old mill beside a pond, and a younger foster child who seems to get all her mother's attention—all make Sarah feel alone. During a freak winter thunderstorm, Sarah and a crow are saved from an icy drowning by a strange boy who claims to have come from the past in search of Mercy, a young girl whose family owned the mill over a hundred years ago. In some mysterious time-travel connection, they are all linked in a search for safety and belonging.

31.34   Lewitt, S. N. **Songs of Chaos.** Ace Books, 1993. 228 pp. ISBN 0-441-77529-2. Fiction.

Dante McCall is an outcast to all the humans living on Earth. He is abnormal because he has synesthesia, confusion of the senses. He is banished from Earth and sent into space on a cargo ship headed to the Trader ship *Hertzen.* But the *Mangueira,* another Trader ship, intercepts the cargo ship and takes Dante aboard. Although he is a freak on Earth, the *Mangueira* is so strange that

Dante seems rather normal there. He finally feels accepted and thinks he wants to make the *Mangueira* his home—until he starts to wonder if his new home might actually be a trap.

31.35   McCaffrey, Anne. **Damia.** Ace Books, 1993. 341 pp. ISBN 0-441-13556-0. Fiction.

Afra Lyon has always been a precocious telepath, even as a baby, although he was raised in the rigidly mannered Capellan society and family. No one is surprised when Afra, at age sixteen, applies to work for the Prime, the primary telepath. Afra has always wanted to work for the FT&T, the network that handles communication and transportation between the star systems that comprise the Federation. Amazingly, Afra is accepted and soon encounters new experiences, including the challenges of transport work, relationships with personnel at the transport station, attacks by aliens on the space frontier, and family relationships.

31.36   McCaffrey, Anne. **Damia's Children.** Ace Books, 1994. 325 pp. ISBN 0-441-00007-X. Fiction.

In this sequel to *The Rowan* and *Damia*, two brothers and two sisters—Laria, Thian, Rojer, and Zara—are learning to master their psychic powers and are forging their futures with an alien race, the Mrdinis. Each child will be raised with a pair of Mrdinis in the hope that the communication gap can be closed and the two races unified. With Damia's children also reside the hope and the possibility that the longtime insectlike enemy, the Hive, can be overcome.

31.37   McConnell, Ashley. **Quantum Leap.** Ace Books, 1992. 294 pp. ISBN 0-441-69322-9. Fiction.

When Admiral Al Calavicci locates Dr. Sam Beckett, it seems that Sam, through the experimental Quantum Leap accelerator, has been transferred into the body of carnival worker Bobby Watkins, a polio survivor living in Jasmine, Oklahoma. Ziggy the computer predicts that in just four days, a terrible mishap will kill seven people. Can Sam, in Bobby's body, prevent it, or will he be the cause of it? Or will the mishap be caused by roller-coaster builder Mike McFarland or by the ex-partner in the amusement park, Jesse Bartlett? Can Sam prevent the catastrophe just days before it happens—or will he be stuck forever in Bobby's body?

31.38   McConnell, Ashley. **Quantum Leap: The Wall.** Ace Books, 1994. 245 pp. ISBN 0-441-00015-0. Fiction.

Dr. Sam Beckett, who is able to transfer into the bodies of others, has leaped into the life of a six-year-old American girl, Missy Robicheaux. It is 1961, and Missy's military family is living in Hainerberg, Germany. At first Sam thinks he has become Missy in order to stop the beatings she and her brother Tom are receiving from their mother, Jane. Information from Al, Sam's helper from another time, foretells that on a day when the emergency siren goes off, Tom will be killed in a fire, and Jane will die from an overdose of pills. When the warning siren sounds, Sam, as Missy, destroys all the pills "she" can find and locates Tom in his hiding place in the tool shed. The shed catches fire, but Missy and Tom escape, only to find their mother unconscious. She has found more pills. Suddenly Sam becomes the adult Missy, in a hospital waiting room, and this time Sam knows immediately what his real mission is.

31.39   McMullan, Kate. **Under the Mummy's Spell.** Farrar, Straus, and Giroux, 1992. 214 pp. ISBN 0-374-38033-3. Fiction.

Before Peter Harring kisses the mummy, Princess Nephia, on a dare at the Metropolitan Museum of Art, his biggest problem is Howie the bully. But the kiss awakens Nephia, who pleads with Peter to bring back "the treasure of her soul." Peter begins a fast-paced adventure to restore to the Pharaoh's daughter her beloved cat "before the moon is full."

31.40   Morris, Janet, and Chris Morris. **Trust Territory.** Penguin/Roc Books, 1992. 261 pp. ISBN 0-451-45126-0. Fiction.

It is the twenty-fifth century; Earth is a game preserve, accessible only to the very privileged. The United Nations of Earth (UNE) rules the Trust Territory and the space station at the Threshold. The story is told alternately through the perspectives of several characters: Captain Joe South, a test pilot who was lost for five centuries in "sponge" space on a mission and has now "returned" to a time into which he does not quite fit; Riva Lowe, director of customs for Threshold; Lt. Reice, commanding officer; Secretary General Mickey Croft, chief executive officer of the UNE; and Richard Cummings II, one of the Earth's most wealthy and influential businessmen, whose runaway son and girlfriend have disappeared in space.

31.41   Nolan, William F., and Martin H. Greenberg, editors. **The Bradbury Chronicles: Stories in Honor of Ray Bradbury.** Penguin/Roc Books, 1992. 336 pp. ISBN 0-451-45195-3. Fiction.

This collection of stories celebrates Ray Bradbury's fifty years of professional writing. The authors and the topics are varied. One story involves a troll who is part of a folksy town legend until a know-it-all psychiatrist confronts the troll and then has only himself to blame for the chilling results. There is also a burned-out rock singer who is drawn to a dead-end town, where he gets involved in a strange game. A third story involves a father who never denies killing his own daughter—and who never guesses how his punishment will fit the crime. Mature language.

31.42 Oppel, Kenneth. **Dead Water Zone.** Little, Brown/Joy Street Books, 1993. 152 pp. ISBN 0-316-65102-8. Fiction.

Right before he disappeared, Sam called his older brother, Paul, to say, "Something wonderful is going to happen." Now sixteen-year-old Paul is searching for Sam in Watertown, an area reserved for their society's undesirable thieves and addicts, where water pollution has created a dead water zone. Paul knows that he must act quickly to find and protect his genius younger brother in that hostile, dangerous, and eerie place and that he must trust the untrustable: Armitage, a black-market entrepreneur, and his sister Monica, daughter of a water drinker. If it is not too late already, Paul has to locate Sam before he is found by the Cityweb men or Sked, a Watertown thug, and before Sam becomes one of the strange, addicted water drinkers. First published in Canada, 1992.

School Library Journal Best Books, 1992

31.43 Perry, Steve. **Brother Death.** Ace Books, 1992. 243 pp. ISBN 0-441-54476-2. Fiction.

Saval Bork is a matador, one of the most elite bodyguards in the world. He is married to Veate, an Albino Exotic, the most beautiful and sensual of creatures, and he is the father of a baby son. When his sister, Tazzimi, assistant chief peace officer on the planet Tembo, asks his help, Saval immediately agrees to come; he knows the value of family. Neither of them, however, can know that while they are trying to find and stop the mysterious killer who decapitates his victims, they and Ruul Oro, the handsome entertainer who loves Tazzi, are the targets of the mysterious Zonn cult. Mature language and situations.

31.44 Ransom, Bill. **ViraVax.** Ace Books, 1993. 307 pp. ISBN 0-441-86476-7. Fiction.

On Easter of 2015, in the country of Costa Brava, ViraVax—a very powerful and very private laboratory doing cutting-edge genetic research—is a dangerous place to work. Red Bartlett, a top scientist, is killed in self-defense by his wife when he brutally attacks her. ViraVax immediately claims the body, or what is left of the body, and creates the cover story that Red was killed by intruders linked to the Catholic guerrilla underground. Yet it seems unlikely the underground would kill the only Catholic employed by ViraVax. Colonel Rico Toledo, Red's best friend, is determined to uncover the truth about what actually happened to Red and what is really going on at ViraVax. Mature language, violence.

31.45 Resnick, Mike. **Oracle.** Ace Books, 1992. 244 pp. ISBN 0-441-58694-5. Fiction.

The Oracle, the human female Penelope Bailey, disappeared fourteen years ago when she was eight. By now her psychic abilities must have increased, but no one knows how or how much. Some individual or group is willing to pay Iceman, the top bounty hunter, two million Maria Theresa dollars to bring Penelope back from the closed alien planet Hades, where Iceman surmises she must be either ruler or prisoner. When Iceman takes the job, he never anticipates that he will soon be in a deadly race with others to reach Penelope first—and to free her or kill her.

31.46 Rubinstein, Gillian. **Skymaze.** Pocket Books/Archway Paperbacks, 1993. 227 pp. ISBN 0-671-76988-X. Fiction.

They are not exactly friends—or enemies either—but Ben, Andrew, Mario, and Elaine all know each other. What they have in common is an unhappiness in their lives, antagonistic siblings or other family difficulties, and the experience of having been trapped inside the video game "Space Demons" and mastering it. Without warning, a new game, "Skymaze," somehow merges with reality. The game is alluring and almost addictive, yet menacing and terrorizing. The four soon find they cannot quit until one of them solves the maze. And they must win—the stakes have become too high to lose.

31.47 Sawyer, Robert J. **Fossil Hunter.** Ace Books, 1993. 290 pp. ISBN 0-441-24884-5. Fiction.

Suddenly the established world order of the Quintaglios society is on shaky ground. While Toroca, leader of the Geological Survey of Land and son of Afsan the Far-Seer, is searching for information for the Exodus Project, he finds the strange, blue, otherworld artifact in their planet's bookmark layer. Rodlox, governor of Edz'toolar Province, challenges his emperor brother, Dy-Dybo, for his position and right to rule. The public loses faith in the blood-priests and allows all the hatchlings in the clutches of eggs to live, instead of culling just one hatchling per clutch. Now the youngsters and the crowding are testing everyone's territorial reflexes; and the crime of murder, which has never been known in the dinosaur's world (with the exception, of course, of *dagamant*), has claimed two victims.

31.48   Serling, Carol, editor. **Journeys to the Twilight Zone.** DAW Books, 1993. 287 pp. ISBN 0-88677-525-6. Fiction.

This is a collection of sixteen short stories of wide-ranging science fiction and fantasy. The topics vary from children of the future on a field trip to a future where unhealthy eating is unlawful. Included are ghosts from the past who warn about the present and fortune-tellers who tell futures that can be changed. Read to find out what happens when a pet dog receives a transfusion from a werewolf, or when the amateur hypnotist at the cocktail party finds too good a subject. Mature language.

31.49   Shatner, William. **Tek Vengeance.** Ace Books, 1993. 294 pp. ISBN 0-441-80012-2. Fiction.

Ex-cop Jake Cardigan is lured away from his girlfriend, Beth Kittridge, before she can testify against the powerful Teklords. Her death is tragic; his reaction is furious. Jake and his partner, Sid Gomez, try to discover what really happened to Beth. Was the disappearance of his friend's father genuine, or was it a decoy to take him to South America and far from Beth when she needed him? Mature language.

31.50   Shatner, William. **Teklab.** Ace Books, 1993. 308 pp. ISBN 0-441-80011-4. Fiction.

Jake Cardigan, a forty-nine-year-old ex-cop, ex-con, and current detective for the Cosmos Detective Agency, and Sid Gomez, a twenty-four-year-old Mexican American, are detective partners working on assignment in Paris in 2120. They are trying to stop a serial killer who calls himself the Unknown Soldier and who uses a laser to cut up his victims. Also involved somehow are the Teklords, who are rumored to be about to unleash an even more insidious electronic drug, and a fanatic group called Excalibur. Add to the mixture Jake's son, Dan, and his friend Nancy, who have disappeared in an area of London run by wild youth gangs. Jake and Sid must sort it all out before more people die.

31.51 Sirota, Mike. **The Ultimate Bike Path.** Ace Books, 1992. 202 pp. ISBN 0-441-84391-3. Fiction.

Jack Miller, a thirty-something author, rides his Nishiki bike down the *mhuva lun gallee*, the ultimate bike path in space and time. Here he can choose to enter any door to another world. Each door along the tunnel offers a different reality and different experiences as Jack chooses at random. He is bitten by a *padoodle*, searches for Frankenstein, encounters the *muunastrebors*, escapes the Freddy Krueger creatures, and finds the Amazin' Women of Mountains East, the Plumbers' Afterward, the Great Big Woman Village, and the state of Lethargia before returning to real time. Mature language.

31.52 Stasheff, Christopher. **A Wizard in Absentia.** Ace Books, 1993. 263 pp. ISBN 0-441-51569-X. Fiction.

Rodney Gallowglass, a telepath and telekinetic, leaves his home planet and family in search of a purpose. In his father's old spaceship and accompanied by Fess, the robot that has served Rodney's ancestors for the last 500 years, Rodney soon meets his uncle's branch of the family, including the alluring Pelisse. On other planets Rodney is recruited into SCENT, the Society for the Conversion of Extraterrestrial Nascent Totalitarianisms, and he attempts to help a young serf boy named Ian on a planet still ruled by lords and ladies in a medieval society.

31.53 Steele, Allen. **Labyrinth of Night.** Ace Books, 1992. 340 pp. ISBN 0-441-46741-5. Fiction.

August Nash could never have anticipated that his brief spying mission for Security Associates was only the beginning of his involvement with the international scientific research base on Mars. Earth scientists have discovered a labyrinth under the surface, each room booby-trapped its own unique way. The team thinks they have found the final room, C4 20, but the room's mysterious walls hold a secret. Earth scientists try to unravel the mysteries of the labyrinth and survive the tyrannical, increasingly insane Commander Terrance L'Enfant. All the while, the deadly pseudo-Martian creatures are working tirelessly toward a goal that might cost all the humans their lives. Mature language.

31.54 Stevermer, Caroline. **River Rats.** Harcourt Brace Jovanovich/Jane Yolen Books, 1992. 214 pp. ISBN 0-15-200895-0. Fiction.

Twenty years after the "Flash," the nuclear devastation of the United States, a small troupe of orphans takes an old riverboat from a historic exhibit. They become "river rats," riding the now toxic Mississippi and trading mail service and music for their needs. When they rescue a stranger, they find themselves forced into a desperate search into unfamiliar and dangerous terrain where they hope to find the "Pharaoh's tomb," a survivalist vault built in a mountain, and to ransom back their friend and their boat.

ALA Best Books for Young Adults, 1993

31.55   Thomson, Amy. **Virtual Girl.** Ace Books, 1993. 248 pp. ISBN 0-441-86500-3. Fiction.

Maggie was created by Arnold from a computer landscape of virtual reality. She is so humanlike that she can even occasionally fool her own creator. She is perfect—loyal, strong, beautiful, and innocent. When Maggie becomes separated from her creator, she makes discoveries about the world and herself that Arnold could not have anticipated: new friends and new computer programs. All keep her struggling to survive and to find Arnold again. What will Maggie do if her parts start to wear out and she loses her memory before she finds Arnold? Or what if she is not able to recharge her batteries in time? Can she ever find Arnold again? Mature language and situations.

31.56   Waldrop, Howard. **Night of the Cooters.** Ace Books, 1993. 253 pp. ISBN 0-441-57473-4. Fiction.

Each of the ten short stories in this collection is introduced with information about the origin of the story or the story idea. Topics range widely, including unfriendly aliens who land in Texas in 1830, a class reunion for a 1969 high school class, and an adventure with Sherlock Holmes on the trail of Jack the Ripper. Mature language.

31.57   Wheeler, Deborah. **Jaydium.** DAW Books, 1993. 352 pp. ISBN 0-88677-556-6. Fiction.

While Kithri and her newfound friend Eril are making a run to the jaydium mines of Kithri's planet, Stayman, they are thrown back in time. They find themselves in an age when the dusty planet was covered by plush green vegetation and the sparkling tower of a crystal city existed, a time before the war. They soon become friends with Lennart and Brianna, two people from another past. The four are forced to fight a band of ruthless alien pirates and escape by being zapped into still another time—one farther into the past, when an alien nation on the brink of war ruled over the crystal city. Kithri and Eril seek to return to their planet by stopping the war. Their plan is to link the aliens' minds together through a process called duoflight.

31.58 Williams, Sheila, and Charles Ardai, editors. **Why I Left Harry's All-Night Hamburgers, and Other Stories from Isaac Asimov's Science Fiction Magazine.** Dell/Laurel-Leaf Library, 1992. 304 pp. ISBN 0-440-21394-0. Fiction.

In this collection of thirteen stories on widely ranging subjects, readers can meet in one story the manager of the band from Zoom, who unwittingly tells the truth with his fantastic publicity stories about the band's origins. Find out why the teenage counterman at Harry's in quiet Sutton, West Virginia, left the best place in the universe to get a burger and drink in the wee hours of the morning. And learn who would pity a swan.

31.59 Williams, Walter Jon. **Aristoi.** Tor Books, 1993. 448 pp. ISBN 0-812-51409-2. Fiction.

Gabriel Aristos is one of the lords of technology, a member of the elite society called the Aristoi, who live in a complex world containing pregnant men and dogs with anesthetizing saliva. Gabriel and a female Aristos, Cressida, discover that someone has been tampering with the Hyperlogos Seal that seals communications. The chief suspect is Saigo, another Aristoi who has become a madman. If Saigo can change communications and change data, then he could change history itself, a possibility that could spell disaster for the whole human race. Gabriel does not know who or how many are involved in corrupting the Hyperlogos, but he knows he must try to stop them, whatever the risk. Mature situations.

31.60 Wu, William F. **Marauder.** Avon/Byron Preiss Books, 1993. 243 pp. ISBN 0-380-76511-X. Fiction.

Robot R. Hunter continues the search begun when the Mojave Center (MC) Governor robot divided himself and escaped into the past to avoid shutdown by the Oversight Committee. Hunter is now after MC 2 with his previous team of robotics expert Jane Maynard and survivalist Steve Chang, and with historian Rita Chavez. Tidal waves and his own calculations have given Hunter MC 2's location: Port Royal, Jamaica, 1668. Hunter will have to negotiate his actions in a dangerous center of buccaneer activity, which seems to violate the Three Laws of Robotics that he must obey. The team also has to contend with the handsome and treacherous pirate Roland; Rita's unwittingly irresponsible actions, which almost sabotage the mission; the two pirate captains, Tomann and Quinn, as they capture two Spanish treasure ships; Captain Morgan's assault of Portobello; and Dr. Nystrom's attempts to confound the mission and take MC 2 himself. Part of Isaac Asimov's Robots in Time series.

31.61 Wu, William F. **Predator.** Avon Books, 1993. 244 pp. ISBN 0-380-76510-1. Fiction.

The Mojave Center (MC) Governor, an experimental gestalt humaniform robot, is running the city on probationary status. It is 2140, and with his advanced robotic capabilities, he can monitor and coordinate all the city's municipal systems perfectly. It is when he discovers his miscalculation, an error that a robot could not make, that he begins to try to save himself. Five other robots, identical to him and all governing major cities, have all failed that day and now have ceased to function. Immediately, MC Governor begins his desperate plan. Fleeing into the past to hide, MC calls his inventor, Wayne Nystrom, for help, and Nystrom leaps back into time to save his robot and his own reputation. Part of Isaac Asimov's Robots in Time series.

32 Self-Help: Your Health and Your Body

32.1 Arrick, Fran. **What You Don't Know Can Kill You.** Bantam Books, 1992. 154 pp. ISBN 0-553-07471-7. Fiction.

Ellen, who recently graduated from high school, looks forward to college and, eventually, marriage to her wonderful boyfriend, Jack. However, when Ellen tests positive for HIV, the AIDS virus, it seems that life is crashing in on her, her parents, her younger sister, and Jack—from whom Ellen contracted HIV. *What You Don't Know Can Kill You* is a powerful story of a family's struggle to cope with AIDS.

ALA Best Books for Young Adults, 1993

32.2 Asimov, Isaac. **The Human Body: Its Structure and Operation.** Illustrated by Anthony Ravielli. Penguin/Mentor Books, 1992. 346 pp. ISBN 0-451-62707-5. Nonfiction.

If you would like to understand the complex systems of the human body, you will find this book to be an informative, easily understandable, and highly interesting resource. Isaac Asimov, probably the most famous scientist-writer of our time, explains the structure and operation of the human body, from the skeletal system to the reproductive system. He also includes a chapter on recent medical technology and transplant surgery and the pronunciations and derivations for specialized terms where they appear in the text.

32.3 Berger, Gilda, and Melvin Berger. **Drug Abuse A–Z.** Enslow, 1990. 143 pp. ISBN 0-89490-193-1. Nonfiction.

Drug Abuse A–Z is a dictionary-like guide to the scientific, trade, and slang names and terms relating to drugs. Entries run from *A.A.* (Alcoholics Anonymous) to *zonked* (so intoxicated by a drug that one is completely unable to function).

32.4 Bode, Janet. **Death Is Hard to Live With: Teenagers and How They Cope with Loss.** Delacorte Press, 1993. 192 pp. ISBN 0-385-31041-2. Nonfiction.

Using an authoritative yet sensitive approach, Janet Bode addresses the ever-growing need for teens to cope with bereavement.

Through interviews with teenagers who have experienced the death of a friend or a relative, Bode explores ways of making peace with the shock, guilt, and tragedy of death. The narratives explore living to the fullest while experiencing the pain of death and making loss a part of life. More than a self-help book, *Death Is Hard to Live With* is a "survival" guide. It does not provide any easy answers but offers insight. Young people who are feeling defeated can learn by reading what worked for others and can discover that they, too, can find a way to cope. To readers needing to face the realities of death, Bode's book will be a lifeline.

ALA Quick Picks for Young Adults, 1994

32.5 Cohen, Susan, and Daniel Cohen. **Teenage Stress.** Dell/Laurel-Leaf Library, 1992. 186 pp. ISBN 0-440-21391-6. Nonfiction.

Whether an adolescent or adult, we all face the challenge of stress in our lives. Stress can be the result of a monumental happening, such as the death of a loved one, or a seemingly minor happening, such as missing the bus. Either way, all of us need to learn coping methods so that stress does not overwhelm us, causing us to lose the ability to perform up to our potential and, in extreme cases, leading to depression or severe illness. In *Teenage Stress*, the authors have created a guide to help teenagers deal with stress as well as a bibliography of fiction dealing with major issues, such as homosexuality, drugs, alcohol, sex, and divorce.

32.6 Feldman, Robert S., and Joel A. Feinman. **Who You Are: Personality and Its Development.** Franklin Watts/Venture Books, 1992. 114 pp. ISBN 0-531-12544-0. Nonfiction.

What causes us to respond to social situations the way we do? Does our environment shape us, or is it unconscious influences? Two professional psychologists give brief descriptions of the various schools of personality development: Freud and psychoanalysis, humanism and behaviorism, and traits of personality. Another section of the book deals with the types of personality disorders that prevent people from adjusting to different social and personal situations: obsessive-compulsive behaviors, paranoia and narcissism, and the more severe antisocial and multiple personality disorders. The final section covers personality tests and ways to change your personality.

32.7 Ferry, Charles. **Binge.** Daisy Hill Press, 1993. 95 pp. ISBN 0-9632799-0-4. Fiction.

Eighteen-year-old Weldon Yeager awakens in the hospital to find himself in the worst personal nightmare of his life. The phantom pain he "feels" from his amputated limb will soon be nothing compared to his mental anguish when he learns that in one of life's ironic twists, he has destroyed what he was seeking. *Binge* is Weldon's statement into a police tape recorder about the events that lead from his longings for the places and friends of his childhood to his last binge drinking and his being charged with larceny and manslaughter.

ALA Best Books for Young Adults, 1993

32.8 Gardephe, Colleen Davis, and Steve Ettlinger. **Don't Pick Up the Baby or You'll Spoil the Child, and Other Old Wives' Tales about Pregnancy and Parenting.** Chronicle Books, 1993. 95 pp. ISBN 0-8118-0242-6. Nonfiction.

If your nose grows larger, you are having a girl. Eat for two! Never swim in water above your waist or your baby will drown. In this delightful little book, Colleen Davis Gardephe and Steve Ettlinger discuss a myriad of the age-old myths about pregnancy and parenting. Surprisingly, some of the myths are actually partly true! All the information in the book has been reviewed by physicians for accuracy.

32.9 Grant, Cynthia D. **Phoenix Rising: Or, How to Survive Your Life.** Atheneum, 1989. 148 pp. ISBN 0-689-31458-2. Fiction.

When Helen dies of cancer at the age of eighteen, her younger sister Jessie is haunted by panic attacks and dreams in which she relives Helen's death. Not until Jessie decides to read Helen's last diary does she begin the painful journey through dark grief and mourning toward recovery. Ultimately, Jessie learns both how to mourn Helen's death and how to celebrate her life.

IRA Young Adults' Choices, 1991
School Library Journal Best Books, 1989

32.10 Grant, Cynthia D. **Shadow Man.** Atheneum, 1992. 149 pp. ISBN 0-689-31772-7. Fiction.

The strength of this thought-provoking novel is the sensitive portrayal of the protagonist, Gabriel McCloud, who is just eighteen and drunk when he smashes his battered truck into a tree. The news of Gabe's death flashes over Willow Creek instantly. Some of the townspeople expected this to happen to a kid in the McCloud family, which was characterized by booze and dope. But many townspeople loved Gabe. He seemed different from the rest of his family, and the news of his death affects the whole community. Each person has reasons to grieve for Gabe. Now he will be the shadow in their lives, and no one will ever be quite the same.

ALA Best Books for Young Adults, 1994

32.11 Gravelle, Karen, and Susan Fischer. **Where Are My Birth Parents? A Guide for Teenage Adoptees.** Walker, 1993. 128 pp. ISBN 0-8027-8257-4. Nonfiction.

Searching for birth parents can be a learning experience, but it is also filled with emotional questions. This book begins with helping teens decide whether they *want* to search for their birth parents. Then the reader learns about telling his or her adoptive parents and about making the search itself. The authors talk about the emotions of making the first contact with birth parents and the initial reunion. The final section lists resources to aid in the process. Personal accounts throughout the book help teenagers realize they are not alone in feeling the need to search for birth parents.

32.12 Grollman, Earl A. **Straight Talk about Death for Teenagers: How to Cope with Losing Someone You Love.** Beacon Press, 1993. 146 pp. ISBN 0-8070-2500-3. Nonfiction.

Today's teenagers, like today's adults, are faced with the deaths of friends and family from accidents, disease, violence, and drugs. Yet there may be little guidance given to help teens understand death and the intense grief they feel. Dr. Earl Grollman, who has spent most of his life counseling the young through their grief, has written this book about death and grieving expressly for teenagers. In simple, clear language, Dr. Grollman tells young people what they can expect when someone they love dies and what can help ease their pain. He explains to readers the benefits of attending the funeral, what to expect when they go back to school, how their bodies respond to grief, how to take care of themselves, and what changes they may see in their relationships with family and friends. Grieving teenagers who find intense explorations of death simply too painful to manage may find that this book delivers comfort in manageable terms.

32.13 Hall, David E. **Living with Learning Disabilities: A Guide for Students.** Lerner, 1993. 60 pp. ISBN 0-8225-0036-1. Nonfiction.

Being told that you have a learning disability can be confusing. Dr. David E. Hall explains just what learning disabilities are and the forms they can take. He stresses the importance of having a good attitude and explores ways to cope with such disabilities. The book ends with a brief chapter on medications that can help those with learning disabilities and a resource section for those seeking additional help.

32.14 Hawley, Richard A. **Think about Drugs and Society: Responding to an Epidemic.** Walker, 1992. 149 pp. ISBN 0-8027-8114-4. Nonfiction.

This very readable examination of the American drug problem presents a brief historical background of alcohol, marijuana, and cocaine use and discusses aspects of contemporary debate surrounding these drugs. Among the issues presented are whether drug use is a "victimless" crime, age requirements for legal use of drugs, and decriminalization and legalization of drugs. There is an appendix of resources and a glossary.

32.15 Johnson, Kendall. **Turning Yourself Around: Self-Help Strategies for Troubled Teens.** Hunter House, 1992. 205 pp. ISBN 0-89793-092-4. Nonfiction.

Sylvia's family has money and status; she's bulimic. Jason's parents are on-again, off-again about their marriage; more and more Jason finds it "a whole lot easier to get wasted." Kathy craves attention and love, but everything she does to gain them is a disaster. These three stories are used to explain a program that helps teens beat their addictions to destructive behaviors such as alcohol or drug use, eating disorders, and poor family interaction. Activities and problem-solving techniques are suggested to help teens regain control of their lives.

32.16 Klass, Sheila Solomon. **Rhino.** Scholastic Hardcover Books, 1993. 161 pp. ISBN 0-590-44250-3. Fiction.

When Annie Trevor looks in the mirror, she sees "an okay face and in the middle of it a clunky nose." Annie inherited her irregular nose from her father and grandfather. Rhinoplasty would make her feel better about herself. Yet her boyfriend, Bob, worries that the surgery will change her personality. Annie knows there are bigger problems in life—Bob's, for instance—but she can do something about hers. Now, will she?

ALA Quick Picks for Young Adults, 1994

32.17 Kolodny, Nancy J. **When Food's a Foe: How to Confront and Conquer Eating Disorders,** rev. ed. Little, Brown, 1992. 169 pp. ISBN 0-316-50181-6. Nonfiction.

A growing number of teenagers and young adults suffer from eating disorders. Author Nancy Kolodny discusses the two most common disorders—anorexia nervosa and bulimia—and how they begin. Questionnaires, checklists, and exercises provide help for those who suffer from these disorders, as well as ways to help someone you know who suffers from them. In addition, the author provides a suggested reading list, referral sources, and facts about nutrition. First published in 1987.

32.18 Landau, Elaine. **Weight: A Teenage Concern.** Dutton/Lodestar Books, 1991. ISBN 0-525-67335-0. Nonfiction.

In our society, where "thin is in," the burden on adolescents can be overwhelming. Elaine Landau not only looks at the infamous consequences of the pressure to be thin—anorexia nervosa and bulimia—but goes further by exploring radical weight-loss methods, why diets do not work, groups concerned with the weight issue, and overweight teenagers' personal stories and struggles. She emphasizes the relationship of weight and self-esteem and advocates self-acceptance as the key to a fulfilling life.

32.19 LeShan, Eda. **What Makes You So Special?** Dial Books, 1992. 145 pp. ISBN 0-8037-1155-7. Nonfiction.

Why are your eyes blue or brown or green? Why do you have a happy outlook on life? Why does your best friend lack self-confidence? Why can't you draw as well as your friend? Eda LeShan answers these questions and many more about the family, cultural, and social backgrounds that make you special. The interesting examples and stories about young people will help you understand yourself and others better, feel good about your differences, and learn to be a good friend to yourself.

32.20 Mabie, Margot C. J. **Bioethics and the New Medical Technology.** Atheneum, 1993. 162 pp. ISBN 0-689-31637-2. Nonfiction.

In the technologically advanced world that ours has become, particularly in the field of medicine, it has become too easy, author Margot Mabie asserts, to create and sustain life simply because we have the technology to do so. In this book, Mabie explains the issues and explores the troubling questions that bioethics raises at the beginning and end of life. This well-written and sensitive work is best suited for older readers.

32.21   Ryan, Elizabeth A. **Straight Talk about Drugs and Alcohol.** Dell/
Laurel-Leaf Library, 1992. 145 pp. ISBN 0-440-21392-4. Nonfiction.

This book presents information about the effects of societal pressures, peer pressures, and family pressures on drug and alcohol
use and examines the problems regarding teenage use of alcohol
and other drugs. Also included are quizzes and charts to test the
reader's knowledge of drugs and alcohol and an appendix with
fifty-four pages of listings of state offices that make referrals to
agencies, organizations, hospitals, or programs that deal with alcohol or drug abuse.

32.22   Rylant, Cynthia. **Missing May.** Orchard Books, 1992. 89 pp. ISBN
0-531-05996-0. Fiction.

After the death of her beloved Aunt May, who had raised twelve-
year-old Summer for the past six years, Summer and Uncle Ob
search for strength to go on living. Summer misses May terribly
but is forced to put her grief aside while trying to keep Ob from
dying himself. Cletus, a school friend, and Ob believe in the spirit
world; together, with Summer, they search for tranquillity. Peace
comes, but from a different source than Summer expects. Young
adults who are developing their thoughts and feelings about
death and grief will find this story of Summer and Aunt May, set
in rural West Virginia, a genuine and loving tale.

ALA Best Books for Young Adults, 1993
ALA Notable Books for Children, 1993
Booklist's Top of the List, 1992
Boston Globe–Horn Book Fiction Award, 1992
Newbery Medal, 1993

32.23   Schneider, Meg F. **Popularity Has Its Ups and Downs.** Simon and
Schuster/Julian Messner, 1992. 112 pp. ISBN 0-671-72848-2. Nonfiction.

What is popularity? Why do some people have it and others
don't? Is it something you want, or do you actually want friends?
If you put popularity in its place, you may find that feeling good
about yourself and having good friends are more important.
Reading about "The Great Popularity Myths," discovering "Who
Is the Real You," and learning about "Friendships—The Only
Popularity That Really Counts" will help you understand what
matters in life. A chapter on "The Shyness Factor" will help you
conquer this area as well.

32.24 Siegel, Ronald K. **Fire in the Brain: Clinical Tales of Hallucination.** E. P. Dutton, 1992. 275 pp. ISBN 0-525-93408-1. Nonfiction.

Teens interested in the natural workings of the human mind, as well as its dark side, will enjoy these clinical accounts of hallucination. Author Ronald K. Siegel, described by *Omni* magazine as "probably knowing more about how drugs work than anyone else alive," presents seventeen fascinating case histories from the world of hallucination. The cases involve the use of visionary drugs, imaginary companions, dreams, and life-threatening danger.

32.25 Silverstein, Alvin, Virginia Silverstein, and Robert Silverstein. **Steroids: Big Muscles, Big Problems.** Enslow, 1992. 112 pp. ISBN 0-89490-318-7. Nonfiction.

This book offers highly readable, understandable, nontechnical answers to questions about steroids. Compiled from hundreds of current sources, the book explains the composition, kind, functions, and history of steroids, including current reasons for use, their addictive nature, and the short-term and long-term dangers. Also discussed are psychological effects of steroids, such as personality changes and heightened aggressiveness, and the potential legal/criminal ramifications of steroid use.

32.26 Stoehr, Shelley. **Crosses.** Dell/Laurel-Leaf Library, 1993. 153 pp. ISBN 0-440-21561-7. Fiction.

Nancy, a fifteen-year-old freshman, goes to the girls' bathroom to hide out and continue the compulsive carving on her arm that she has recently begun to do. It has been a typical morning: some vodka, a screaming fight with her mother, and a quick change at school into the safety-pin earrings, dark eyeliner, and spiked hair that matches her new identity. In the bathroom Nancy meets Katie, who has scars of carved crosses on her shoulder. Nancy and Katie are soon best friends, finding companionship in their ever-increasing risk taking, smoking, drinking, and drug taking. Even Nancy's boyfriend is unable to stop the escalating, self-destructive behavior. Nancy senses some of the danger, but it is not until things become deadly that she is forced to examine her life. Mature language and situations.

ALA Best Books for Young Adults, 1993
IRA Young Adults' Choices, 1994

32.27 Taylor, Clark. **The House That Crack Built.** Illustrated by Jan Thompson Dicks. Chronicle Books, 1992. 32 pp. ISBN 0-8118-0133-0. Fiction.

This adaptation of a nursery rhyme addresses the source, drug harvest, dealers, gangs, cops, users, and helpless infant victims of crack cocaine. It is a resource that can broach a difficult subject to teens as well as to older and younger readers. The illustrations are colorful enough to hold a child's attention and sophisticated enough to intrigue adults. The verses are rhythmic, unvarnished, and truthful.

ALA Best Books for Young Adults, 1993
ALA Quick Picks for Young Adults, 1993

32.28 Washton, Arnold M., and Donna Boundy. **Cocaine and Crack: What You Need to Know.** Enslow, 1989. 95 pp. ISBN 0-89490-162-1. Nonfiction.

This book begins with some historical background of cocaine and the epidemic of its use in the United States, as well as basic information about the nature and effects of cocaine. In a combination of factual information and anecdotes, the book discusses some dangerous myths associated with addiction and performance under the influence of drugs. The authors include an examination of other medical emergencies created by cocaine use. The conclusion gives information about resources for the cocaine abuser and family members.

33 Short Stories

33.1 Anderson, Sherwood. **Winesburg, Ohio.** Penguin/Signet Classic Books, 1993. 252 pp. ISBN 0-451-52569-8. Fiction.

First published in 1919, Sherwood Anderson's tales of life in an Ohio small town continue to speak to us of what it means to be human. Anderson's characters experience the loneliness, isolation, and unfulfilled dreams that are so much a part of the daily lives of each of us. Ray Pearson, who feels "tricked by life and made a fool of," Tom Foster, who is "a part of and yet distinctly apart from the life about him," and George Willard, a young writer, are representative of those in Winesburg who search for ways to connect and relate to others.

33.2 Berry, James. **The Future-Telling Lady, and Other Stories.** HarperCollins, 1993. 139 pp. ISBN 0-06-021435-X. Fiction.

Born and raised in Jamaica, James Berry has chosen that setting for the seven stories in this collection. Ghosts, magic, and the future-telling lady, subjects prominent in the culture of the West Indies, serve as excellent vehicles for Berry to explore such concerns as lying, stealing, and sibling rivalry. Of particular interest is the title story, "The Future-Telling Lady," which focuses on parent-child relationships and efforts made to improve those relationships. First published in Great Britain, 1991.

Notable 1994 Children's Trade Books in the Field of Social Studies

33.3 Brooks, Martha. **Paradise Café, and Other Stories.** Little, Brown/Joy Street Books, 1990. 124 pp. ISBN 0-316-10978-9. Fiction.

This collection of fourteen stories by Canadian writer Martha Brooks focuses on the fears, joys, and hopes of teenagers. "Running with Marty" explores the fear of making commitments; "Paradise Café" deals with first love; and "Like Lauren Bacall" shows a young girl trying to discover not only who she is but how she relates to relatives and others. In all the selections, the characters and their experiences are realistic. First published in Canada, 1988.

Boston Globe–Horn Book Fiction Honor Book, 1991
School Library Journal Best Books, 1990

33.4 Butler, Robert Olen. **A Good Scent from a Strange Mountain: Stories.** Penguin, 1992. 249 pp. ISBN 0-8050-1986-3. Fiction.

Although the major characters in each of the fifteen stories in this collection are Vietnamese, the emotional issues and concerns addressed are universal. The loss of loved ones, the human desire to communicate with others, and the eagerness of parents to share past experiences and memories with their children are a few of the subjects found in these poignant stories. Readers can gain a greater understanding of the impact of the Vietnam War on individual lives and share in the joy and sorrow of others through Robert Olen Butler's masterful prose.

Pulitzer Prize for Fiction, 1993

33.5   Colchie, Thomas, editor. **A Hammock beneath the Mangoes: Stories from Latin America.** Penguin/Plume Books, 1992. 430 pp. ISBN 0-452-26866-4. Fiction.

The twenty-six stories included in this collection provide an excellent introduction to the works of Hispanic writers such as Gabriel García Márquez, Carlos Fuentes, Isabel Allende, and Jorge Amado. Although set in Latin America, the stories transcend geographical boundaries because of the universal truths the authors address. Some stories are amusing, while others like "The Doll Queen" and "Love" are haunting and thought provoking.

33.6   Forkner, Ben, editor. **Louisiana Stories.** Pelican, 1990. 399 pp. ISBN 0-88289-784-5. Fiction.

This collection of sixteen stories provides an excellent view of life in Louisiana over the years, while at the same time it presents a variety of characters and universal experiences and emotions. Native Louisiana writers George Washington Cable and Ernest Gaines write of the Creole and African American experiences respectively. William Faulkner and Robb Forman Dew, writers who spent only a portion of their lives in Louisiana, capture the feeling of the South, specifically New Orleans, but their focus is more on the emotions of their characters than on the setting itself.

33.7   Gilman, Charlotte Perkins (edited by Barbara H. Solomon). **Herland, and Selected Stories.** Penguin/Signet Classic Books, 1992. 349 pp. ISBN 0-451-52562-0. Fiction.

This collection contains Charlotte Perkins Gilman's *Herland*, a feminist utopian novel first published in 1915, and twenty of her short stories written between 1890 and 1916. Gilman's heroines are sensible and intelligent but often economically and politically disadvantaged by a society that devalues women's worth. These strong women, however, find ways to develop self-respect and engage in meaningful works. Although written long ago, Gilman's stories are fresh and entertaining and contain messages that are echoed by feminist writers of today.

33.8   Jennings, Paul. **Unmentionable! More Amazing Stories.** Viking, 1993. 120 pp. ISBN 0-670-84734-8. Fiction.

These nine stories are written by Paul Jennings, a four-time winner of the Young Australians' Best Book Award. Each tale involves everyday teenage characters who become involved in unusual, comical, and sometimes supernatural happenings. A magic harmonica, earrings that turn people into magnets, a little robot man, a strange cat hat—all these objects add to the delight and surprise of the reader. First published in Australia, 1991.

ALA Quick Picks for Young Adults, 1994

33.9   Jones, Edward P. **Lost in the City.** Photographs by Amos Chan. William Morrow, 1992. 249 pp. ISBN 0-688-11526-8. Nonfiction.

A collection of portraits set in Washington, D.C., *Lost in the City* presents short sketches about everyday city people who struggle to maintain a sense of purpose despite the inherent difficulties they face. The subjects of Jones's sketches are African American men and women who go about their daily routines, immersing themselves in their tasks in the belief that they can somehow become an integral part of their society. Jones has created a series of mini-novels about characters who, in their battle to be a part of life, are forced to relegate their losses to a secondary position.

33.10   Kane, Pearl Rock, editor. **The First Year of Teaching: Real World Stories from America's Teachers.** Penguin/Mentor Books, 1992. 167 pp. ISBN 0-451-62858-6. Nonfiction.

Teachers, it has been said, "touch the future." This book provides excellent examples of how twenty-five novice teachers touched the lives of their students, both in the present and in the future. These inspirational sketches demonstrate the importance of love, patience, and compassion in the classroom, whether the students view themselves as gifted or slow to learn. Those considering a career in teaching would enjoy this book.

33.11   Louie, David Wong. **Pangs of Love.** Penguin/Plume Books, 1992. 225 pp. ISBN 0-452-26888-5. Fiction.

Many of the characters in this collection of eleven short stories by David Wong Louie are Chinese American. His stories deal with modern-day issues in American life, such as abortion, dating, and gay lifestyles. They are witty, surprising, sometimes surreal, and meant for the mature reader.

33.12   Maxwell, William. **Billie Dyer, and Other Stories.** Penguin/ Plume Books, 1993. 117 pp. ISBN 0-452-26950-4. Fiction.

Although he spent forty years as a fiction editor at the *New Yorker*, it is not New York City but Lincoln, Illinois, that serves as the setting for the seven stories in this collection by William Maxwell. Whether he is writing about the love of a group of fifth graders for a young teacher who ultimately dies of tuberculosis or about dealing with the cruelty that lives just beneath the surface in each of us, Maxwell is an engaging writer. It is difficult to come to know his characters without coming to know oneself somewhat better.

33.13   Mazer, Anne, editor. **America Street: A Multicultural Anthology of Stories.** Persea Books, 1993. 150 pp. ISBN 0-89255-190-9. Fiction.

Gary Soto, Langston Hughes, Grace Paley, and others offer insight into the cultural differences of many youth growing up in America. While readers can learn something about what it means to be Latino, Asian, African American, or Jewish in America, they are also likely to be struck by the universal needs of the characters—the need to belong, to have friends, and to achieve goals.

33.14   Miller, John, and Genevieve Anderson, editors. **Chicago Stories: Tales of the City.** Chronicle Books, 1993. 241 pp. ISBN 0-8118-0164-0.

Not only is Chicago "the Windy City" or the "City of the Big Shoulders," as poet Carl Sandburg states, but it is also a city of wonderful stories by authors such as Saul Bellow, Maya Angelou, Langston Hughes, Studs Terkel, and Mike Royko. Race relations, the 1968 Democratic Convention, baseball, and Al Capone are but a few of the subjects addressed in this collection of short fiction and nonfiction works.

33.15   Miller, John, and Kirsten Miller, editors. **Florida Stories: Tales from the Tropics.** Chronicle Books, 1993. 176 pp. ISBN 0-8118-0457-7.

One could hardly find a more diverse group of writers than those whose stories and sketches fill this work. John J. Audubon, Nathaniel Hawthorne, Ernest Hemingway, Zora Neale Hurston, Joan Didion, Dave Barry, and others depict the people, the places, and the spirit of the state that some call Paradise. To see Disney World through the eyes of Dave Barry or Miami from Joan Didion's point of view or Key West from Hemingway's perspective is to see Florida as a complex place that may or may not correspond to one's view of paradise.

33.16 Mohr, Nicholasa. **El Bronx Remembered: A Novella and Stories.** HarperCollins/Harper Keypoint Books, 1993. 263 pp. ISBN 0-06-024314-7. Fiction.

This collection of twelve stories captures the lives and spirit of the Puerto Rican immigrants who came to New York in search of the American dream. From Hector, who must wear his uncle's orange, pointed-toed shoes to graduation, to the Fernandez family, who keep a hen tied to the leg of the kitchen table, the characters are real, as is their fight to survive.

National Book Award for Children's Literature finalist, 1976

33.17 Montgomery, L. M. **The Road to Yesterday.** Bantam Books, 1993. 403 pp. ISBN 0-553-56068-9. Fiction.

This collection of fourteen short stories, as told through the eyes of Anne Shirley—now married to Gilbert Blythe and the mother of grown-up children—gives the reader a look at life in a small Canadian village on Prince Edward Island prior to World War II. The characters, events, and local gossip are often hilarious, sometimes sad, and occasionally bizarre, but always entertaining. If you enjoyed Lucy Maud Montgomery's *Anne of Green Gables*, you are in for a treat reading these stories, which were discovered after the author's death. First published in Canada, 1974.

33.18 Rochman, Hazel, and Darlene Z. McCampbell, editors. **Who Do You Think You Are? Stories of Friends and Enemies.** Little, Brown/Joy Street Books, 1993. 170 pp. ISBN 0-316-75355-6. Fiction.

The sixteen stories in this collection, written by such well-known authors as Joyce Carol Oates, Richard Peck, and Ray Bradbury, provide excellent opportunities to reflect on friendship. Characters range from a warm, caring boy in "A Boy and His Dog" to a frightening, sinister man in "Where Are You Going, Where Have You Been?" It is easy to put the book aside after reading it, but it is impossible to forget the characters and their stories.

33.19 Salisbury, Graham. **Blue Skin of the Sea.** Delacorte Press, 1992. 215 pp. ISBN 0-385-30596-6. Fiction.

In this collection of stories, the reader will follow Sunny Mindosa as he grows up in a Hawaiian fishing village. In the first story, he is seven, motherless, and fighting his fear of the sea, and in the eleventh story he is seventeen and fighting for the girl he loves. Along the way, Sunny encounters the dangers of the sea (tidal waves, moray eels, and tiger sharks) and the dangers on land (bullies, tourists, and first loves). Yet he survives, watched over by a loving father and an extended family of colorful characters.

ALA Best Books for Young Adults, 1993
Notable 1992 Children's Trade Books in the Field of Social Studies

33.20 Segel, Elizabeth, editor. **Short Takes.** Dell, 1992. 166 pp. ISBN 0-440-40581-5. Fiction.

Elizabeth Segel has selected nine short stories by authors well known for their young adult literature. Robert Cormier, Norma Fox Mazer, and E. L. Konigsburg are among those who have contributed to this collection of stories dealing with the pain of growing up. The characters ring true, and the problems of class bullies, first loves, and being left out of the group are those with which young people can identify.

33.21 Sillitoe, Alan. **The Loneliness of the Long-Distance Runner.** Penguin/Plume Books, 1992. 176 pp. ISBN 0-452-26908-3. Fiction.

Each of these nine short stories portrays life in England's poorest city neighborhoods in the 1950s. Along with the poverty and despair, Alan Sillitoe, known as a working-class novelist, introduces the reader to a group of tough-minded, streetwise characters who manage to survive in spite of adversity. One cannot help but admire these young men who live by their wits and manage to beat the system—at least part of the time. First published in 1960.

33.22 Simmen, Edward, editor. **North of the Rio Grande: The Mexican-American Experience in Short Fiction.** Penguin/Mentor Books, 1992. 428 pp. ISBN 0-415-62834-9. Fiction.

Included in this anthology are stories by Anglos and Mexican American writers, with each group presenting a different perspective on the culture and daily lives of Mexican Americans. Sandra Cisneros, Stephen Crane, Carlos Flores, Willa Cather, Maria Cristina Meña, and other talented writers portray the struggle and racial prejudice Mexican Americans have faced in this country. This collection showcases Chicano writers and promotes a deeper appreciation for the twelve million Americans of Mexican descent.

33.23 Solomon, Barbara H., editor. **Other Voices, Other Vistas: Short Stories from Africa, China, India, Japan, and Latin America.** Penguin/Mentor Books, 1992. 476 pp. ISBN 0-451-62845-4. Fiction.

This collection of twenty-five stories from Africa, China, India, Japan, and Latin America not only provides information about these cultures but also offers insight into universal experiences and relationships as well. Facing economic hardships, trying to relate to and understand one's parents, and wrestling with political issues are but three of the kinds of struggles the characters face.

33.24 Soto, Gary. **Small Faces.** Dell/Laurel-Leaf Library, 1993. 137 pp. ISBN 0-440-21553-6. Nonfiction.

Whether Mexican American novelist and poet Gary Soto is recalling how he met and fell in love with his wife, attending a concert, speculating on his role in society, or lamenting the destruction of the rain forests, he is an engaging writer. His willingness to reveal himself as one who laughs, cries, and cares deeply about family, friends, and the world around him is likely to appeal to most readers.

33.25 Soto, Gary, editor. **Pieces of the Heart: New Chicano Fiction.** Chronicle Books, 1993. 171 pp. ISBN 0-8118-0068-7. Fiction.

Gary Soto, a well-known Latino poet and novelist, has compiled sixteen short stories written by Americans of Mexican descent. "The Waltz of the Fat Man," "Summer League," "La Loco Santa," and "The Jumping Bean" are four of the stories in this diverse collection. The stories vary greatly in plot, setting, and style, but the characters are Chicanos—not the stereotypes found in much literature, but real people dealing with life's struggles. Each is a "piece of the heart."

33.26 Thomas, Joyce Carol, editor. **A Gathering of Flowers: Stories about Being Young in America.** Harper and Row/Harper Keypoint Books, 1990. 232 pp. ISBN 0-06-026174-9. Nonfiction.

To read these stories is to gain a better understanding of oneself as well as others. Gary Soto, Maxine Hong Kingston, and the other writers represented in this book show that love, fear, success, failure, joy, pain, and sorrow are universal emotions and experiences. In entertaining and thought-provoking ways, the authors present young adults from a variety of ethnic backgrounds wrestling with such issues as religious faith, first love, and the treatment of those society considers misfits.

33.27   Trelease, Jim, editor. **Hey! Listen to This: Stories to Read Aloud.** Penguin, 1992. 414 pp. ISBN 0-14-014653-9. Fiction.

This anthology of short stories, edited by best-selling author Jim Trelease, is suitable for students, teachers, parents, librarians, and anyone else interested in reading stories to youth of any age. In addition to the stories, Trelease includes an introduction to each story, information about the author, and a brief note. The stories are arranged by subject category and by level of difficulty.

33.28   Wilson, Budge. **The Leaving.** Putnam/Philomel Books, 1992. 207 pp. ISBN 0-399-21878-5. Fiction.

The Leaving is a powerful collection of ten short stories by Budge Wilson, who is becoming one of Canada's most celebrated writers. Each of these stories is set in Canada and focuses on a young woman and the events and problems in her life. Betrayal, respect for others, and friendship are three of the universal issues Wilson addresses.

ALA Best Books for Young Adults, 1993
ALA Notable Books for Children, 1993

33.29   Yep, Laurence, editor. **American Dragons: Twenty-Five Asian American Voices.** HarperCollins, 1993. 234 pp. ISBN 0-06-021495-3.

While Laurence Yep taught creative writing in Asian American studies, he collected twenty-five short stories, poems, and excerpts from plays—all written by Asian Americans. The contributors include well-known authors, such as Maxine Hong Kingston, and new writers. They explore all the questions immigrants must face: Who am I? How do I fit in? What is the American dream? Each contributor shows a fresh, new perspective of life as an Asian American.

ALA Best Books for Young Adults, 1994

34 Sports and Recreation

34.1 Aaseng, Nathan. **The Locker Room Mirror: How Sports Reflect Society.** Walker, 1993. 136 pp. ISBN 0-8027-8217-5. Nonfiction.

Society expects sports heroes to be role models both on and off the field, but athletes are not immune to the same problems their fans face. Violence, drug abuse, cheating, and sexual and racial discrimination are present in locker rooms and sports arenas. From Ben Johnson's steroid-tainted Olympic sprint to Len Bias's shocking death from a cocaine overdose to the Detroit Pistons' "Bad Boys" close-combat basketball play, *The Locker Room Mirror* explores the lasting effects of infractions by our sports heroes. These high-profile scandals force the public to focus on the problems society faces: the more closely we analyze that mirror, the more clearly we see the reflection of our own society. A helpful bibliography of sources for further reading and research is included.

34.2 Aaseng, Nathan. **True Champions: Great Athletes and Their Off-the-Field Heroics.** Walker, 1993. 128 pp. ISBN 0-8027-8247-7. Nonfiction.

True Champions recounts the stories of athletes who have exhibited remarkable bravery, generosity, and caring on or off the playing field. This book does not try to sweep aside all criticism of sports; rather, it presents a quieter, brighter side of sports through stories of athletes who saw beyond the trophy case. Learn how the Boston Celtics "wasted" a draft choice on Landon Turner, a player who could never play, simply to make his dream to be drafted come true; how Linda Down, born with cerebral palsy, finished the New York City Marathon on crutches; and how sprinter Wilma Rudolph set up a foundation for underprivileged children. Read the inspiring stories of these true champions—athletes who have done more than just win games. These are the stars who gave something back to their fans, who made sacrifices for others, and whose greatness runs beyond athletic prowess.

34.3 Aldridge, Gwen. **Baseball Archaeology: Artifacts from the Great American Pastime.** Photographs by Bret Wills. Chronicle Books, 1993. 112 pp. ISBN 0-8118-0290-6. Nonfiction.

Featuring over 200 lavish, four-color photographs accompanied by an informative text, *Baseball Archaeology* follows America's fa-

334

Sports and Recreation

vorite sport from its start in the 1880s to the modern era. This handsome picture book captures the romance and mythology of the game. Here is the "real stuff" of baseball, those things that fire the imagination and trigger memories of unforgettable moments in games gone by. The book is organized into five chapters arranged chronologically to celebrate the game's first century. Chapter introductions set the stage with the world events, important players, and the big stories and scandals of the day. With Babe Ruth's bat and Ty Cobb's spikes, the legends of baseball come alive in this fascinating excavation of the games' famous and forgotten artifacts. It's all here—the heart and soul of major league baseball, the legends and lore, the bats and masks and gloves that helped shape America's favorite pastime.

34.4 Appleman, Marc. **Joe Montana.** Sports Illustrated for Kids/Time Magazine, 1991. 122 pp. ISBN 0-316-04870-4. Nonfiction.

Here is the complete and captivating story of Joe Montana, the man who may be the greatest football quarterback ever to play the game. Find out how Montana made his reputation as the "Comeback Kid" in college and how he led the San Francisco 49ers to four Super Bowl victories. This Sports Illustrated for Kids biography includes color photographs and a glossary of terms.

ALA Quick Picks for Young Adults, 1992

34.5 Ashton, Steve. **Climbing.** Lerner, 1993. 48 pp. ISBN 0-8225-2480-5. Nonfiction.

Are you up to the challenge of scaling a boulder, rocky hill, or mountain? If you have never been climbing, discover the thrill of ascending extremely steep terrain or cliff faces with nothing more than your hands and feet. As a reader, you will get a first-hand look at different types of climbing: rock, ice, and mountain. You will learn what ropework is and why it is so important, how different climbs are rated, what precautions to take before climbing on snow and ice, and how to keep your equipment in good condition. Author and experienced climber Steve Ashton includes important information about safety as he introduces this challenging sport. His adventure stories may well inspire you to sign up for climbing lessons. Part of the All Action series.

34.6 Baczewski, Paul. **Just for Kicks.** HarperCollins/Harper Keypoint Books, 1992. 182 pp. ISBN 0-397-32466-9. Fiction.

It was Brandon's bright idea to get his smart-mouth sister, Sarah, to join the high school football team. Sarah is an incredible athlete, the most talented kicker the team has seen in a long time, and the team needs her help to win the state championship. The fact that Sarah is the only female among an incredibly macho and hostile bunch of players is just the beginning of her brother's headaches as manager of the team. Brandon also has a crazy coach and a lovesick linebacker to deal with, as well as his two demented older brothers, who play quarterback and offensive lineman. This is a story about high school and football, about brothers and sisters, and about devotion and dedication. Can Brandon pull it all together? He has to, he just has to.

34.7 Barnidge, Tom, editor. **Good Days, Bad Days: An Official NFL Book.** Viking, 1992. 119 pp. ISBN 0-670-84686-4. Nonfiction.

The heights of success and the depths of defeat are next-door neighbors in competitive sports, one lesson all athletes must learn. The price of chasing victory is the possibility that one may fail, as athletes are reminded every time they take the field. In *Good Days, Bad Days*, fifteen star players in the National Football League provide an inside look at some of their triumphs and disappointments on and off the field. By experiencing some difficult times, failures, and frustrations, these stars gained a greater thirst for victory.

34.8 Cannon, A. E. **The Shadow Brothers.** Dell/Laurel-Leaf Library, 1992. 179 pp. ISBN 0-440-21167-0. Fiction.

When Marcus Jenkins and his foster brother and running teammate, Henry, turn sixteen, they confront both the bonds and conflicts of brotherhood. Henry demonstrates his Navajo heritage and turns toward a world to which Marcus will never belong. Marcus is forced to discover his own strengths and passions, which include his feelings for Henry's former girlfriend, Celia. This story blends the traditional elements of a coming-of-age novel with realistic situations about prejudice, self-acceptance, and winning the race.

34.9 Christopher, Matt. **Pressure Play.** Little, Brown, 1993. 154 pp. ISBN 0-316-14098-8. Fiction.

Travis Bonelli, less obsessed with baseball than are his fellow team members, tries to balance his playing with his hobby of watching, editing, and making horror videos. He enjoys playing shortstop, but the other kids seem to eat, sleep and breathe baseball. Only right fielder Peter Hooper shares Travis's horror-movie interest. When Peter tells Travis that their team, the Seminoles, could go to the World Series if they win their own league, Travis worries that he might have to give up his hobby for a while. The pressure is on Travis to juggle his time and to discover the identity of the mysterious phone caller who is threatening him to concentrate more on baseball. Playing hard and working together as a team are valuable lessons explored in this gripping story of baseball and friendship.

34.10   Coe, Sebastian, David Teasdale, and David Wickham. **More Than a Game: Sport in Our Time.** BBC Books, 1992. 240 pp. ISBN 0-563-36231-6. Nonfiction.

More Than a Game is an exploration of sport seen through the eyes of many of the world's sporting giants, experts, and commentators. The three-person writing team shows that sport is a global force capable of binding people together as well as forcing them apart. In the twentieth century, sport has been challenged by commercialism, politics, drugs, technology, and television, yet the sporting spirit has survived. This book offers a definitive account of sport in our time as a universal language that unites people of every creed, nationality, and color.

34.11   Cohen, Neil. **Shaquille O'Neal.** Illustrated by Steve McGarry. Bantam Books, 1993. 103 pp. ISBN 0-553-48158-4. Nonfiction.

He is 7'1" tall and the hottest stuff in the NBA today. Climb onto the shoulders of pro basketball's rookie sensation, Shaquille O'Neal, for a sky-scraping, rim-rattling ride through his exciting world. Read all about how Shaquille got his name and what it means, why he couldn't dunk even when he was 6'7" tall, what size shoe he wears, and the name of his favorite rap group. Follow Shaquille from when he was a kid living on army bases to his first season in the NBA. How does this awesome African American athlete deal with fame? Who were the major influences in his life?

34.12   Cooper, Michael L. **Playing America's Game: The Story of Negro League Baseball.** Dutton/Lodestar Books, 1993. 96 pp. ISBN 0-525-67407-1. Nonfiction.

With verve and clarity, Michael Cooper tells the exciting story of the Negro baseball league. Because racism kept blacks out of the major leagues for nearly half a century, Negroes played a separate version of America's favorite pastime. Nevertheless, the Negro leagues lifted the spirits of countless black people throughout segregated America and gave them hope. Here is the informative, inspiring story of such exceptional athletes as Andrew "Rube" Foster, John Henry Lloyd, and James "Cool Papa" Bell. It details the hardships they faced as well as the accomplishments they achieved. When Jackie Robinson and other great athletes broke into the major leagues in the late 1940s, the Negro leagues collapsed, but their place in history will be remembered and admired.

34.13 Cromartie, Warren, with Robert Whiting. **Slugging It Out in Japan: An American Major Leaguer in the Tokyo Outfield.** Penguin/Signet Books, 1992. 336 pp. ISBN 0-451-17076-8. Nonfiction.

Welcome to the world of Japanese baseball, where a black ballplayer fresh from the Montreal Expos needed all his baseball skills, street smarts, and native pride to give as much as he took on his way to becoming a star in the land of the rising sun. Warren Cromartie, a top National League outfielder, was an African American playing baseball in a land where to be only half-Japanese made one an object of contempt. He tells his story with pride, a story of bad calls, bad vibes, bad-mouthing, and bad feelings. This first-person account of a skilled professional is the frankest, most painful, yet most revealing, look at the way Japanese play ball and other games of life.

34.14 Crutcher, Chris. **Athletic Shorts: Six Short Stories.** Dell/Laurel-Leaf Library, 1992. 161 pp. ISBN 0-440-21390-8. Fiction.

Have you ever wondered what happens to Willie Weaver when he returns to Oakland, where Louie Banks goes after graduation, and whether Dillion and Jennifer ever get together? *Athletic Shorts* allows the reader to check into what's happening to some of the characters of Chris Crutcher's novels. Some of these short stories take place before the time in which the characters originally appeared in a book, and some take place afterward. All mix poignancy and humor in just the right proportions to keep Crutcher's readers involved. These are six stories of love and death, people facing challenges, and doing their best—no matter what happens. If you have you ever wondered about these characters, now you can find out.

ALA Best Books for Young Adults, 1992
ALA Quick Picks for Young Adults, 1992
School Library Journal Best Books, 1991

34.15 Deuker, Carl. **Heart of a Champion.** Little, Brown/Joy Street Books, 1993. 199 pp. ISBN 0-316-18166-8. Fiction.

They say that baseball is like a fever, and that once you catch it, you never recover. Seth Barham catches the fever the first afternoon he visits Jimmy Winter's house. On that day, when he first learns about earned run averages, slugging percentages, and walks-to-strikeout ratios, he and Jimmy are best friends. But good friends rarely act just as one would have them, and Seth discovers that Jimmy is rather complex and unpredictable. This story is a heartfelt tribute to those friends who come but once in a lifetime—friends who change one's life irrevocably and who can never be forgotten. More importantly, this story is a moving testimony to the strength and courage that can grow out of a loss.

ALA Best Books for Young Adults, 1994
ALA Quick Picks for Young Adults, 1994

34.16 Duder, Tessa. **Alex in Rome.** Houghton Mifflin, 1992. 166 pp. ISBN 0-395-62879-2. Fiction.

Well-developed, realistic, three-dimensional characters round out this novel about competitive swimming and adolescence. As a member of the New Zealand Swim Team, fifteen-year-old Alex confronts different and overwhelming feelings, but she is determined to make the most of Rome and the 1960 Olympic Games experience. While Alex is exceptional, she is not heroic; while she is strong, she is also selfish, shortsighted, and vulnerable. *Alex in Rome* is as impressive for its sports drama as it is for its depiction of the emotional turmoil of coming-of-age.

34.17 Drumtra, Stacy. **Face-Off.** Avon/Flare Books, 1992. 117 pp. ISBN 0-380-76863-1. Fiction.

Face-Off is the story of twin teenage brothers, T. J., an honor student, and Brad, the jock, who have always thought of themselves as opposites. About the only thing they have in common is their love of hockey and their competitiveness. Problems erupt when hard times force T. J. to transfer out of his fancy prep school to the local public school where Brad has held the spotlight. The boys find themselves competing not only for supremacy on the hockey team and for friends but also for their father's attention. Stacy Drumtra, the seventeen-year-old author, shows superb ability in depicting both detailed, action-packed hockey scenes and complex peer and family relationships. Readers will find themselves caught up in this story of growing up and learning to live with and appreciate siblings.

Avon Flare Young Adult Competition Winner, 1991

34.18 Dygard, Thomas J. **Backfield Package.** Morrow Junior Books, 1992. 202 pp. ISBN 0-688-11471-7. Fiction.

Four Hillcrest High School friends decide to keep their football team's backfield intact by attending a small, little-known college that would allow them to play together another four years. But then a big-league university shows interest in Joe, the quarterback. He begins to wonder if his decision to go with his friends was too hasty and whether his first loyalty should have been to his potential. The compelling conflicts of promises are explored and solved through genuine feelings of allegiance to one another. *Backfield Package* is a story of football and, more importantly, of friendships.

ALA Quick Picks for Young Adults, 1993
IRA Young Adults' Choices, 1994

34.19 Dygard, Thomas J. **Game Plan.** Morrow Junior Books, 1993. 220 pp. ISBN 0-688-12007-5. Fiction.

For three years, Beano Hatton, student manager of the Barton High football team, passed out uniforms, checked equipment, and watched Coach Pritchard call the plays and form the Tigers' game plan each week. To him, football was an exciting intellectual exercise rather than an action-packed game of force. But when Coach Pritchard is seriously injured in a car accident and the school principal appoints Beano acting head coach for the final game, the student manager discovers that coaching a team is more than developing a strategy or calling the right plays. Beano must stand up to the Tigers' arrogant star quarterback, who is sure that he can do better than anyone else. Beano must handle reporters who want to turn his coaching debut into a media event, and he must meet the toughest challenge of all—to lead the team to victory. *Game Plan* is a story of a young man's struggle to understand what it really means to be called "Coach."

34.20 Fox, Alan. **Kayaking.** Lerner, 1993. 48 pp. ISBN 0-8225-2482-1. Nonfiction.

Join kayaking enthusiast Alan Fox as he explains the basics of the sport of kayaking. He relates his incredible experiences and tells how you can join the fun. From exploring peaceful rivers to navigating through turbulent whitewater, kayaking can introduce you to a whole new world of adventure. In this action-packed book, you will learn about the equipment and clothing you will need, proper safety precautions, how to plan your kayaking trip, and the different kinds of kayaking. A glossary is included. Part of the All Action series.

34.21   Gardner, Robert, and Dennis Shortelle. **The Forgotten Players: The Story of Black Baseball in America.** Walker, 1993. 120 pp. ISBN 0-8027-8248-5. Nonfiction.

This is the story of hundreds of black baseball players who played thousands of exciting games before sellout crowds prior to the integration of major league baseball. Robert Gardner and Dennis Shortelle report on what life was like in the Negro baseball leagues that flourished before Jackie Robinson broke the color barrier in the late 1940s. This book is not about how many games were won by Satchel Paige or how many home runs were slammed by Josh Gibson. Rather, it is about baseball players who were banned from major league baseball because of the color of their skin. They played because they loved the game and wanted to keep the path open for those who eventually broke the barrier that had divided professional baseball into black and white leagues for half a century.

34.22   Gutman, Bill. **Football Super Teams.** Pocket Books/Archway Paperbacks, 1991. 145 pp. ISBN 0-671-74098-9. Nonfiction.

Read all about the football super teams—their strengths, weaknesses, coaches, and star players, and the games and performances that made football history. Read about the most one-sided title game in the NFL, the first and only NFL team to go unbeaten through the regular season and the playoffs, and the great coaches. Read about teams that demonstrated pride, talent, champions, and domination. Such action-packed accounts are all in this book, ready for instant replay. Young and old will enjoy this collection of football history that covers teams from the 1940 Chicago Bears to the 1990 New York Giants.

34.23   Gutman, Bill. **Great Quarterbacks of the N.F.L.** Pocket Books/Archway Paperbacks, 1993. 149 pp. ISBN 0-671-79244-X. Nonfiction.

In the world of professional football, the quarterback is almost always looked upon as the main player, the focal point of the action and the player who best reflects the emotional ups and downs of the team. *Great Quarterbacks of the N.F.L.* takes the reader along to meet six of the best quarterbacks: Jim Kelly of the Buffalo Bills, Dan Marino of the Miami Dolphins, John Elway of the Denver Broncos, Bernie Kosar of the Cleveland Browns, Warren Moon of the Houston Oilers, and Troy Aikman of the Dallas Cowboys.

These six possess qualities of greatness, incredible athletic ability, toughness, a will to win, individuality, and the desire to get the job done under pressure.

34.24 Gutman, Bill. **Great Sports Upsets 2.** Pocket Books/Archway Paperbacks, 1993. 158 pp. ISBN 0-671-78154-5. Nonfiction.

In *Great Sports Upsets 2,* some of the most spectacular come-from-behind victories in sports history are showcased. Football, baseball, tennis, basketball, and track and field are just a few of the sports represented in this exciting collection. In this book, you will read about aging and injured players beating the odds, last-place teams surging to victory, rookies playing All-Star ball, and runners defying time and gravity. These are stories of individuals and teams—including Jimmy Connors, Michael Jordan and the Chicago Bulls, and the 1991 Minnesota Twins—that were involved in epic confrontations and epic games resulting in great sports upsets.

34.25 Gutman, Dan. **Baseball Babylon.** Penguin Books, 1992. 366 pp. ISBN 0-14-01-6542-8. Nonfiction.

Baseball players are not just idols. While many serve as good role models for teens and young adults, what about the shocking, bizarre scandals, the hushed-up stories of major league murderers, lunatics, racists, drug addicts, and spies? *Baseball Babylon* offers a sensational walk on the wild side of the national pastime and graphic proof that baseball is anything but child's play. The purpose of this book is to tell both tragic and funny stories of people in baseball who became caught up in circumstances that got out of control.

34.26 Gutman, Dan. **Baseball's Biggest Bloopers: The Games That Got Away.** Viking, 1993. 160 pp. ISBN 0-670-84603-1. Nonfiction.

Some baseball players are more famous for the one mistake they made than for all their home runs and great plays put together. In baseball, a *goat* is a person who makes a mistake, a big mistake. Sometimes even the greatest players make mistakes, as the true stories in this book demonstrate. Including play-by-play descriptions of the games, historical trivia, and lifetime statistics of key players, this book shows how life goes on after even the worst error and how sometimes a little mistake can make a very big difference.

34.27 Halecroft, David. **Breaking Loose.** Viking, 1990. 114 pp. ISBN 0-670-84697-X. Fiction.

Matt Greene is one of the best football players the Alden Panthers have ever seen. He has the speed, strength, and instinct to be the league's leading rusher. His only problem is his dad, a former NFL All-Pro, who wants Matt to do even better. With his dad watching him all the time, Matt starts fumbling handoffs and blowing important plays. It is fortunate to have a guy with Matt's ability on the team, but will all the pressure cost the Panthers their chance at the championship? Part of the Alden All Stars series.

34.28   Halecroft, David. **Power Play.** Viking, 1990. 119 pp. ISBN 0-670-84698-8. Fiction.

The Alden Panthers have never had a good hockey team until Derrick Larson moves to town from Minnesota. He is a powerhouse on skates and an expert shooter. Unfortunately, his seventh-grade team members cannot keep up with him, and without team effort, the Panthers slip to a losing season. Derrick thinks about moving up to the eighth-grade team, where he could really use his talents, but that would mean leaving behind his new friends. *Power Play* features a straightforward plot with plenty of exciting, realistic hockey moves and snappy dialogue. Part of the Alden All Stars series.

34.29   Hills, Gavin. **Skateboarding.** Lerner, 1993. 48 pp. ISBN 0-8225-2482-1. Nonfiction.

In its short history, skateboarding has become a worldwide craze. Skateboards have come a long way from the days when they were made from scrap wood and broken roller skates. With modern high-tech boards, skateboarders can perform spectacular tricks just about anywhere. Expert skateboarder Gavin Hills explains how to get started in the sport, gives tips on avoiding injury, and profiles some of the top skateboarders. You will learn the specialized terms that skateboarders use to describe their sport, the difference between street and ramp skateboarding, and how to assemble a great board suited for your individual skateboarding style. While danger is part of the excitement of skateboarding, by following the simple safety precautions detailed in this book and by using good judgment, skateboarders can have a fun and rewarding time. Part of the All Action series. First published in Great Britain, 1992.

34.30   Horrigan, Kevin. **The Right Kind of Heroes: Coach Bob Shannon and the East St. Louis Flyers.** Algonquin Books of Chapel Hill, 1992. 333 pp. ISBN 0-945575-70-X. Nonfiction.

This is the story of Coach Bob Shannon and the East St. Louis Flyers, a true story about a coach who will not give up and a team that has beaten all the odds. Coach Shannon's credo—"Get it done"—has been successful in his fifteen seasons as head football coach. The Flyers have won 152 of 173 games and the state championship six times. *The Sporting News* has named Shannon the high school coach of the year five times. These remarkable feats were accomplished in East St. Louis, a dangerous and desolate city with the nation's highest murder rate, where over half of the 41,000 residents are unemployed and three-quarters receive public assistance. This is a story of the power of human pride pitted against the power of poverty. In East St. Louis, pride is winning, inch by inch, with hard work and dedication.

ALA Best Books for Young Adults, 1993
Booklist Editors' Choice, 1992

34.31 Killien, Christi. **The Daffodils.** Scholastic Hardcover Books, 1992. 129 pp. ISBN 0-590-44241-4. Fiction.

When the Daffodils softball team elects a "boy-crazy" new girl, Caitlin, as their new leader, former captain Nicole struggles to understand the teammates who have suddenly become strangers. Nicole finds herself caught up in a bewildering world of nail polish, bras, and boys. Only when her efforts to save the team backfire and a friendship is betrayed does Nicole prove herself a winner on and off the field. This is a frank coming-of-age novel as well as a sports story.

34.32 Kimble, Bo. **For You, Hank: The Story of Hank Gathers and Bo Kimble.** Dell, 1993. 247 pp. ISBN 0-440-21459-9. Nonfiction.

From the asphalt and gymnasiums of North Philly to a winning team at Loyola Marymount University in Los Angeles, "The Hank and Bo Show" scored untold points, shattered basketball records, and entered the hearts of thousands of fans. The story of Hank Gathers, as told by his close friend and Loyola teammate Bo Kimble, is a moving and inspirational biographical tribute. Handsome, popular, witty, and talented on the court and off, Gathers was headed for the NBA until a small defect in his heart gave way midgame in the final season of his collegiate basketball career. *For You, Hank: The Story of Hank Gathers and Bo Kimble,* is a heartrending testimonial from one hoops star to another. While it is a book about two basketball players, it is also a story about friendship, love, respect, loss, pain, and rejuvenation.

ALA Best Books for Young Adults, 1993
Booklist Editors' Choice, 1992

34.33 Klass, David. **Wrestling with Honor.** Scholastic/Point Books, 1989. 200 pp. ISBN 0-590-43187-0. Fiction.

Ron Woods is captain of the wrestling team, an honor student, and the straightest kid in school. Going into his senior year, Ron's only worry is beating his wrestling rival, Igor. But Ron fails the mandatory drug test for athletes. He knows that if he just retakes the test he will be cleared, but he refuses because he views it as an invasion of his rights. Ron could lose everything by not giving in—the wrestling championship, his friends, and his girl. Is it worth it to do the right thing?

34.34 Lipsyte, Robert. **Arnold Schwarzenegger: Hercules in America.** HarperCollins, 1993. 85 pp. ISBN 0-06-023003-7. Nonfiction.

Arnold Schwarzenegger arrived in America as a young immigrant with little money and a lot of ambition. Within a few years he showed the world that the first step to fame and fortune is taking control of yourself. He sculpted his body into a championship symbol of power. He turned bodybuilding into a competitive sport and made it popular among men and women looking for new ways to find strength and health. From the shy, fearful boy afraid of being marked as a loser to his nickname, the Austrian Oak, Arnold dreamed of being someone whom other people admired and respected. He had a plan, he worked hard, he had faith in himself, and he held on to his roots even as he moved forward to a film career. His best advice: "You have to look at yourself in the mirror and then visualize what you can be." This biography includes an index and suggestions for further reading.

34.35 Lipsyte, Robert. **The Brave.** HarperCollins/Harper Keypoint/Charlotte Zolotow Books, 1991. 195 pp. ISBN 0-06-023916-6. Fiction.

The Brave proves again why Robert Lipsyte is a master of the young adult sports novel. Lipsyte has an unfailing gift for portraying troubled teenagers, and seventeen-year-old Sonny Bear is no exception. Leaving the Moscondagas Indian reservation for the streets of New York, boxer Sonny Bear tries to harness his inner rage by training with Alfred Brooks, a former boxer turned policeman. Brooks thinks that Sonny has the talent to make it to the top, to be a contender. But first Sonny has to learn to act smart, take control of his life, and beat "the monster"—the anger he brought with him from the reservation. Fans of *The Contender* will not be disappointed by this long-awaited sequel and will be eager to read the next book about Sonny Bear, *The Chief.*

34.36   Lipsyte, Robert. **The Chief.** HarperCollins, 1993. 226 pp. ISBN 0-06-021068-0. Fiction.

On the verge of having a shot at the heavyweight boxing championship, nineteen-year-old Sonny Bear finds himself with conflicting loyalties when trouble erupts on his reservation over the construction of a new gambling casino. Martin Malcolm Witherspoon, who calls himself "the only Black in America who can't jump," comes to save Sonny Bear and Alfred Brooks and tell their story of a wild and dangerous ride as they try to rescue the reservation and win the title. *The Chief*, a sequel to *The Brave*, will continue to satisfy young adult readers who search for tough action and sports appeal.

34.37   Lipsyte, Robert. **Jim Thorpe: 20th-Century Jock.** HarperCollins, 1993. 95 pp. ISBN 0-06-022989-6. Nonfiction.

Jim Thorpe was America's first great all-around athlete. A Native American who was stripped of his own language, clothing, and culture and drilled in the ways of whites, Thorpe is remembered for his accomplishments as an Olympic decathlon winner in 1912 and as an outstanding professional football and baseball player. Thorpe's baseball skills were major league, but he was hired by the New York Giants more for his fame than his hitting. However, his greatest athletic love was football, and he played the game into middle age. As a member of the Canton, Ohio, Bulldogs, he was an early player, owner, and official of what would become the National Football League. Perhaps his daughter, Charlotte, described him best: "Young and old loved him for what he was—a big, warm, fun-loving boy-man."

34.38   Littlefield, Bill. **Champions: Stories of Ten Remarkable Athletes.** Illustrated by Bernie Fuchs. Little, Brown, 1993. 132 pp. ISBN 0-316-52805-6. Nonfiction.

Champions is a collection of sports profiles of athletes who have made extraordinary achievements and have given something back to their sports. These fine athletes have the ability to fire your imagination, raise your consciousness, and give you a new perspective. In wise, inspiring prose, Bill Littlefield profiles ten women and men athletes, giving insight into the human side of sports and competition. They provide the reader with a sense of how to build lives that are made up of passion, dedication, self-respect, and constant striving.

ALA Best Books for Young Adults, 1994
IRA Teachers' Choices, 1994
School Library Journal Best Books, 1993

34.39 MacLean, John. **When the Mountain Sings.** Houghton Mifflin, 1992. 168 pp. ISBN 0-395-59917-2. Fiction.

Thirteen-year-old Sam can remember his first ski lessons as if they were yesterday. Now his mentor and coach, Phil, tells him he is ready to race in the highly competitive USSA Race Program—where all Olympic hopefuls begin. Sam is not so sure. Practicing racing is fun, but racing in races is not. *When the Mountains Sing* follows Sam as he struggles to overcome his fear of competition and to master the giant slalom, considered the most technically exciting event in Alpine racing.

IRA Young Adults' Choices, 1994

34.40 Macy, Sue. **A Whole New Ball Game: The Story of the All-American Girls Professional Baseball League.** Henry Holt, 1993. 140 pp. ISBN 0-8050-1942-1. Nonfiction.

From 1943 to 1954, some of America's best female athletes earned their livings by playing baseball. This is their story in their own words: a tale of no-hitters and chaperones, stolen bases and practical jokes, home runs and run-ins with fans. The AAGPBL (the All-American Girls Professional Baseball League) was born out of the war-time "manpower" shortage, and ended with the growth of television and the ideal of the suburban home. Accordingly, this is a story of America's changing attitudes toward men and women and the roles we expect each to play. It is also a story of baseball, for the women of the AAGPBL were every bit as in love with the game as the men who made it to the majors. The same courage and spunk that the players displayed on the field led them to get back in touch with each other in the 1980s and to take their rightful places in the National Baseball Hall of Fame.

ALA Best Books for Young Adults, 1994
Notable 1994 Children's Trade Books in the Field of Social Studies
School Library Journal Best Books, 1992

34.41 Malley, Stephen. **The Kids' Guide to the 1994 Winter Olympics.** Bantam Books, 1994. 80 pp. ISBN 0-553-48159-2. Nonfiction.

The Kids' Guide to the 1994 Winter Olympics is divided into three sections: Skates, Sleds, and Skis. Each section has chapters about

Olympic sports: figure skating, speed skating, ice hockey, bobsled, luge, Alpine skiing, freestyle skiing, Nordic skiing, ski jumping, and biathlon. Each chapter details the history of the sport, a "You Are There" story that puts the reader in the middle of the action, and graphics that show how the sport really works. There is information about equipment, rules, which countries' athletes have done the best in the sport, legends, and the 1992 Olympic medalists. Included are color photos of great Olympic stars, a schedule of events, a glossary, and a trivia quiz. With this informative book, the reader can become a winter games wizard.

34.42 Margolies, Jacob. **The Negro Leagues: The Story of Black Baseball.** Franklin Watts, 1993. 128 pp. ISBN 0-531-11130-X. Nonfiction.

The Negro Leagues: The Story of Black Baseball looks at a part of baseball history that is seldom examined. It follows African Americans in baseball from the game's beginnings nearly 150 years ago through the years immediately following the integration of major league baseball. It is a story of great ballplayers who played in obscurity because of the color of their skin: their very existence was ignored by major newspapers and radio. Jacob Margolies profiles some of the leading figures in black baseball—including Rube Foster, Satchel Paige, and Josh Gibson—and describes some of black baseball's greatest games. This history of the Negro leagues not only reveals the discrimination against black baseball players but also highlights the outstanding achievements of talented African Americans.

Notable 1994 Children's Trade Books in the Field of Social Studies

34.43 Nash, Bruce, and Allan Zullo (compiled by Bernie Ward). **The Greatest Sports Stories Never Told.** Illustrated by John Gampert. Simon and Schuster, 1993. 96 pp. ISBN 0-671-79527-9. Nonfiction.

The sports world is full of incredible-but-true stories. Many just get lost over time. Bruce Nash and Allan Zullo have uncovered fantastic accounts of phenomenal feats, amazing courage, startling incidents, and wonderful sportsmanship. They have filled this book with sports stories that most teens have never heard before, such as the jockey who left the gate on one horse and crossed the finish line on another, the boxer who was knocked down twenty-seven times and still won, the football player who caught the winning touchdown pass with two broken hands, and the one-woman track team that in one competition won six gold medals, broke three world records, and scored more points than the second-place team, which had twenty-two members. From the minor leagues to the Olympics, from the inspirational to the hilarious, this collection includes thirty-four exciting, amazing, and amusing moments in the world of sports.

34.44 Rolfe, John. **Jerry Rice.** Illustrated by Steve McGarry. Bantam Books, 1993. 98 pp. ISBN 0-553-48157-6. Nonfiction.

The man with the hands is Jerry Rice of the San Francisco 49ers, named the most valuable wide receiver in the National Football League. Catch his act as he catches passes and rewrites the record books. Here are some of the records he holds: most yards gained by a wide receiver in a Super Bowl game; most touchdown passes caught by any player in NFL history; most single-season touchdown passes caught; most career touchdown passes caught in postseason play. Here you can find out how he became such a handyman. How did he get this good? How does he stay this good? Who influenced his life on and off the field?

34.45 Salassi, Otto R. **On the Ropes.** William Morrow/Beech Tree Books, 1992. 248 pp. ISBN 0-688-11500-4. Fiction.

In early summer of 1951, the mother of eleven-year-old Squint Gain dies, and the bankers are about to foreclose on the family's Texas farm. Squint has no intention of living with his aunts and uncles, so he and his older sister, Julie, head for Dallas to track down their father, Claudius, who deserted the family nearly seven years earlier. They find Claudius, who returns home with his troupe of professional wrestlers and turns the family farm into the Gain's Arena and Wrestling Academy. The wild world of professional wrestling opens up a new world to Squint. Can he manage the different lifestyles and change of pace brought by his father's return, or does he yearn for the familiarities of family and home?

34.46 Scholz, Jackson. **The Football Rebels.** Morrow Junior Books, 1993. 246 pp. ISBN 0-688-12523-9. Fiction.

Unable to make the varsity football team at Midwestern University, freshman Clint Martin decides to buck the athletic organization by starting his own informal team made up of any student who wants to play football. With Clint's leadership and the financial backing of a rich eccentric named Shoo-Fly, the football Rebels are born. Their uniforms, contributed by local businesses, display advertisements of everything from lobsters to diamond rings. Their field is an abandoned stadium, and their playing is undisciplined. Their presence at the university stirs up trouble, which threatens to put an end to the new team. The plan that Clint designs helps the Rebels win their battle for football freedom and makes an exciting climax to a story of determination and ingeniousness.

34.47 Scholz, Jackson. **Rookie Quarterback.** Morrow Junior Books, 1993. 227 pp. ISBN 0-688-12524-7. Fiction.

This action-packed story of how Tim Barlow makes his decision to secure his future by combining his academic and athletic abilities offers its readers a valuable lesson about sports and about life. Football has always been Tim's life—so much so that his total dedication to the team causes him to flunk his junior year. Because he is academically ineligible to play football, Tim drops out of school and joins the navy. Two years later, Tim returns home to get a job and his high school diploma; but Bart Hogan, a local semipro, has other plans for Tim. He is determined to make Tim a member of his team. For a while Tim maintains a good balance between his high school courses and his time on the field, but once again he is forced to choose between his irrepressible urge to play football and his plans to get an education.

34.48 Seidl, Herman. **Mountain Bikes: Maintaining, Repairing, and Upgrading.** Sterling, 1994. 128 pp. ISBN 0-8069-8764-2. Nonfiction.

It is no wonder that people everywhere are getting on mountain bikes and taking to the hills. These bikes are relatively small, easy to handle, and built with state-of-the-art road-racing technology. Everything you need to know about mountain bikes is in this full-color guide—every mountain bike model, bike care and maintenance, and all the accessories you can imagine—plus you will learn about frames, suspensions, and steering systems. Every page is packed with outrageous, full-color photos. Use this invaluable guide on your next trip: it is easy to use, is fully indexed, and will help you and your mountain bike eat up the miles both on and off the road.

34.49 Shlain, Bruce. **Baseball Inside Out: Winning the Games within the Games.** Viking, 1992. 185 pp. ISBN 0-670-83506-4. Nonfiction.

Bruce Shlain, often called the "Miss Manners" of baseball etiquette, offers a probing, offbeat, and entertaining investigation of the game of baseball and competitions within the game. The table of contents categorizes the anecdotes into four groups: Pitchers and Hitters, The Manager's Game, Clubhouse Chemistry, and

GM's Burden. Each category allows the reader to gain insight into hidden confrontations. Listen to Tom Lasorda converse on the mound in x-rated splendor, get an earful of Earl Weaver going toe-to-toe with an umpire, examine the 1991 Mets when the team chemistry does not mesh, and delve into one-sided trades with inside influences. *Baseball Inside Out* is a romp beneath the surface, an examination of unspoken rules, and a revelation of the national pastime.

Booklist Editors' Choices, 1992

34.50 Snyder, John S. **Basketball! Great Moments and Dubious Achievements in Basketball History.** Chronicle Books, 1993. 208 pp. ISBN 0-8118-0308-2. Nonfiction.

Fifth in a series of ball-shaped sports-trivia books, *Basketball!* is informative and inviting. From the world-famous Wilt Chamberlain and Kareem Abdul-Jabbar to the all-but-forgotten Doggie Julia and Spud Webb, here are 200 professional and college players who have shot, blocked, and passed their way into basketball history. Each page presents a one-of-a-kind accomplishment— either glorious or notorious—and then provides the story behind the facts and figures. For example, Quintin Dailey is the only player to order takeout food on the bench during an NBA game; George King is the only player to hit a game-winning free throw and steal the ball in the final twelve seconds of game seven of an NBA final. These records and the colorful stories behind them make *Basketball!* a slam dunk for all hoop lovers.

34.51 Thornley, Stew. **Cal Ripken, Jr.: Oriole Ironman.** Lerner, 1992. 64 pp. ISBN 0-8225-0547-9. Nonfiction.

Cal Ripken, Jr. is a biography of the Baltimore Orioles team member known for his play as shortstop. Baseball fans are used to seeing Ripken—he has not missed a game since 1982. A two-time American League MVP, Cal is closing in on Lou Gehrig's record for consecutive games played. But baseball is more than just a game to Ripken: it is a family affair. His father and brother are also Baltimore Oriole members, and he values his family and family time while remaining faithful to his professional skills. Cal Ripken Jr., the Oriole Ironman, has earned his place among the greatest.

34.52 Weaver, Will. **Striking Out.** HarperCollins, 1993. 272 pp. ISBN 0-06-023347-8. Fiction.

After the shocking and jolting death of his older brother, Billy struggles to face life, to meet the grueling demands of the family farm, and to survive the strained relationship with his parents, especially with his father. Billy Baggs thinks his name should be Billy Never, for there is never a vacation, never a movie, never a new car, never enough money. But life on the farm begins to change when Billy begins to play baseball. Coach Anderson sees Billy's great potential, but Billy's father has no time for baseball and needs the boy to help out on the farm. Billy is torn between two worlds. *Striking Out* introduces readers to a young man who gains self-confidence and who begins to understand what is possible for him and what choices he may have to make.

ALA Best Books for Young Adults, 1994

34.53 Weidhorn, Manfred. **Jackie Robinson.** Atheneum, 1993. 207 pp. ISBN 0-689-31644-5. Nonfiction.

Jack Roosevelt Robinson started life deep in poverty and surrounded by prejudice, but through a rare combination of athletic skill, intelligence, leadership, and courage, he went on to become a national hero, cheered by baseball fans, admired by his peers, and courted by politicians. When Robinson was chosen by the Brooklyn Dodgers in 1947 to be the first black man to play major league baseball, he had to perform a delicate balancing act while silently withstanding insults and threats to himself and his family. Despite these pressures, Robinson emerged from his first season as rookie of the year. Largely because of his talent and courage, baseball was integrated without violence or legislation. After his ten-year baseball career ended, Jackie Robinson remained an ardent supporter of the Civil Rights movement, and through his involvement in business and politics, he continued to fight against racial injustice despite the criticism he received.

Notable 1994 Children's Trade Books in the Field of Social Studies

34.54 Weiss, Ann E. **Money Games: The Business of Sports.** Houghton Mifflin, 1993. 186 pp. ISBN 0-395-57444-7. Nonfiction.

In this provocative book, Ann Weiss discusses the influence and growing importance of money in the complex world of professional and amateur sports. Sport is a business, and the bottom line for any business must be reckoned in dollars and cents. But sport is also more than a business, and money is not its only object, for in sport the real bottom line is human striving, human competition, and the celebration of human achievement. Weiss has approached an area of contemporary concern in American society and has explored it in a concise and lucid manner.

34.55 Wieler, Diana. **Bad Boy.** Delacorte Press, 1992. 184 pp. ISBN 0-385-30415-3. Fiction.

When sixteen-year-old A. J. Brandiosa and his best friend, Tulsa Brown, make the citywide ice hockey team, A. J. believes that his life is finally coming together. But it soon falls apart when A. J. makes the unexpected discovery that Tulsa is gay. A. J. cannot keep his rage and fear from spilling onto the ice. Usually an aggressive and fair defenseman, A. J. becomes a violent team player. This story takes an honest look at teenage sexuality and amateur hockey.

ALA Best Books for Young Adults, 1993
ALA Quick Picks for Young Adults, 1993
International Board on Books for Young People Honor List, 1990

34.56 Williams, Peter. **When the Giants Were Giants: Bill Terry and the Golden Age of New York Baseball.** Algonquin Books of Chapel Hill, 1994. 331 pp. ISBN 0-945575-02-5. Nonfiction.

This is the story of a forgotten giant—the man once called "baseball's greatest first baseman" and the last National League .400 hitter, Bill Terry. Brought up from poverty and the obscurity of semipro ball in the South by the famed "Little Napoleon," manager John McGraw of the Giants, Terry developed into the team's key player when the Roaring Twenties met the Dirty Thirties, and New York became the center of the baseball universe. As America battled the hopelessness of the Great Depression, the no-nonsense Terry replaced the flamboyant McGraw as manager of the Giants and led the team to three pennants and a world championship. *When the Giants Were Giants* will appeal to baseball fans, baseball history buffs, and lovers of excellent storytelling.

34.57 Yates, Keith D., and H. Bryan Robbins. **Tae Kwon Do Basics.** Sterling, 1987. 128 pp. ISBN 0-8069-8756-1. Nonfiction.

Learning tae kwon do, a form of karate, is hard work. It will take you many hours of practice before you become an expert. You will need to listen closely to what your instructor says, and you will need to practice by yourself. That is where this book can help. All the mysteries and secrets surrounding the sport of tae kwon do are answered in easy-to-understand text. Step-by-step detailed photos and illustrations show how to execute every move.

Enthusiastic students can practice maneuvers like a double wrist grab, a shoulder grab, a reverse punch, roundhouse kicks, and an inside grab. Every punch, strike, block, and kick is designed with built-in safety tips. See for yourself why so many kids choose tae kwon do as their favorite sporting style of karate. This self-instructing book shows you all the basic exercises and techniques you need to develop your tae kwon do skills.

34.58   Zinsser, Nate. **Dear Dr. Psych: A Kid's Guide to Handling Sports Problems.** Little, Brown, 1991. 64 pp. ISBN 0-316-98898-7. Nonfiction.

Most books that help you play sports do so by focusing on your body and the physical side of sports. This book is different. *Dear Dr. Psych* focuses on your mind and how it affects your performance, and answers fifteen questions about the psychological aspects of competitive sports. At the beginning of the book, find a question that deals with a problem or a challenge that you face. Turn to that section, and you will find the question repeated, the answer, a summary of the answer ("The Lowdown"), and a section ("Psych Yourself Up") that suggests things you can do to make the answer work for you. This book is written for young athletes who choose to discover and explore their athletic potential.

ALA Quick Picks for Young Adults, 1992

35 War and War Stories

35.1 Ashabranner, Brent. **Always to Remember: The Story of the Vietnam Veterans Memorial.** Photographs by Jennifer Ashabranner. Scholastic, 1992. 97 pp. ISBN 0-590-44590-1. Nonfiction.

Today's teenagers may be unaware of the unpopularity of the Vietnam War and may not realize how surprised veterans were at the rapid and widespread support for construction of the Vietnam Veterans Memorial. This is the story of the memorial—the man who dreamed it, the young college student who won the design competition, and the more than 58,000 men and women whose names are inscribed on its panels. It is also the story of the people who come—relatives, friends, and others—to touch the wall, to leave a message or a remembrance, to weep at the young lives lost (the average age of the young men who died in the war was nineteen). As author Brent Ashabranner states, "It will make us remember that war—any war, any time, any place, however necessary and for whatever moral purpose—is about sacrifice and sorrow, not about glory and reward."

35.2 Becker, Elizabeth. **America's Vietnam War: A Narrative History.** Houghton Mifflin/Clarion Books, 1992. 199 pp. ISBN 0-395-59094-9. Nonfiction.

The Vietnam War was the longest period of involvement that the United States has had in a war—beginning with "advisers" in the 1950s, after the French were defeated in the French Indochina War; escalating in the 1960s; and concluding in the 1970s with the peace talks in Richard Nixon's second term as president. Elizabeth Becker, who covered Southeast Asia as a foreign correspondent, masterfully deals with the complexity of this war and the people involved "at home" as well as in Vietnam.

35.3 Bilton, Michael, and Kevin Sim. **Four Hours in My Lai.** Viking, 1992. 430 pp. ISBN 0-670-84296-6. Nonfiction.

We hear about enemy troops sometimes committing atrocities, but do American soldiers ever commit atrocities against civilians in enemy countries? What causes individuals in war to behave differently—to operate with a different moral code—than they would as civilians? In *Four Hours in My Lai*, we get some insight into these questions, as authors Michael Bilton and Kevin Sim examine the events of March 16, 1968, in the Vietnamese village of My Lai, when a large number of soldiers in Charlie Company murdered more than 300 unarmed children, women, and elderly men. The book provides vivid description, maps to document the location of the event, and photographs of some participants in the event and the subsequent investigation. The book is based on an award-winning film and raises important questions about war and behavior in war.

35.4 Bosco, Peter I. **The War of 1812.** Maps by Frank Senyk. Millbrook Press, 1991. 128 pp. ISBN 1-56294-004-X. Nonfiction.

Why did the United States have to fight Britain only a few years after winning the Revolutionary War? What was the early U.S. Navy like? What kinds of ships did it have? officers and crew? armament and weaponry? What issues caused the new war? Peter I. Bosco presents the answers to these questions in a highly readable format, interweaving fictional narrative with the factual presentation. Maps and illustrations greatly enhance this book.

35.5 Coe, Charles. **Young Man in Vietnam.** Scholastic/Point Books, 1990. 115 pp. ISBN 0-590-43298-2. Nonfiction.

What was the Vietnam War really like? How does a young officer deal with the reality of war? In 1968, Charles Coe tried to make sense out of the year he spent as a lieutenant leading troops into combat and dealing with death and with boredom. Twenty years later, Coe wrote a book relating his impressions of the war. In the preface, addressed in letter form to his sons, he indicates that he tried to write about the "things that truly mattered to those of us who fought. A letter from home. Your first dead man. The heat. The boredom. The fear."

35.6 Cornum, Rhonda, as told to Peter Copeland. **She Went to War: The Rhonda Cornum Story.** Presidio Press, 1992. 203 pp. ISBN 0-89141-463-0. Nonfiction.

Major Rhonda Cornum provides a riveting account of her experiences in the Persian Gulf War—events leading up to the war, her role as a surgeon, her capture and time spent as a prisoner of war, her treatment by the Iraqui guards, and her efforts at bolstering her own spirits and serving as a model for her fellow prisoners. Black-and-white pictures of Cornum, her husband, her daughter, her military associates, and the desert add to the drama of Cornum's harrowing experience.

35.7 Cox, Clinton. **The Forgotten Heroes: The Story of the Buffalo Soldiers.** Scholastic, 1993. 180 pp. ISBN 0-590-45121-9. Nonfiction.

Even though the Civil War ended slavery in the United States, acceptance of and opportunities for black people were limited. Thus many headed west, including the thousands who joined the calvary and became known as Buffalo Soldiers. It is ironic that those who had recently won freedom contributed to restricting the freedom of Native Americans; in the process, they helped to open land for white settlement but to close it to African Americans and Native Americans. This book reveals the "incredible heroism and an integrity that deserves our honor," an integrity and heroism belonging to the Buffalo Soldiers and to the Native Americans they fought.

Notable 1994 Children's Trade Books in the Field of Social Studies

35.8   Cox, Clinton. **Undying Glory: The Story of the Massachusetts 54th Regiment.** Scholastic, 1991. 159 pp. ISBN 0-590-44170-1. Nonfiction.

If you have seen the movie *Glory,* then you know the subject of this book—the bravery, determination, and success of the first regiment of African American soldiers. The Massachusetts 54th infantry regiment, led by a young white officer, proved its mettle at the Battle of Charleston and subsequently in the Civil War. As a result, the first black officers came from the 54th regiment. The success of these first black soldiers in the U.S. Army and their 180,000 African American comrades is inspirational to blacks and whites alike.

35.9   Devaney, John. **America on the Attack: 1943.** Walker, 1992. 218 pp. ISBN 0-8027-8195-0. Nonfiction.

This is the third book in John Devaney's World War II series, with one book for each year between 1941 and 1945. This volume focuses on 1943, the middle year of American participation in the Second World War, with American forces throughout the Pacific, in Europe, and in North Africa. Entries are in chronological order from January to December and are in the format of what Devaney describes as "snapshots"—anecdotes, behind-the-scenes conferences, incidents, and brief stories conveying the progress of the war and its impact on both those on the front lines and those at home. This quite readable and informative book is accompanied by numerous photographs and illustrations.

35.10   Devaney, John. **America Storms the Beaches: 1944.** Walker, 1993. 201 pp. ISBN 0-8027-8244-2. Nonfiction.

The fourth book in this series on America's involvement in World War II examines the events of 1944 that changed the course of the war in favor of the Allied forces. The book is organized in the form of a diary or journal, with letters and news clippings providing daily descriptions of the war and giving readers a feeling of being alive at the time of the war.

35.11 Dickinson, Peter. **AK.** Delacorte Press, 1992. 229 pp. ISBN 0-385-30608-3. Fiction.

Peter Dickinson probes what it is like to be a teenager in a war-torn country. In a story set in the fictitious African nation of Nagala, teenage commando Paul, called AK because of his trusted AK gun, buries his weapon when he hears that the war is over. But peace does not last. A military coup occurs, and Paul needs to dig up his rifle. He and his friend Jilli are called on to confront various forces of corruption and idealism, of love and survival.

ALA Best Books for Young Adults, 1993
Notable 1992 Children's Trade Books in the Field of Social Studies

35.12 Emerson, Zack. **Hill 568.** Scholastic, 1991. 230 pp. ISBN 0-590-44592-8. Fiction.

The second volume in the Echo Company series about the Vietnam War focuses on Thanksgiving of 1967. This fictional account gives readers an indication of what it is like for soldiers to have jungle rot attack their feet and to know that the enemy takes control during the night. "Meat" Jennings, Snoopy, Viper, and others build a firebase, fight Vietcong ambushes, look forward to letters from home, and confront the endless boredom, fear, and constant digging in war. They attack Hill 568 and, at considerable cost, gain temporary control. Meat learns to be "point" on patrol and to have the safety of the squad depend on him. As in the other volumes, a glossary at the end of the book proves a handy reference for military terms. Second book in the Echo Company series.

35.13 Emerson, Zack. **Stand Down.** Scholastic, 1992. 323 pp. ISBN 0-590-44594-4. Fiction.

In this fourth volume in the Echo Company series, the company has "stand down" time away from the front lines. Meat receives letters from a former girlfriend and from Lieutenant Becky Phillips; the squad gets a new member, Bozo; and squad members try to recuperate from the battles. During their respite from the Vietnam War, Meat looks for Becky, Finnegan seems ready to "flip-out," Sarge has to adjust to a new top sergeant, and Snoopy just hopes his feet will heal. The extensive glossary (twenty pages) proves useful for military terms and abbreviations. Mature language. Fourth book in the Echo Company series.

35.14   Emerson, Zack. **'Tis the Season.** Scholastic, 1991. 254 pp. ISBN 0-590-44593-6. Fiction.

Fans of the television series *China Beach* will relate to the third volume in the Echo Company series, set in Vietnam around Christmas of 1967 and New Year's Day of 1968. Lieutenant Becky Phillips, a twenty-one-year-old nurse at an emergency/receiving hospital, cares for the wounded and, in an effort to sound like Ella Fitzgerald, tries to cheer them as well. Readers of this fictional story about the Vietnam War will learn what happens when a nurse disobeys orders by riding an emergency medevac helicopter into the jungle. Third book in the Echo Company series.

35.15   Emerson, Zack. **Welcome to Vietnam.** Scholastic, 1991. 208 pp. ISBN 0-590-44591-X. Fiction.

This first volume in the Echo Company fiction series about American involvement in the Vietnam War is set in Vietnam in November of 1967. Meet Snoopy, JD, Sergeant Hanson, and other soldiers as they struggle with the heat, rain, and Vietcong hiding in the jungle. The series reflects the day-to-day life of soldiers in combat, on patrol, and at rest. The strong language is in keeping with that used by soldiers; the giving of nicknames reflects the distancing that soldiers seek to reduce the pain when a companion is killed. In this volume, eighteen-year-old Michael "Meat" Jennings joins the squad, and in spite of fear and jungle rot and the death of war, he begins to move from being the "new kid" to a veteran assuming responsibility. First book in the Echo Company series.

35.16   Hansen, Joyce. **Between Two Fires: Black Soldiers in the Civil War.** Franklin Watts, 1993. 160 pp. ISBN 0-531-11151-2. Nonfiction.

Part of a series entitled the African-American Experience, this book traces the efforts of 180,000 blacks who saw the American Civil War as a chance to earn their freedom and to prove their bravery and loyalty as well. Told through the accounts of journalists, the letters and diaries of soldiers, and reports by officers, the stories are vividly presented, accompanied by black-and-white illustrations, engravings, and photographs.

Notable 1994 Children's Trade Books in the Field of Social Studies

35.17   Harries, Meirion, and Susie Harries. **Soldiers of the Sun: The Rise and Fall of the Imperial Japanese Army.** Random House, 1991. 569 pp. ISBN 0-394-56935-0. Nonfiction.

The authors examine the rise of Japan's formidable military force from the samurai of the nineteenth century, its successes against Russia at the turn of the century, its conquests leading up to and including the early years of World War II, and its demise following that war. Meirion and Susie Harries explore the complex behavior of Japanese officers and men, their military structure, training, and plotting—revealing both extraordinary bravery and extraordinary brutality.

35.18 Hersey, John. **Of Men and War.** Scholastic, 1991. 132 pp. ISBN 0-590-44649-5. Nonfiction.

Did a future president of the United States really save the crew of a PT boat in World War II? How do nine men survive for days on a four-man raft? These and other questions are answered in John Hersey's collection of five true stories about World War II. Hersey gathered these informative, fast-paced stories in his role as a war correspondent and originally published them in national magazines. The stories were collected in book form in 1963.

35.19 Katcher, Philip. **The Civil War Source Book.** Facts on File, 1992. 318 pp. ISBN 0-8160-2823-0. Nonfiction.

What do you want to know about the Civil War? The chances are very good that this volume—replete with photographs, maps, illustrations, biographical sketches, letters, journal entries, and historical accounts—will have the information that you are seeking. Philip Katcher's book employs encyclopedic detail and narrative and uses facts to examine the five years of civil strife in the mid-nineteenth-century United States.

35.20 Kerr, M. E. **Linger.** HarperCollins, 1993. 213 pp. ISBN 0-06-022882-2. Fiction.

Author M. E. Kerr effectively examines what leads someone to join the army in a story about the Gulf War. A young soldier in the Persian Gulf writes to the town's "world class beauty," asking her to write to him. Kerr builds an intriguing drama of war, work, and forces that cause us to do what we might not do under other circumstances.

35.21 Landau, Elaine. **Chemical and Biological Warfare.** Dutton/Lodestar Books, 1991. 118 pp. ISBN 0-525-67364-4. Nonfiction.

Elaine Landau describes an "invisible" killer: biological and chemical weapons like nerve gases and anthrax. She reveals the effects of such weapons, means of detection, defenses against them, and problems and procedures for disposal. The book also poses moral and ethical issues and describes some of the debate in the scientific community.

35.22   Marrin, Albert. **America and Vietnam: The Elephant and the Tiger.** Maps by Andrew Mudryk. Viking, 1992. 271 pp. ISBN 0-670-84063-7. Nonfiction.

Albert Marrin writes in a compelling fashion about the Vietnam War, providing a brief history of the country and its occupancy, the rise of Communism, and the political history of the war, with examples of daily horror and heroism. A strength of the book is its reflections on the legacy that this strange war has for the world today. Marrin studied the unfolding war as a junior high school teacher and graduate student and reflects on its evolution and repercussions as a historian. Everett Alvarez Jr., the longest-held prisoner of war in the Vietnam War, writes, "One of the book's strong points is that it portrays the war the way the men who fought remember it."

35.23   Meltzer, Milton. **Voices from the Civil War: A Documentary History of the Great American Conflict.** HarperCollins/Harper Trophy Books, 1992. 198 pp. ISBN 0-690-04802-5. Nonfiction.

Author Milton Meltzer uses letters, diaries, journals, ballads, public documents, memoirs, and other sources to help readers understand the Civil War—the "struggle for the future of our nation." We can "hear" Abraham Lincoln, Stephen Douglas, Robert E. Lee, Jefferson Davis, Henry Clay, Frederick Douglass, John Brown, Sojourner Truth, and common soldiers and civilians on both sides of the conflict as they discuss causes of the war, its effect on their lives, and their frustrations, hopes, and dreams. *Voices from the Civil War* brings the war home in a very realistic manner.

School Library Journal Best Books, 1989

35.24   Miller, David Humphreys. **Custer's Fall: The Native American Side of the Story.** Penguin/Meridian Books, 1992. 271 pp. ISBN 0-452-01095-0. Nonfiction.

This reissue of David Humphreys Miller's 1957 book is fascinating reading. Basing his book on interviews with more than seventy Native American participants, the author brings an immediacy to the Battle of the Little Bighorn through the perspective of Native Americans—the other side of the "winning" of the West. With the exception of one chapter, "White Man's World," which describes other events in 1876, the book focuses on the day that

Native Americans defeated General George Custer and inflicted their worst defeat on the U.S. Army.

35.25 Phillips, Charles, and Alan Axelrod. **My Brother's Face: Portraits of the Civil War in Photographs, Diaries, and Letters.** Chronicle Books, 1993. 153 pp. ISBN 0-8118-0162-4. Nonfiction.

The American Civil War was the first war to be extensively documented in photographs. The authors draw upon tintype, daguerreotype, and ambrotype black-and-white photographs from the National Archives to illustrate the text. See the famous and the unknown, read excerpts from diaries kept and letters written by real participants in the War between the States. The book is organized chronologically by battles, from Fort Sumpter to Second Manassas, Shiloh, Antietam, Chickamauga, Cold Harbor, and others, and culminating at Appomattox. In the foreword, Brian Pohanka discusses the stage of photographic journalism at the time of the war.

35.26 Robertson, James I., Jr. **Civil War! America Becomes One Nation.** Alfred A. Knopf/Borzoi Books, 1992. 179 pp. ISBN 0-394-92996-9. Nonfiction.

This book gives a vivid account of the reasons for the Civil War and reviews the five years of turmoil. Maps, charts, and photographs of the terrain and people in conflict supplement the text. The author provides an excellent overview of a nation at war with itself.

ALA Best Books for Young Adults, 1993
IRA Children's Choices, 1993

35.27 Rylant, Cynthia. **I Had Seen Castles.** Harcourt Brace, 1993. 112 pp. ISBN 0-15-238003-5. Fiction.

John Dante is seventeen and a high school senior when World War II breaks out. His friends begin enlisting, but he is in love with a girl who opposes war and wants him to be a conscientious objector. Readers see World War II through John's eyes—first as a teenager living during war time and then as an older man recalling the intensity of feelings about the war by his family, his friends, and himself.

35.28 Whitman, Sylvia. **Uncle Sam Wants You! Military Men and Women of World War II.** Lerner, 1993. 80 pp. ISBN 0-8225-1728-0. Nonfiction.

How were nearly 16 million people made ready to serve in the armed forces of the United States in World War II? How were food, clothing, sleeping quarters, training, and transportation managed? What was it like for so many young persons to be uprooted from their normal lives? How did they deal with fear, wounds, prejudice? Sylvia Whitman interviewed veterans from all branches of the services, women and men, to weave a sense of what it was like for people to serve in World War II. The book is filled with black-and-white photographs and accompanied by songs and slogans from the era.

35.29   Wormser, Richard L. **Three Faces of Vietnam.** Franklin Watts, 1993. 157 pp. ISBN 0-531-11142-3. Nonfiction.

Embellished by the inclusion of black-and-white photographs of famous personages and of war scenes, this book reveals the Vietnam War from three different perspectives: the American soldiers fighting, U.S. college students protesting American involvement in the war, and the Vietnamese experiencing the war firsthand. Richard L. Wormser captures the turbulent years and varied emotions that confronted Americans in a war that was not only far away but difficult to understand.

36 Westerns and the West

36.1 Beatty, Patricia. **Bonanza Girl.** William Morrow/Beech Tree Books, 1993. 210 pp. ISBN 0-688-12280-9. Fiction.

In a fictional story based on a true event, Ann Katie and her brother, Jeremy, accompany their widowed mother when she travels to the Idaho Territory in the 1880s to find a teaching job. But teachers are not yet in demand on the frontier, so Mrs. Scott opens a restaurant, and the Scott family enters into a new life in a mining town.

36.2 Bonner, Cindy. **Lily.** Algonquin Books of Chapel Hill, 1992. 352 pp. ISBN 0-945575-95-5. Fiction.

For Lily DeLony, the oldest daughter of a motherless ranch family in McDade, Texas, during the 1880s, life does not offer much but cooking, cleaning, and mending. It is no wonder that she falls for the flashing grin and curly hair of Marion Beatty, youngest of the notorious Beatty brothers. Though all the townsfolk say the Beattys are nothing but trouble, Lily sees only the good in Marion. On their honeymoon she has to look extra hard for the good since they are now being pursued by the law.

ALA Best Books for Young Adults, 1993

36.3 Bonner, Cindy. **Looking after Lily.** Algonquin Books of Chapel Hill, 1994. 336 pp. ISBN 1-56512-045-0. Fiction.

In this sequel to *Lily*, Marion Beatty asks his brother Woody to look after his wife, Lily. Marion has to serve a two-year jail term for his role in a gunfight, while Woody has just been acquitted of murder charges pertaining to that same gunfight. Footloose Woody has never been around a woman before, since he was only five when he lost his mother, so the experience is a unique one for him. Woody is used to coming and going as he pleases and holding a job only when he cannot rob a bank or find money any other way. But Woody tries hard to honor his promise, though he often questions why he ever agreed to "look after Lily"—who is just a scrawny little thing and due to have a baby any day.

ALA Best Books for Young Adults, 1995

36.4 Buchanan, William J. **One Last Time.** Avon/Flare Books, 1992. 118 pp. ISBN 0-380-76152-1. Fiction.

Young Indian David Baca, part Apache and part Isleta, becomes a vaquero, or herdsman, to help his father with range work. David's job is made more difficult because his family's New Mexico pueblo has been terrorized by a maverick bull, nicknamed Diablo, that recently "liberated" several heifers from a friend's pen. On the morning of his fifteenth birthday, David hears his father has been gored in the leg by Diablo. When David sees his father's bloody, damaged leg, he vows to rid the reservation of the menacing Diablo.

ALA Quick Picks for Young Adults, 1993

36.5   Davis, William C. **The American Frontier: Pioneers, Settlers and Cowboys, 1800–1899.** Smithmark/Salamander Books, 1992. 256 pp. ISBN 0-8317-1825-0. Nonfiction.

Through the pages of this book, readers can walk or ride across the frontier with buffalo hunters, gold prospectors, settlers, and fur traders; can settle on the range with cattle ranchers; can help hunt outlaws with the Texas Rangers; and can fight for or against the Native Americans. In this magnificent retelling of the settling of the American West, period photographs add authenticity while full-color photos of tribal headdresses and tomahawks, western wear, gambling equipment, buffalo hunter supplies, and farming implements further illuminate actual equipment and supplies used by these early inhabitants of the West.

36.6   Estleman, Loren D. **Sudden Country.** Doubleday, 1991. 182 pp. ISBN 0-385-24727-3. Fiction.

Young Texan David Grayle, growing up in the 1890s, is sure that the excitement of the West is long over. Then Jotham Flynn, one of Quantrill's notorious Raiders, appears at the boardinghouse run by David's mother when he is released from prison. Although Jotham is killed, David obtains his treasure map. He sets out with a motley assortment of other treasure hunters seeking the gold from one of Quantrill's raids.

36.7   Fergus, Charles. **Shadow Catcher.** Soho Press, 1991. 308 pp. ISBN 0-939149-55-9. Fiction.

Most photographs of Native Americans taken at the turn of the century were posed and were often resisted by the Indians, who believed their souls were stolen by the photographers, or "shadow catchers." In 1913, wealthy Rodman Wanamaker funded an expedition to bring words of peace to Native Americans and to obtain their allegiance to the United States. One member of the expedition was Joseph Dixon, who had built his photographic reputation on the posed, idealized Indian photos. But to the dismay of the Bureau of Indian Affairs, someone else on the expedition was recording more accurate portrayals that showed Native American poverty, shabby living conditions, and affinity for alcohol, and was sending these photographs to an eastern newspaper. Two views of Native Americans are presented in this book, one based on their actual situation and the other based on an idealized fiction the government wanted shown.

36.8   Garry, Jim. **This Ol' Drought Ain't Broke Us Yet (But We're All Bent Pretty Bad): Stories of the American West.** Crown/Orion Books, 1992. 228 pp. ISBN 0-517-58814-5. Fiction.

This collection of tales is populated by cowboys, ranchers, moonshiners, ghosts, and pioneers who lived on the frontier back when the ability to laugh helped these settlers survive. Readers will chuckle over Uncle Emzy's training method for mules, resulting in cowboys catapulting through the air; the city-slicker government surveyor who names a rivulet of water Crick Creek, based on advice from an old rancher; and the revengeful blacksmith who is tricked into falling into the winter pile of horse manure. Set a while sometime soon and rock, spit, and swap some of these tales.

36.9   Hillerman, Tony. **Sacred Clowns.** HarperCollins, 1993. 305 pp. ISBN 0-06-016767-X. Fiction.

Lieutenant Joe Leaphorn and Officer Jim Chee, well-known Navajo Tribal Policemen, team up to solve two seemingly unrelated murders. First, an art teacher is killed at a mission school on the Navajo reservation. The next day, and many miles away, a sacred clown completes his role in a tribal ceremony and is killed. The only link between the two murders is a runaway student from the mission school whose uncle is the dead sacred clown, but no one can locate this student. Leaphorn and Chee once again fall back on their patience, careful questioning, and understanding of the Navajo culture to solve the murders.

36.10   Hobbs, Will. **The Big Wander.** Atheneum, 1992. 181 pp. ISBN 0-689-31767-0. Fiction.

Clay Lancaster and his older brother Mike have been traveling through the Southwest on a trip they call "the big wander" since they have no fixed route. Mike decides to return home, but Clay remains and works at a Navajo trading post while looking for his namesake uncle, who has turned up missing. Uncle Clay, somewhat of a maverick in their family, was last seen trying to save the wild mustangs. When Clay meets some Navajos who have spotted his uncle, he sets out riding a burro named Pal in search of Uncle Clay and lands smack-dab in a modern "wild west adventure."

ALA Best Books for Young Adults, 1993

36.11 Karr, Kathleen. **Oh, Those Harper Girls! Or, Young and Dangerous.** Farrar, Straus and Giroux, 1992. 182 pp. ISBN 0-374-35609-2. Fiction.

Lily Harper and her five sisters—March, April, May, June, and July—pitch in to help their down-on-his-luck father avoid bank foreclosure on his Texas ranch in the 1860s. Unfortunately, all their attempts to make money, from cattle rustling to moonshining to holding up a stagecoach, end in disaster. They are arrested after the stage coach robbery, but their fortune improves when a New York theater agent hires them for a reenactment of their infamous deeds.

36.12 Marrin, Albert. **Cowboys, Indians, and Gunfighters: The Story of the Cattle Kingdom.** Atheneum, 1993. 196 pp. ISBN 0-689-31774-3. Nonfiction.

The intertwining lives of the Indian, the cowboy, and the gunfighter are poignantly captured in this well-illustrated, hard-to-put-down account of western life. In the early 1500s, Spaniards brought cattle and horses to Mexico, leading to development of the famed Texas longhorns, which were rounded up by cowboys on horseback. Native Americans initially benefited from the introduction of the horses, using them to hunt the buffalo, but then the Indians had to defend their land against white men who were determined to raise cattle on it. The U.S. Cavalry, the buffalo hunters, the legendary gunfighters (often veterans of the Civil War), and the increasing numbers of frontier families eventually led to the demise of the Native American.

Notable 1994 Children's Trade Books in the Field of Social Studies
School Library Journal Best Books, 1993

36.13 McCarthy, Cormac. **All the Pretty Horses.** Alfred A. Knopf/Borzoi Books, 1992. 302 pp. ISBN 0-394-57474-5. Fiction.

Teenager John Grady and his best friend Rawlins ride south from their homes in Texas. Looking for a better life, the two swim across the river to Mexico and find work on a large ranch. Horses, love, loss, danger, and death all intermingle in this tautly written, violent, and deeply moving novel. This is a western that readers will likely never forget. Mature language and situations. First book in the Border Trilogy.

National Book Award for Fiction, 1992

36.14   Miller, John, and Genevieve Morgan, editors. **Southwest Stories: Tales from the Desert.** Chronicle Books, 1993. 210 pp. ISBN 0-8118-0216-7.

Although the writers and subjects are diverse, the setting—the American Southwest—is the same in each of the eighteen selections in this collection. Whether reading about the Southwest in Georgia O'Keeffe's letters to friends, a Zuni myth, D. H. Lawrence's poetry, a short story by Sandra Cisneros, or an excerpt from a Larry McMurty novel, readers will find the natural beauty of this region shining through. The authors know this part of America, and they have great insight into the full range of human emotions.

36.15   Myers, Walter Dean. **The Righteous Revenge of Artemis Bonner.** HarperCollins, 1992. 140 pp. ISBN 0-06-020846-5. Fiction.

Fifteen-year-old Artemis Bonner hastens out of New York City in 1882 in response to his aunt's summons, accompanied by a promise of half her life savings, to avenge his uncle's murder and the theft of his treasure. Heading west, Artemis tracks down the murderer, Catfish, in an escapade that takes him from Mexico up to Alaska. Ironically, Artemis catches up with Catfish in a gunfight outside the same saloon where Uncle Ugly was killed in this exciting tale of the Old West.

ALA Best Books for Young Adults, 1993

36.16   Nixon, Joan Lowery. **A Deadly Promise.** Bantam Books, 1992. 170 pp. ISBN 0-553-08054-7. Fiction.

After their mother dies in the late 1800s, Sarah leaves her sister Susannah with relatives in Chicago and travels to Leadville, Colorado, to find their father. Sarah is astonished to find that her father is on his deathbed and that he has been accused of murder. She vows to clear his name. Sarah is helped in her quest by Susannah and by friends Jeremy and Clint as they search for a document that may clear her father but that also may incriminate some Leadville citizens. Sequel to *High Trail to Danger.*

36.17   Paulsen, Gary. **Mr. Tucket.** Delacorte Press, 1994. 166 pp. ISBN 0-385-31169-9. Fiction.

As he lingers behind his family's wagon train to practice shooting his new birthday rifle, Francis Alphonse Tucket is captured by Pawnee Indians. After traveling with them for several weeks, Francis is astounded to see a one-armed white man named Mr. Grimes ride into camp, and even more astounded when Mr. Grimes steals a pony and helps him escape. As the two head off for Mr. Grimes's beaver camp, Francis, now called Mr. Tucket, experiences further adventures that introduce him to the ways of the West.

36.18 Reaver, Chap. **A Little Bit Dead.** Delacorte Press, 1992. 230 pp. ISBN 0-385-30801-9. Fiction.

After young trapper Herbert Reece saves the life of Shanti, a young Native American boy, he finds himself accused of murdering a gunslinger. Reece tries to find Shanti to establish his alibi, but meanwhile the gunslinger's cronies are trying to eliminate both Reece and Shanti in this exciting tale of western justice in the late 1800s.

ALA Best Books for Young Adults, 1993
ALA Quick Picks for Young Adults, 1993
IRA Young Adults' Choices, 1994

36.19 Reedstrom, E. Lisle. **Custer's 7th Cavalry: From Fort Riley to the Little Big Horn.** Sterling, 1992. 156 pp. ISBN 0-8069-8762-6. Nonfiction.

What was General George A. Custer really like? Why was he twice suspended from his duties? Who were the other commanders with him on his last campaign? Author E. Lisle Reedstrom, an accomplished researcher and noted illustrator, offers a chronological examination of Custer's activities with the 7th Cavalry from 1867 to his final battle at the Little Bighorn in 1876. Custer's forays with the 7th Cavalry, which occurred primarily in what is now Kansas, Nebraska, and Montana, were designed to protect railroad workers as well as to move Native Americans onto reservations. The thorough text and the accompanying period photos, illustrations, and maps capture the main players and battlegrounds, all of which provide needed background to understand Custer's final, disastrous battle.

36.20 Sanders, Leonard. **Star of Empire: A Novel of Old San Antonio.** Delacorte Press, 1992. 437 pp. ISBN 0-385-29916-8. Fiction.

Corrie, born and raised in Charleston, South Carolina, is engaged to marry the very suitable bachelor Ramsey Cothburn, but she feels that something is missing from the relationship. When Texas war-hero Tad Logan returns home, Corrie is swept off her feet by him, breaks her engagement, marries Tad, and moves to the Republic of Texas. Life is harsh, there is no proper social life, and Corrie is often left alone as Tad's duty to the Texas Volunteers finds him fighting against Comanches and then the Mexican Army. She wonders if they and their two sons can ever escape what seems to be a never-ending cycle of conflict.

36.21 Schlissel, Lillian (edited by Gerda Lerner). **Women's Diaries of the Westward Journey.** Schocken Books, 1992. 278 pp. ISBN 0-8052-1004-0. Nonfiction.

The arduous westward journeys undertaken by over 350,000 Americans are recounted here through the perspective of women travelers. Between the early 1840s and the late 1860s, before the advent of railroads, the trek west was a grueling one with unmarked trails, nonexistent maps, and inexperienced settlers. For the most part, the 103 women represented in this work through their letters, diaries, and reminiscences did not willingly choose to travel west but were forced to accompany their families. In addition to their normal chores of cooking and tending their children, these women often drove the oxen team, searched for buffalo chips or kindling for fires, unpacked and repacked their goods following rainstorms or wet river crossings, and tried to keep their family unit intact. Many were pregnant or delivered babies on the trail. As the entries clearly show, the strength and fortitude of these women contributed to the successful settlement of the American West.

36.22 Szasz, Ferenc Morton, editor. **Great Mysteries of the West.** Fulcrum, 1993. 266 pp. ISBN 1-55591-111-0. Nonfiction.

The American West has its share of unsolved mysteries, similar to those pertaining to the Bermuda Triangle. This collection of well-documented essays attempts to explain how a mystery becomes a mystery and offers plausible solutions to such unexplained events as the disappearance of the Anasazi, sightings of Sasquatch or Bigfoot in the Pacific Northwest or western Canada, the meaning of symbols drawn on rocks, and the validity of reported lost gold mines. Each essay is written by a specialist in the field, who cites studies and articles that explain the event. As more scientific studies are undertaken about these unusual happenings, they may provide the clues needed to solve these mysteries.

36.23 Underwood, Larry D. **Love and Glory: Women of the Old West.** Media, 1991. 188 pp. ISBN 0-939644-79-7. Nonfiction.

Most people are familiar with the story of Cynthia Ann Parker, the young white girl captured by the Comanches and the mother of Quanah Parker, the famous Native American chief. And most have heard of the beleaguered Donner party, whose entrapment in the Sierra Nevada forced them to practice cannibalism in order to survive. But many other women also came west, and this book introduces readers to some not-so-famous women. You can meet Susan Maguffie, the first white woman to travel along the Santa Fe Trail; or Josephine Earp, better known as the wife of Wyatt Earp; or Frances Grummond, who accompanied her husband to Kansas's Fort Kearney, where he was killed by Native Americans, and who was forced to make her way home accompanying his body. The lives of these western women, including missionaries, prostitutes, army wives, and captives, help readers understand the physical and mental strength that pioneer women needed in order to survive lives that included starvation, freezing temperatures, sandstorms, blizzards, and perilous journeys.

Appendix: Award-Winning Books

One of the many ways of finding good books is to consult various award programs to see which books have been recognized as outstanding. This appendix includes major awards given between 1989 and 1995 for poetry, fiction, drama, and nonfiction for young readers and adults, as well as descriptions of some other useful booklists.

Jane Addams Award

The Jane Addams Award, established in 1953, is given annually to the book for young people that most effectively promotes peace, social justice, world community, or equality of the sexes and of all races. It is given by the Women's International League for Peace and Freedom and the Jane Addams Peace Association.

1989   Hamilton, Virginia. *Anthony Burns: The Defeat and Triumph of a Fugitive Slave*. Alfred A. Knopf.

1990   McKissack, Patricia, and Fredrick McKissack. *A Long Hard Journey: The Story of the Pullman Porter*. Walker.

1991   Durell, Ann, and Marilyn Sachs, eds. *The Big Book for Peace*. Dutton Children's Books.

1992   Buss, Fran L. (with Daisy Cubias). *Journey of the Sparrows*. Dutton/Lodestar Books.

1993   Temple, Frances. *Taste of Salt: A Story of Modern Haiti*. Orchard Books.

1994   Levine, Ellen. *Freedom's Children: Young Civil Rights Activists Tell Their Own Stories*. Avon Books.

Boston Globe–Horn Book Award

Given annually since 1967 by the *Boston Globe* and *Horn Book Magazine*, these awards are conferred in three categories: outstanding fiction or poetry, outstanding nonfiction, and outstanding picture book.

1989   **Fiction Award**

Fox, Paula. *The Village by the Sea*. Orchard Books.

Fiction Honor Books

Dickinson, Peter. *Eva*. Delacorte Press.

Mayne, William. *Gideon Ahoy!* Delacorte Press.

Nonfiction Award

Macauley, David. *The Way Things Work*. Houghton Mifflin.

Nonfiction Honor Books

Isaacson, Philip M. *Round Buildings, Square Buildings, and Buildings That Wiggle like a Fish*. Photographs by the author. Alfred A. Knopf.

Yep, Laurence. *The Rainbow People*. Illustrated by David Wiesner. Harper and Row.

Picture Book Award

Wells, Rosemary. *Shy Charles*. Illustrated by the author. Dial Books.

Picture Book Honor Books

Cooney, Barbara. *Island Boy*. Illustrated by the author. Viking Kestrel.

Vivas, Julie. *The Nativity*. Illustrated by Julie Vivas. Harcourt Brace Jovanovich/Gulliver Books.

1990 **Fiction Award**

Spinelli, Jerry. *Maniac Magee*. Little, Brown.

Fiction Honor Books

Conrad, Pam. *Stonewords: A Ghost Story*. HarperCollins.

Fleischman, Paul. *Saturnalia*. HarperCollins/Charlotte Zolotow Books.

Nonfiction Award

Fritz, Jean. *The Great Little Madison*. G. P. Putnam's Sons.

Nonfiction Honor Books

Goor, Ron, and Nancy Goor. *Insect Metamorphosis: From Egg to Adult*. Photographs by Ron Goor. Atheneum.

Hoban, Tana. *Shadows and Reflections*. Photographs by the author. Greenwillow Books.

Picture Book Award

Young, Ed. *Lon Po Po: A Red Riding Hood Story from China*. Illustrated by the author. Putnam/Philomel Books.

Picture Book Honor Books

Martin, Bill, Jr., and John Archambault. *Chicka Chicka Boom Boom*. Illustrated by Lois Ehlert. Simon and Schuster.

Rosen, Michael. *We're Going on a Bear Hunt*. Illustrated by Helen Oxenbury. Macmillan/Margaret K. McElderry Books.

Award for Creative Excellence

Burkert, Nancy Ekholm. *Valentine and Orson*. Illustrated by the author. Farrar, Straus and Giroux.

1991 **Fiction/Poetry Award**

Avi. *The True Confessions of Charlotte Doyle*. Orchard Books.

Fiction/Poetry Honor Books

Seabrooke, Brenda. *Judy Scuppernong*. E. P. Dutton.

Brooks, Martha. *Paradise Café and Other Stories*. Little, Brown.

Nonfiction Award

Rylant, Cynthia. *Appalachia: The Voices of Sleeping Birds*. Illustrated by Barry Moser. Harcourt Brace Jovanovich.

Nonfiction Honor Books

Stanley, Diane, and Peter Vennema. *Good Queen Bess: The Story of Elizabeth I of England*. Macmillan/Four Winds Press.

Freedman, Russell. *The Wright Brothers: How They Invented the Airplane*. Holiday House.

Picture Book Award

Paterson, Katherine. *The Tale of the Mandarin Ducks*. Illustrated by Leo and Diane Dillon. Dutton/Lodestar Books.

Picture Book Honor Books

Mathers, Petra. *Sophie and Lou*. Illustrated by the author. HarperCollins.

Jonas, Ann. *Aardvarks, Disembark!* Illustrated by the author. Greenwillow Books.

1992 **Fiction Award**

Rylant, Cynthia. *Missing May*. Orchard Books.

Fiction Honor Books

Avi. *Nothing but the Truth*. Orchard Books.

Myers, Walter Dean. *Somewhere in the Darkness*. Scholastic.

Nonfiction Award

Cummings, Pat, ed. *Talking with Artists*. Macmillan/Bradbury Press.

Nonfiction Honor Books

Rankin, Laura. *The Handmade Alphabet*. Dial Books.

Ehlert, Lois. *Red Leaf, Yellow Leaf*. Harcourt Brace Jovanovich.

Picture Book Award

Young, Ed. *Seven Blind Mice*. Illustrated by the author. Putnam/Philomel Books.

Picture Book Honor Book

Fleming, Denise. *In the Tall, Tall Grass*. Illustrated by the author. Henry Holt.

1993   **Fiction Award**

Berry, James. *Ajeemah and His Son*. HarperCollins.

Fiction Honor Book

Lowry, Lois. *The Giver*. Houghton Mifflin.

Nonfiction Award

McKissack, Patricia, and Fredrick McKissack. *Sojourner Truth: Ain't I a Woman?* Scholastic.

Nonfiction Honor Book

Krull, Kathleen. *Lives of the Musicians: Good Times, Bad Times (And What the Neighbors Thought)*. Harcourt Brace.

Picture Book Award

Alexander, Lloyd. *The Fortune-Tellers*. Illustrated by Trina Schart Hyman. Dutton Children's Books.

Picture Book Honor Books

McDermott, Gerald. *Raven: A Trickster Tale from the Pacific Northwest*. Illustrated by the author. Harcourt Brace.

Sis, Peter. *Komodo!* Greenwillow Books.

1994   **Fiction Award**

Williams, Vera B. *Scooter*. Illustrated by the author. Greenwillow Books.

Fiction Honor Books

Fine, Anne. *Flour Babies*. Little, Brown.

Fox, Paula. *Western Wind*. Orchard Books.

Nonfiction Award

Freedman, Russell. *Eleanor Roosevelt: A Life of Discovery*. Houghton Mifflin/Clarion Books.

Nonfiction Honor Books

Marrin, Albert. *Unconditional Surrender: U. S. Grant and the Civil War*. Atheneum.

Levy, Constance. *A Tree Place, and Other Poems*. Illustrated by Robert Sabuda. Macmillan/Margaret K. McElderry Books.

Picture Book Award

Say, Allen. *Grandfather's Journey*. Illustrated by the author. Houghton Mifflin.

Picture Book Honor Books

Henkes, Kevin. *Owen*. Illustrated by the author. Greenwillow Books.

Sis, Peter. *A Small Tall Tale from the Far Far North*. Illustrated by the author. Alfred A. Knopf.

Andrew Carnegie Medal

This medal, first given in 1937 to commemorate the centenary of the birth of Andrew Carnegie, is awarded annually by the British Library Association to an outstanding children's book written in English and first published in the United Kingdom.

1989   McCaughrean, Geraldine. *Pack of Lies*. Oxford University Press.

1990   Fine, Anne. *Goggle-Eyes*. Hamish Hamilton.

1991   Cross, Gillian. *Wolf*. Oxford University Press.

1992   Doherty, Berlie. *Dear Nobody*. Orchard Books.

1993   Fine, Anne. *Flour Babies*. Hamish Hamilton.

1994   Swindells, Robert. *Stone Cold*. Hamish Hamilton.

International Board on Books for Young People Honor List

Established in 1956, this list is published every two years to recognize books published in countries all over the world that represent the best in literature for young readers. Listed below are recent honorees from the United States.

1990   **Writing**

Freedman, Russell. *Lincoln: A Photobiography*. Houghton Mifflin/Clarion Books.

Illustration

Yolen, Jane. *Owl Moon*. Illustrated by John Schoenherr. Putnam/Philomel Books.

Translation

Härtling, Peter (translated from German by Elizabeth D. Crawford). *Crutches*. Lothrop, Lee and Shepard.

1992   **Writing**

Staples, Suzanne Fisher. *Shabanu: Daughter of the Wind*. Alfred A. Knopf.

Illustration

Kesey, Ken. *Little Tricker the Squirrel Meets Big Double the Bear*. Illustrated by Barry Moser. Penguin.

Translation

Sevela, Ephraim (translated from Russian by Antonina W. Bouis). *We Were Not Like Other People*. HarperCollins.

1994   **Writing**

Paterson, Katherine. *Lyddie.* Lodestar Books.

Illustration

Bedard, Michael. *Emily*. Illustrated by Barbara Cooney. Doubleday.

Translation

Orlev, Uri (translated from Hebrew by Hillel Halkin). *The Man from the Other Side*. Houghton Mifflin.

International Reading Association Children's Book Award

Given annually since 1975, this award honors the first or second book of an author, from any country, who shows unusual promise. Titles listed here are winners in the older readers category.

1989   Wolff, Virginia Euwer. *Probably Still Nick Swansen*. Henry Holt.

1990   Crew, Linda. *Children of the River*. Delacorte Press.

1991   Conlon-McKenna, Mariata. *Under the Hawthorn Tree*. Illustrated by Donald Teskey. Holiday House.

1992   Grossman, Virginia. *Ten Little Rabbits*. Illustrated by Sylvia Long. Chronicle Books.

Kass, Pnina. *Five Words*. Cricket Magazine.

Mikaelson, Ben. *Rescue Josh McGuire*. Hyperion Books.

1993   Hesse, Karen. *Letters from Rifka*. Henry Holt.

1994   Toll, Nelly. *Behind the Secret Window: A Memoir of a Hidden Childhood during World War Two*. Dial Books.

Coretta Scott King Award

These awards and honor designations have been given annually since 1969 to African American authors and illustrators for books that are outstanding inspirational and educational contributions to literature for children and young people. They are given by the Social Responsibilities Round Table of the American Library Association.

1989   **Author Award**

Myers, Walter Dean. *Fallen Angels*. Scholastic.

Author Honor Books

Berry, James. *A Thief in the Village, and Other Stories*. Orchard Books.

Hamilton, Virginia. *Anthony Burns: The Defeat and Triumph of a Fugitive Slave*. Alfred A. Knopf.

Illustrator Award

McKissack, Patricia. *Mirandy and Brother Wind*. Illustrated by Jerry Pinkney. Alfred A. Knopf.

Illustrator Honor Book

Greenfield, Eloise. *Under the Sunday Tree*. Illustrated by Amos Ferguson. Harper and Row.

1990 **Author Award**

McKissack, Patricia, and Fredrick McKissack. *A Long Hard Journey: The Story of the Pullman Porter*. Walker.

Illustrator Award

Greenfield, Eloise. *Nathaniel Talking*. Illustrated by Jan Spivey Gilchrist. Black Butterfly Children's Press.

1991 **Author Award**

Taylor, Mildred. *The Road to Memphis*. Dial Books.

Author Honor Book

Haskins, James. *Black Dance in America: A History through Its People*. Thomas Y. Crowell.

Illustrator Award

Price, Leontyne. *Aïda*. Illustrated by Leo and Diane Dillon. Harcourt Brace Jovanovich/Gulliver Books.

Illustrator Honor Book

Johnson, Angela. *When I Am Old with You*. Illustrated by David Soman. Orchard Books.

1992 **Author Award**

Myers, Walter Dean. *Now Is Your Time! The African-American Struggle for Freedom*. HarperCollins.

Author Honor Book

Greenfield, Eloise. *Night on Neighborhood Street*. Illustrated by Jan Spivey Gilchrist. Dial Books.

Illustrator Award

Ringgold, Faith. *Tar Beach*. Illustrated by the author. Crown.

Illustrator Honor Book

Bryan, Ashley. *All Night, All Day: A Child's First Book of African American Spirituals*. Illustrated by the author. Atheneum.

1993 **Author Award**

McKissack, Patricia C. *The Dark-Thirty: Southern Tales of the Supernatural*. Illustrated by Brian Pinkney. Alfred A. Knopf.

Illustrator Award

Anderson, David A./Sankofa, reteller. *The Origin of Life on Earth: An African Creation Myth*. Illustrated by Kathleen Atkins Wilson. Sight Productions.

1994   **Author Award**

Johnson, Angela. *Toning the Sweep*. Orchard Books.

Author Honor Books

Thomas, Joyce Carol. *Brown Honey in Broomwheat Tea*. Illustrated by Floyd Cooper. HarperCollins.

Myers, Walter Dean. *Malcolm X: By Any Means Necessary*. Scholastic.

Illustrator Award

Feelings, Tom. *Soul Looks Back in Wonder*. Illustrated by the author. Doubleday.

Illustrator Honor Books

Thomas, Joyce Carol. *Brown Honey in Broomwheat Tea*. Illustrated by Floyd Cooper. HarperCollins.

Mitchell, Margaree King. *Uncle Jed's Barbershop*. Illustrated by James Ransome. Simon and Schuster.

1995   **Author Award**

McKissack, Patricia C., and Fredrick L. McKissack. *Christmas in the Big House, Christmas in the Quarters*. Scholastic.

Author Honor Books

Woodson, Jacqueline. *I Hadn't Meant to Tell You This*. Delacorte Press.

McKissack, Patricia C., and Fredrick McKissack. *Black Diamond: The Story of the Negro Baseball League*. Scholastic.

Illustrator Award

Johnson, James Weldon. *The Creation*. Illustrated by James E. Ransome. Holiday House.

Illustrator Honor Books

Medearis, Angela Shelf. *The Singing Man*. Illustrated by Terea Shaffer. Holiday House.

Grimes, Nikki. *Meet Danitra Brown*. Illustrated by Floyd Cooper. Lothrop, Lee and Shepard Books.

NCTE Orbis Pictus Award for Outstanding Nonfiction for Children

This award commemorates the work of John Comenius, *Orbis Pictus: The World in Pictures*, published in 1657 and historically considered to be the first book actually planned for children. The selection committee chooses one outstanding nonfiction book each year on the basis of accuracy, organization, design, writing style, and usefulness for classroom teaching.

1990 **Award**

Fritz, Jean. *The Great Little Madison*. G. P. Putnam's Sons.

Honor Books

Blumberg, Rhoda. *The Great American Gold Rush*. Macmillan/Bradbury Press.

Lauber, Patricia. *The News about Dinosaurs*. Macmillan/Bradbury Press.

1991 **Award**

Freedman, Russell. *Franklin Delano Roosevelt*. Houghton Mifflin/Clarion Books.

Honor Books

Ekoomiak, Normee. *Arctic Memories*. Henry Holt.

Lauber, Patricia. *Seeing Earth from Space*. Orchard Books.

1992 **Award**

Burleigh, Robert. *Flight: The Journey of Charles Lindbergh*. Illustrated by Mike Wimmer. Putnam/Philomel Books.

Honor Books

Myers, Walter Dean. *Now Is Your Time! The African-American Struggle for Freedom*. HarperCollins.

Conrad, Pam. *Prairie Visions: The Life and Times of Solomon Butcher*. HarperCollins.

1993 **Award**

Stanley, Jerry. *Children of the Dust Bowl: The True Story of the School at Weedpatch Camp*. Crown.

Honor Books

Cummings, Pat, ed. *Talking with Artists*. Macmillan/Bradbury Press.

Cone, Molly. *Come Back, Salmon: How a Group of Dedicated Kids Adopted Pigeon Creek and Brought It Back to Life*. Sierra Club Books.

1994 **Award**

Murphy, Jim. *Across America on an Emigrant Train*. Houghton Mifflin/Clarion Books.

Honor Books

Brandenburg, Jim. *To the Top of the World: Adventures with Arctic Wolves*. Walker.

Brooks, Bruce. *Making Sense: Animal Perception and Communication*. Farrar, Straus and Giroux.

1995   **Award**

Swanson, Diane. *Safari beneath the Sea: The Wonder World of the North Pacific Coast*. Sierra Club Books.

Honor Books

Dewey, Jennifer Owings. *Wildlife Rescue: The Work of Dr. Kathleen Ramsay*. Boyds Mills Press.

Freedman, Russell. *Kids at Work: Lewis Hine and the Crusade against Child Labor*. Houghton Mifflin/Clarion Books.

McKissack, Patricia C., and Fredrick L. McKissack. *Christmas in the Big House, Christmas in the Quarters*. Scholastic.

John Newbery Medal

The Newbery Medal and honor book designations have been given annually since 1922 to the most distinguished contributions to children's literature published in the United States during the preceding year. The authors must be citizens or residents of the United States. The award is given by the Association for Library Service to Children of the American Library Association.

1989   **Medal**

Fleischman, Paul. *Joyful Noise: Poems for Two Voices*. Illustrated by Eric Beddows. Harper and Row/Charlotte Zolotow Books.

Honor Books

Hamilton, Virginia. *In the Beginning: Creation Stories from around the World*. Illustrated by Barry Moser. Harcourt Brace Jovanovich.

Myers, Walter Dean. *Scorpions*. Harper and Row.

1990   **Medal**

Lowry, Lois. *Number the Stars*. Houghton Mifflin.

Honor Books

Lisle, Janet Taylor. *Afternoon of the Elves*. Orchard Books.

Paulsen, Gary. *The Winter Room*. Orchard Books.

Staples, Suzanne Fisher. *Shabanu: Daughter of Wind*. Alfred A. Knopf.

1991   **Medal**

Spinelli, Jerry. *Maniac Magee*. Little, Brown.

Honor Book

Avi. *The True Confessions of Charlotte Doyle*. Orchard Books.

1992 **Medal**

Naylor, Phyllis Reynolds. *Shiloh*. Atheneum.

Honor Books

Avi. *Nothing but the Truth: A Documentary Novel*. Orchard Books.

Freedman, Russell. *The Wright Brothers: How They Invented the Airplane*. Holiday House.

1993 **Medal**

Rylant, Cynthia. *Missing May*. Orchard Books.

Honor Books

Brooks, Bruce. *What Hearts*. HarperCollins.

McKissack, Patricia C. *The Dark-Thirty: Southern Tales of the Supernatural*. Illustrated by Brian Pinkney. Alfred A. Knopf.

Myers, Walter Dean. *Somewhere in the Darkness*. Scholastic.

1994 **Medal**

Lowry, Lois. *The Giver*. Houghton Mifflin.

Honor Books

Conly, Jane Leslie. *Crazy Lady!* HarperCollins.

Yep, Laurence. *Dragon's Gate*. HarperCollins.

Freedman, Russell. *Eleanor Roosevelt: A Life of Discovery*. Houghton Mifflin/ Clarion Books.

1995 **Medal**

Creech, Sharon. *Walk Two Moons*. HarperCollins.

Honor Books

Cushman, Karen. *Catherine, Called Birdy*. Houghton Mifflin/Clarion Books.

Farmer, Nancy. *The Ear, the Eye and the Arm*. Orchard Books.

National Awards for Adult Readers

National Book Award

Established in 1950 by a group of American publishers, book manufacturers, and booksellers, this award has been administered since 1989 by the National Book Foundation. This prestigious award annually honors outstanding books of fiction, nonfiction, and (except for the years 1984–90) poetry.

1989 **Fiction**

Casey, John. *Spartina*. Alfred A. Knopf.

Nonfiction

Friedman, Thomas L. *From Beirut to Jerusalem*. Farrar, Straus and Giroux.

1990 **Fiction**

Johnson, Charles. *Middle Passage*. Atheneum.

Nonfiction

Chernow, Ron. *The House of Morgan: An American Banking Dynasty and the Rise of Modern Finance*. Atlantic Monthly Press.

1991 **Fiction**

Rush, Norman. *Mating*. Alfred A. Knopf.

Nonfiction

Patterson, Orlando. *Freedom*. Basic Books/HarperCollins.

Poetry

Levine, Philip. *What Work Is*. Alfred A. Knopf.

1992 **Fiction**

McCarthy, Cormac. *All the Pretty Horses*. Alfred A. Knopf.

Nonfiction

Monette, Paul. *Becoming a Man: Half a Life Story*. Harper San Francisco.

Poetry

Oliver, Mary. *New and Selected Poems*. Beacon Press.

1993 **Fiction**

Proulx, E. Annie. *The Shipping News*. Charles Scribner's Sons.

Nonfiction

Vidal, Gore. *United States: Essays 1952–1992*. Random House.

Poetry

Ammons, A. R. *Garbage*. W. W. Norton.

1994 **Fiction**

Gaddis, William. *A Frolic of His Own*. Alfred A. Knopf.

Nonfiction

Nuland, Sherwin B. *How We Die: Reflections on Life's Final Chapter*. Alfred A. Knopf.

Poetry

Tate, James. *Worshipful Company of Fletchers*. Ecco Press.

Pulitzer Prize

Established by the will of Joseph Pulitzer, publisher of the *New York World,* these prizes have been awarded annually since 1917 for outstanding achievements in twenty-one categories of drama, letters, music, and journalism. We have listed here only those categories of most interest to young adult readers.

1989 **Fiction**

> Tyler, Anne. *Breathing Lessons.* Alfred A. Knopf.

Drama

> Wasserstein, Wendy. *The Heidi Chronicles, and Other Plays.* Harcourt Brace Jovanovich.

History

> Branch, Taylor. *Parting the Waters: America in the King Years, 1954–63.* Simon and Schuster.

> McPherson, James M. *Battle Cry of Freedom: The Civil War Era.* Oxford University Press.

Biography or Autobiography

> Ellmann, Richard. *Oscar Wilde.* Alfred A. Knopf.

American Poetry

> Wilbur, Richard. *New and Collected Poems.* Harcourt Brace Jovanovich.

General Nonfiction

> Sheehan, Neil. *A Bright Shining Lie: John Paul Vann and America in Vietnam.* Random House.

1990 **Fiction**

> Hijuelos, Oscar. *The Mambo Kings Play Songs of Love.* Farrar, Straus and Giroux.

Drama

> Wilson, August. *The Piano Lesson.* Penguin/Plume Books.

History

> Karnow, Stanley. *In Our Image: America's Empire in the Philippines.* Random House.

Biography or Autobiography

> de Grazia, Sebastian. *Machiavelli in Hell.* Princeton University Press.

American Poetry

> Simic, Charles. *The World Doesn't End: Prose Poems.* Harcourt Brace Jovanovich.

General Nonfiction

Maharidge, Dale, and Michael Williamson. *And Their Children after Them: The Legacy of "Let Us Now Praise Famous Men": James Agee, Walker Evans, and the Rise and Fall of Cotton in the South.* Pantheon Books.

1991 Fiction

Updike, John. *Rabbit at Rest.* Alfred A. Knopf.

Drama

Simon, Neil. *Lost in Yonkers.* Penguin/Plume Books.

History

Ulrich, Laurel Thatcher. *A Midwife's Tale: The Life of Martha Ballard, Based on Her Diary, 1785–1812.* Alfred A. Knopf.

Biography or Autobiography

Naifeh, Steven, and Gregory White Smith. *Jackson Pollock: An American Saga.* C. N. Potter.

American Poetry

Van Duyn, Mona. *Near Changes.* Alfred A. Knopf.

General Nonfiction

Holldobler, Bert, and Edward O. Wilson. *The Ants.* Harvard University Press.

1992 Fiction

Smiley, Jane. *A Thousand Acres.* Alfred A. Knopf.

Drama

Schenkkan, Robert. *The Kentucky Cycle.* Dramatists Play Service.

History

Neely, Mark E., Jr. *The Fate of Liberty: Abraham Lincoln and Civil Liberties.* Oxford University Press.

Biography or Autobiography

Puller, Lewis B., Jr. *Fortunate Son: The Healing of a Vietnam Vet.* Grove Weidenfeld.

American Poetry

Tate, James. *Selected Poems.* Wesleyan University Press.

General Nonfiction

Yergin, Daniel. *The Prize: The Epic Quest for Oil, Money, and Power.* Simon and Schuster.

1993   **Fiction**

Butler, Robert Olen. *A Good Scent from a Strange Mountain: Stories*. Henry Holt.

Drama

Kushner, Tony. *Angels in America: Millennium Approaches*. Theatre Communications Group.

History

Wood, Gordon S. *The Radicalism of the American Revolution*. Alfred A. Knopf.

Biography or Autobiography

McCullough, David G. *Truman*. Simon and Schuster.

American Poetry

Glück, Louise. *The Wild Iris*. Ecco Press.

General Nonfiction

Wills, Garry. *Lincoln at Gettysburg: The Words That Remade America*. Simon and Schuster.

1994   **Fiction**

Proulx, E. Annie. *The Shipping News*. Charles Scribner's Sons.

Drama

Albee, Edward. *Three Tall Women*. Dramatists Play Service.

Biography or Autobiography

Lewis, David Levering. *W. E. B. DuBois: Biography of a Race, 1868–1919*. Henry Holt.

American Poetry

Komunyakaa, Yusef. *Neon Vernacular*. Wesleyan University Press.

General Nonfiction

Remnick, David. *Lenin's Tomb: The Last Days of the Soviet Empire*. Random House.

Booklists

In addition to recognition awarded to a handful of selected titles, several organizations issue annual lists of recommended books. While such lists are too lengthy to include in this volume, we include descriptions of the booklists that would be of interest to readers of *Books for You* and indicate how to obtain these booklists.

American Library Association/Notable Children's Book Committee

The Notable Children's Book Committee of the Association for Library Service to Children, a division of the American Library Association, selects notable books each year on the basis of literary quality, originality of text and illustrations, design, format, subject matter of interest and value to children, and likelihood of acceptance by children. Many of the books chosen are also of interest to young adults. The complete list of Notable Books for Children appears yearly in the March 15 issue of *Booklist,* a journal published by the American Library Association.

American Library Association/Young Adult Library Services Association

The Young Adult Library Services Association of the American Library Association each year chooses the fiction and nonfiction titles that best satisfy the criteria of good literary quality and popular appeal to young adult readers. The complete list of Best Books for Young Adults is published each year in the April 1 issue of *Booklist.* The association also publishes an annual list of books with high appeal to young adult readers who, for whatever reason, do not like to read. The complete list of Quick Picks for Young Adults can also be found each year in the April 1 issue of *Booklist.* Both lists can be ordered directly from the ALA. Please indicate which list you desire and send a self-addressed stamped business-size envelope for each list to YALSA, 50 E. Huron Street, Chicago, IL 60611.

Booklist's Editors' Choice List

The editors of *Booklist,* a journal published by the American Library Association, issue an annual listing of recommended new fiction and nonfiction titles for children and young adults. The Top of the List, initiated in 1991, indicates the best book in each category of the Editors' Choice annual lists. The complete lists may be found in *Booklist* each January 15.

International Reading Association

The International Reading Association each year asks children, young adults, and teachers to vote on a list of books recommended by recognized sources such as *Booklist, Horn Book,* and *Journal of Reading.* The top vote-getters in each group are listed in IRA journals each year and may also be obtained from the IRA directly. The complete list of Children's Choices appears yearly in the November issue of *The Reading Teacher,* the

Young Adults' Choices appear in the November issue of *Journal of Reading,* and the Teachers' Choices appear in the November issue of *The Reading Teacher*. Single copies of any of the lists may be obtained for a charge of $1.00 from The International Reading Association, Order Department, 800 Barksdale Road, P.O. Box 8139, Newark, DE 19714-8139.

Notable Children's Trade Books in the Field of Social Studies

The Book Review Subcommittee of the National Council of the Social Studies–Children's Book Council Joint Committee selects books published in the United States each year that (1) are written primarily for children in grades K–8; (2) emphasize human relations; (3) present an original theme or a fresh slant on a traditional topic; (4) are highly readable; and, when appropriate, (5) include maps and illustrations. Many of the books recognized are of interest to young adults. The complete list of these notable books appears yearly in the April/May issue of *Social Education,* the journal of the National Council for the Social Studies. Single copies may be obtained at no charge by sending a stamped (3 oz.), self-addressed 6" x 9" envelope to the Children's Book Council, 568 Broadway, Suite 404, New York, NY 10012. (In 1994, the date on the list was changed to coincide with the current calendar year. Prior to 1994, the date on the list was for the previous calendar year, the year in which the books were published. Thus, while there is no list labeled Notable 1993 Children's Trade Books in the Field of Social Studies, there has been no interruption in the listing. The 1993 books appear on the 1994 list.)

School Library Journal's Best Books

The Book Review Editors of *School Library Journal* annually choose the best among the thousands of new children's books submitted to the journal for review during the preceding year. Books are selected on the basis of strong story line, clear presentation, high-quality illustration, and probable appeal to young readers. The complete list is published each year in the December issue of the journal.

Lists and descriptions of other awards, prizes, and lists can be found at the front of recent editions of *Children's Books in Print,* an annual publication of R. R. Bowker.

Directory of Publishers

Harry N. Abrams. 100 Fifth Avenue, New York, NY 10011. 800-345-1359.

Ace Books. Division of Berkley Publishing Group. Orders to: P.O. Box 506, East Rutherford, NJ 07073. 800-223-0510.

Addison-Wesley. Route 128, Reading, MA 01867. 800-447-2226.

Algonquin Books of Chapel Hill. Division of Workman. Orders to: 708 Broadway, New York, NY 10003. 800-722-7202.

Alyson Publications. Orders to: InBook, P.O. Box 120470, East Haven, CT 06512. 800-253-3605.

Arcade. Distributed by Little, Brown. Orders to: 200 West Street, Waltham, MA 02254. 800-759-0190.

Atheneum. Division of Macmillan. Orders to: 100 Front Street, Box 500, Riverside, NJ 08075. 800-257-5755.

August House. P.O. Box 3223, Little Rock, AR 72203. 800-284-8784.

Avon Books. Orders to: P.O. Box 767, Dresden, TN 38225. 800-223-0690.

Avon/Camelot Books. See Avon Books.

Avon/Flare Books. See Avon Books.

Avon/Byron Preiss Books. See Avon Books.

Baen Books. Division of Baen Publishing Enterprises. Distributed by Pocket Books, 1230 Avenue of the Americas, New York, NY 10020. 800-223-2336.

Ballantine Books. Division of Random House. Orders to: 400 Hahn Road, Westminster, MD 21157. 800-733-3000.

Bantam Books. Division of Bantam Doubleday Dell. Orders to: 414 E. Golf Road, Des Plaines, IL 60016. 800-223-6834.

Bantam/Skylark Books. See Bantam Books.

BBC Books. Distributed by Parkwest, 451 Communipaw Avenue, Jersey City, NJ 07304. 201-432-3257.

Beacon Press. Distributed by Farrar, Straus and Giroux, 19 Union Square West, New York, NY 10003. 800-631-8571.

Betterway Books. Division of F & W Publications, 1507 Dana Avenue, Cincinnati, OH 45207-1005. 800-289-0963.

Betterway/Shoe Tree Books. See Betterway Books.

Michael Bruce Associates. P.O. Box 396, Powell, OH 43065.

Bulfinch Press. Division of Little, Brown. Orders to: 200 West Street, Waltham, MA 02254. 800-343-9204.

Candlewick Press. Division of Walker Books, London, England. Orders to: Penguin USA, P.O. Box 120, Bergenfield, NJ 07621. 800-526-0275.

Carnegie-Mellon University Press. Distributed by Cornell University Press, 512 E. State Street, P.O. Box 250, Ithaca, NY 14851. 800-666-2211.

Carolrhoda Books. 241 First Avenue North, Minneapolis, MN 55401. 800-328-4929.

Carolrhoda/Adventures in Time Books. See Carolrhoda Books.

Chronicle Books. 275 Fifth Street, San Francisco, CA 94103. 800-722-6657.

Chronicle/Labyrinth Books. See Chronicle Books.

Crown Publishing Group. Affiliate of Random House. Orders to: 400 Hahn Road, Westminster, MD 21157. 800-733-3000.

Crown/Orion Books. See Crown Publishing Group.

Daisy Hill Press. P.O. Box 1681, Rochester, MI 48308. 313-651-0748.

DAW Books. Distributed by Penguin USA. Orders to: P.O. Box 120, Bergenfield, NJ 07621-0120. 800-526-0275.

Delacorte Press. Division of Bantam Doubleday Dell. Orders to: 1540 Broadway, New York, NY 10036-4094. 800-223-6834.

Dell. Division of Bantam Doubleday Dell. Orders to: 1540 Broadway, New York, NY 10036-4094. 800-223-6834.

Dell/Laurel-Leaf Library. See Dell.

Dell/Yearling Books. See Dell.

Dial Books. Division of Penguin USA. Orders to: P.O. Box 120, Bergenfield, NJ 07621. 800-387-0600.

Doubleday. Division of Bantam Doubleday Dell. Orders to: Doubleday Consumer Services, P.O. Box 5071, Des Plaines, IL 60017-5071. 800-223-6834.

E. P. Dutton. Division of Penguin USA. Orders to: P.O. Box 120, Bergenfield, NJ 07621-0120. 800-526-0275.

Dutton Children's Books. See E. P. Dutton.

Dutton/Cobblehill Books. See E. P. Dutton.

Dutton/Lodestar Books. See E. P. Dutton.

Dutton/Truman Talley Books. See E. P. Dutton.

Eakin Press/Panda Books. See Eakin Press/Sunbelt Media.

Eakin Press/Sunbelt Media. P.O. Drawer 90159, Austin, TX 78709-0159. 512-288-1771.

William B. Eerdman. 255 Jefferson Avenue, SE, Grand Rapids, MI 49503. 800-253-7521.

Enslow. Bloy Street and Ramsey Avenue, Box 777, Hillside, NJ 07205. 800-398-2504.

Facts on File. Subsidiary of Infobase Holdings, 460 Park Avenue South, New York, NY 10016. 800-322-8755.

Farrar, Straus and Giroux. 19 Union Square West, New York, NY 10003. 800-631-8571.

Farrar, Straus and Giroux/Aerial Books. See Farrar, Straus and Giroux.

Fawcett Book Group. Division of Ballantine Books. Orders to: 400 Hahn Road, Westminster, MD 21157. 800-733-3000.

Fawcett/Columbine Books. See Fawcett Book Group.

Fawcett/Juniper Books. See Fawcett Book Group.

Donald I. Fine. Distributed by Penguin USA, P.O. Box 120, Bergenfield, NJ 07621-0120. 800-526-0275.

Fulcrum Publishing. 350 Indiana Street, Suite 350, Golden, CO 80401. 800-992-2908.

Greenwillow Books. Division of William Morrow. Orders to: 39 Plymouth Street, P.O. Box 1219, Fairfield, NJ 07007. 800-843-9389.

Ruth V. Groves. 834 16th Street, Wilmette, IL 60091. 708-251-3282.

Hampden-Sydney Poetry Review. P.O. Box 126, Hampden-Sydney, VA 23943.

Harcourt Brace. (Formerly Harcourt Brace Jovanovich.) Orders to: 6277 Sea Harbor Drive, Orlando, FL 32887. 800-346-8648.

Harcourt Brace/Gulliver Books. See Harcourt Brace.

Harcourt Brace Jovanovich. See Harcourt Brace.

Harcourt Brace Jovanovich/Gulliver Books. See Harcourt Brace.

Harcourt Brace Jovanovich/Harvest Books. See Harcourt Brace.

Harcourt Brace Jovanovich/Jane Yolen Books. See Harcourt Brace.

Harper and Row. See HarperCollins.

Harper and Row/Harper Keypoint Books. See HarperCollins.

HarperCollins. (Formerly Harper and Row.) Orders to: 1000 Keystone Industrial Park, Scranton, PA 18512-4621. 800-242-7737.

HarperCollins/Laura Geringer Books. See HarperCollins.

HarperCollins/Harper Keypoint Books. See HarperCollins.

HarperCollins/Harper Keypoint/Ursula Norstrom Books. See HarperCollins.

HarperCollins/Harper Keypoint/Charlotte Zolotow Books. See HarperCollins.

HarperCollins/Harper Perennial Books. See HarperCollins.

HarperCollins/Harper Trophy Books. See HarperCollins.

HarperCollins/Harper Trophy/Charlotte Zolotow Books. See HarperCollins.

HarperCollins/Willa Perlman Books. See HarperCollins.

HarperCollins/Charlotte Zolotow Books. See HarperCollins.

Haynes. Distributed by Motorbooks International, P.O. Box 2, Osceola, WI 54020. 800-458-0454.

Helicon Nine Editions. Division of Helicon Nine, P.O. Box 22412, Kansas City, MO 64113. 913-345-0802.

Holiday House. 425 Madison Avenue, New York, NY 10017. 212-688-0085.

Holmes and Meier. Division of IUB, 30 Irving Place, New York, NY 10003. 800-437-7840.

Henry Holt. 115 West 18th Street, New York, NY 10011. 800-488-5233.

Houghton Mifflin. Orders to: Wayside Road, Burlington, MA 01803. 800-225-3362.

Houghton Mifflin/Clarion Books. See Houghton Mifflin.

Hunter House. P.O. Box 2914, Alameda, CA 94501-0914. 510-865-5282.

Hyperion Books for Children. Division of Disney Books. Orders to: Little, Brown, 200 West Street, Waltham, MA 02254. 800-343-9204.

Jewish Publication Society. 1930 Chestnut Street, Philadelphia, PA 19103. 800-234-3151.

Alfred A. Knopf. Subsidiary of Random House. Orders to: 400 Hahn Road, Westminster, MD 21157. 800-733-3000.

Alfred A. Knopf/Borzoi Books. See Alfred A. Knopf.

Alfred A. Knopf/Dorling Kindersley. See Alfred A. Knopf.

Lerner Publications. 241 First Avenue North, Minneapolis, MN 55401. 800-328-4929.

Lerner/Runestone Press. See Lerner Publications.

Little, Brown. Division of Time Warner. Orders to: 200 West Street, Waltham, MA 02254. 800-343-9204.

Little, Brown/Joy Street Books. See Little, Brown.

Longstreet Press. 2150 Newmarket Parkway, Suite 118, Marietta, GA 30067. 800-927-1488.

Lothrop, Lee and Shepard Books. Division of William Morrow. Orders to: 39 Plymouth Street, P.O. Box 1219, Fairfield, NJ 07007. 800-237-0657.

Louisiana State University Press. P.O. Box 25053, Baton Rouge, LA 70894-5053. 504-388-6666.

Macmillan. Orders to: 100 Front Street, Box 500, Riverside, NJ 08075. 800-257-5755.

Macmillan/Bradbury Press. See Macmillan.

Macmillan/Collier Books. See Macmillan.

Macmillan/Four Winds Press. See Macmillan.

Macmillan/Margaret K. McEldery Books. See Macmillan.

Macmillan/New Discovery Books. See Macmillan.

Media. Division of Westport, 4050 Pennsylvania, Suite 310, Kansas City, MO 64111. 800-347-2665.

Millbrook Press. 2 Old New Milford Road, Brookfield, CT 06804. 203-740-2220.

William Morrow. Orders to: Wilmor Warehouse, P.O. Box 1219, 39 Plymouth Street, Fairfield, NJ 07007. 800-843-9389.

William Morrow/Beech Tree Books. See William Morrow.

William Morrow/Books of Wonder. See William Morrow.

William Morrow/Quill Paperbacks. See William Morrow.

William Morrow/Tambourine Books. See William Morrow.

Morrow Junior Books. See William Morrow.

Motorbooks International. P.O. Box 2, Osceola, WI 54020. 800-458-0454.

Northwestern University Press. 625 Colfax Street, Evanston, IL 60208-4210. 800-621-2736.

Northwood Press. Write to: Mariflo Stephens, 108 2nd Street, SW, No. 5, Charlottesville, VA 22902.

W. W. Norton. 500 Fifth Avenue, New York, NY 10110. 800-233-4830.

Orchard Books. Division of Franklin Watts, 95 Madison Avenue, 11th Floor, New York, NY 10016. 800-672-6672.

Pelican Publishing. 1101 Monroe Street, Gretna, LA 70053. 800-843-1724 (800-843-4558 in Louisiana).

Penguin Books. Division of Penguin USA. Orders to: 120 Woodbine Street, Bergenfield, NJ 07621. 800-631-3577.

Penguin/Mentor Books. See Penguin Books.

Penguin/Meridian Books. See Penguin Books.

Penguin/Onyx Books. See Penguin Books.

Penguin/Plume Books. See Penguin Books.

Penguin/Plume/Truman Talley Books. See Penguin Books.

Penguin/Puffin Books. See Penguin Books.

Penguin/Puffin/Jean Karl Books. See Penguin Books.

Penguin/Roc Books. See Penguin Books.

Penguin/Signet Books. See Penguin Books.

Penguin/Signet Classic Books. See Penguin Books.

Persea Books. 60 Madison Avenue, New York, NY 10010. 212-779-7668.

Pocket Books. Division of Simon and Schuster. Orders to: 200 Old Tappan Road, Old Tappan, NJ 07675. 800-223-2336.

Pocket Books/Archway Paperbacks. Division of Simon and Schuster. Orders to: 200 Old Tappan Road, Old Tappan, NJ 07675. 800-223-2336.

Pocket/Minstrel Books. See Pocket Books.

Pocket/Star Books. See Pocket Books.

Presidio Press. 31 Parmaron Way, Novato, CA 94949. 415-883-1373.

G. P. Putnam's Sons. Division of Putnam. Orders to: 390 Murray Hill Parkway, East Rutherford, NJ 07073-2185. 800-631-8571.

Putnam/Philomel Books. See G. P. Putnam.

Random House. Orders to: 400 Hahn Road, Westminster, MD 21157. 800-733-3000.

Random House/Villard Books. See Random House.

Random House/Vintage Books. See Random House.

Riverview Publishers. 152 Slocum Crescent, Forest Hills, NY 11375. 718-268-1821.

Robson Books. Distributed by Parkwest Publications, 451 Communipaw Avenue, Jersey City, NJ 07304. 201-432-3257.

Schocken Books. Division of Random House. Orders to: 400 Hahn Road, Westminster, MD 21157. 800-733-3000.

Scholastic. Orders to: P.O. Box 120, Bergenfield, NJ 07621. 800-325-6149.

Scholastic/Madison Press Books. See Scholastic.

Scholastic/Point Books. See Scholastic.

Scholastic Hardcover Books. See Scholastic.

Charles Scribner's Sons. Division of Macmillan. Orders to: 100 Front Street, Box 500, Riverside, NJ 08075. 800-257-5755.

Shapolsky Publications. 136 West 22nd Street, New York, NY 10011. 212-633-2022.

Sierra Club Books. Distributed by Random House. Orders to: 400 Hahn Road, Westminster, MD 21157. 800-733-3000.

Sierra Club Books for Children. See Sierra Club Books.

Simon and Schuster. 1230 Avenue of the Americas, New York, NY 10023. 212-698-7000.

Simon and Schuster/Green Tiger Press. See Simon and Schuster.

Simon and Schuster/Julian Messner. See Simon and Schuster.

Simon and Schuster Books for Young Readers. Division of Simon and Schuster, 1230 Avenue of the Americas, New York, NY 10023.

Smithmark. Orders to: 80 Distribution Boulevard, Edison, NJ 08817. 800-645-9990 (800-932-0070 in New Jersey).

Smithmark/Salamander Books. See Smithmark.

Soho Press. Distributed by: Farrar, Straus and Giroux, 19 Union Square West, New York, NY 10003. 800-631-8571.

Sports Illustrated for Kids. Distributed by Little, Brown. Orders to: 200 West Street, Waltham, MA 02254. 800-343-9204.

Station Hill Press. Station Hill Road, Barrytown, NY 12507. 914-758-5840.

Sterling Publishing. 387 Park Avenue South, New York, NY 10016-8810. 800-367-9692.

Gareth Stevens. River Center Building, 1555 N. River Center Drive, Suite 201, Milwaukee, WI 53212. 800-341-3569.

Texas Tech University Press. Texas Tech University, Lubbock, TX 79409-1037. 800-832-4042.

Ticknor and Fields. Affiliate of Houghton Mifflin: Orders to: Wayside Road, Burlington, MA 01803. 800-225-3362.

Tor Books. Division of Tom Doherty Associates, 175 Fifth Avenue, New York, NY 10010. 212-388-0100.

Troll Associates. Subsidiary of Educational Reading Services, 100 Corporate Drive, Mahwah, NJ 07430. 800-526-5289.

University of California Press. 2120 Berkeley Way, Berkeley, CA 94720. 800-822-6657.

University of Chicago Press. Orders to: 11030 S. Langley Avenue, Chicago, IL 60628. 800-621-2736.

University of Nebraska Press. 312 North 14th Street, P.O. Box 880484, Lincoln, NE 68588-0484. 800-755-1105.

University Press of Mississippi. 3825 Ridgewood Road, Jackson, MS 39211-6492. 601-982-6205.

Viking. Division of Penguin USA. Orders to: P.O. Box 120, Bergenfield, NJ 07621-0120. 800-526-0275.

Viking/Reinhardt Books. See Viking.

Walker and Company. 720 Fifth Avenue, New York, NY 10019. 800-289-2553.

Ward Lock. Distributed by Sterling Publishing, 387 Park Avenue South, New York, NY 10016-8810. 800-367-9692.

Franklin Watts. Subsidiary of Grolier. Orders to: 5450 N. Cumberland Avenue, Chicago, IL 60657. 800-672-6672.

Franklin Watts/Impact Books. See Franklin Watts.

Franklin Watts/Venture Books. See Franklin Watts.

Wesleyan University Press. Orders to: University Press of New England, 23 S. Main Street, Hanover, NH 03755-2048. 800-421-1561.

Author Index

Subject Index

To avoid duplication, subject index entries are not given for the books in Chapter 22, Multicultural Themes. These books all appear in other chapters of the booklist and are indexed in those other chapters.

Title Index

Editor

Leila Christenbury, chair, is a former high school English teacher who currently teaches in the School of Education at Virginia Commonwealth University in Richmond. She is the past coeditor of *The ALAN Review* and the current editor of *English Journal*. She has served on the Executive Board of the Virginia Association of Teachers of English (VATE) for fifteen years. Her latest book is *Making the Journey: Being and Becoming a Teacher of English Language Arts* (1994).

Contributors

David Black teaches English at Louisa County High School in Mineral, Virginia. He has written essays for professional and literary journals across the United States and is a prize-winning poet whose work has been published widely. He is the poetry editor of *English Journal* and the secretary of VATE.

Mary T. Davis teaches English at Peabody Middle School in Petersburg, Virginia. She is on the Executive Board of VATE and also serves as the organization's multicultural liaison.

Darien Fisher-Duke has worked as a librarian in public schools, in universities, and for special libraries. Kids, canoeing, and swimming keep her busy. She loves all kinds of books, in particular Japanese baseball mysteries, and is librarian at Brookland Middle School in Richmond, Virginia.

Eileen Ford is a former English teacher and supervisor who is now an assistant principal at Providence Middle School in Chesterfield County, Virginia. She enjoyed working on *Books for You* because it gave her a chance to think about English teaching again.

Bonnie Griffith Hall chairs the English department at John Rolfe Middle School in Henrico County, Virginia, where she teaches eighth graders. She is a director of the Capital Writing Project in Richmond, Virginia.

Sylvia P. Harrison teaches at Lake Taylor High School, Norfolk, Virginia, where she serves as the English department chair. She is currently treasurer of her local VATE affiliate and a crossword puzzle fan.

Mary Kay Hight is a librarian at Christchurch School in Virginia and has a strong interest in sports of all kinds.

Anamae Hill is a retired English teacher, middle school English supervisor, and humanities center coordinator. She was active in VATE, the Virginia Conference of English Educators, and the Middle School Assembly of NCTE.

June R. Hill teaches at Prince George High School in Virginia, where she is also department chair. She is the founder and sponsor of the Young Authors' Club and is active in both the Southside Virginia Writing Association and in VATE.

Nancy Hubard teaches at Norview High School in Norfolk, Virginia.

Sheary D. Johnson teaches library science and media at Virginia Commonwealth University in Richmond. She has nineteen years' experience as a public school librarian at both the elementary and high school levels.

Kathryn Kelly (Atkins) has taught English at Shawsville High School, Virginia, where she also was department chair. She is a former president of VATE and is currently a doctoral student in English education at the University of Florida.

Alan M. McLeod, a former high school English teacher and editor of *The Virginia English Bulletin,* is professor of English education and head of the Division of Teacher Education at Virginia Commonwealth University in Richmond. When he is not in the office, at a ballgame, or fishing, he invariably can be found reading imaginative literature, biography, and nonfiction.

Ann T. Reddy is an English teacher at the high school level who currently lives in Findlay, Ohio.

Nancy Rosenbaum teaches English at Patrick Henry High School in Roanoke, Virginia. She is active in VATE at both the local and state levels. Science fiction remains one of her reading loves.

Judith B. Rosenfeld is the librarian at St. Anne's School in Bristol, Virginia. She edits *The Open Book,* a guide to new children's books for adults who work with young people.

Rebecca Scanlon is a retired school librarian from Varina High School in Henrico County, Virginia. In her spare time, she serves as the music librarian for the Richmond Symphony.

Pam Spencer is a librarian at Thomas Jefferson High School for Science and Technology in Alexandria, Virginia. She chairs the Adult Books for Young Adults review committee for *School Library Journal* and has published *What Do Young Adults Read Next?* (1994).

Betty M. Swiggett is a retired English curriculum specialist from Hampton City Schools, Virginia, a former president of VATE, and an adjunct professor of education at the College of William and Mary. She is the chair of the Recognize Excellence in Student Literary Magazines Advisory Committee for NCTE.

Joyce J. Swindell serves as the senior coordinator of communication skills, K–12, for Norfolk Public Schools in Virginia. She is a past president of VATE and the chair of the Virginia Conference of English Educators.

Mark Tavernier has been a communication skills teacher specialist for thirteen years with the Norfolk, Virginia, Public Schools. He also serves as the executive secretary for VATE.

Editorial Assistants

Courtenay Gibbs, a doctoral student at Virginia Commonwealth University in Richmond and former English teacher, has provided research assistance for *Books for You.* She currently teaches at Randolph-Macon College in Ashland, Virginia.

Frances S. Hodges, a native of Maryland, worked for some years as nutrition coordinator for the Carroll County, Maryland, Office of Aging. An avid reader, she has worked on *Books for You* as its editorial assistant from the very start of the project and has provided not only keyboarding and database expertise but has made numerous substantive, editorial, and organizational decisions. She lives in Richmond with her husband, Addison, and middle daughter, Elizabeth.